THE WOMAN IN THE PITH HELMET

A TRIBUTE TO ARCHAEOLOGIST NORMA FRANKLIN

THE WOMAN IN THE PITH HELMET
A TRIBUTE TO ARCHAEOLOGIST NORMA FRANKLIN

edited by

Jennie Ebeling and Philippe Guillaume

LOCKWOOD PRESS

2020

THE WOMAN IN THE PITH HELMET
A TRIBUTE TO ARCHAEOLOGIST NORMA FRANKLIN

Copyright © 2020 by Lockwood Press

ISBN: 978-1-948488-33-4

Cover design by Susanne Wilhelm. Cover art by Noga Blockman. Photograph courtesy of Shimon Gibson.

Library of Congress Control Number: 2020919304

Printed in the United States of America on acid-free paper.

CONTENTS

Excavating Jezreel

Martha Hellander

Like reapers at harvest,
We advance across the golden field.
Wielding pickaxes and *tourias*
We attack the wild oat-straw,
Slash the yellow-petaled mustard,
Flay the tough-stemmed fennel;
Scrape topsoil, pry stones,
Evict gerbils and scorpions that flee our blows,
To lay out squares at *Tel Jezreel*.

Points marked and string untangled,
Loci assigned and buckets tagged,
We unspool the wide black cloth,
Tie canopies to poles with cryptic knots
For life-giving shade:
Our *Beyt-haYaar-haLevanon*.
A sigh of morning breeze
Brushes our bare arms;
Long-buried ones sense our presence and stir,
As the sun rises over *Ein Jezreel*.

We lay siege to the shrine,
Five centimeters at a time.
We tell tales, interpret finds:
This limestone boulder shaped by an adze—
A foundation stone of Ahab's palace!
These rock-cut limestone pits—
The winery of the *tzaddick* Naboth!

I come seeking Jezebel.
Daughter of Tyre, garden city on an island,
Sent to marry Ahab, king in dusty Israel,
To seal a covenant with family ties,
Far from her beloved sea.
Dispatched in a coup at Jezreel,
Or so the story goes.

Jezebel stands at her window,
Adorned in Hathor headdress,
With sacred mask of malachite and kohl,
Her necklace the Tears of Isis.
The people pass below,
Mourning the young god whose death
Is reenacted each spring—
Communal grief, in which all have a share,
Gives way to joy at resurrection—
Jezebel leading the dance.

Jezebel as priestess hears the grieving citizens,
Jezebel as goddess blesses their sacred tears.
When her killer drives up,
Chariot wheels smoking for full effect,
Jezebel as Queen Mother calls out *murderer*
And stares him down.

Horseshoe nails dug from the road to the tell suggest Jehu's horses.
Their sharp hooves dismembered Jezebel's body,
Devoured by Ashera's sacred dogs,
Leaving only the sacrificial parts:
Her skull, her hands, her feet,
Or so the story goes.

At the bottom of a cistern,
The skeleton of a dog.

Might this cleft be Jezebel's tomb,
Divined by porcupine quills,
With amethyst scarab and dedicated jug?
Might that hollowed shard be her skull?
Narrow flints honed from rubbing glaze on pots

Evoke her finger bones, delicate and long,
Tracing lines of text as she reads the law
In the royal archives of Tyre.

Long before Jezebel's time,
Basalt was shaped and smoothed here,
Into standing stones and offering bowls,
Grinding stones and basins.
Holiness imbues this place
Above the sacred spring.
The Gilboa, an arrow's flight away,
Lies like a recumbent goddess
Who disdained holy war
And gathered peace-loving kings
Into her body, the first temple.

The bowls, the standing stones, the pots
Topple and shatter in the holy wars
In the blood-soaked Valley of Jezreel.
They bear the weight of war-horses.
Our voices awaken them.
We lift the relics, hold them aloft.
They enjoy a brief moment in the sun,
And begin to tell their secret Things:
How the people hulled and threshed the emmer,
Made beer, fermented mash for the dead;
How incense smoldered in the stone vessel;
How the grapes were borne aloft and trampled,
Yielding wine for the great festivals
Of harvest and thanksgiving.
An ancient *baetyl*,
Its slender curve of finely-honed basalt
Set upright after millennia underground,
With the warm skin of a mother held close,
Summons unexpected tears.

We share among ourselves
Words of trees and whispers of stone,
Glimpses of holiness
That abided here,
Long before the gods had names.

By mid-day our shades flap and strain, saying
Leave this stony outcrop to bake
A few more centuries, let the basalt
Crumble and cleave in the burning sun.
The shades long to join the black storks
That soar over the *tel*,
In the hot wind from *Beth She'an*.

On the dig, discipline prevails.
Artifacts are handed in,
Measured, weighed,
Labeled, drawn,
Photographed and wrapped,
Packed into crates dark inside
As the earth they came from.
The shades are neatly folded.
The pickaxes, the *tourias*,
The buckets, the survey tools,
Decommissioned, yet ever imbued
With the dust of Jezreel.

Introduction: Norma Franklin, Renaissance Woman with a Pith Helmet

Sheila Bishop, Deborah Cantrell, Jennie Ebeling, and Ann Stehney

The youngest child of Nora and Henry Kremer, Norma Franklin was born in London and travelled around quite a lot with her parents from a young age. On her first trip to Greece, Norma saw the Parthenon and decided that she would someday become an archaeologist; while visiting Israel for the first time in 1962, at age eleven, she decided that she would become an archaeologist in Israel. Norma was an active part of the swinging sixties scene in London while still in school, and, when she finished, refused to go to University. Instead, she looked for opportunities to earn enough money to get to Israel and start a life there. When she was nineteen, her father gave her the opportunity to sell fire escape equipment and, with a bit of luck and a lot of hard work, Norma started Automated Rescue Equipment, Ltd. (AREL) in 1969 in order to manufacture and sell them. To demonstrate these contraptions, Norma overcame all fear of heights and learned to propel herself from hydraulic cranes, or "cherry-pickers," and land easily and safely on the ground. Since some of this equipment was installed in Sandringham House, Norma was a contractor of sorts to the Queen of England.

Norma married her now ex-husband David and, in 1974, they spent two months driving their Volvo station wagon to Israel via Europe, sailing from Venice. They hung out in Tel Aviv, sleeping on the beach, before enrolling in a Hebrew *ulpan* in Arad. They bought their first flat in Ramat Aviv and their son Yoni was born in 1976; shortly after, they moved to Raanana and had their daughter Avital in 1979 and son Amitai in 1982. Norma commuted to London to run her fire escape business, sometimes taking the three children with her. She studied to become a tour guide in Israel and made sure that her family saw the whole of the country, from the green north to the desert south, almost every Saturday. Norma was the engine behind these happy sunny days, deciding on the route and packing everyone up in the car early. They went to the sand dunes of Netanya almost every year in time to see the big black irises and the kids rolled down the sand dunes between them. They visited ancient sites all over Israel, traveling from one tell to another and hearing many stories. Norma's curiosity for places and people didn't end in Israel, however. The family traveled all over Europe visiting museums and seeing many beautiful places, including Pompeii and Mount Vesuvius, where the kids could feel the soles of their shoes starting to melt slightly from the heat of the volcano. According to Avital:

> Nothing ever seems to scare my mum: her curiosity is what leads her and no fear ever seems to stand in her way. I remember visiting the Far East and seeing mum's excitement at the mud huts with straw mats on the floor, always learning and searching for answers to the great mysteries of archaeology. Her curiosity would sometime put her in awkward situations, however. Once, when we were in a small village in Tibet, she happily tasted some homemade alcohol out of a big barrel only to find out that they fermented it by chewing the grains and spitting them out into the barrel. Mum is always up for an adventure.

After selling her business in 1989, Norma got down to fulfilling her childhood dream and enrolled in the BA program in archaeology at Tel Aviv University. A few years later, she was one of the founding members of Tel Aviv University's Megiddo Expedition.

Hold Your Horses: Norma Is in the (Dig) House

Deborah Cantrell

I first met Norma Franklin at the Megiddo Expedition in the summer of 2000. As we dirty diggers staggered down the tell for breakfast and announcements, a blur in a pith helmet, wearing combat boots and a utility belt, sped past me, talking a blue streak to the cadre of students trying to keep up with her. Upon arriving, tired and hungry, at the shaded picnic pavilion, I saw this dynamo dart from table to table, person to person, smiling, laughing, pointing, and waving, while she busily "sorted things out," from lost laundry to weekend transport to Jerusalem, to "please call your mother," to missing passports, and "use earplugs if your roommates snore." Who in the world is this obviously "Most Important Woman," I wondered. Then I noticed that the three kingpins, David Ussishkin, Israel Finkelstein, and Baruch Halpern, answered almost every question from the volunteer diggers with only two words: "Ask Norma." "Ah!" I thought, "She runs this place." And, indeed, I was correct. Norma was the engine (fig. 1).

Norma organized the Megiddo dig, top to bottom. She secured housing for hundreds of volunteers, and arranged food, transport, equipment, supplies, pottery washing, educational programs, and weekend trips to other archaeological sites, as well as to Jerusalem and Tel Aviv. She also planned the evening lectures by famous historians, scientists, and archaeologists, as well as overseeing the graduate school credit courses taught on site in the afternoons. And, during the day, she was an area supervisor on the dig, teaching and training other aspiring archaeologists who were learning to love Israel

Figure 1. Norma observing Gallery 629 at Megiddo. Photo courtesy of Norma Franklin.

more with each scrape of the trowel. And, now I know this was her intentional, secret mission: sharing her love of Israel.

I saw Norma again at the Society for Biblical Literature conference in Nashville, Tennessee in the fall of 2000. I invited Israel Finkelstein and Norma to tour our riding stables in Nashville to witness first-hand evidence of "cribbing" and see the mountains of dung created by fewer than one hundred horses to bolster my arguments that Megiddo was a hugely important equestrian center in the Iron Age. Somehow, due largely to the behind-the-scenes machinations of Jack Sasson and Doug Knight, my advisors at Vanderbilt Divinity School, Israel Finkelstein and David Ussishkin learned that I had some ideas about the function of the mangers and columns still in situ at Megiddo, based on my many decades of equestrian activities and horse ownership. My input while a digger at Megiddo eventually helped settle an academic disagreement between the two, and Israel was convinced that, indeed, the stables were a highly functioning reality in Iron Age Megiddo. Norma believed the site was also used as a trading and sale locale for horses and donkeys, much like the "horse fairs" in Ireland, which she later took me to experience, thereby broadening my horizons considerably.

In 2001, we all joined forces to present a session at the Toronto SBL, dedicated to the rechristened Megiddo stables, which former editor-in-chief of *Biblical Archaeology Review* magazine, Hershel Shanks, had entitled "Horsing Around in Megiddo" with lectures to be presented by Israel Finkelstein, David Ussishkin, Baruch Halpern, Norma Franklin, and Lord Allenby. The night before our session, when we met for drinks to discuss the logistics of our upcoming program, Lord Allenby, Viscount of Megiddo, raised a toast to the reborn stables at Megiddo and then enthusiastically asked, "I say, Deborah, I know you are discussing the stable vice of 'cribbing' tomorrow, but are you discussing 'wind-sucking' … or should I?" I felt an elbow to my ribs and Norma whispered, "Let him do that!" And this was my introduction to Norma's wicked sense of humor.

After that wonderful session in Toronto, Norma and I made it a practice to meet at conferences and lectures, then tour the city and countryside. For over a decade, while completing our PhDs, we gave lectures in San Diego, Denver, Boston, San Antonio, Atlanta, Chicago, Philadelphia, Washington DC, London, Vienna, Berlin, Amsterdam, and Cambridge, including sessions at the Smithsonian and the British Museum. Although I always lectured on equine matters, Norma's topics were varied and fascinating, for example, mason marks, the tombs of the Israelite kings in Samaria, the contribution of famous archaeologists in Israel, the sex life of the date palm, the winery production facilities at Jezreel, and, more recently, full circle back to revisiting the stables at Megiddo.

Norma, as did I, had a life before archaeology captured us: I as an attorney; she as an entrepreneur. In the 1970s and 1980s, Norma was CEO of a British company that she founded that manufactured collapsible fire escapes used by various businesses in the United States and Europe, and even installed in one of the Queen's private residences. Norma commuted from Tel Aviv to London several times a month, sometimes with her three young children, to supervise this enterprise. After she sold the business, she decided to pursue her dream of becoming an archaeologist and enrolled in Tel Aviv University.

I was thrilled and not in the least surprised when, in 2012, Norma and Jennie Ebeling organized and administered an important dig for the University of Haifa and the University of Evansville at Jezreel. They brought years of field experience and advanced scholarship to the project. Once again, Norma organized and orchestrated the "on the ground" logistics, making the experience unique and worthwhile for the volunteers. They arranged weekend tours, not only to other archaeological sites, but also many historical and biblical locations, as well as tours to Jordan and Petra. Their discovery of the largest Iron Age wine producing facility and the hundreds of storage enclosures around Jezreel has sparked articles and lectures about Naboth's vineyard and King Ahab and even revitalized the scholarship around Jezebel and her death under the hooves of Jehu's horses.

Norma, my brilliant friend, you are a phenomenon! You delight in showing us all—scholars, students, laymen, tourists—where history happened. Plus, you explain the how and why, with zeal and patience … well, maybe not with that much patience. But we get the message. The message is Israel, with its beauty, vitality, history, and spiritual connection to the entire world. And when we are fortunate enough to circle within the realm that you, Norma, have touched with your amazingly gifted scholarship, our lives are forever enriched and our minds enlightened. Thank you.

Have You Lost Your Mind?

Sheila Bishop

I clearly remember the day I went to Tel Jezreel with Shimon Gibson to meet with Norma Franklin to consider re-digging the site. We toured the site, which had been dug previously by David Ussishkin and John Woodhead during the 1990s. There were weeds higher than our heads, there were open cisterns every few feet, there were cow patties everywhere, and it was around 110 degrees Fahrenheit with no shade in sight. "Have you lost your mind?" I wondered if it might be true. After the tour, we went to a nearby restaurant on the road up to Gilboa. As I looked at the beautiful countryside, I thought to myself: "Norma, if you really want to dig that site, I will do all I can to help you; but there is no way I would ever spend a day digging there." Of course, I would. It would be irresistible.

When I discovered the world of biblical archaeology, my desire was to help bring about projects that would make the pages of the texts come alive. I was too old to do much with that desire—or so I thought. I certainly had no desire to return to university at age 40 to pursue a degree in archaeology. I opted for a role in support—a facilitator, as it were, with as much digging as possible on the side. And so I did. Norma must have been in a similar position entering the field later in life. Norma, however, opted for the gold. Norma wanted to do the work, get the degree, think outside the box, write about it—and do a dig. And so she did.

Norma was already planning a dig, co-directed by Jennie Ebeling. In no time at all, a survey was underway. The following season, I, too, would dig. We were fortunate to have a senior digging team. I will not name names. We know who we are. We are pretty good, and we got some good assignments from Norma.

No, we did not find a palace or an inscription saying, "Jezebel was here," but we did find a wonderful amethyst scarab—the kind of artifact that any digger loves. Although it will not get much notice, there is no denying the connection. Jezebel was a Phoenician princess, and the amethyst scarab (typically from Phoenicia) was prevalent in jewelry-making in multiple countries for five hundred years or more. And no, we did not find an inscription saying, "Naboth's vineyard." However, the site is not in question and the combination of that unique winery overlooking a plot of land ideally suited to growing grapes near the ancient spring was one of the most delightful things I ever had the privilege to dig. And as Norma would become a video superstar, thanks to that winery, I would become a Covergirl at 60 on the cover of *Artifax Magazine*, as if I were a three-thousand-year-old artifact myself.

While Norma's goal may have been relentless pursuit of the archaeology and history of Israel (and I do mean relentless pursuit of every little detail of historical fact from beginning to end), she did much to fulfill my goal of seeing the pages of the Bible come to life. Although it is unlikely that Jezreel will be on the tourist route any time soon, Jezreel might be the site that most exemplifies "text jumping off the page," with so many characters and stories connected to the site. In reality, it is Norma and her amazing abilities that make the text jump off the page.

Little did I know the years would pass so quickly, or that the Jezreel team would become not only my friends but also my family as I would lose my own. However, the new paradigm of digging six years and publishing is a good one and also a prudent one. And, certainly, I could not have known that Norma had lost her mind long before that fateful day at Jezreel: she lost it when she decided to become a modster-hippie in 1960s London; when she decided to relocate to Israel; when she decided to sell her business and go back to university to study archaeology. The Jezreel Expedition has amazing directors—as well as great staff, students, and senior volunteers—all at a great kibbutz in one of the loveliest places to work. Thank you, Norma, for having the vision to take us there, as well as the energy and the tenacity to make it all happen. It was fun.

A View from the Dig Office

Ann Stehney

The first indication that the culture of the Jezreel Expedition would be different was when Norma Franklin welcomed us not as students, volunteers, and staff, but as Team Members.[1] The designation appealed to me; class distinctions make me uncomfortable, even in the classroom. I would be digging with the pros, and Norma had established a spirit of collaboration between people with all levels of education and experience.

My friend Deborah Appler, professor at the Moravian Theological Seminary, recommended the Jezreel experience to me. She had joined the expedition in the initial survey season and assured me that I would "love it," although the reasons were a bit vague. I applied to be a Visiting Student, duly submitting the required forms through the University of Evansville. My *Skills and Experience Summary* was largely blank, reporting academic degrees and occupational skills that seemed irrelevant, noting brief seasons in the field at two other sites (with little or no responsibility), and promising to contribute my fervor as a life-long learner. I was accepted.

I "met" Norma by email. She wrote to provide the newcomers with essential information and friendly advice: What to Bring, Directions to Afula, Where to find Coffee and Wi-Fi when you arrive, and more. With characteristic attention to detail, she provided prices for everything in both shekels and dollars, attaching photos of the bus station (inside and out) and the nearby Café Shani (ditto). Norma takes care of her team,

---

1. Full Disclosure: I'm neither an archaeologist nor a biblical scholar but a retired mathematics professor and college administrator. My perspective here is that of an outsider, a friend of archaeology with some dig experience, one of those curious laypersons who form the public audience for professional archaeologists, a consumer if you will. I want to share the ways that Norma Franklin has impacted me and others at Jezreel, with the hope that readers will recognize in these observations the Norma they know and admire.

Figure 2. Norma giving a tour through the impressive undergrowth at Jezreel. Photo courtesy of Deborah Cantrell.

in ways large and small. In fact, she still takes care of me, regularly recommending journal articles of interest (complete with links to Academia.edu) and recently researching the perfect smart phone for me (with price and vendor) after I ignored her hints that my ten-year-old flip phone was somehow inadequate.

Norma gave each season's new team members an introductory tour of Greater Jezreel—starting at the upper tell with its grand view of the Jezreel Valley, past installations previously unearthed, winding down to the current dig site near Ein Jezreel—during which she wove biblical and historical narratives through an account of the findings of past and present excavations (fig. 2). Anyone who has been on a field trip with Norma won't be surprised to learn that she is a licensed tour guide, having passed the rigorous Israeli requirements for that role before taking up archaeology. She is a natural storyteller, and her love of the land and its history is discernible. A visit to Megiddo, enlivened by Norma's accounts of their time there and vouched for by her colleagues, was always a highlight of the Jezreel season.

When it comes to recognizing talent, Norma is something of a genius. As her vision for renewed excavations at Jezreel was taking hold in 2011, a recent op-ed by Jennie Ebeling entitled *Where are the Female Dig Directors in Israel?* caught her attention. She brought Jennie onboard as the Co-Director of the new Jezreel Expedition and picked a core team from among her Megiddo associates. It was a diverse group from five countries on four continents, most of whom continued through the last excavation season. As Field Director Ian Cipin confirms, it was a good fit for everyone. In the team as a whole, not everyone was a practicing or aspiring archaeologist or biblical scholar. Norma believed that the work was enriched by enthusiasts from varied backgrounds, and she found ways for each to contribute in their own way. The fact that Norma ran a successful business in the UK from Israel is an indication of her trust in the expertise and dedication of others.

Norma is an educator by instinct, engaging her team in ways that are known in higher-ed jargon as high-impact experiences. She, Jennie, and Ian fostered a culture of individual responsibility, seeing that everyone had the opportunity to try new things and learn first-hand. "You found it, you dig it" was their mantra. No matter how significant a find might appear, you were not only *allowed* to dig it but *expected* to. To quote a team member who arrived one season with a seminary group and returned twice on her own, "Norma turned theology students into responsible diggers."

Under the leadership of Norma and Jennie, the Jezreel Expedition Field School was certified by the Register of Professional Archaeologists, the first program in Israel to earn this distinction, in recognition of the program's curriculum and research design. Like other field schools, Jezreel's program included excursions, lectures by specialists, regular updates on the excavation, and the opportunity to observe pottery reading. The Jezreel difference, it seems to me, was an extraordinary expectation of engagement on the part of everyone. Ian's field manual laid out the strategies and procedures to be understood and practiced by all, including the registration system for documenting the excavation. Team members were expected to participate in recording data in the field and to engage fully in pottery reading. The square supervisors, many of them BA students, organized the reading of pottery from their own loci, until less-experienced coworkers felt comfortable with the process and with interacting with the experts at that close range.

Norma's impact on team members extends well beyond their seasons at the site. Enabled by international communication channels and the social media that she embraced early on, she continues to inspire and mentor Jezreel alumni. For faculty and students at consortium institutions, who were introduced to biblical archaeology at Jezreel, she offers scholarly guidance and recommends sources of information. Generous with her time, Norma recently had a significant role in facilitating the work of students in Jennie's 2019 seminar who chose to report on artifacts from Jezreel. According to Jennie, the results were impressive—their papers have the scope and depth to be the basis for published articles, thanks to Norma.

Midway through my first season at Jezreel, I asked what was done with all the data being recorded on those myriad paper sheets. "It's a problem," I was told, so I offered to help transcribe the information. I admit to having an ulterior motive: I hoped to have an opportunity to analyze the data when the time came, so I had a personal stake in a first-rate database. By the next day, I was spending my mornings in the field and the afternoons immersed in Excel files. Before the next season, Norma asked me to be the dig's registrar and office manager, with responsibility for record-keeping and preparing the collection of finds for specialists. Skeptical but reassured that she, Jennie, and Ian would teach me whatever I needed to know, it was an offer I couldn't refuse. Now, my wish has come true, and as my colleagues prepare for publication, this data junkie has a supporting role.

Those of you who have worked or partied or bunked with Norma will have your own stories about her sense of humor, her beloved car, her earring collection, her frustrations with technology, and her eccentricities. Like other team members, I did things at the Jezreel Expedition that I didn't know I could do. My life is enriched by having been a member of Team Norma.

Your Dates Are Off: An Appreciation of Norma's Scholarly Contributions

Jennie Ebeling

Norma's publication record is fascinating. Since she came to archaeology as a second career and did not pursue a teaching position in an Israeli university, Norma has had the freedom to research, write, and present on topics that interest her. Her doctoral dissertation for Tel Aviv University–*State Formation in the Northern Kingdom of Israel: Some Tangible Symbols of Statehood*–was published in a series of articles in the early 2000s. Passionately dedicated to, in her own words, "killing sacred cows," Norma challenged a number of long-accepted ideas about the Iron Age chronology at three key sites in the Northern Kingdom of Israel (Samaria, Megiddo, and Jezreel) in her dissertation and in the many publications that followed (e.g., Franklin 2001b, 2003, 2004a, 2004b, 2005, 2006).

While the most sensational claim she made was identifying what could be the tombs of the kings of Israel at Samaria, it was also remarkable that her reassessment of the Iron Age chronology of Samaria and Megiddo prompted David Ussishkin, with whom she had been working at Megiddo for years, to publish a 22-page (!) rejoinder (Ussishkin 2007b) criticizing her ideas. Norma was far from unhappy with this rejoinder and another that Ussishkin (2007a) wrote in response to her article "Lost Tombs of the Israelite Kings" in *BAR* (Franklin 2007). She continued to develop her ideas and publish them, including a critique of Ussishkin's dating of the Iron Age enclosure at Jezreel (Franklin 2008). Although her understanding of various Iron Age elements at Megiddo is not accepted by all, Norma put forward a methodology for distinguishing between ninth and eighth century BCE Israelite architecture and prompted scholars to reexamine their preconceived notions.

Although Norma has described herself as "happiest with complex stratigraphy," her work belies an interest in diverse historical and art historical subjects relating to the Iron Age. A brief survey of just a few of her publications in print and online is instructive. She identified the city of Samaria in the Room V wall reliefs in Sargon II's palace in Khorsabad (Franklin 1994, 2001a). After examining the masons' marks on stone ashlars at Megiddo and Samaria, she suggested they originated with Carian builders (Franklin 2001). She identified the design of stone volutes (commonly known as "pro-to-Ionic capitals") as date-palm bases that could not have served as structural capitals (Franklin 2011). She reexamined the meaning of the term "Ophel" and suggested that the Ophel in Jerusalem should be identified with the Stepped Stone Structure (Franklin 2013b). She also revealed the important and pervasive presence of the Twenty-Fifth Kushite Dynasty in eighth century Judah, shown by, among other things, the winged sun-disks on LMLK stamped seal impressions (Franklin 2018a). These insights and many more complement the stratigraphic and chronological studies that dominate her research program.

Our discoveries at Jezreel 2012–2018 led Norma to engage with new research questions. After researching parallels at Samaria and Gibeon, she suggested that the majority of the *ca.* 100 bell-shaped pits identified at Jezreel functioned as grain silos rather than water cisterns, as many have assumed (Franklin 2018b). Our discovery of a large Iron Age winery complex led her to investigate the important role of wine production in the context of the ninth-eighth century military center(s) at Jezreel (Franklin et al. 2015, 2017, 2020). Norma also developed her ideas about the relationship between Megiddo and Jezreel in the latter half of the eighth century BCE and the changing function of these cities under Assyrian domination (Franklin 2019). Although her research has been more collaborative in recent years, especially with members of the Jezreel Expedition, she continues to forge her own original research trajectory.

I would also like to highlight Norma's commitment to engaging with the public about the archaeology of Israel. Norma is an exceptional public speaker with years of experience as a tour guide in Israel. She has probably given hundreds of tours of Megiddo over the years and has a singular ability to engage diverse audiences—from groups of student excavators to well-heeled participants in exclusive private tours of Israel—with the history of the site and its colorful excavators. Norma was also a popular virtual guide and "talking head" in numerous biblical archaeology videos. During the "golden age" of such programs (the 1990s and early 2000s), Norma could be seen striding through Megiddo in her familiar pith helmet, her calm, reasoned, British-accented voice tempering the bluster of some of her colleagues. Her iconic look—not only the pith helmet, but also her giant scarves and jewelry, colorful shoes, and diminutive stature—is a perfect foil to the typical appearance of other field archaeologists in Israel. A 2014 issue of *BAR* magazine included a photo of Norma—the only woman among five male archaeologists (including contributor Eric Cline)—in her signature headgear in a piece called "Indiana Jones: Fashion Icon." The irony is that Norma was the only person pictured who was NOT wearing a fedora; we must conclude that it was impossible to find a female dig director wearing *Raiders of the Lost Ark* cosplay! Norma was even the subject of one of Facebook video star Nas Daily's 1,000 one-minute videos—which begins "She has the hardest job"—in 2017, at age sixty-six.

Norma has broken the mold in more ways than one. Importantly, in my opinion, she broke it first with her original research.

Norma's colleagues and friends who contributed essays to this volume have been inspired by her scholarship and many have worked closely alongside her at Megiddo (1994–2010) and/or Jezreel (2012–2018). Co-editor Philippe Guillaume and I would like to thank all of those who contributed essays and art to this volume and those who supported it in other ways. Special thanks go to Sheila Bishop, Deborah Cantrell, Geoffrey Cowling, Judith Hadley, and Ann Stehney; Avital Franklin-Machlev and Amitai Franklin; Billie Jean Collins and Lockwood Press; and members of Kibbutz Yizrael.

Selected Works by Norma Franklin

1994   "The Room V Reliefs at Dur-Sharrukin and Sargon II's Western Campaigns." *TA* 21.2:255–75.

2000   "Relative and Absolute Chronology of Gallery 629 and the Megiddo Water System: A Reassessment." Pages 515–23 in *Megiddo III: The 1992–1996 Seasons*. Edited by Israel Finkelstein, David Ussishkin, and Baruch Halpern. Tel Aviv: Emery and Claire Yass Publications in Archaeology.

2001a "A Room with a View: Images from Room V at Khorsabad, Samaria, Nubians, the Brook of Egypt and Ashdod." Pages 257–77 in *Studies in the Archaeology of the Iron Age in Israel and Jordan*. Edited by Amihai Mazar. JSOTSupp 331. Sheffield: Sheffield Academic.

2001b "Masons' Marks from the Ninth Century BCE Northern Kingdom of Israel: Evidence of the Nascent Carian Alphabet?" *Kadmos* 40:107–16.

2003   "The Tombs of the Kings of Israel: Two Recently Identified 9th Century Tombs from Omride Samaria." *ZDPV* 119:1–11.

2004a "Samaria: From the Bedrock to the Omride Palace." *Levant* 36:189–202.

2004b "Metrological Investigations at 8th and 9th Century Samaria and Megiddo, Israel." *Mediterranean Archaeology and Archaeometry* 4.2:83–92.

2005   "Correlation and Chronology: Samaria and Megiddo Redux." Pages 310–22 in *The Bible and Radiocarbon Dating: Archaeology, Text and Science*. Edited by Thomas E. Levy and Thomas Higham. London: Equinox.

2006   "Revealing Stratum V at Megiddo." *BASOR* 342:95–111.

2007   "Lost Tombs of the Israelite Kings," *BAR* 33.4:26, 28–35.

2008   "Jezreel: Before and After Jezebel." Pages 45–53 in *Israel in Transition: From Late Bronze II to Iron IIa (ca. 1250–850 B.C.E.)*. Vol. 1: *The Archaeology*. Edited by Lester L. Grabbe. New York: T&T Clark.

2008   "Trademarks of the Omride Builders?" Pages 45–54 in *Bene Israel: Studies in the Archaeology of Israel and the Levant during the Bronze and Iron Ages in Honour of Israel Finkelstein*. Edited by Alexander Fantalkin and Assaf Yasur-Landau. CHANE 31. Leiden: Brill.

2011   "From Megiddo to Tamassos and Back: Putting the 'Proto-Ionic Capital' in Its Place." Pages 129–49 in *The Fire Signals of Lachish: Studies in the Archaeology and History of Israel in the Late Bronze Age, Iron Age, and Persian Period in Honor of David Ussishkin*. Edited by Israel Finkelstein and Nadav Na'aman. Winona Lake, IN: Eisenbrauns.

2013a "Who Really Built the Water System at Megiddo?" *The Ancient Near East Today* 1/7.

2013b "Dispelling the Fog around the Ophel. Exploring the Narrative: Jerusalem and Jordan in the Bronze and Iron Ages." Pages 286–296 in *Exploring the Narrative: Jerusalem and Jordan in the Bronze and Iron Ages; Papers in Honour of Margreet Steiner*. Edited by Eveline van der Steen, Jeanette Boertien, and Noor Mulder-Hymans. LHB/OTS 583. Bloomsbury T&T Clark.

2017   "Entering the Arena: The Megiddo Stables Reconsidered." Pages 87–102 in *Rethinking Israel: Studies in the History and Archaeology of Ancient Israel in Honor of Israel Finkelstein*. Edited by Oded Lipschits, Yuval Gadot and Matthew J. Adams. Winona Lake, IN: Eisenbrauns.

2018a "The Kushite Connection: The Destruction of Lachish and the Salvation of Jerusalem." Pages 680–95 in *Tell It in Gath: Studies in the History and Archaeology of Israel; Essays in Honor of Aren M. Maeir on the Occasion of His Sixtieth Birthday*. Itzhaq Shai, Jeffrey R. Chadwick, Louise Hitchcock, Amit Dagan, Chris McKinny, and Joe Uziel. ÄAT 90. Münster: Zaphon.

2018b "Exploring the Function of Bell-Shaped Pits: With a View to Iron Age Jezreel." Pages 76*–82* in in *Eretz Israel, Lawrence E. Stager Volume*. Edited by Joseph Aviram, Amnon Ben-Tor, and Jodi Magness. Eretz Israel 33. Jerusalem: Israel Exploration Society (Hebrew).

2019   "Megiddo and Jezreel Reflected in the Dying Embers of the Northern Kingdom of Israel." Pages 189–208 in *The Last Days of the Kingdom of Israel*. Edited by Shuichi Hasegawa, Christoph Levin, and Karen Radner. Berlin: de Gruyter.

Franklin, Norma, Jennie Ebeling, and Philippe Guillaume

2015   "An Ancient Winery at Jezreel." *Bet Mikra* 60.1:9–18.

Franklin, Norma, Jennie Ebeling, Philippe Guillaume, and Deborah Appler

2017   "Have We Found Naboth's Vineyard at Jezreel?" *BAR* 43.6:49–54.

2020   "An Ancient Winery at Jezreel, Israel." *Journal of Eastern Mediterranean Archaeology and Heritage Studies* 8.1:58–78.

Ussishkin, David (rejoinders to Norma Franklin)

2007a "The Disappearance of Two Royal Burials." *BAR* 33.6:60–70.

2007b "Megiddo and Samaria: A Rejoinder to Norma Franklin." *BASOR* 348:49–70.

Abbreviations

AASOR	Annual of the American Schools of Oriental Research
ÄAT	Ägypten und Altes Testament
ABS	Archaeology and Biblical Studies
ADAJ	Annual of the Department of Antiquities of Jordan
A&L	Ägypten und Levante
AIL	Ancient Israel and Its Literature
AJA	American Journal of Archaeology
AntW	Antike Welt
BA	Biblical Archaeologist
BagM	Baghdader Mitteilungen
BAR	Biblical Archaeology Review
BASOR	Bulletin of the American Schools of Oriental Research
BCH	Bulletin de Correspondance Hellénique
CBR	Currents in Biblical Research
CHANE	Culture and History of the Ancient Near East
CRAI	Comptes Rendus de l'Académie des Inscriptions et Belles-Lettres
DDL	Edwin M. Yamauchi and Marvin R. Wilson. Dictionary of Daily Life in Biblical and Post-Biblical Antiquity. Peabody, MA: Hendrikson, 2016
DJD	Discoveries in the Judaean Desert
DSD	Dead Sea Discoveries
ErIsr	Eretz-Israel
HA-ESI	Hadashot Arkheologiyot. Excavations and Surveys in Israel
HALOT	The Hebrew and Aramaic Lexicon of the Old Testament. Vol. 2. Leiden: Brill, 1995.
HR	History of Religions
IAA	Israel Antiquities Authority
IEJ	Israel Exploration Journal
JAEI	Journal of Ancient Egyptian Interconnections
JAOS	Journal of the American Oriental Society
JBL	Journal of Biblical Literature
JBQ	Jewish Bible Quarterly
JCS	Journal of Cuneiform Studies
JESHO	Journal of the Economic and Social History of the Orient
JHebS	Journal of Hebrew Scriptures

JHS	*Journal of Hellenic Studies*
JMA	*Journal of Mediterranean Archaeology*
JNES	*Journal of Near Eastern Studies*
JPR	*Journal of Prehistoric Religion*
JPS	Jewish Publication Society
JQR	*The Jewish Quarterly Review*
JRA	*Journal of Roman Archaeology*
JSOT	*Journal for the Study of the Old Testament*
JSOTSup	Journal for the Study of the Old Testament Supplement Series
KTU	M. Dietrich, O. Loretz, and J. Sanmartín, *Die keil-alphbetischen Texte aus Ugarit.* AOAT 24.1. Kevelaer: Butzon und Bercker; Neukirchen-Vluyn: Neukirchener Verlag, 1976
LHBOTS	The Library of Hebrew Bible/Old Testament Studies
MNDPV	*Mitteilungen und Nachrichten des deutschen Palästina-Vereins*
NEA	*Near Eastern Archaeology*
NEAEHL	*The New Encyclopedia of Archaeological Excavations in the Holy Land* 5. Edited by E. Stern. Jerusalem: Israel Exploration Society.
OEAE	*The Oxford Encyclopedia of Ancient Egypt*
OJA	*Oxford Journal of Archaeology*
OTL	Old Testament Library
PEF	Palestine Exploration Fund
PEFQS	*Palestine Exploration Fund Quarterly Statement*
PEQ	*Palestine Exploration Quarterly*
QDAP	*Quarterly of the Department of Antiquities of Palestine*
RDAC	*Report of the Department of Antiquities, Cyprus*
RevB	*Revue Biblique*
RevQ	*Revue de Qumran*
SAAB	*State Archives of Assyria Bulletin*
SAOC	Studies in Ancient Oriental Civilization
TA	*Tel Aviv*
TCS	Texts from Cuneiform Sources
TBL	Themes in Biblical Literature
UF	*Ugarit Forschungen*
VT	*Vetus Testamentum*
VTSup	Supplements to *Vetus Testamentum*
ZDPV	*Zeitschrift des deutschen Palästina-Vereins*

PART ONE

JEZREEL, ZER'IN, AND YIZRAEL

Women, Water, and Walkways: Preliminary Findings from the Jezreel Expedition in Light of Biblical and Archaeo-Ethnographic Evidence

Deborah Appler, Julye Bidmead, and Marilyn Love

Abstract: In the Hebrew Bible, young women draw water and gain blessings and husbands (Gen 21:14–20; 24:10–27; 29:1–11; Exodus 2:15–19). Yet, the meeting at the well was more than a biblical betrothal type-scene. Rather, it was a gender-specific and time-consuming task that was essential to the household and community. Cross-cultural ethnographic data from nineteenth and early twentieth century Levant also depict women as the water carriers. Exploring the textual mentions of water-carrying in the Hebrew Bible, clues from ancient iconography, nineteenth- and early twentieth-century representations of Middle Eastern women, and an experiment conducted at Tel Jezreel, this paper evaluates the amount of time devoted to carry water, methods of conveyance, and types of vessel employed in Iron Age Israel.

Keywords: water carrier, women, vessels, experimental archaeology

In ancient Israel, the limited rainfall over the summer months made water collection vitally important to society's subsistence. That role fell primarily to women. Almost every aspect of daily life depended on collecting and conserving of water—agricultural activities, raising animals, cooking, personal use, and so forth. Water was obtained from natural sources such as streams and springs, as well as from boreholes dug to reach subterranean water and would then be fed into water systems, reservoirs and plastered cisterns, all of which are found at several archaeological excavations. There is extensive archaeological evidence for underground water systems fed by natural springs or internal subterranean pools such as those found at the biblical sites of Megiddo, Hazor, Gezer, and Beersheva. Whereas these large urban societies had complex water systems, pastoral and more-rural communities relied on smaller wells and cisterns as their main sources of water.

Cisterns (bor), small structures often cut into the limestone bedrock, provided an efficient means of catching and storing rainwater. In the Bible, cisterns are frequently

3

mentioned in both domestic and agricultural contexts. (Deut 6:10–11; 2 Kgs 18:31; Isa 36:16; Neh 9:25; 2 Chr 26:10; Eccl 2:4–6). Plaster-lined cisterns are found in early Iron Age (ca. 1200 BCE) settlements where springs or other natural sources were lacking or inadequate. Natural springs and wells were likely preferred as they provided fresh underground water, whereas water from cisterns, though efficient as a method of collecting and storing rainfall, often became stagnant and contaminated (Edelman and Ghantous 2014: 25).

Wells (be'er) are of central importance in the Hebrew Bible not only for their practicality but also because they serve multiple literal and metaphorical functions throughout the Torah, Nevi'im, and Ketuvim (Hyman 2006: 187). Wells (and other sources of centralized water) function as locales of social gathering and meeting places, especially for future spouses, and define identity as well as sociopolitical and geographic boundaries.

Drawing water from wells was "an important task assigned to young women" (Hyman 2006: 182), which makes Moses drawing water for the daughters of Midian (Exod 2:19) all the more striking. Wells also serve as a locus for the iconic betrothal type-scene in the Hebrew Bible: the groom journeys to a foreign land; he encounters a girl (or several of them) at a well; someone draws water; the girl runs home to announce the visitor's arrival; the visitor is invited to a meal (Cook 1997: 11).

The stories of three biblical couples fit this type-scene. Abraham's servant Eliezer stopped at a well and met Rebekah there to set up her marriage to Isaac (Gen 24:10–27). Jacob met Rachel at a well where she came to water her father Laban's flock of sheep (Gen 29:1–11). Moses too met Zipporah at a well when she arrived with her sisters to water their father's flock (Exod 2:15–22). In addition to these betrothal scenes, Saul met young women who were on their way to draw water while he was searching for his father's donkeys (1 Sam 9:3–12). Even Jesus, finding respite at a well in Samaria, conversed with a Samaritan woman who was drawing water. Their conversation turned to the subject of her marriages (John 4:1–26). As literal and metaphorical sustainers of life, women at the well are central to the continuation of the patriarchal line of descent and to the fulfillment of the "divine promise of descendants to Abraham and Sarah" (Cook 1997: 13).

Water as a crucial life-sustaining element is illustrated by the occasion when Hagar and Ishmael were in dire need. Besides the sheer need for water, the scene described in Gen 16:7 speaks of the "elation and jubilation that resulted from digging a successful well" (Hyman 2006: 181) and of the need to be accepted by the god of the Israelites. Hagar is the first person in the Hebrew Bible to name a deity, naming him at a well, and naming the well after him: "Therefore the well was called the Well of the Living One Who sees me" (Gen 16:13–14).

Wells were also loci for social custom and cooperation. They united communities over the need for a consistent source of water. The location and usage of wells defined who belonged to a community and who did not—much as in Hagar's case. The geographic location of wells was an important heirloom that was passed down through the generations: "the name of the well and the name of the place became one and the same" (Hyman 2006: 184). Given that the task of drawing water was assigned to young women, it is easy to imagine that the location of wells was knowledge that was passed down through the generations of women, maintaining the livelihood of their pastoral communities.

In the Nevi'im and Ketuvim, wells serve as metaphors for feminine beauty and the dangers of female sexuality (Hyman 2006: 185). The young fool is advised to beware of the bittersweet words of the loose woman and to drink from his own well (Prov 5:15). The beloved in the Song of Solomon (4:15) is described as "a garden fountain, a well of living water, and flowing streams from Lebanon." These metaphors confirm the association of wells, water, and young women as is the case in Canaanite literature (Marsman 2003: 420). In the Ugaritic Legend of Aqhat, Pughatu is referred to as "She who carries water on her shoulder" (KTU 1.19:11.1, see Pardee 1997a: 352). In the Kirta Epic, Thatmanatu, the youngest daughter of King Kirtu, "went out at dusk to draw water" (KTU 1.16:1.50–51; see Pardee 1997b: 340).

One thing biblical narratives do not tell us is how water was collected and what type of vessel was employed. According to King and Stager (2001: 125), women used a vessel attached to a rope "and carried the water from the well in jars (*kaddim*) on their head or shoulder." Getting water from a spring might have been similar—a woman would lower the vessel to collect the water and then carry the filled vessel in some manner back home. This interpretation is problematic when examined more closely.

Here is where we posed a number of research questions, such as how was water for domestic usage gathered, carried, and stored in Iron Age Israel? In order to answer this question, several others must be raised. Exactly what type of vessel was used for carrying water, particularly for use when women or children were drawing water from a central source for domestic use? In what manner did they actually carry these vessels? What type of vessel was initially used to collect the water? Might it be some sort of a one-handled jug or, perhaps, a two handled jug tied on each side, and then transferred to a larger vessel? How were the jars/jugs carried? Why do we assume that it is on the head (or the shoulder?) Was the smaller vessel used for gathering something that was left at the well for everyone's use or did the women carry this vessel with them also?

Vocabulary

What types of jars and vessels were used for transporting and storing water? Using the biblical text alone, reconstructing the method and type of vessels employed for carrying water in ancient Israel is a challenging task. The Hebrew text is not consistent in its usage of specific terminology to describe the water-carrying vessels. Additionally, there is little evidence that the ancients classified different types of jars and storage vessels as we do, nor do these classifications necessarily match standard pottery typologies.

The most common word for a water-carrying vessel in the Hebrew Bible is *kad*. The same word is used in Ugaritic for both a vessel and a measure (Kletter 2017: 30). The *kad* was probably a medium size clay vessel often translated in English as "jug" or "jar." Yet, the *kad* that Rebekah was carrying on her shoulder (כד על שכמה), and which she used to water the camels (Gen 24:15) would likely have been a larger and heavier vessel than a small jug. The *kaddim* into which Gideon and his men hid torches (Judg 7:16–20) would have been smaller than Rebekah's *kad* because they were held in their hands (Judg 7:19). On Mount Carmel, Elijah also has four *kaddim* of water poured over his sacrifice. Four jugs would not have drenched the bull and the wood. These texts indicate that *kaddim* are large enough to hold torches and substantial amounts of water, yet light enough for a woman to carry when filled with water.

The *ṣappaḥah* David takes from King Saul (1 Sam 26:12) is designated as a water vessel (צפחת המים). Again it is a portable vessel. The *ṣappaḥah* of the widow of Zarephath might be larger as it was used to store oil (1 Kgs 17:12–14). The remaining meal was stored in a *kad*, though in 1 Sam 26 it contained water.

In the same story, Elijah asks for a little water in a *keli* to drink (1 Kgs 17:10). This word has a very wide semantic range from weapons to any type of tool and implements (HALOT 2:478–79). Here it refers to a small drinking vessel more like a cup.

The Hebrew Bible refers to six other types of vessels for storing and transporting various liquids. The *kōr* is mentioned as a measure of oil and of grain as well as the corresponding square plot sown with that amount of grain. If the *kor* was a vessel too, it would have been a large storage jar with an estimated capacity between 350 and 450 liters (HALOT 2: 496), far too heavy for transport (Lipschits et al. 2010: 455). Kletter (2017: 29) argues that the *kor* could never have been a vessel but must be understood as a measuring unit.

The *bath* (occurring thirteen times in the Bible) was mass produced in the late eighth century BCE (Lipschits et al. 2010: 457–58). The Hebrew Bible uses it as a fixed capacity, although in reality the jars recovered in archaeological contexts have no uniform capacity (Kletter 2017: 30–31).

Another fixed-capacity measure in the Hebrew Bible is the *hin*, possibly reserved for cultic use since it does not appear in economic contexts (Lipschits et al. 2010: 454). It parallels the Egyptian *hnw*, which was also a fixed measure with its beginning in the Egyptian New Kingdom. *Hin/hnw* is present on wall drawings and in excavations as well as in the Amarna Letters and on an Iron II alabaster from Samaria (Kletter 2017: 30). Related to the *hin* is the *log*, in parallel with the Ugaritic *lg/lgm*, which was used for measuring and storing wine and oil. A seventh century BCE Hebrew inscription on an alabaster fragment from Susa denotes "one *hin* and one half *log* and a quarter *log*" (Kletter, 2017: 30).

The *ḥemet* Hagar fills with water when God showed her the well (Gen 21:19) was a portable water carrier, probably a skin, and thus a likely container for water transport thanks to its light weight. As these water skins are not normally found in the archaeological record, this line of inquiry is moot.

Related to the *ḥemet* is the *nebel*, which was most likely a clay vessel used for transporting liquids on journeys (1 Sam 1:24, 10:3, 25:18; 2 Sam 16:1). As skins are much lighter than clay vessels for transporting liquids, one would surmise that the *nebel* is a skin like the *ḥemet*. The Septuagint has indeed rendered the *nebel* as ἀσκός "skin" in Jer 13:12, though it merely transliterated it as νεβελ in 1 Sam 1:24 and 2 Sam 16:1. In Isa 30:14, however, the *nebel* is associated with the potter and it is shattered in pieces (Lipschits et al. 2010: 470). As is the case with the *bath*, the *kad*, and the *kor*, the *nebel* appears as a vessel as much as a measure, which is hardly surprising from the point of view of the ancient users, but produces intractable problems when we want to fit these different terms in standardized measuring systems. Therefore, biblical texts cannot be expected to provide a coherent classification of vessels. The same term may have been used for different vessels and measures at different times and in different locations, while two different terms can be used to refer to the same vessel as is the case today. A "cuppa tea" may be served in a mug, a fine-bone china cup, or a bowl.

The pottery typology developed by archaeologists is hardly more precise. A jug is a type of vessel with a pouring lip, mouth, or spout, or a deep container for liquids with a narrow mouth. It can also be defined as a cylindrical container with a handle and a lip. A jar, in contrast, tends to be larger and has a wider mouth than a jug. Function can only be inferred from shape and size, however, and archaeological terminology is hardly more precise than biblical terms.

Iconographic Sources

We have little comparative iconographical ancient Near Eastern evidence of women carrying water vessels. No women are shown carrying water vessels on their heads. In the Lachish reliefs segment 4, for example, the scenes of the Israelite captives exiting the city show men, women, and children carrying their possessions over their shoulders with one hand clutching a small jug, perhaps for water?

The earliest pictorial evidence of women carrying water on their heads comes not from the ancient Near East but from classical Greece. Several decorated *hydriai* show women collecting and transporting water in *hydriai* resting on their heads. The *hydria* is a rounded terracotta vessel with three handles—two at the sides and one at the back— used, as its name indicates, for fetching water (Hemingway and Hemingway 2000). A 510 BCE Athenian *hydria* shows two women with (presumably) full vessels upright while another woman's hydria (perhaps empty) is tilted (fig. 1). Another hydria shows five women conversing while another fills her vessel at the fountain (fig. 2).

These images might be purely stylistic. They indicate that carrying a vessel on the head was the canonical Greek way to portray women fetching water, which says little about actual practice. As is the case with terminology and measurements, a wide range

Figure 1. Attic black-figure
hydria. Louvre Museum;
© 1993 RMN / Hervé
Lewandowski.

Figure 2. Women drawing
water at the fountain house.
Terracotta hydria, ca.
510–500 BCE. Metropolitan
Museum of Art.

Figure 3. Abraham's Servant Meeteth Rebecca, ca. 1896–1902, by James Jacques Joseph Tissot.

of practices can be expected at any given time and place. Ethnographic studies can be valuable, but they need to be approached carefully with an understanding that Iron Age Israelite society varies from today's cultures and practices. Another instance of the need for caution concerns the artistic representations of women at the well in the "maiden and the water jar" scenes in nineteenth and early twentieth-century travel accounts in biblical lands (Kenaan-Kedar 2013).

Jacques Joseph (James) Tissot visited the Middle East at the end of his life (between 1886 and 1896) after a religious experience. Famous for his representations of fashionably dressed women, the biblical scenes to which he turned after the death of his Irish mistress and his return to France became iconic among Anglo-Saxon religious communities. Though he likely observed women carrying water on their shoulders during his travels in Palestine, Tissot's *Abraham's Servant Meeteth Rebecca* depicts Rebekah and a row of other women in the background each with a jar on her head (fig. 3). As with the models of his prereligious phase, Rebekah is an alluring young woman with bare feet and pouting lips that retains a provocative pose behind the modesty of the veil and robes with which she has been decked.

These paintings should not be taken as representations of actual methods of water carrying. The advent of photography introduced a new technique but not a new approach to the subject. Western perceptions of biblical women were so colored by the paintings of the previous centuries that early twentieth century photographs were necessarily staged due to the time it took to impress the plates. Technical constraints and the popular "Maiden and the Jar" scene led Tel Aviv photographers in the 1920s and 1930s to use immigrant young women posing "as Arab women wearing traditional Arab costume—embroidered dresses and head covering embellished with coins, and holding water jars" (Kenaan-Kedar 2013: 52). Fashionable as they were, the likelihood that these early photographs and prints reflected actual practices is slim. In his nineteenth century travelogue, Reverend F. W. Farmer describes how the women of Zer'in, the biblical Jezreel, were drawing the day's water from the village's spring with large earthen vessels:

> ... and we met the entire procession of them bearing their pitchers, sometimes simply balanced on the head, sometimes supported with one arm. There were none who, like Rebekah, carried their pitchers on the shoulder— a mark, I believe, of higher rank. (Farrar 1871: 442–42)

Contrary to Tissot, Farrar remained faithful to the biblical scene and remembered that Rebekah carried her jar on her shoulder (Gen 24:16). Farrar did note that some Zer'ini women were not balancing their pitcher on their head, but what mattered most was to underline the gap between the noble bearing of the imagined biblical figure and the actual conditions he encountered in Zer'in, which he describes as "wretched" (Farrar 1871: 381; also Ebeling in this volume). These living conditions would have not been far removed from those in rural backwaters at home, but Westerners saw them as illustrations of a decline they attributed to Islam and to the infamous Ottoman "sick man of Europe."

Turning to current ethnographic studies on water carrying, especially in rural communities in Africa, researchers have found that 90 percent of water (and wood) gathering is carried out by women. This percentage bears a striking similarity to what we suspect was the case in biblical times and such studies can be fruitful to our understanding of ancient water-carrying practices. For example, researchers of the Kikuyu and Luo tribes in East Africa found that women who were accustomed to carrying loads on their heads did so more efficiently than people who did not (Dweck

2010). Comparing the rates of exertion and energy consumption of these women while they were carrying loads on their heads and on their backs with the same rates for army recruits and other Westerners carrying the same loads, revealed that these women exerted less energy than the Westerners while carrying heavy loads in general. Additional studies found that the gait mechanics of the women from these tribes resulted in a near-perfect transfer between potential and kinetic energy while carrying loads on their heads. This demonstrates that the Kikuyu and Luo women found a way of bodily transporting loads that exerted the least amount of energy.

Nevertheless, carrying such heavy loads of water continuously results in numerous health problems for women. "In some parts of Africa, where women expend as much as 85 percent of their daily energy intake fetching water, the incidence of anaemia and other health problems are very high" (UNESCO 2004). It is likely that Iron Age Israelite women were plagued with similar health issues, which can account for reproductive and fertility problems. If biblical women carried water on their shoulders like Rebekah, they would have exerted themselves even more than the women of these African tribes who carried their loads on their heads.

An experimental archaeological test was conducted at Tel Beth Shemesh after archaeologists noted an anomalously large number of broken pottery bases in the silt at the bottom of the reservoir among twelve whole or broken vessels and 1,495 indicative sherds (Bunimovitz, Lederman, and Manor 2009: 133). The large number of base sherds found within the silt suggested that they resulted from the manner in which the water was drawn from the reservoir. The majority consisted of the lower parts of the jugs revealing a unique breakage pattern with "the handle with the upper part of jug, including its mouth, broken off as if forcefully torn away (134).

Assuming that this type of broken jug was used to gather water, the archaeologists speculated that the intact jugs were probably tied to ropes and then dropped into the reservoir via a shaft. On the way, the vessels would have hit against the walls of the shaft. To test the theory, a potter produced four replicas of the jugs using local clay similar to the ancient jugs. These jugs, like the original, could hold about 2.2 liters of water. Having found a bottle-shaped cistern nearby, the archaeologists tied the jugs to a rope and lowered them down. One of the problems was where and how to tie the jug. Tying it to a handle resulted in water spillage on the way up. Tying the rope under and around the protruding ridge of the neck was the most successful method. Lifting a water-filled jug out of the cistern soon revealed that any careless movement caused the vessel to hit against the cistern's side, causing the base of the jug to break off and sink down into the cistern leaving only the upper part of the vessel tied to the rope when lifted out. The experiment resulted in three out of four of the replica jugs with the same breakage pattern as the excavated remains. Experiments like this provide possible clues as to the method of gathering water from a well or cistern, but questions regarding the manner of transport remain open.

Figure 4. Palestinian women on the way to the well.
Source: Palestine in Pictures, C.E. Raven, 1929, p. 3.
Library of Congress Prints and Photographs Division,
G. Eric and Edith Matson Photograph Collection.

In early Palestinian villages, water was drawn from wells in buckets with two handles tied to a rope (Ziffer 2013). Water was then carried home in a *jarrah* (Arabic), a large jar with a body resembling a sack with two handles and a short cup-form neck (fig. 4). These *jarrahs* were anywhere from 29–50 cm in height. The women carried the full water jars on their heads, covered with a kerchief to pad their heads. Ziffer observed that on their way to the well, the women would carry the empty jar on their shoulder with the mouth facing down. From a distance it would be easy to tell whether the jars were full or empty and if the women were returning or going to the well. Once at home, the water was stored in larger water jars about 50–70 cm high with a flat base and two to four handles. A dipper type jug was then used to retrieve water from the large jar. No less than four different types of vessels are used for water gathering and storage, which goes a long way to explain the difficulties in identifying the names and holding capacity of vessels in the Bible.

Our excavation at Jezreel conducted a simple experimental archaeological investigation during the 2015 season. Tel Jezreel has no large-scale water system, but it does have at least 68 pits, some dated to the Iron Age (Franklin 2017). Though some of these pits may have served as grain silos rather than water cisterns (Franklin 2018: 78), the distance between the village and the perennial spring makes the use of some of the pits for storage of run-off rain water likely.

As one of the goals of the 2014 expedition was to discover the ancient path that ran from the spring to the tell that is visible in the LiDAR scan, sections of the path were excavated near the lower tell (Area S) and another on the slope above (Area P). These paths meet on the slope north–northeast of Zerʻin. The width of the path leading to the spring is not uniform. In some places it is extremely narrow—0.6 to 1 m—where the topography allows it to widen out to approximately 3 to 4.5 m. In the narrower stretches, the rock face may have been cut to widen the path to allow enough room for two people to pass. Sandal and horseshoe nails dating from the Roman to the Ottoman

Figure 5. Local roads connecting Tel Jezreel with 'Ein Jezreel. Courtesy of the Jezreel Expedition.

periods speak to the continued importance of this path as a major way to the spring (Feinberg Vamosh 2015).

The distance between the spring of Ein Jezreel and the Iron Age compound on the upper tell is a little over 1 km with a rise of more than 90 m (fig. 5). Walking at an average pace without any additional carried weight takes about 20 minutes. During the 2015 excavation season at Jezreel, the authors wanted to figure out how water may have been transported in biblical (and later) periods. Assuming that young women would have carried the water for daily use from the spring to their households, we recruited three young women from the excavation to carry water from the spring up the winery complex located northwest of the spring (Franklin et al. 2017: 54), but less than half-way to the center of Zer'in. Our goal was to ascertain whether or not young women would have been physically capable of carrying this much water on a daily basis and how strenuous it might have been.

Putting our theory to the test, the young women began their hike right before sun-down, remaining consistent with the only piece of textual evidence we have regarding the time women would go out to retrieve water: "the time of the evening that women go out to draw water" (Gen 24:11). Practically, this also made sense as it is a cooler time of the day, especially during the hot summers, and there was still some daylight to walk the darkened path. Due to time constraints, budgetary reasons, and uncertainty as to which type of vessels were employed, we focused on the assumed weight of the water rather

Figure 6. Beginning the walk. Photo courtesy of the authors.

than the actual shape of vessel. While not scientific by any means, we loaded three vinyl laundry baskets used in the excavation to wash pottery sherds and packed each one with six liters of plastic water bottles (figs. 6–8). Using the size of a typical liquid storage vessel based on ethnographic research, we assumed that a woman would have carried approximately six to eight liters of water each time on each trip. At first, the young women bore their 7–8 kilo burden effortlessly. After a few minutes in the upward climb, they began shifting the weight on their heads, on their shoulders, or against their hips. No method was preferred but they all agreed that carrying the vessels on their heads was the least strenuous, though this approach would have taken more skill and practice. Obviously, the plastic laundry baskets were not easy to balance on heads without

Figure 7. Walking along the excavated area of Tel Ein Jezreel. Photo courtesy of the authors.

Figure 8. Arrival at the Iron Age winery. Photo courtesy of the authors.

padding and previous practice. Without the exact type of vessel, we could not predict the actual carrying method.

Given the necessary confinement of women in the village to avoid impregnation by strangers, women could have experienced water chores as a time of limited freedom away from flies, smoke, crying babies, pestering men, and in-laws, a time purposely made longer by chatting, discreet personal hygiene by the fresh water, and free gossip; remember that young women who had survived long enough to be able to carry water would have been the fittest.

While awaiting more precise data, we cannot assume that our Jezreelite ancestresses carried water on their heads, or only on their heads. We know very little about the types of vessels they used, but we should not expect any uniformity across time and place. More experiments are needed in the somewhat prosaic matter of water transport, though that is precisely this kind of focus that holds much potential to recover a sense of daily life in biblical times.

References

Bunimovitz, Shlomo, Zvi Lederman, and Dale W. Manor. 2009. "The Archaeology of Border Communities: Renewed Excavations at Tel Beth-Shemesh. Part 1: The Iron Age." *NEA* 72:114–42.

Cook, Joan E. 1997. "Wells, Women, and Faith." *Proceedings of the Eastern Great Lakes and Midwest Biblical Societies* 17:11–18.

Dweck, Jessica. 2010. "Head Case: The Art and Science of Carrying Things on Your Head." Slate Magazine, https://slate.com/news-and-politics/2010/08/the-art-and-science-of-carrying-things-on-your-head.html

Edelman, Diana V., and Hadi Ghantous. 2014. "Cisterns and Wells in Biblical Memory." Pages 177–96 in *Memory and the City in Ancient Israel*. Edited by Diana V. Edelman and Ehud Ben Zvi. Winona Lake, IN: Eisenbrauns.

Farrar, F. W. 1871. "Days in the Holy Land." *The Quiver: An Illustrated Magazine for Sunday and General Reading* 6:293–98.

Franklin, Norma. 2017. "The Story of Naboth's Vineyard and the Ancient Winery in Jezreel." TheTorah.com. https://www.thetorah.com/article/the-story-of-naboths-vineyard-and-the-ancient-winery-in-jezreel

———. 2018. "Exploring the Function of Bell-Shaped Pits: With a View to Iron Age Jezreel." *Eretz-Israel* 33:76–82.

Franklin, Norma, Jennie Ebeling, Philippe Guillaume, and Deborah Appler. 2017. "Have We Found Naboth's Vineyard at Jezreel?" *BAR* (November/December):49–54.

Hemingway, Colette, and Seán Hemingway. 2000. "Greek Hydriai (Water Jars) and Their Artistic Decoration." *Heilbrunn Timeline of Art History*. New York: The Metropolitan Museum of Art, http://www.metmuseum.org/toah/hd/gkhy/hd_gkhy.htm

Hyman, Ronald. 2006. "Multiple Functions of Wells in the Tanakh." *JBQ* 34:180–89.

Kenaan-Kedar, Nurith. 2013. "The Maiden and the Jar as an Israeli Image." Pages 49–58 in *To the Fountain: The Maiden and the Jar; A Local and Multi-cultural Image*. Edited by N. Kenaan-Kedar. Tel Aviv: Eretz-Israel.

King, Philip, and Lawrence Stager. 2001. *Life in Biblical Israel*. Louisville, KY: Westminster John Knox.

Kletter, Raz. 2017. "Vessels and Measures: The Biblical Liquid Capacity System." *IEJ* 64:22–37.

Lipschits, Oded, Ido Koch, Arie Shaus, and Shlomo Guil. 2010. "The Enigma of the Biblical

Bath and the System of Liquid Volume Measurement during the First Temple Period." *UF* 42:453–78.

Marsman, Henni J. 2003. *Women In Ugarit and Israel: Their Social and Religious Position in the Context of the Ancient Near East.* Leiden: Brill.

Pardee, Dennis. 1997a. "The 'Aqhatu Legend." Pages 343–56 in *Canonical Compositions from the Biblical World.* Vol. 1 of *The Context of Scripture.* Edited by William W. Hallo. Leiden: Brill.

———. 1997b. "The Kirta Epic." Pages 333–43 in *Canonical Compositions from the Biblical World.* Vol. 1 of *The Context of Scripture.* Edited by William W. Hallo. Leiden: Brill.

UNESCO Water Portal. 2004. "Facts about Women and Water." GWAnet, http://gender.cawa-ter-info.net/what_is/facts_e.htm

Vamosh, Miriam Feinberg. 2015. "Path Perfect: Reclaiming Jezreel." Online: http://miriamfeinbergvamosh.com/wp-content/uploads/2015/01/Jezreel-from-The-Bible-and-Interpretation.pdf

Ziffer, Irit. 2013. "Water Vessels in Traditional Arab Pottery." Pages 25–40 in *To the Fountain: The Maiden and the Jar; A Local and Multi-Cultural Image.* Edited by N. Kenaan-Kedar. Tel Aviv: Eretz-Israel.

IN THE LAND AND IN THE DIRT:
THE VALUE OF FIELD-SCHOOL EXPERIENCE
FOR DIVINITY SCHOOL STUDENTS

Tony W. Cartledge

Abstract: This essay is a testimony on the impact of active participation in an archaeological field school such as the Jezreel Expedition on divinity school or seminary students and volunteers.

Keywords: biblical archaeology, field school, holy land, pilgrimage

There is the land upon which we gaze, the ground upon which we stand, and the dirt in which we dig: for divinity school students embarking on their first excavation, all of them are holy.[1] Such students are pilgrims as well as researchers. They come not only for the technical training involved in modern methods of archaeology, but also for the experience of working and eating and sleeping in the land where Hebrew ancestors scratched out a living. They want to walk in the land where Jesus walked and ponder the ways in which they feel called to follow his teachings.

As team members from one world who travel to another for a time of living and working together, they experience the full measure of what anthropologist Victor Turner called *communitas*, a liminal experience of transcending space and time between the quotidian world of daily life and the immersive experience of digging in sacred ground (Turner 1973; Turner and Turner 1978).

Participating in an archaeological field school takes divinity school students a step beyond pilgrim travelers, increasing the likelihood of "crossing over" from the ordinary

---

Submitted with grateful appreciation to Norma Franklin not only for her many contributions to the field of archaeology, but for her helpful and welcoming approach to involving students in the field, insisting that all participants are members of the team.

1. I write from the perspective of a Protestant Christian professor who brought students from Campbell University Divinity School to participate in the 2018 season of excavations of the Jezreel Expedition. Campbell University has historic Baptist ties, but students come from a variety of Christian traditions, most of them Protestant.

through a convergence of phenomena to experience the kind of intense and emotive experiences that Jane Bennett (2001: 31) describes as "enchantment."

Recent studies on the relationship of pilgrimage and archaeology have emphasized the importance of encounters with objects as well as with people and places (Scousen 2018). For religiously oriented students excavating at a biblical location, the objects encountered are on another level than icons, images, or buildings that encrust the surface of sacred sites: they are the very stuff of ancient life, preserved in the time capsule of archaeological strata.

The benefits of field-school participation go beyond an encounter with the past, however. Students whose opinion of Israel and the West Bank may have been shaped almost entirely by pro-Zionist preachers or politicians have the opportunity to experience life on the ground in a very small country made even smaller by walls, fences, and border crossings designed to keep displaced Palestinians and their Israeli occupiers apart. This may lead to a new appreciation of the sociopolitical situation and the inherent obstacles to peace in the land. For some, it may help them realize, for the first time, that "Israeli" and "Israelite" are not synonymous terms.

In sum, participation in a field-school excavation offers a smorgasbord of benefits for divinity school students. Intellectually, they gain an "on the ground" appreciation for the geography and climate of the land. They learn the techniques of archaeology and an appreciation for the mixed parade of cultures that have inhabited the biblical world. On a more personal level, they have the opportunity to make spiritual connections through hands-on encounters with holy dirt, the artifacts it holds, and the stories it tells. On yet another level, it exposes them to realities that can make them more informed and compassionate citizens of the world.

In support of this view, I offer as a case study the experience of thirteen persons associated with Campbell University Divinity School (CUDS) who participated in the 2018 season of the Jezreel Expedition, led by co-directors Norma Franklin of the Zinman Institute of Archaeology at the University of Haifa, and Jennie Ebeling of the University of Evansville, Indiana.

Six members of the team had taken my archaeology course at CUDS prior to the dig, and the others had been prepared through advance orientation and reading of the Jezreel Expedition Field Manual. The team arrived midway through the four-week dig and worked for the remainder of the season, lodging with other team members at nearby Kibbutz Yizre'el and attending evening lectures.

Franklin, Ebeling, and Field Director Ian Cipin oriented team members to the geographical setting and strategic history of the site, to its various biblical connections, and to the history of excavations at Jezreel. Following Franklin's philosophy that learning is maximized through a broadening of connections, Campbell volunteers were assigned to work in different squares so that they could interface with team members from other schools and other countries, most from the University of Evansville and University College, London.

Square supervisors offered hands-on training, and team members readily took instruction, blending smoothly into the work flow. Whether clearing an ancient pavement; chasing walls; uncovering a workshop for basalt implements; articulating mud brick; lowering a living surface; identifying and preserving pottery, flint, and bones; or washing and helping to classify ceramic finds, the team worked efficiently and cooperatively with supervisors and other students.

Even when assigned to the less glamorous and physically demanding work of backfilling squares that have been fully excavated with dirt from the spoil pile, team members worked without complaint and learned different kinds of lessons.

Daily digging followed a predictable schedule, beginning at 5:00 a.m. and continuing until around 1:00 p.m. Active squares were located in two nearby areas on the lower tel, near the spring, where most residents probably lived in antiquity.

Areas of the excavation explored in 2018 were primarily on a level from the Early Bronze Age (about 3600–2600 BCE), though later usage and a sloping terrain made the excavation challenging. Refuse pits and the robber trenches yielded broken pottery from the Middle and Late Bronze Age, Iron Age, Persian, and Hellenistic periods, as well as Roman and Mamluk times.

Pottery washing at Jezreel offered a more pleasant experience than at most digs, where buckets of pottery are schlepped back to the camp and filled with water to soften the dirt before being washed later in the day with the help of a second bucket of water that quickly becomes muddy. The lower tell at Jezreel is little more than 100 m uphill from a small park at ʿEin Jezreel, the spring that supported life in the area for thousands of years. The original spring has gone dry, but water is pumped in from another nearby spring, traveling through a concrete sluice and into a pool. Franklin conceived the innovative idea of collecting pottery in open plastic baskets that could be set into the stream and easily swirled about to remove excess dirt. Though tired after a morning of digging, team members could sit in the shade with their feet in cool water to wash the sherds onsite. Sherds were then returned to the baskets, carried back to the kibbutz and spread in the sun to dry, allowing team members to avoid the hot and muddy chore of washing pottery later in the afternoon. Divinity school participants, without exception, found all aspects of the experience to be rewarding, as revealed in reflection papers submitted following the dig.[2]

Muriel Lasater, a December 2018 graduate, was gratified by the tangible connection to ancient peoples: "Even though archaeological digging can be strenuous and exhausting, it can also be very enlightening. I love how this process connects us to humanity at large and allows us to gain insight into their lives by studying pottery, artifacts, and figurines. It's amazing how this connects us to people who lived thousands and thousands of years ago." Digging through Bronze Age remains reminded participants

2. A feature article about the Jezreel Expedition including some of the student quotes used here appeared earlier in *Nurturing Faith Journal and Bible Studies* 36.5 (Sept.–Oct. 2018), 46–48.

that the Hebrews controlled the land for only a few hundred years during the Iron Age, and even that was not uniform. Other peoples were in the land long before them, lived alongside them, and have remained ever since.

David Helms, pastor of First Baptist Church in Southern Pines, NC and an adjunct professor at CUDS, also felt a connection to the ancients: "The experience of digging in the dirt, separating stones, and placing pottery shards aside brings me closer to those ancient people the Bible calls 'the people of the earth,' reminding me that we are all simply 'people of the earth.'"

David Brantley of Raleigh, who left a successful business career to study theology, believed the dig would prove helpful in his future ministry. He had previously experienced Israel through a study tour, but wrote: "the practical experience of participating in an actual dig has not only been an experience of a lifetime, but has provided insights into Canaanite, Israelite, and even Roman history that will surely assist my ministry in the future." Prior to the dig, participants engaged in a three-day "mini-tour" of southern Israel, Jerusalem, Qumran, and Samaria. They examined the ruins of Lachish, walked barefoot on the Lithostratos, prayed at the Western Wall, pondered the remains of Qumran, and drove through the Samarian hill country to stand atop Mount Gerizim and look down on the teeming Balata refugee camp in the city of Nablus. During breaks in digging, they took in the views from Mount Carmel and Mount Tabor. They had the rare treat of touring Megiddo with Franklin, who excavated there for nearly two decades before moving to Jezreel.

John Robert Harris, a recent graduate who is associate pastor of Faith Fellowship Church in Kinston, NC, found visiting those sites to be an invaluable adjunct to the dig experience. Both brought him closer to the biblical narratives. "Stepping into an ongoing archaeological dig in Jezreel has furthered my connection with the Bible as well as scratched my itch for discovery," he said. Like several other participants, Harris kept a journal of his experiences. "My time here will forever stay with me," he said, "and I pray will continue to teach me years from now."

For Victor Knight, the spiritual benefit of the dig came as a surprise. Knight took Divinity School courses during his last semester as an undergraduate at Campbell before entering a master's degree program at Yale University, where he plans to study Ugaritic. "For me, coming here was an academic affair," he wrote, noting that his academic side was in fact challenged through field-school lectures and the discipline of digging. "Nevertheless, in a much more unexpected way, the trip has affected me spiritually. From standing on the Mt. of Olives to watching pilgrims driven to tears, I have come to have a more complete picture of the Bible."

Dale Belvin, a CUDS graduate and pastor of the Rose of Sharon Freewill Baptist Church in Bear Grass, NC, also appreciated the dual benefits: "This has been both an academic experience and a spiritual experience," he wrote. "It is academic because I have learned so much. I have learned about Israel and Jerusalem in biblical times as well as modern-day Israel. I have learned some of the finer details about some of my favorite biblical stories like David fighting Goliath and some of the traditions around the death, burial, and resurrection of Jesus. I have learned a great deal about Neolithic, Bronze Age, and Iron Age living. It is a spiritual experience because this is the land of the Bible. Nearly every city, town, village, landmark, mountain, or area has significance. I have found the work of excavating to be very spiritual as we have gotten into the dirt and put in a good day's work."

The experience of simply being in the land was as important as the dig itself for some students. For Ryan Craddock, a CUDS student who works as a counselor in a halfway house, getting to Israel was the primary goal. "I would have washed camels to reach it," he wrote. "My main desire was to step into the scenery of the stories I love, that formed my faith, ancient tales that have shaped the world," he related. "I was quickly immersed in a place where the past meets the present, and where people from all nations, faith traditions and ideologies converge to experience and discover something uniquely human and deeply personal."

Craddock found that the experience went even deeper: "For me, the whole trip is like an excavation of the soul. With some work, guidance and gracious assistance from others, stone and soil are cleared away to reveal ancient realities and bring new insight."

But it isn't just encountering artifacts of the past that provides connections. Karie Parkes, a CUDS graduate and current Director of Student Activities for Campbell's undergraduates, found the community aspect of living in a kibbutz and getting to know other people to be especially gratifying. While others may have bemoaned the tedium of washing pottery, she considered it her favorite activity because it was easier to talk and connect with team members who were excavating in other squares.

Experiences such as these are multiplied hundreds of times over by volunteers at other excavations, especially those that have biblical connections. For divinity school or seminary students especially, whether on the surface of the land or beneath it, participants can find the field-school experience to be a most rewarding part of their personal, professional, and spiritual journeys.

To Norma Franklin and other dig directors who willingly embrace students as members of the excavation team and work to make the experience mutually beneficial, may these reflections serve as an expression of gratitude and respect for the blessing you have been—and continue to be—to others.

References

Bennett, Jane. 2001. *The Enchantment of Modern Life: Attachments, Crossings, and Ethics.* Princeton, NJ: Princeton University.

Scousen, B. Jacob. 2018. "Rethinking Archaeologies of Pilgrimage." *Journal of Social Archaeology* 18:264–65.

Turner, Victor. 1973. "The Center Out There: The Pilgrim's Goal." *HR* 12:191–230.

Turner, Victor, and Edith Turner. 1978. *Image and Pilgrimage in Christian Culture: Anthropological Perspectives.* Oxford: Blackwell.

The Secret Life of the Archaeological Field School: The Jezreel Expedition as a Case Study

Ian Cipin

Abstract: Archaeological field schools have been an integral part of excavation projects in the Southern Levant for many years now, having evolved and developed since William Dever invited students to earn credit for taking part in archaeological fieldwork at Gezer in 1966. An essential source of funding for many excavations, archaeological field schools in Israel attract hundreds of students each year who are eager to earn credits while also gaining valuable fieldwork experience. Archaeology has changed tremendously since Dever's first field school, and this paper asks whether or not archaeological field schools in the region have kept pace with these developments. Using the Jezreel Expedition as a case study, I argue that the innovative approach to the archaeological field school adopted there, while challenging to implement, offered students the opportunity not only to obtain credit, but also to achieve a broader understanding of the archaeological process and solid preparation for a career in archaeology.

Keywords: field school, students, volunteers, education, field manual, methodologies, syllabus

Although I first met Norma Franklin in 2006, it was not until 2008 that I worked directly for her. Unbeknownst to me at the time, Norma's ethos on what a dig experience should be was already shaping my own values on this topic. From the very beginning, one referred to people attending as "volunteers" at one's peril. They were "team members" who had come to participate, contribute and, perhaps most importantly in the context of this essay, learn. People who were investing time and money to participate in an excavation were to be valued, with importance placed on both their pastoral and educational experience.

On reading the title of this article, one would be excused for thinking that this is an exposé detailing lurid revelations about scandalous activities that have gone on in the many field schools in Israel. There are others much more qualified than I to do this. The purpose of this essay, then, is to offer some observations on the life of the archaeological field school from its first appearance in the 1960s to the present day.

Since the first field school in Israel in 1966, the field-school experience has been "a rite of passage" (Adler 2002: 21). Yet, little or no consensus exists as to what constitutes good practice. Although supporting organizations, such as the American Schools of Oriental Research (ASOR) and the Institute for Field Research (IFR), have developed statements on codes of conduct, they have had little to say with regard to learning outcomes. It is not my intention to advocate the design of the perfect field school. Indeed, each project needs to tailor what it can offer according to the location of the site, the excavation strategy, and the periods of occupation, to name a few variables. Nevertheless, we have an obligation to those entrusted to our charge to ensure we are doing the maximum we can within the limited time we have to prepare them to be successful in the field. I believe that this means we, in turn, have an obligation continually to challenge our boundaries to ensure that the modern-day field school remains fit for purpose.

Background

For most of us who studied archaeology and continue excavating with students, the archaeological field school is an integral part of an archaeologist's training (Adler 2002: 21) even though, in some cases, it is not a requirement of the course or degree being taken. Even so, many universities, particularly in the United States, offer or accept credit for participating in a recognized field school. Personally, I attended university in the United Kingdom and, while gaining credit from a field school was not a requirement, accruing a prescribed number of fieldwork days from an approved excavation was.

It is entirely by chance that I stumbled upon issues surrounding field schools and why I felt they were falling short of what they should be achieving. My own experience on field schools had been both rewarding and stimulating, but once I began being involved in the tutoring of students and sharing these experiences with others, I came to realize that experiences are varied indeed.

I recently met with a friend who I knew had excavated at a well-known site in Israel some years ago while a student. This site has well-known and respected directors and staff and produces fascinating archaeology. As is inevitable in these circumstances, we started to compare our experiences. Paraphrasing somewhat the conversation, my friend said quite emphatically "That was the worst dig I ever went on." I was not a little surprised and asked why, since it is such an interesting site. "Absolutely, the site is really cool" was the answer. "Did you have an issue with the directors and the way they acted?" I asked. "No, they were impressive and always spoke well to the volunteers." "So, were your supervisors mean to you or were they just not very good at what they were doing?" "Oh no, they really knew their stuff and I never saw them being mean to anyone. To the contrary actually. They were popular." Perplexed I asked, "in the light of all that, why do you feel it was the worst dig you went on then?" "I learnt nothing!"

It transpires that no engagement with the archaeology was offered beyond moving dirt. My friend had no involvement with the recording process, was not shown how it was done and was not included in wider discussions about what was going on either in his section or in the area as a whole. In short, the volunteer's role was simply to move dirt. Those of us who are passionate about archaeology and the study of the past will not deny that this alone is an incredibly enjoyable and fulfilling experience, but one cannot but wonder if we are using these people as glorified laborers. To me, this means that the project had failed in its responsibilities as a field school. It cannot be right that team members go home feeling that they have learnt nothing.

As mentioned, organizations such as ASOR have education as central in their mission statements. Clearly there is a disconnect between the standards expected from supporting organizations and the experiences of students. In order to understand how this has come to be, a short review of the history of field schools in Israel is necessary.

A Brief History of the Field School

In the early days of the twentieth century, large-scale excavations were carried out in the region but they looked quite different to what we do today. Directors had their students assisting them as staff members with the bulk of the manual work and dirt shifting carried out by locally hired workers, many of whom were skilled excavators in their own right. The priority of early dig directors was to reveal the secrets held by the dirt, not to educate student excavators.

This is aptly illustrated with Breasted's excavations at Megiddo, commencing in 1926 on behalf of the Oriental Institute of the University of Chicago. Rather than providing field training for undergraduate students, the search for biblical Armageddon was the sole driving force. Reports of the day proudly tell us of the vast number of workers employed to carry out this large-scale excavation. Such is the interest in the spectacle of these excavations that they have now become the story itself (Cline 2020).

The field school as we know it today was born, it seems, in 1966. While reporting on the renewed excavations at Gezer in an article published in *Biblical Archaeologist* (Dever 1967), Dever explained that many of the students participated in a unique educational venture, attending lectures in the afternoons and evenings on field methodology, the archaeological history of Palestine, and the excavations past and present at Gezer. Those who completed a paper after the conclusion of the season received two hours of graduate credit through Hebrew Union College. This program was so successful that it was continued in future years (Dever 1967: 54).

The motives and inspiration for this "unique educational venture" are not stated, but the training given at Gezer was further formalized with the publication of a manual specifically written for archaeologists working in the field (Dever and Lance 1982). The editors were almost apologetic for the manual being so site specific (Dever and Lance 1982: i), each chapter being authored by a staff member according to his particular expertise at Gezer, and less like Wheeler's *Archaeology from the Earth* (1966). Written primarily for his students and originally published in 1954, Wheeler admirably attempted to write a field manual but it was written entirely from his own experience. It serves well as a general manual and we would be well served to take heed of several of his insights even though many years have passed since its writing. However, it makes no attempt to address student education in the field. Dever and Lance's manual addresses this issue.

By 1976, field schools were established at several other sites, including Lahav. Although not reported on until 2015, the Lahav field school was clearly regarded as significant enough to warrant mention in the methodological description of the Lahav report some forty years later. Clearly, logistical and functional forces were at play where, after prescreening, the participants' "motivation had been further demonstrated by a willingness to pay for their own travel to and support at the dig camp" (Cole 2015: 4). Already in 1976, students and volunteers were also drawn into discussions of digging strategy and the interpretation of the materials they were uncovering, and they had the opportunity to share in the field-recording duties or to learn additional skills by assisting staff specialists in the processing and analysis of materials (Cole 2015: 4). The benefits of such a strategy in enabling the staff to excavate with a higher degree of confidence and accuracy are clearly acknowledged.

What We Know about Digs Today

While it is unclear to what extent this applies to students, several excavations now produce comprehensive Staff Field Manuals or Field Manuals for Area Supervisors. For example, the Tel Dor Excavation Project produced a comprehensive 177-page Staff Manual with a detailed description of the history of excavations as well as excavation and recording methodologies.[1] As this manual seems very much written for the benefit of all taking part in the excavation, why refer to it as a "Staff Manual" rather than a "Field Manual"? This would surely encourage students to engage more with the methodologies of the excavation. It is, however, very encouraging to see the document available open access on the project's website.

Turning our attention to the structure of a field school, very little information is available either for the general enquirer or the prospective student. One exception is the syllabus for the forthcoming (2020) season at Tel Abel Beth Maacah Excavations available for download from IFR's website.[2] Though brief, this manual provides a clear idea of what students can expect to learn during the field school.

Adler (2002: 21) points out the "education-vs-skill" disconnect that derives from the reward structure within academic departments where primary importance is given to research and publication. This scenario must be familiar to many readers. So where does that leave the field school? Offering credit for the completion of such an activity is a useful way to generate income and it would seem that the formal obligation of a given

---

1. Tel Dor Excavation Project, 2013, http://dor.huji.ac.il/Download/Tel_Dor_Staff_Manual/Tel_Dor_Staff_Manual_2013.pdf.

2. https://ifrglobal.org/program/israel-abel-beth-maacah-short-sessions/

project ceases there. I suggest that, morally, it does not. If the position of the directors of prominent sites such as Gezer and Lahav is anything to go by, I am not alone.

Today, there are dozens of excavations in Israel each year offering "for credit" field schools. Many are listed on respected websites and publications. For example, *Biblical Archaeology Review*, the popular magazine published by the Biblical Archaeology Society, each year dedicates a section to digs for the forthcoming season in the region, often including links to the official project site detailing how many credits are available for attending and the costs involved.[3] There are, however, no details about what to expect from the field school. It is all about the number of credits obtained in exchange for participation—the field school seemingly being little more than a vehicle to obtain a product. Including some information on how participants can achieve their goals is not necessarily the responsibility of the Biblical Archaeology Society, but providing these details could enhance the value of the service.

The work of organizations in promoting field schools and offering grants to students should not be undervalued. Since 2007, ASOR has awarded more than $850,000 in excavation grants, dig fellowships, travel scholarships and other research fellowships. A recent circular communication from ASOR (11 January 2020) reports that, in 2019 alone, ASOR awarded $52,000 in dig scholarships. I personally know students who would not have been able to attend field schools in Israel were it not for such assistance. Given that ASOR is such a major funding source for students in the field, what policies are in place to ensure that these funds are spent wisely and students are receiving an appropriate educational experiences in the field?

The main vehicle for ASOR's compliance strategies is the Committee on Archaeological Research and Policy (CAP). CAP governs a whole range of the organization's activities, including setting standards and policies for professional conduct[4] and codes of conduct for fieldwork projects,[5] including a statement of general standards for projects that are associated with ASOR.[6] I wish for the moment to give some attention to the latter.

The opening sentence of CAP's Statement of Purpose and Principles acknowledges that "archaeological fieldwork is an important element of training and professional practice for many ASOR members" (www.asor.org). Nothing more is mentioned with regard to the training aspect of field work. The rest of the policy statement focuses on safety, ethical conduct and matters of equality. A robust code of conduct is indeed essential and ASOR is to be applauded for having comprehensive and detailed protective standards. But should the responsibility of an organization as important as ASOR stop there? Besides ensuring that all fieldwork participants undertake their activities in a

---

3. Biblical Archaeology Society, https://www.biblicalarchaeology.org/digs/.

4. http://www.asor.org/about-asor/policies/policy-on-professional-conduct/.

5. http://www.asor.org/about-asor/policies/code-of-conduct-for-fieldwork-projects.

6. http://www.asor.org/initiatives-projects/asor-affiliated-archaeological-projects/standards-policies/.

safe environment, expected standards of training given at field schools should be provided, especially those that carry an affiliation with the organization.

The Institute for Field Research (IFR) produces pamphlets for both students and potential partners. As stated above, the Tel Abel Beth Maacah Excavations is a rare project in Israel that provides a syllabus with defined learning outcomes. What was the situation at the Jezreel Expedition 2013–2018?

Jezreel as a Case Study

At Jezreel, we believed that a field school should not only offer participants the experience of taking part in an archaeological excavation, but also that participants should be taught to be archaeologists. It is they, after all, who will be the supervisors and field directors of tomorrow. It was after two seasons of excavation that I came to the conclusion that we had to change how we were doing things. I no longer wanted to work with a registrar; instead, I wanted to make the team members responsible for their own work, which implied changing our working practices. I spent the off-season redesigning the paperwork so that it was both easier to follow and easier on the eye. I knew that for this to work it had to be user friendly and simple to comprehend. A fieldwork manual was also written (Cipin n.d.) detailing some basic archaeological principles as well as our methodology, including a detailed guide on how recording and registration were to be carried out.

Our system was to work as follows. Each square had a designated square supervisor, selected for having some experience in the field, who was to maintain overall control. In agreement with the area supervisor, each square supervisor was responsible for taking out locus numbers from the register, starting the locus and finds sheets, taking opening and closing levels, writing tags, and issuing artifact numbers as needed and when appropriate. Ensuring that all finds found their way to where they needed to be was also under the square supervisor's jurisdiction. Clearly, this responsibility was not delegated to these team members lightly. Although they may have had prior experience, they were still beginners, mostly undergraduates students. Even if they had dug in the region before, it was highly unlikely that they had any previous experience in registration. If this was to work, I knew my coaching skills would have to be at the top of their game.

As the beginning of the 2014 season approached, when all this was to be implemented for the first time, I was worried. I was terrified. The time had come for me to put my money where my mouth was and basically hand over the registration of a research excavation to largely inexperienced team members. It did not take long for my fears to be quashed. I cannot deny that it was incredibly hard work, made easier by the fact that in this season we were working with a relatively small team numbering in the twenties. But there were still six squares and six square supervisors who had not worked in this way before. It took no more than a week to get everybody up to speed (fig. 1). I did this by sticking to the simple "Explain-Demonstrate-Practice" mantra. An initial

Figure 1. Jezreel Expedition field director Ian Cipin briefs team members at the start of the excavation season.

Figure 2. Jezreel team members fill out paperwork for their squares.

comprehensive briefing was given to them followed by my filling out the first couple of sheets (and associated material, tags, finds, etc). Next, they made their first attempts under my guidance and watchful eye. As the locus numbers started to be issued, their competence and confidence increased (fig. 2).

Figure 3. Jezreel team member Stephanie Marcotte enters data into her field notebook.

Figure 4. Jezreel Expedition co-director Norma Franklin at a pottery reading with team members.

As I could not be in every single square at every moment, these square supervisors were at the "coal face." Their briefings back to me were invaluable in helping me with interpretation. The new locus sheets had plenty of space to write whatever they wanted to add. Any thoughts, musings, ideas with the final interpretation were only given in consultation with the area supervisor. Whatever opinions they had, they were encouraged to include in the form. At the postexcavation stage, when I was making my final interpretations in the reports, I found these insights particularly useful.

Conclusions

Young emerging talents are with us for a short time, a matter of a few weeks. It is impossible for us to train them to be archaeologists in such a short time but we still have an obligation to give them the best possible foundation. This needs a clear vision as to what the outcomes should be when we are teaching practical skills in field archaeology (fig. 3). The better we prepare our students, the better archaeologists they will become and the better team members we will have in future seasons.

This essay has offered only a snapshot of field schools in Israel. Those of us working in the region should be proud that excavation projects and the field schools they offer continue to be regarded as part and parcel of archaeological students' essential education. While much progress has been made since the days of Dever's first field school at Gezer in 1966, there is still a great deal to be done to ensure that we are offering the best value to students both financially and educationally. I suggest that the time has come for a thorough review of practices throughout the region, an enormous task perhaps best undertaken by an organization such as ASOR. They have already formulated guidelines on best practices that can now expand to include the educational side of the field school. A one-size-fits-all standard would be too much to expect, however. The methods and techniques employed on a paleolithic site differ immeasurably from that on a classical site. Nevertheless, broadly defined standards and learning outcomes tailored to the needs of digs of varying types is within our grasp. We just have to understand that we have a responsibility to do it.

The legacy that we leave behind is the impact we have on others. Few have dedicated themselves more to making field schools in Israel a rewarding, enriching, and educational experience than the honoree of this volume (fig. 4).

References

Adler, M. 2002. "Teaching the Past in the Present: Archaeological Field Training in the 21st Century." *Proceedings of the Society for California Archaeology* 16:21–23.

American Schools for Oriental Research. http://www.asor.org/initiatives-projects/asor-affiliated-archaeological-projects/about-asors-cap-committee/

Statement of Purpose and Principles, http://www.asor.org/about-asor/policies/code-of-conduct-for-fieldwork-projects

Cipin, Ian. no date. *The Jezreel Expedition Fieldwork Manual*. Unpublished report.

Cline, Eric H. 2020. *Digging up Armageddon: The Search for the Lost City of Solomon*. Princeton: Princeton University Press.

Cole, D. P. 2015. Lahav V: The Iron, Persian, and Hellenistic Occupations within the Walls at Tel Halif-Excavations in Field II, 1977–1980. Winona Lake, IN: Eisenbrauns.

Dever, William G. 1967. "Excavations at Gezer." *The Biblical Archaeologist* 30.2: 47–62.

Dever, William G., and H. L. Lance, eds. 1982. *A Manual of Field Excavation: Handbook for Field Archaeologists*. Cincinnati, OH: Hebrew Union College.

Wheeler, Mortimer. 1966. *Archaeology from the Earth*. Penguin: Harmondsworth.

GONE TO THE DOGS:
ZER'IN THROUGH WESTERN EYES

Jennie Ebeling

Abstract: Many western travelers to Palestine in the nineteenth century visited Zer'in, the site of ancient Jezreel, on their tours to sites of biblical significance. Although dozens of published accounts by Christian pilgrims and other visitors record information about the contemporary Arab settlement and its inhabitants, the focus of these accounts is the ancient remains, or, more accurately, the lack thereof. Travelers made note of decorated sarcophagi lying at the entrance to the village and a "tower" standing at its center, but they drew a stark contrast between the imagined splendor of Ahab and Jezebel's Jezreel and the general squalor and ruin they witnessed at Zer'in. This survey reveals how nineteenth-century travelers experienced the site through the lens of the biblical stories set at Jezreel, particularly those about Jezebel, and explained the conditions at the site on the biblical curse placed on Ahab and his evil queen.

Keywords: Zer'in, Jezreel, nineteenth-century Palestine, Jezebel, Naboth

From her early conception of a new archaeological project at Jezreel, Norma Franklin believed that it would be impossible to undertake a comprehensive study of greater Jezreel from its earliest period of occupation without first understanding its recent settlement history. So, in preparation for our survey season in June 2012, she gathered maps, plans, illustrations, photographs, written accounts, and oral histories of Zer'in—the Palestinian village located on the western part of Tel Jezreel until 1948—along with relevant material from salvage excavations conducted by the Israel Antiquities Authority in 1987–1988 and in 2007 and the Tel Aviv University-British School of Archaeology in Jerusalem excavations 1990–1996. Although the Jezreel Expedition team unearthed relatively few remains dating to the nineteenth and twentieth century CE during its 2013–2018 excavation seasons, Norma consistently incorporated the recent history of the site in publications and presentations and enthusiastically supported the analysis of modern material recovered, among them weapons-related artifacts that may provide information about the battles at Zer'in in 1948. This essay focuses on nineteenth-century western travelers' observations of Zer'in and its antiquities. It is intended to celebrate Norma's impressive career and thank her for inviting me to embark on this wild journey when we met for coffee at the Ramat Aviv Mall in summer 2011.

35

Located at the narrowest point of the Jezreel Valley in Lower Galilee, Jezreel sits relatively neglected and unprotected today, overshadowed by the nearly equidistant and well-developed tourist sites of Megiddo and Bet She'an. Visitors to the site consist mainly of groups of Israeli students who are dropped off in the parking lot of the upper tell and, led by local guides, walk down the northern slope along one of the ancient paths to the spring below. 'Ein Yizre'el, one of several springs in this part of the valley, is now a pleasant spot for school groups and families to enjoy a picnic or a dip in the pool under the shade of eucalyptus trees. There is very little preserved ancient architecture to see at Jezreel, and the excavated areas on the upper tell are now pits with overgrown vegetation and crumbling baulks rather than restored and signposted buildings such as those at Megiddo and Bet She'an. Despite its unimpressive ancient remains, however, the identity of biblical Jezreel was lost for only a few hundred years after the medieval period: visitors from as early as the Roman period recognized the site as the setting for stories of Naboth, Ahab, Jezebel, and Elijah in 1 and 2 Kings, and, beginning in the 1830s, western travelers who visited Zer'in identified it as ancient Jezreel (Robinson and Smith 1841: 164 n. 4).

This study investigates how nineteenth-century western travelers experienced Zer'in through the lens of the biblical stories set at Jezreel—particularly those about Jezebel. This is seen in descriptions of one or more sarcophagi that lay near the entrance to the village, the tower that stood among the village houses, and the dogs that prowled around the tower and the village cemetery. In keeping with the desolation motif common in nineteenth-century travelers' accounts, visitors drew a stark contrast between the imagined splendor of Ahab and Jezebel's city and conditions in the modern village; this is particularly evident in the engravings, photographs, and other illustrations of Zer'in that contradict details in the accompanying narrative accounts. The widespread belief among nineteenth-century Christian pilgrims that Palestine was a cursed land inspired some visitors to explain the exaggerated squalor, desolation, and ruin they observed at Zer'in on the biblical curse placed on Ahab and his wicked queen Jezebel.

Jezreel in the Historical Accounts

Although other researchers have surveyed the historical references to Jezreel (Robinson and Smith 1841; Khalidi 1992; Ussishkin and Woodhead 1992; Pringle 1993; Moorhead 1997; Peterson 2002), I will briefly summarize them here to provide context for western encounters with biblical Jezreel in the nineteenth century. Eusebius, Bishop of Caesarea, referred to Esdraela in his *Onomasticon* (ca. 324 CE) as a "most famous (very great) village in the great plain located between Legeon [near Megiddo] and Scythopolis [Bet She'an]" (Eusebius of Caesarea 1971). In the *Itinerarium Burdigalense*, the anonymous Bordeaux Pilgrim (ca. 333 CE) identified Istradela, located ten miles from Maximianopolis (Megiddo) and twelve miles from Scythopolis, as the place where King Ahab lived and Elijah prophesied (Bordeaux Pilgrim 1887: 17). Likely based on the writings of the Christian nun and pilgrim Egeria (ca. 381–384 CE), Peter the Deacon (ca. 1137 CE) wrote: "In Jezreel [Iezrael] there is nothing left of Naboth's vineyard but its well, and the foundations of a tower. The tomb of Jezebel is stoned by everyone to this very day" (Wilkinson 1981: 201).

Fretellus (ca. 1137) referred to the site as Zarain and reported a monument (*pyramis*) of Jezebel there (Fretellus 1971: 31). John of Wurzburg (ca. 1165) referred to the site as Zaraim, also commonly called Little Gallina, and said of it: "Of this city was Jezebel, the most wicked queen, who took away Naboth's vineyard from him, who for her covetousness was cast down from the top of her palace and slain, whose *pyramis* is to be seen at this day" (Wurzburg 1890: 6). Theoderich (ca. 1175) also mentioned a *pyramis* by the name of Jezebel at the site, which was then called Ad Cursum Gallinarum (Theoderich 1896: 63). Another pilgrim referred to the site as Zaraim and related that Jezebel's monument could still be seen in his day (*Anonymous Pilgrims* 1897: 57). This close association between Jezebel and standing architecture at the site disappeared with the Crusader occupation and reemerged in the writings of nineteenth-century travelers from Europe and the United States, as will be shown below.

Around 1165, Benjamin of Tudela identified Serain as the ancient Jezreel and reported that one Jewish dyer lived there (Asher 1840: 80). The Crusaders called the site Le Petit Gérin and may have constructed fortifications of some kind (Abu Shama 1898: 246). Ralph of Diceto recorded a *villa* of the Templars at the site, which he called Parvum Gerinum (1876: 28) and, according to Roger of Wendover (1886: 33), the site was owned and defended by the Templars.

Salah ed-Din attacked and destroyed the village of Zer'ain in 1183 and again in 1184; it fell a third time to his nephew Husam al-Din Muhammad in 1187 after the battle of Hattin (Pringle 1993: 227). After his victory over the invading Mongols in the nearby Battle of 'Ain Jalut in 1260, Baybars reportedly restored a mosque and tower in the village (Khalidi 1992: 339). In 1283, Burchard of Mount Sion (1896: 48) wrote of the settlement:

> It stands on a somewhat high spot, and was once one of the royal cities of Israel, but at this day it scarce has thirty houses. It is now called Zaraein, and stands at the foot of Mount Gilboa, on the west side thereof. Before its gate is still shown the field of Naboth the Jezreelite.

Estori HaParhi (ca. 1280–1366) also identified Zer'in with biblical Jezreel (Luncz 1897: 290). During the thirteenth century, the site was one of the stops on the postal route between Jenin and Irbid (Sauvaget 1941: 74–75).

Ottoman records and the writings of European historians document some aspects of the settlement from the sixteenth through the eighteenth century. Nine households were recorded in a 1538 survey and a tax survey of 1596/97 lists four heads of household (Grey 2012: 353). Adrichom (1628: 73) reported thirty houses in the late sixteenth century and Dapper (1688: 89) recorded that the settlement in his time contained some one-hundred fifty houses occupied by both Moors and Jews (Ussishkin and Woodhead 1992: 6). By 1815, some fifty houses were said to cluster around the tower (Grey 2012: 353).

To summarize, we learn from several textual sources that there was some sort of monument (a tomb?) associated with Jezebel at the site in the twelfth century. Although it is presumed that Peter the Deacon (ca. 1137 CE) used the fourth-century Egeria's descriptions of her travels in his writings, his association of standing architecture with a monument related to Jezebel is in line with the descriptions of his twelfth-century contemporaries. That he mentions the foundations of a tower in addition to Jezebel's tomb suggests that two presumably ancient structures could be seen at Jezreel before the Crusader occupation of the site. Other medieval sources refer to fortifications built by the Crusaders in the twelfth century that were apparently destroyed in a series of attacks in the 1180s. Baybars is credited with restoring a tower and a mosque in the village in the late thirteenth century. Interestingly, the church first investigated by Schumacher and later excavated by the 1990s excavation team at Tel Jezreel is not mentioned in any written account until its existence was reported in a 1902 issue of the *American Journal of Archaeology* (see further below).

Jezreel Rediscovered in the Early Nineteenth Century

Jezreel reappears in the accounts of western writers in the early nineteenth century when the east opened up to European and American travelers. However, the earliest western visitors did not immediately identify Zer'in as the site of biblical Jézreel. Turner (1820: 151), who traveled through Palestine in 1815, mentioned the small village of Zerekin occupied by Muslims immediately after relating that the monks of Nazareth told him "the city of Jezreel, and Naboth's vineyard" are in the plain of Esdraelon. He did not identify this Zerekin with Jezreel, however. Buckingham (1821: 495) visited Zaraheen during his travels in 1816 and described sarcophagi and a tower in the center of a town with perhaps fifty houses. Like Turner, Buckingham did not connect the site to Jezreel and reported very little on the place and its inhabitants. As noted by Robinson and Smith (1841: 164 n. 5), most early nineteenth-century travelers believed nearby Jenin to be the site of biblical Jezreel.

Although Robinson and Smith are credited as the first modern scholars to identify Jezreel with Zer'in, they conceded that several earlier travelers had made the connection "apparently on mere conjecture" (1841: 164) before their important journey through Palestine in 1838. One of them was Charles Boileau Elliott, who traveled through Palestine in 1836. Elliott offered this description in the second volume of his *Travels in the Three Great Empires of Austria, Russia, and Turkey*:

> At noon we reached Zuraeen, the ancient Jezreel, a miserable little village, surrounded by some magnificent sarcophagi which lie exposed in the valley. It was in this neighbourhood that the battles of Barak and Sisera, of Josiah

and Pharaoh Nechoh, of the armies of Israel, Egypt, and Assyria, were fought. Here, likewise, was the vineyard of Naboth, "hard by the palace of Ahab, king of Samaria;" and here, too was fulfilled the terrible denunciation against his idolatrous wife, "the dogs shall eat Jezebel by the wall of Jezreel." Now, the vineyard and the palace, cultivation and architecture, are alike unknown. All is dilapidation and barrenness. When we visited Jezreel, it was under water; a few half-naked Arabs were the sole representatives of the courtiers who surrounded the palace of the king, and the pastures of his camels and horses were occupied by storks and lizards. (Elliott 1838: 379)

Like most travelers through the nineteenth century, Elliott reported that there was little left of biblical Jezreel and described the village and its inhabitants in a disparaging way. The presumed splendor of Naboth's vineyard and Ahab's palace in 1 Kgs 21 are contrasted with the perceived barrenness of the site, and only some nearby sarcophagi hint to its ancient glory. The desolation motif in particular is repeated frequently by subsequent western visitors (Press 2017b).

Needless to say, Elliott was a product of his time. A lengthy review of his book, however, offers a contemporary assessment of Elliott's perspective. It begins: "We never fell in with a writer who showed such a horror of the inconveniences of foreign travel, yet who with his eyes open had submitted himself to such voluntary discomfort as Mr. Elliott" (Anonymous 1839: 305). The reviewer suggested that Elliott's two volumes

do not disclose nearly so much about the countries they advertise, as about Mr. Elliott himself; or at least their principal charm lies in the relation existing between the traveller and his adventures, in his exquisite appreciation of the worth of every thing of English manufacture ... and his consequent annoyance, dejection, or contempt when he meets with things and persons moulded upon a different standard." (Anonymous 1839: 306)

Indeed, Elliott's derogatory account of Zer'in and its people is no worse than his descriptions of the places and people he encountered in his travels through eastern Europe, Russia, Turkey, and elsewhere in the Levant. Still, the tone of his brief description of Zer'in foretells that of the majority of the Holy Land travel narratives published in the succeeding decades.

Robinson and Smith were clearly travelers of a different sort and their groundbreaking *Biblical Researches in Palestine* (1841) provides a baseline of information about Zer'in at the time of their visit as well as a detailed account of earlier references to it. Robinson and Smith do not describe the site and its inhabitants in a disparaging way and their detailed observations are referred to frequently by subsequent travelers to Zer'in. Like most visitors, they were impressed first and foremost by its location:

It is a most magnificent site for a city; which, being itself thus a conspicuous object in every part, would naturally give its name to the whole region. There could therefore be little question, that in and around Zer'in, we had before us the city, the plain, the valley, and the fountain, of the ancient Jezreel." (Robinson and Smith 1841: 163)

Evidence for the site's antiquities included "a sarcophagus with sculptured ornaments, lying on the left of our path just as we entered the village" (Robinson and Smith 1841: 166). They do not assign a date to "a square tower of some height, partly in ruins" (Robinson and Smith 1841: 166) that they are able to ascend in order to enjoy a panoramic view of the valley. Several local inhabitants informed them of the names of all of the places visible and gave the distance to both el-Lejjun and Beisan at three-and-a-half hours. They describe Zer'in as having "perhaps somewhat more than twenty houses, but they are nearly in ruins, and the place contains few inhabitants" (Robinson and Smith 1841: 166). Like many later travelers to Palestine, Robinson and Smith recounted the biblical stories set at Jezreel in detail in their reports. It is not clear, however, whether or not any of Zer'in's inhabitants with whom Robinson and Smith spoke were aware of the site's connection to events and individuals described in the biblical text.

Zer'in 1840–1900

Western travel to the Holy Land exploded after 1840. American visitors to Palestine alone produced around five hundred travel narratives between 1840 and 1941, with the greatest number published in the second half of the nineteenth century (Rogers 2011: 8). Many scholars have studied the experiences and motivations of western visitors to Palestine in the nineteenth century (see references in Shamir 2013). Shamir suggests that it is easier to examine them through comparison of main thematic and stylistic strands in their writings rather than the author's religious motivations. These strands include

> dry-toned, guidebook-style information about Palestine's geography and history; romantic Arabian-Nights-inspired exotica; a recollection of a biblical story or event triggered by a specific Holy Land site; a farcical or patronizing account of an encounter with locals (dragomen and Turkish soldiers are favorite targets); a sentimental outpouring prompted by sacred geography and often tinged with nostalgia; an expression of disappointment by the landscape's small proportions or desolation; a self-critical description of western tourists as boorish or vandalistic; an argument with or revision of an earlier traveler's exegesis of the land; and skepticism over the authenticity of sites or relics held sacred by Catholic or Orthodox Christians. (Shamir 2013: 125)

Accounts might contain any or all of these thematic strands regardless of the traveler's religious or other motivations for visiting Palestine. This is clear in the dozens of accounts of visits to Zer'in by explorers, Christian pilgrims, and other travelers published between 1840 and 1900.

The following uses information gleaned from these accounts to show how western visitors experienced Zer'in through the lens of biblical events set at Jezreel, particularly those related to Jezebel. Information about the archaeological remains as they appeared at that time, details about the village and its environs, and anecdotal information about its inhabitants are woven into the discussion throughout. I then argue that travelers' inaccurate and/or exaggerated descriptions of squalor, desolation, and ruin are intended as evidence that the site and its inhabitants still suffer the curse placed on the House of Ahab.

Despite the lack of visible remains from antiquity, many visitors report one or more sarcophagi and a tower located in the center of the village. The other presumably ancient remains mentioned by some writers, including caves, quarries, cisterns, and wine presses, will not be included in this discussion.

The Sarcophagi

Stone sarcophagi are the only ancient artifacts reported by nineteenth century visitors. Buckingham (1821: 495) saw "several sarcophagi, both plain and sculptured" at the site. Elliott (1838: 379) noted "magnificent sarcophagi" lying exposed in the valley. More specific information about the location of these objects is provided by Robinson and Smith (1841: 166), who mention "a sarcophagus with sculptured ornaments, lying on the left of our path as we entered the village." Although Robinson and Smith were probably aware of the antiquity of the sarcophagus they observed, Thomson (1859: 180) explicitly identified them as ancient: "and these large sarcophagi are certainly relics of old Jezreel." Some travelers to Zer'in actively sought out the sarcophagi, probably aware of their existence through their familiarity with the work of Robinson and Smith (see Ritter 1866: 324). J. Wilson (1847: 303), for example, described riding around town "in search of the sarcophagi which are said to be found in its neighbourhood, and altogether we found eleven of them, entire or in fragments, a number greater than we expected. They are doubtless of great antiquity, and may even be Israelitish."

In another version of his popular volume *The Land and the Book*, Thomson (1882: 177) mentioned that his party's tents were pitched near the sarcophagi, which were located close to but outside of the village. Guérin (1868: 312) described a lidless and damaged marble sarcophagus carved on all four sides and measuring 3 feet 3 inches by 7 feet 6 inches near a shallow *birket* ("pool") west of the village. Guérin's description of pitching his tent near a pool and sarcophagus suggests that this location marked a common campsite for travelers. Farrar (1871: 442) described seeing the sarcophagi somewhere near his camp after dark: "We strolled into the open air as the moon rose in a splendid orb over the mud hovels and mounds of rubbish which once were Jezreel, lighting up the broken sarcophagi and fragments of ruin scattered here and there around it."

The incorporation of the sarcophagi into a campground used by travelers is also supported by the fact that some visitors reported one or more sarcophagi being used as watering troughs (Phelps 1863: 327; Tristram 1865: 131; Tristram 1871: 211; Bartlett 1876: 476; Miller 1892: 242). In a rare description of the children of Zer'in, Tristram

(1865: 131) reported that "a number of Arab boys were playing at hockey, near a marble sarcophagus, now converted into a horse-trough." Most writers described them specifically as horse-troughs, a detail that may have been intended to relate the sarcophagi to biblical Jezreel and, more specifically, to Jezebel.

Several writers provided more, detailed descriptions of the sculptured decoration and suggested a specific connection between these artifacts and Jezreel's biblical inhabitants. Tristram (1865: 131–32) reported that, in addition to the one repurposed as a horse-trough, there was one other complete and several broken sarcophagi strewn about, "sculptured with the figure of the crescent moon, the symbol of Ashtaroth, the goddess of the Zidonians." In a later publication, Tristram (1871: 211) expanded his discussion of the sarcophagi and connected them specifically to Jezebel: "Many old sarcophagi, or marble coffins, lay strewn about, some converted into horse-troughs, and several richly sculptured with the figures of the crescent-moon, the symbol of Ashtoreth, the goddess of the Zidonians; but these are the only relics of the ancient beauty of Jezreel." A bit later in his discussion, Tristram (1871: 212) asserted that "At Jezreel she [Jezebel] maintained a grove and temple of Ashtoreth, the abomination of the Zidonians, with her 400 priests," thus explicitly linking the Phoenician princess and Israelite queen to the sarcophagi. Manning also connected the crescent moon symbol to Jezebel and went so far as to suggest that she may have been buried in one of them:

> One marble sarcophagus, and the fragments of two or three others, lie outside the modern village. The crescent moon, the familiar symbol of the goddess of the Zidonians, is sculptured on them. It is possible, perhaps even probable, that these very coffins once held the bones of the royal house which 'taught Israel to sin'. (Manning 1874: 171–72)

According to Bartlett (1876: 476–77), "not a vestige of the ancient glory can be seen here—unless we except some broken sarcophagi, sculptured with the crescents that symbolized the Zidonian goddess Ashtaroth, and two that were whole, one of them now used as a horse-trough."

In *Picturesque Palestine*, Sir Charles Wilson (1881: 266) described "many marble sarcophagi strewn about, some of them still perfect, many finely sculptured with figures of the crescent moon, the symbol of Ashtaroth." He called these sarcophagi the only relics of the site's ancient beauty, and "all that is left by which we can say, 'This is Jezreel.'" According to Miller (1892: 242–43), "A few handsomely carved sarcophagi, at present used as watering-troughs, alone tell of the former splendour of this place; while the form of the crescent moon, visible on one or two of them, helps to remind us that here once an important worship was rendered to the goddess Ashtoreth, 'the abomination of the Zidonians,' under the patronage of the wicked Phoenician and Israelitish Queen, Jezebel." There is some tension in identifying these beautiful relics from ancient Jezreel with the detestable Jezebel; perhaps, then, describing their reuse as horse-troughs and intentionally invoking the horses who were ultimately responsible for her death mitigate this.

Conder and Kitchener did not mention the sarcophagi in their *Survey of Western Palestine* (1882) and Schumacher's report of the medieval church (1902) does not make reference to them. Exposed sarcophagi were apparently known to archaeologists in the Department of Antiquities of Mandatory Palestine, however, as Antiquities Report N. 2115 made by inspector N. Makhouly on 11/7/35 includes the note "no traces to the marble sarcophagus." A Roman-Byzantine cemetery lies under Kibbutz Yizrael to the west of the site and several complete sarcophagi and numerous fragments have been discovered and documented in the twentieth century (Moorhead 1997: 150–54). The assemblage of sarcophagus fragments published by Moorhead and some of those on display in Kibbutz Yizre'el and in the Beit Shturman Museum and Institute of Regional Knowledge in nearby Kibbutz Ein Harod may include some of those seen by the nineteenth century travelers.

The Tower

A building is mentioned in nearly all western travelers' accounts from the medieval period through the nineteenth century. Although the monument (*pyramis*) mentioned by the medieval writers cannot be identified with any certainty, it may lie under the ruined building—often called a tower by nineteenth century visitors—on the western part of Tel Jezreel. Pringle (1997: 56) suggests that two vaults known as "el-Uqud" seen under the standing tower by Department of Antiquities of Mandatory Palestine inspector S.A.S. Husseini in 1941 were from the destroyed Crusader castle, although Peterson (2001: 322) suggests that they could be Mamluk in origin. The building described by the nineteenth-century travelers is featured in numerous engravings, photographs, and other illustrations from the period and remains the most identifiable feature at the site today. The only archaeological investigations in the immediate vicinity of the tower to date appear to have been carried out by Charles Wilson in 1866 on behalf of the Palestine Exploration Fund, according to the 1 May 1866 issue of *The Scattered Nation*: "At Zerin (Jezreel) some small excavations were made near the large square building in the village, but without result" (Grove 1866: 121; see further below). For now, the date of the tower's construction is unknown and little can be said of what lies beneath it.

While Buckingham (1821: 495) did not recognize Zaraheen as Jezreel when he visited the site in 1816, he mentioned "a high modern building in the centre ... and perhaps about fifty dwellings around it." Interestingly, Elliott (1838: 379) did not mention the tower, going so far as to say: "Now, the vineyard and the palace, cultivation and architecture, are alike unknown." Beginning with Robinson and Smith, the tower was accessible to foreign visitors, and some reported ascending the building and observing the panoramic view from the top. Wilson (1847: 87), for example, apparently paid a few piastres to the tower's (unnamed) owner for permission to ascend it. The view inspired a number of them to recount the biblical stories and historical events that took place at Jezreel, nearby sites, and in the valley below.

None of the writers specified the name of the owner(s) of the building, but several mentioned its function. According to the first edition of Josias Porter's *A Handbook for Travellers in Syria and Palestine* (1858: 337), part of the popular series of *Murray's Handbooks for Travellers* (called *Blue Guides* starting in the early twentieth century), "[t]he only sightly building is a square tower of some antiquity, now used as a *Medafeh*, or 'Inn,' where travellers are treated to bare walls, fleas *ad libitum*, and a supper at the public expense." That this description is repeated verbatim by other writers (e.g., Blaikie 1859: 354; Whitney 1875: 245) demonstrates the popularity of this and other early travel guides and the habit of some travelers of incorporating specific details of previously published accounts in their own writings. Guérin (1868: 311) described a square building in the center of the village as the residence of the Sheikh, and Farrar (1871: 440, 442) related that, when his party pitched their tents on the slope below the city, his guide "asked for the Sheykh, who, when travellers come without tents, superintends the hospitalities (?) of the Medafeh, or square tower, which serves as a sort of inn ...." An engraving of Zer'in in *Picturesque Palestine* (Wilson 1881: 265) bears the caption: "The Castle of Zerin (Jezreel). Now used as a *manzal* or inn, literally "a place for unloading," open to all wayfarers." Thomson (1882: 177) called it a "square tower now used as a mudafeh, or inn." According to Geikie (1891: 748), "There is nothing to be seen in the present village but the tower, which is used for a khan, or resting-place for travellers."

Most provided only very brief descriptions of the tower, including Robinson and Smith (1841: 166), who identified it matter-of-factly as "a square tower of some height, partly in ruins," and Conder and Kitchener (1882: 88), who wrote: "A modern tower or taller house stands in the centre of the village." Some described the tower in particularly disparaging terms: "this apology for a castle" (Thomson 1859: 180), "a shattered tower" (Porter 1866: 257), "an old ruined tower" (Burt 1869: 324–25), "there is a square tower, but it is a poor affair, and cannot boast of any great antiquity" (Kean 1895: 218). Yet, the illustrations that accompany some of these accounts show the tower's impressive appearance on the highest point of the site among the village houses (fig. 1). Although some engravings clearly exaggerate the tower's size and position (fig. 2), early photographs provide more objective documentation of the state of the building during the second half of the nineteenth century (fig. 3).

Although most visitors recognized that the tower they observed was not particularly ancient, it reminded many of the tower from which Jezebel was defenestrated according to 2 Kgs 9:

> There is a tower in Jezreel to this day—the only building of any note in it—and though not the ancient one, it served at least to remind us of the graphic incident which occurred in the days of Ahab's son and successor, Joram, and which the sacred historian thus describes... (Buchanan 1859: 348)

Figure 1. Zerʻin. From Thomson 1882.

Figure 2. Zerʻin. From Temple 1888.

Temple (1888: 206) wrote of Zerʻin: "In the midst is a tower, reminding the traveller of the far finer tower which must have stood thereabouts in the day when the watchman decried Jehu driving furiously in the chariot."

Some speculated that this tower, located as it is on the highest part of the site, may sit on the ruins of the older tower from which Jezebel was thrown or incorporate some of the earlier, biblical-period structure in its lower courses. According to Thomson (1859:

Figure 3. The earliest-known photograph of Zer'in, by Corporal H. Phillips, R.E. (Wilson 1865). Courtesy of the Palestine Exploration Fund.

180): "This apology for a castle may now stand upon the spot of that watch-tower from which the rebel Jehu was first seen driving furiously up the valley of Jezreel." Phelps (1863: 327), describing Jehu's entrance into Jezreel, stated: "his own furious driving being watched from the tower that stood perhaps where this old tower now stands." Wilson (1881: 28) asserted that the tower, while not very old, "occupies probably the site of the old Migdol, or watch-tower, are all that make up modern Jezreel." Manning (1874: 170) suggested that "The ruins of an ancient tower probably mark the spot where the watchman stood looking out along the valley toward the Jordan, and saw Jehu driving furiously toward the city. Though only the lower courses of the original migdol or watch-tower remain, yet a view may be gained for miles." More careful observers noted that Jezebel's tower must have been on the eastern side of the site according to the story in 2 Kgs 9, however. Guérin (1868: 311–12), for example, related that the tower on the western part of the site appeared to be of Arab origin and may have replaced an older tower and believed that the biblical tower must have stood instead on the eastern part of the site, since Jehu arrived at the site from the east in pursuit of Joram.

Edward L. Wilson offered a strange and possibly unique description of the meaning of the tower for the inhabitants of Zer'in:

> Their houses are dreadfully humble and comfortless, and all the wealth of the town seems to have been used for the preservation of the ancient tower which stands among the houses. It seems a strange place among such a benighted people, and serves to show with what reverent care they preserve what they consider holy. If Ahab and his four hundred priests worshiped Astarte here, and Herod kept up the unholy rites, it is a holy place in the eyes of the present dwellers at Jezreel, but none the more holy because Jesus did missionary work among their predecessors. The same crescent moon that shone as

a symbol of Astarte shines for Mohammed their prophet, and for this they honor and preserve Jezreel's tower. (Wilson 1890: 741–42)

Interestingly, he did not mention seeing sarcophagi at Zer'in although he most certainly would have been familiar with earlier travelers' accounts of one or more sarcophagi decorated with the image of the crescent moon described above. Still, it is unclear how he made a connection between the tower—which is called "The Castle of Jezreel" in the accompanying illustration—and the Prophet Mohammed, and, perhaps more importantly, why he understood the tower to be a holy place for both the ancient and modern inhabitants.

Gone to the Dogs

Descriptions of the tower provided an opportunity for a number of writers to relate one of the more horrifying biblical stories set at Jezreel: Jezebel's ravaging by dogs. Some made their retelling more vivid by connecting the modern dogs seen prowling around Jezreel to those who ate Jezebel:

> We look to that tower which is standing a ruin on the hill, and although it has of course nothing to do with Ahab's palace, yet one shudders at it, for the form of a Jezebel, as 'she painted her face, and tired her head, and looked out at a window,' rises before the imagination, and the sickening details of that horrible story make one turn aside for the wild pariah dogs, just as Stanley saw them, and as any traveler may see them any day prowling round the spot, and the scene becomes painfully realistic. (Hodder 1874: 244)

Hodder was referring to Stanley's retelling of the story of Jezebel who, in describing the locations of specific biblical events, wrote

> how in the open place ... the body of the Queen was trampled under the hoofs of Jehu's horses; how the dogs gathered round it, as even to this day, in the wretched village now seated on the ruins of the once splendid city of Jezreel, they prowl on the mounds without the walls for the offal and carrion thrown out to them to consume. (Stanley 1857: 34–42)

In his retelling of the story of Jezebel's death, Phelps (1863: 328) wrote "Around the dead queen the voracious dogs gathered and feasted, as to this day they prowl about these old mounds for whatever may be thrown out to them." A few decades later, Kean (1895: 219) reported that "a pile of white bones lies by the back of the dead wall near by the tower—they recall the terrible death of Jezebel, who was thrown from a window here, and devoured by dogs. All these bones have been cleaned by the dogs."

The theme of dogs persists beyond descriptions of the tower, and dogs seen roaming around the village in general reminded some visitors of Jezebel's dogs. According to Charles (1866: 265–66), "The dogs howl and prowl around it as they do around all

Arab villages, and as they did in the days of Jezebel and Ahab, and of the murdered Naboth." Geikie (1891: 748) related that "The town dogs follow you with hideous uproar
as you go through the streets—if one can use the word for such a collection of hovels."
And, according to Bartlett (1876: 476–77), "The starving dogs of the village are still
numerous enough to devour Jezebel in a single night."

Porter, the author of one of the *Murray's Handbooks for Travellers*, specifically located dogs in the village cemetery on the eastern part of the site. In one account (Porter
1864: 598), he connected the dogs he saw in the cemetery with the story of Jezebel's
death: "As the writer rode away from it he saw a number of ravenous-looking dogs
prowling among the tombs in the little cemetery, which painfully revived the story of
Jezebel and Ahab." In an account published two years later, the dogs are contemporary
witnesses to the truth of Elijah's oracle:

> On approaching the little village which occupies the site of the ancient city of
> Jezreel, I rode through a modern cemetery, which lies open and neglected on
> the hill-side. There I saw a troop of dogs burrowing into a new-made grave,
> while two huge vultures were perched on a cliff not a hundred yards distant.
> The place seemed deserted; there was none 'to fray them away.' Did it not
> look like an illustration of the prophetic curse and the historic narrative given
> in the Bible? – 'In the portion of Jezreel shall dogs eat the flesh of Jezebel'
> (2 Kings ix. 36; compare 1 Kings xxi. 23). (Porter 1866: 252)

Although it is impossible to know if there is any truth to this account, his intent is clearly to bring to the reader's mind the image of dogs consuming Jezebel's body.

It is interesting that the cemetery vignette in not found in his earlier *Murray's
Handbook*, which confines the description of the dogs of Zer'in to those that "prowl on
the mounds without the walls for the offal and carrion thrown out to them to consume"
(Porter 1858: 354). Perhaps Porter's attempt to connect modern dogs to ancient ones
by describing the desecration of a fresh grave at Zer'in would have been a bit too mor-
bid to include in an official guidebook to Palestine!

As discussed above, the tower is described by some writers in a particularly disparaging way that belied its fine condition and impressive appearance on the landscape as
seen in numerous illustrations and photographs from the period. Accounts of the other
buildings in Zer'in—the private houses usually described as clustering around the
tower—vary widely in number and condition. While Buckingham (1816) estimated
fifty houses, Robinson and Smith (1841: 166) recorded "somewhat more than twenty
houses," J. Wilson (1847: 87) saw "thirty or forty rude houses," Buchanan (1859: 348)
described "a little hamlet of twenty houses," and Hodder (1874: 243–44) counted
"thirty or forty miserable dwellings on the hill." Conder and Kitchener reported twenty
or thirty "modern houses" at Zer'in in their *Survey of Western Palestine* (1882: 88), and
Thomson (1882: 177) related that "there are now not more than twenty-five or thirty

wretched hovels all told." This variability might be an accurate reflection of the fluctuating settlement sizes during this period attested in Ottoman sources.

Those who offer less precise counts seem to intentionally downplay the true number of houses in the village. In the same way that the illustrations and photographs of the tower contradict the derogatory description that usually accompanies them, late nineteenth-century photographs bear witness to a greater number of houses than most travelers describe. For example, Prime (1874: 339), who traveled in 1855 and 1856, recorded "a few mud huts," Phelps (1863: 327) "a cluster of wretched houses," Porter (1866: 257) "a dozen miserable houses," Burt (1869: 324–25) "a few wretched hovels," Farrar (1871: 381) "the few miserable huts," C. Wilson (1881: 28) "a few flat-topped hovels," Geikie (1891: 748) "a collection of hovels," Stewart (1899: 125) "a collection of miserable hovels," and Withrow (1894: 432) "a few squalid Arab huts." As mentioned above, E. L. Wilson (1890: 741–42) reported that "Their houses are dreadfully humble and comfortless." It is difficult to imagine how he would know this, since no traveler—including Wilson—specifically described entering any of the buildings at Zer'in but the tower.

The disparaging language used to describe Zer'in is the same used to describe many other villages in Palestine. In western eyes, Zer'in is miserable (Elliott 1838: 379; Bonar 1858: 391), wretched (J. Wilson 1847: 304; Van de Velde 1854: 327; Stanley 1857: 342; Newton 1875: 134), squalid (Farrar 1871: 381), and "covered with modern hovels" (Wilson and Warren 1871: 356). According to Seaton (1895):

> The present village is by no means a pleasant place to visit; the little half-mud huts are anything but tidy, and the whole place is disorderly, if not filthy. I would have refused to pass through its narrow and crooked lanes, had it not been for the ancient history attaching to it. (Seaton 1895: 308).

Another visitor who failed to notice Zer'in's economic standing considered it among the lowest he had witnessed on his travels:

> As you approach the place, you are struck with its squalid appearance: your way lies through manure heaps and giant weeds. Beyond these rise the hovels of the villagers – poorer than almost any you have ever seen; this place might take a prize for squalour. The village on the site of Samaria city was bad enough: this is below the lowest depths you could have conceived. (Kean 1895: 218)

What the visitors interpreted as filth may in fact have been indicators of a prosperous farming community measured by the size of its manure heaps and the weeds growing around them. Although repellant to western eyes, an untidy place may in fact bear witness to a thriving economy.

Another motif in descriptions of the site is desolation. As Press (2017a) notes, by the time Mark Twain published *The Innocents Abroad* in 1869, "desolate Palestine" was a cliché of travel writing. Although Twain's book, by far the most famous of the nine-teenth-century travelers' accounts, satirizes the genre, it played a major role in popular-izing the idea of a desolate Palestine and continues to be cited today. The exaggerated scenes of desolation described by Porter and others (Press 2017b) were intended to show the fulfillment of biblical prophecy, even if this picture was at odds with reality. Porter's description of Zer'in is similar to his accounts of other places in Palestine such as Ashkelon, where he first described a fertile landscape with gardens and rich pro-duce before concluding that it was desolate (Press 2017b). For Porter (1866: 252–53), Zer'in was a "scene of desolation, in the centre of one of the finest plains in the world," whose "slopes immediately round the village are bare and barren as a desert." Like Por-ter, who called the site's position "a noble one, worthy of a royal city" (1866: 252), Tris-tram (1865: 130) described it as "a lovely position for a capital city, but not a vestige of it remains. The very ruins have crumbled from desolate heaps to flat turf-clad hillocks."

Although Twain visited Zer'in, he had very little to say about it and apparently did not even enter the village. All Twain related of his visit to Zer'in is "Presently we came to a ruinous old town on a hill, the same being the ancient Jezreel (1869: 547)." Although his description is brief, it relates another common cliché: ruin. Despite the tower, houses, and cemetery, and the villagers who are sometimes described in and around the village and spring, the place is described as a ruin, or a ruin so ruined that it is *without* ruins! So wrote Porter (1866: 252): "The city is utterly ruined. Its very ruins have disappeared." Several writers singled out Jezreel as the most ruined ruin they saw in Palestine. According to Tristram (1865: 130), "no destruction has been more com-plete and utter, even in this land of ruins, than that of Jezreel." Similarly, Wilson wrote in *Picturesque Palestine* (1881: 28): "While no locality in the land has been more indis-putably identified than Zerin, there is scarcely, even in this land of ruins, a destruction more complete and utter than that of Jezreel."

What is the reason for this state of affairs—the squalor, the desolation, the com-plete ruin? Jezreel was cursed. A common belief among visitors, especially Christian pilgrims, was that Palestine as a whole was under a curse. According to Press (2017b), Christian visitors familiar with both the biblical imagery of Palestine as a land flow-ing with milk and honey and the negative accounts of previous travelers saw a land fallen into disrepair and desolation. While many understood its decline as the result of a curse that had been foretold by biblical prophets, some who visited Zer'in explained its condition on the biblical curse on the House of Ahab. For example, after briefly describing the general conditions in the village and offering a lengthy recounting of the biblical stories set at Jezreel, Buchanan (1859: 349), concluded that "The curse that fell so justly on Ahab's house, seems to rest still on Jezreel." After retelling the scene of dogs desecrating a recent grave, Porter (1866: 252) concluded that "The blood shed, and the crimes committed there, would seem to have brought a double curse upon Jezreel." And, perhaps unique in identifying some clues to Zer'in's prosperity, Burt (1869: 324–

25) noticed in the place of Ahab's palace "a dense mass of weeds," which he attributed to "a soil made fertile by human gore."

Jezreel "Rediscovered" by Archaeologists

Reports of a lack of visible ancient architecture at Zer'in apparently resulted in little interest in the site among early archaeologists in Palestine. As mentioned above, Charles Wilson explored the site on behalf of the Palestine Exploration Fund in 1866, but did not find enough to justify an excavation:

> At Zer'in (Jezreel) some small excavations were made near the large square building in the village, but without result. In and around the village are more than 300 cisterns or subterranean granaries for corn; a number of these were visited at various points, in the hope that some remains of the old town might be found in them, but neither there nor in the large accumulation of rubbish round the village could any foundations or remains be seen of sufficient importance to justify the commencement of excavations on a large scale. The examination of the mound is quite practicable, but would require much time and money (Grove 1866: 121).

The next archaeological study of the site was carried out by Gottlieb Schumacher, who had until that time published reports of the archaeological remains of the areas he surveyed in preparation for the construction of the Damascus-Haifa railway. According to the first report of the Managing Committee of the American School for Oriental Study and Research in Palestine, H. G. Mitchell—who had recently been appointed Director of the School in Jerusalem—was the first to report the existence of ancient architectural remains at Zer'in:

> While at Haifa I heard that natives had uncovered an ancient structure at Zerin. I at once engaged Dr. Schumacher as an expert to go to the place and ascertain what had been discovered. He found that it was the remains of an interesting Christian church. His report, with drawings, was forwarded to the Committee. (Moore and Mitchell 1902)

Schumacher's report included an introductory paragraph apparently written by the editor of the journal, the classical scholar J. H. Wright, Professor of Greek and Dean of the Graduate School of Arts and Sciences at Harvard University at the time:

> The village of Zer'in stands upon the site of the ancient city of Jezreel, a favorite residence of the Israelite kings of the dynasty of Omri. In the fourth century of our era it was "a fine village." It is mentioned more than once by the crusading historians under the name "parvum Gerinum," but hitherto no Christian remains have been observed there. Recently, however, the ruins of a church were discovered among the hovels of the village by Dr. G. Schum-

acher, who examined them at the instance of the Director of the School in
Jerusalem … (Schumacher 1902: 338)

Apparently based on Eusebius's description, Wright calls the fourth century settlement a "fine village" but goes on to describe the recently discovered church as situated among the hovels of the inhabitants of the early twentieth-century village. Even a
scholar of renown like Wright could not avoid invoking the derogatory image of Zer'in
common in nineteenth-century travel accounts in the earliest report of scientific excavations at Jezreel.

Although inspectors from the Department of Antiquities of Mandatory Palestine visited Zer'in several times and local archaeologist N. Zori conducted surveys in
the area as early as 1941, archaeological work would not be resumed at the site until
1987, after bulldozers damaged ancient architecture during the preparation of areas
to the east of the tell for the construction of a museum dedicated to the history of
the Jewish-Zionist settlement of the Jezreel Valley. Discoveries made during salvage
excavations conducted by the Israel Antiquities Authority in 1987 and 1988 led to
the excavation project co-directed by D. Ussishkin and J. Woodhead at Tel Jezreel
1990–1996 (Ussishkin and Woodhead 1992: 6–10). From the start, the team led by
Ussishkin and Woodhead focused their efforts on uncovering remains from the tenth
through eighth centuries BCE (p. 11), when, according to the biblical accounts, Jezreel was an Israelite royal city. Thus, the primary intent of the first large-scale excavation project was the same as that of most nineteenth century travelers to Zer'in:
to identify archaeological remains associated with Ahab and Jezebel. And, like the
nineteenth-century travelers who associated Zer'in's ancient relics and standing architecture with Israelite royalty, the archaeologists found what they were looking for
(Franklin 2008: 45–53; 2018).

Acknowledgements

I thank Maggie Sullivan, Abigail Miles, and other undergraduate archaeology students
enrolled in the "Jezreel Analysis and Publication" course I taught at the University of
Evansville in spring 2019 for their contributions to the research for this essay.

References

Abu Shama. 1898. *Recueil des historiens des Croisades*. Vol. 4: *Historiens orientaux*. Paris: Imprimerie nationale.
Adrichom, Christian. 1628. *Theatrum Terrae Sanctae et biblicarum historiarum, cum tabulis geographicis*. Cologne: Hermann Mylius.
Anonymous. 1839. Review article of C.B. Elliott, *Travels in the Three Great Empires of Austria,
    Russia, and Turkey.*" *British Critic and Quarterly Theological Review* 25:305–20.
Anonymous. 1897. *Anonymous Pilgrims (11th and 12th Centuries)*, vol. 6. Translated by A. Stewart. London: Palestine Pilgrims' Text Society.

Asher, Adolf. 1840. *The Itinerary of Rabbi Benjamin of Tudela*. London: Asher.

Bartlett, Samuel C. 1876. *From Egypt to Palestine through Sinai, the Wilderness and the South Country*. New York: Harper.

Blaikie, William G. 1859. *Bible History, in Connection with the General History of the World*. London: Nelson & Sons.

Bonar, Horatius. 1858. *The Land of Promise: Notes of a Spring Journey from Beersheba to Sidon*. London: James Nisbet.

Bordeaux Pilgrim. 1887. *Itinerary from Bordeaux to Jerusalem*. Translated by A. Stewart. London: Palestine Pilgrims' Text Society.

Buchanan, Robert. 1859. *Notes of a Clerical Furlough, Spent Chiefly in the Holy Land*. London: Blackie.

Buckingham, James S. 1821. *Travels in Palestine, through the Countries of Bashan and Gilead, East of the River Jordan including a Visit to the Cities of Geraza and Gamala, in the Decapolis*. London: Longman, Hurst, Rees, Orme & Brown.

Burchard of Mount Sion. 1896. *A Description of the Holy Land*, vol. 12. Translated by A. Stewart. London: Palestine Pilgrims' Text Society.

Conder, C. R., and H. H. Kitchener. 1882. *The Survey of Western Palestine. Memoirs of the Topography, Orography, Hydrography, and Archaeology*. Volume 2. Sheets VII–XVI. Samaria. London: Palestine Exploration Fund.

Dapper, Olfert. 1688. *Genaue und gründliche Beschreibung des ganzen Palestins*. Nuremberg: Hofmann.

Elliott, C. B. 1838. *Travels in the Three Great Empires of Austria, Russia, and Turkey*, vol. 2. London: Bentley.

Eusebius of Caesarea. 1971. *Onomasticon*. Translated by C. Umhau Wolf. The Tertullian Project http://www.tertullian.org/fathers/eusebius_onomasticon_01_intro.htm

Farrar, F. W. 1871. *Days in the Holy Land*. The Quiver Volume VI. London: Cassell, Petter, & Galpin.

Franklin, Norma. 2008. *Jezreel before and after Jezebel*. Pages 45–53 in *Israel in Transition: From Late Bronze II to Iron IIa (c. 1250–850 B.C.E.)*, vol. 1. Edited by L. L. Grabbe. London: T&T Clark.

———. 2018. "Megiddo and Jezreel Reflected in the Dying Embers of the Northern Kingdom of Israel." Pages 189–208 in *The Last Days of the Kingdom of Israel*. Edited by S. Hasegawa, C. Levin and K. Radner. Berlin: de Gruyter.

Fretellus. 1971. *A Description of the Places Lying Round Jerusalem*. Translated by A. Stewart. London: Palestine Pilgrims' Text Society.

Geikie, Cunningham. 1891. *The Holy Land and the Bible: A Book of Scripture Illustrations Gathered in Palestine*. London: Cassell & Co.

Grey, Tony. 2012. "The Ceramic Legacy of a Palestinian Village During the Ottoman and British Mandate Periods: Zir'in (Tel Jezreel) 1517–1948." *Post-Medieval Archaeology* 46:352–60.

Grove, G. 1866. "Intelligence: Explorations in Palestine." *The Scattered Nation* (May 1):121–22.

Guérin, H. Victor. 1868. *Description géographique, historique et archéologique de la Palestine*. Seconde Partie – Samarie. Tome Premier. Paris: Imprimerie Nationale.

Hodder, Edwin. 1874. *On "Holy Ground."* New York: Nelson & Phillips.

Khalidi, Walid, ed. 1992. *All That Remains: The Palestinian Villages Occupied and Depopulated by Israel in 1948*. Washington D.C.: Institute for Palestine Studies.

Luncz, A. M. 1897. *Estori haParchi: Caftor vaFerach*. Jerusalem: Beit ha-midrash l'halacha bahisyashvus (Hebrew).

Manning, Samuel. 1874. *Those Holy Fields*. London: Religious Tract Society.

Miller, Ellen E. 1892. *Alone through Syria*. 2nd ed. London: Kegan, Paul, Trench, Trubner.

Moore, George F., and H. G. Mitchell. 1902. "First Annual Report of the Managing Committee of the American School for Oriental Study and Research in Palestine." *AJA* 6, Supplement: Annual Reports 1901–1902: 39–47.

Moorhead, T. S. N. 1997. "The Late Roman, Byzantine and Umayyad Periods at Tel Jezreel." *Tel Aviv* 24:129–66.

Peterson, Andrew. 2001. *A Gazetteer of Buildings in Muslim Palestine*, part 1. Oxford: Oxford University Press.

Phelps, S. D. 1863. *Holy Land with Glimpses of Europe and Egypt: A Year's Tour*. New York: Sheldon.

Porter, Josias L. 1858. *A Handbook for Travellers in Syria and Palestine*, part 2. London: Murray.

———. 1864. "Jezreel," Pages 597–99 in *A Cyclopaedia of Biblical Literature*, vol. 2. Edited by W. L. Alexander. 3rd ed. Edinburgh: Black.

———. 1866. *The Giant Cities of Bashan and Syria's Holy Places*. London: Thomas Nelson & Sons.

Press, Michael. 2017a. "How a Mark Twain Travel Book Turned Palestine into a Desert." *Hyperallergic*, https://hyperallergic.com/400528/how-a-mark-twain-travel-book-turned-palestine-into-a-desert/ (accessed 19 June 2020).

———. 2017b. "Struggling to See Palestine," *Aeon* 13, https://aeon.co/essays/biblical-imaginings-have-warped-our-perception-of-palestine (accessed 19 June 2020).

Pringle, Denys. 1993. *The Churches of the Crusader Kingdom of Jerusalem: A Corpus*. Cambridge: Cambridge University.

Ralph of Diceto. 1876. *The Historical Works of Master Ralph de Diceto, Dean of London*. Translated by W. Stubbs. London: Longman, Trübner.

Ritter, Carl. 1866. *The Comparative Geography of Palestine and the Sinaitic Peninsula*, vol. 2. Translated by W. L. Gage. New York: Appleton.

Robinson, Edward, and Eli Smith. 1941. *Biblical Researches in Palestine, Mount Sinai and Arabia Petraea*, vol. 3. Boston: Crocker & Brewster.

Roger of Wendover. 1886. "Flores Historiarum." Page 33 in *Rerum Britannicarum* 84.1. Edited by H. G. Hewlett. London: Longman.

Sauvaget, J. 1941. *La poste aux chevaux de l'Empire des Mamelouks*. Paris: Maisonneuve.

Schumacher, G. 1902. "Remains of a Mediaeval Christian Church at Zer'in." *AJA* 6: 338–39.

Shamir, Milette. 2013. "Encounters of a Third Kind: Mark Twain, William C. Prime and Protestant American Holy Land Narratives." *Quest: Issues in Contemporary Jewish History* 6:116–37.

Temple, Richard. 1888. *Palestine Illustrated*. London: Allen.

Theoderich. 1896. *Description of the Holy Places* (1172), vol. 5/4. Translated by A. Stewart. London: Palestine Pilgrims' Text Society.

Thomson, William M. 1859. *The Land and the Book*, vol. 2. New York: Harper.

———. 1882. *The Land and the Book or Biblical Illustrations Drawn from the Manners and Customs, the Scenes and Scenery, of the Holy Land, Central Palestine and Phoenicia*. New York: Harper.

Tristram, Henry B. 1866. *The Land of Israel: A Journal of Travels in Palestine, Undertaken with Special Reference to Its Physical Character*. London: SPCK.

———. 1871. *The Topography of the Holy Land*. London: SPCK.

Turner, William. 1820. *Journal of a Tour in the Levant*, vol. 2. London: Murray.

Twain, Mark. 1869. *The Innocents Abroad*. Hartford, CT: American Publishing Company.

Upham, Thomas. C. 1857. *Letters Aesthetic, Social, and Moral, Written from Europe, Egypt, and Palestine*. Philadelphia: Longstreth.

Ussishkin, D., and J. Woodhead. 1991. "Excavations at Tel Jezreel 1990–1991: Preliminary Report." *TA* 19:3–56.

Van de Velde, Charles W. M.. 1854. *Narrative of a Journey through Syria and Palestine in 1851 and 1852*, vol. 1. Edinburgh: Blackwood.

Whitney, George H. 1875. *Handbook of Bible Geography*. New York: Hunt & Eaton.

Wilkinson, John. 1981. *Egeria's Travels to the Holy Land*. Rev. ed. Jerusalem: Ariel; Warminster: Aris & Phillips.

Wilson, Charles W. 1865. "List of Photographic Views Taken in Palestine by the First Expedition, November, 1865—May, 1866, Under the Charge of Captain Wilson, Royal Engineers.—Corporal H. Phillips, R.E., Photographer." *PEQ* 1 sup.1: 25–52. DOI: 10.1179/peq.1865.1-2.008

———. 1881. *Picturesque Palestine, Sinai, and Egypt*, vol. 2. New York: Appleton & Co.

Wilson, C. W., and C. Warren. 1871. *The Recovery of Jerusalem*. New York: Appleton & Co.

Wilson, Edward L. 1890. "Some Wayside Places in Palestine." *Century Magazine* 39.5:737–43.

Wilson, John. 1847. *The Lands of the Bible Visited and Described*, vol. 2. Edinburgh: Whyte.

Withrow, William H. 1894. "Tent Life in Palestine." *Methodist Magazine* 39.5:427–41.

Wurzburg, Joannes. 1890. *Description of the Holy Land*, vol. 6. Translated by A. Stewart. London Palestine Pilgrims' Text Society.

Naboth and Moshele:
Reading a Biblical Story in Light
of the Construction of the Memory
# of a Modern Martyr

Philippe Guillaume and Menachem Rogel

Abstract: Jezreel is the scene of two murders, that of biblical Naboth and that of kibbutznik Moshele Orion. Slicing the biblical story and one particular episode of the Israeli-Palestinian struggle in the 1950s, this essay explores the formation of social memory. The fate of the two heroes may help probe deeper the formation of the Naboth tradition and how the memory of Moshele may evolve depending on local political developments.

Keywords: Jezreel, Zerʻin, Samaria, ʻEin Harod, Jenin, Naboth, Har-Zion, infiltrators, social memory, 1 Kgs 19

Three Stones for One Name

An occasional visitor to Kibbutz Yizreel is unlikely to chance upon any of three different inscriptions recording a tragic event in the history of the community. The first inscription, on the eastern outskirts of the kibbutz, stands at the exact spot where Moshele Orion died while on guard duty on March 19, 1955 (fig. 1):

On this spot fell our colleague	במקום זה נפל חברנו
Moshele Orion	משהלה אוריון
while standing guard protecting the kvutsa[1]	בעומדו על משמר הקבוצה
on 25 Adar 5715	כ"ה באדר תשט"ו

Paul Zelas has masterminded this project. Without him, nothing would have happened. We are also grateful to Dany Harpaz, Shimona Matalon, and Omri Zelas for their willingness to share their memories of Moshele. Special thanks are due to Moshele's daughter Orly for a memorable visit at Beit Ha-Shita in June 2018, to Ehud Ben Zvi, in particular for referring us to Efrat Seckbach's work, and to Martha Hellander for improving our English.

1. Properly speaking, Yizreel was a kvutsa until the 1980s. The term "kvutsa" defined the kibbutz

Figure 1. Inscription where Moshele Orion died. All figures courtesy of Philippe Guillaume.

Figure 2. Inscription on Moshele Orion's grave.

The second inscription is the headstone of Moshele's grave in the kibbutz cemetery on the western side of the kibbutz. It records basic information about Moshele's life (fig. 2):

משה ליכט	Moshe Licht
(אוריון)	(Orion)
בן אסתר וחיים	Son of Esther and Chaim
נולד בתל־אביב נפל בקרב	Born in Tel Aviv, fallen in battle
בקבוצת יזרעאל כ״ה אדר	At Kvutza Yizreel on 25 Adar
תשט״ו בן 24 בנפלו תנצב״ה	5715, died at age 24. May his soul be bound in the bundle of life.

Moshele participated in the conquest of the Zer'in stronghold, the ruins of which are still visible east of Yizreel, and lived in the deserted houses of the village following its capture in June 1948. His agricultural training came in useful when the kvutza was established west of Zer'in. The tombstone bears the logo of the Israeli Army, Moshele's rank (sergeant), and his military identity number. He is said to have fallen in battle because he was considered in active service while working at Yizreel.

The third inscription of Moshele's name is found at the top of the stele standing in the *gan ha-zikaron*, the memorial garden (fig. 3). Below Moshele's, the stele bears the name of three other members who died together on the same day during the Yom Kippur War in 1973. It is thanks to this third stone that, over sixty years after his murder, the name Moshele Orion remains familiar at Yizreel, even among the young generation. On the eve of Independence Day, the entire community gathers in the memorial garden to honor those who fell in wars. The memory of Moshele is also kept alive through printed documents.

---

as a more intimate society, against the bigger kibbutzim of the other Kibbutz Movement, Kibbutz Hameuchad.

Heroic Elaborations

The Yizreel library holds a number of records about Moshele's death, most of them gathered in a booklet produced in 2008 by Daniel Orion, Moshele's brother.

The earliest document seems to be an extract from a newspaper's obituary page reporting that in "the days of infiltration of assassins from across the border—he [Moshele] fell on his post on the night of 22 of Adar 1955 and was brought to rest in Yizreel."

A booklet edited for the *shloshim* (thirty-day period of mourning after burial) presents poetic elaborations on the tragic event:

Figure 3. Inscription in the *gan ha-zikaron*.

His voice was silenced. His loud, cheerful, sober voice. He is silenced for us all. The first bearer and puller of the wagon of our group and its cultural life. We are orphaned from a friend that was our guide and teacher in labor and ways of life. (p. 5 §3)

Moshele was abruptly taken, and we need him so much, in the hands of assassins from the west he found his death, while protecting the kvutza, his home that he so loved. His memory will accompany his friends as a decree for the road taken. His home, on whose guard he fell and died, will be our home and it shall grow and blossom and flourish forever. (p. 13)

All his deeds and all his actions were based on the principles of sharing, equality, and helping one's neighbor ... He cared little for himself, his private life—the good of the whole was always right in front of his eyes, and when he started building his private life, the wick of his life was cut short as he stood guard protecting property and the kvutza. This is how Moshele lived and died! As a pioneer, a man of labor and the kvutza. All those who knew him and me in particular, will carry his memory forever. (pp. 14–15)

Moshele was one of the many victims who fell on homeland's altar. He dug the first grave at Yizreel. His grave is still fresh, and on it are tears and a wreath. Many flowers are spread on his face. His image stands erect in front of us, and suggests that our hands shall not be weakened. Our head shall not bow, we shall carry on with our lives, we will work our land, and return to our daily routine, despite this momentous event. It is clear that this despicable murder will not pass quietly. The day of retribution will come. A day of vengeance and retribution (Deut 32:35). Blessed be his memory ... (p. 16)[2]

---

2. Translations from Hebrew by Menachem Rogel.

The eulogies revolve around the theme of sacrifice for the country and the for kvutza for which Moshele's death was a hard blow. His fellows vowed to continue the task and preserve the memory of Moshele's sacrifice by persevering in the development of the kvutza.

The community has gone through ups and downs during the past six decades, and it has grown in numbers and in wealth. Contrary to the majority of kibbutzim, Yizreel retains many of the ideals of its founders and has so far resisted privatization. As a fine illustration of the need for memories of a shared history for social reproduction, the memory of the community's martyrs is kept alive by the yearly ceremony in the *gan ha-zikaron*.

Moshele as a Twentieth-Century Naboth

Moshele is Yizreel's first martyr. As such, he functions as Naboth does in biblical Jezreel.[3] Apart from being remembered as martyrs, the circumstances of their deaths are incomparable. Naboth is said to have been executed by the elders of the local council, whereas Moshele was shot by outsiders. Can the way Yizreel remembers Moshele teach us anything about the biblical story of Naboth written over two millennia earlier?

To be in a position to draw some lessons about the development of the Naboth story, we first use Moshele's case to illustrate how memories are processed and how they evolve within a mere half century.

From Infiltrators to Wars in General: Fading Memories and Recontextualization

The three stelae bearing Moshele's name are hard and fast monuments. Two of these have become physical sites of memory as Moshele's memory is commemorated on a yearly basis at the graveyard and at the memorial garden. Yet, the memory of Moshele changes according to the needs of the community.

In the mid 1950s, Moshele's murder was a hard blow for the fledgling kvutza. It was crucial to elevate the murdered member to the level of model to mobilize the border community's will to survive rather than give up at the height of the infiltration phenomenon (Morris 2001: 281–88). As the one who figuratively "dug the first grave" in the Yizreel cemetery, the kvutza experienced hope at the time by calling for revenge from its enemies "in the west," "across the border" through the evocation of the biblical day of retribution from Deut 32:35.

Three-quarters of a century later, Yizreel is striving. Only the few surviving members who lived in Yizreel at the time can recall in detail the circumstances surrounding Moshele's murder. They explain that Moshele was on guard duty with a colleague a

---

3. "Yizreel" is used for the modern site, and "Jezreel" for the biblical narrative.

few days after Purim.[4] Hiding in a haystack, two infiltrators shot them at close range. Hit in the head, Moshele died instantly while his colleague was injured in the leg and survived.

Members who joined Yizreel after Moshele's death routinely explain that Moshele was shot while on guard duty by infiltrators. The particulars surrounding the event, the haystack, the number of infiltrators, Moshele's colleague, and the type of injuries are not stated.

The term "infiltrator" itself has vanished from what the name Moshele Orion evokes for young Yizreelites today. Instead, their memory of Moshele's death has been recontextualized. The infiltrator has dropped from the vocabulary of the current young generation because the phenomenon of infiltration has been solved by the security fence that runs between Yizreel and Jenin. Instead, Moshele has joined the list of those who fell in the course of the different wars waged since the inception of the State. This is the direct consequence of the annual ceremony in the memorial garden, where the stele lists Moshele together with three men who fell eighteen years later in the Yom Kippur War. The memory of Moshele is not as crucial to the immediate survival of the local community as it was at the time of Moshele's death, but it sustains the national spirit the country needs to face the challenges of the Middle Eastern context.

The changing memories of Moshele illustrate that forgetfulness is the default position. Everything is forgotten, except that which the group decides to make the effort to remember. "Without such an effort and shared memory, the group itself would cease to exist" (Ben Zvi 2017: 2). At first, Yizreel remembered Moshele as the victim of a murder, which called for revenge. Today, Moshele is remembered as the victim of an ongoing war with the neighboring countries. In both cases, Moshele's memory serves the group's reproduction.

Social reproduction, however, differs from biological reproduction. Moshele's wife was pregnant when Moshele was murdered. She left Yizreel soon after the murder for a nearby kibbutz. Moshele's daughter lives not far from Yizreel, but not where her parents lived when she was conceived, nor where the father she never met fell. The social memory of Moshele is generated and maintained apart from the contribution of Moshele's biological family.

From Silage Pit to Swimming Pool: Shifting Locales of the Sites of Memory

The act of remembering also involves the displacement of physical sites of memory. The spot where Moshele actually fell is hardly known today because it is not visible from any of the roads that members and visitors take. The original wooden inscription marking the spot of Moshele's murder had decayed and was replaced by a basalt stele (fig. 4),

---

4. In 1955, Purim occurred ten to eleven days earlier than Moshele's murder, on March 8.

Figure 4. Moshele's stele by the cow sheds.

thanks to the presence nearby of the workshop of the reknown sculptor Berny Fink.[5] Despite its physical sturdiness, the present stele has lost much significance, simply because it is now stuck between silage pits and cowshed. The memory of Moshele relies upon the yearly gatherings in front of the stele standing on the opposite end of Yizreel (fig. 5). Set just above the community's swimming pool, close to the rugby fields of Yizreel's famed team, that stele is more conducive to commemorative gatherings prior to the national holiday than the smells and flies on the dairy side of Yizreel. Remembering requires gathering in a congenial spot for a moment set apart from daily chores. Inscribed in the hearts of every member, the actual spot of Moshele's murder has become irrelevant.

Infiltrators and Meir Har-Zion

Yizreel no longer fears attacks by infiltrators from the west—a direction understood by all as meaning Jenin though Jenin lies in fact some 10 km *south* of Yizreel. Jenin is visible from Yizreel by day and by night and traffic to and from the border crossing at Jalameh passes through the Yizreel junction where the Jenin-Afula main road crosses the Megiddo-Beit-Shean road. Jenin may be ignored but not forgotten.

---

5. Berny Fink won international acclaim for the monument erected at the entrance of the Yad Vashem memorial in Jerusalem. See anonymous 1985: 5–7.

Figure 5. Stele in the *gan ha-zikaron*.

The death of a national hero in March 2014 revived the memory of the period when infiltrators were a threat to border communities such as Yizreel. The media coverage at the occasion of the death of that national hero recalled the affair named after him. The "Har-Zion Affair" derives its name from the activities of Meir Har-Zion, a famous member of Kibbutz 'Ein Harod, also visible from Yizreel, as their fields are adjacent.

Born in Herzliya in 1934, Har-Zion moved to Kibbutz 'Ein Harod in 1948 with his father when his parents separated and his mother and sisters settled at nearby Kibbutz Beit Alfa.[6] Gifted with courage, coolheadedness and extraordinary navigational skills, Har-Zion was one of the very few Israelis of his generation to return from the popular illegal hikes to Petra.[7] Har-Zion also became the most famous member of the short-lived Unit 101 where his skills allowed him to succeed in the most difficult missions.

Unit 101

Unit 101 was created in August 1953 "for carrying out reprisals and deterrence missions across the border" at a time when the army's ineffectiveness in restraining infiltration of Israeli territory created a lack of security in outlying Israeli settlements such as Yizreel, and in some cases the desertion of border settlements (Seckbach 2014: 64).

6. On the foundation of 'Ein Harod, see Shavit 2015: 25–47.
7. On the mythical dimension of Petra for the Palmach generation, see Peters 2015.

To restore State sovereignty and confidence in the army, Unit 101—under the leadership of Ariel Sharon—attacked police, military and civilians across the border in retaliation for Israeli casualties. Unit 101 operated for only five months but brought about radical changes by demonstrating that such actions could indeed force the Jordanian and Egyptian authorities to restrain infiltrations. If these countries did not control their borders, Israel would wreak havoc in their land. The reprisals were also meant to deter potential infiltrators, to reinforce morale in the Israeli public and bolster the position of the Mapai party before the upcoming general elections, in which Mapai suffered a first set-back.

Unit 101 was characterized by its high-level of performance, daring, determination to achieve its goal, strict selection of its members, intensive training, and operation in small groups beyond the Israeli borders. Its soldiers did not wear standard IDF uniforms, and used weapons without the IDF identifying mark (Seckbach 2014: 65). Yet, the methods of Unit 101 were controversial, even in 1950s Israel, and the unit merged with the paratroops in January 1954.

The Har-Zion Affair

A year later, in the middle of February 1955, Har-Zion's sister Shoshana and her boyfriend Oded Wegmeister from Kibbutz Degania Bet were captured and murdered in Wadi al-Ghar, the central section of Nahal Arugot, which ends at 'Ein Gedi. Shoshana and Oded, both eighteen at the time, were on an illegal cross-border hike into Jordanian territory, as reckless youths did in those days. When he heard of the death of his sister, Har-Zion was inconsolable and vowed revenge. On March 4, Ariel Sharon drove Har-Zion and three ex-members of the 890th Battalion to the border. The four then crossed the Armistice Line and reached Wadi al-Ghar—9 km from the border. They captured six Bedouin from the tribe they held responsible for the murder of Shoshana and Oded. Five of them were killed. The sixth was sent back to his tribe to tell what happened.

On their return, Har-Zion and three of his companions were held in custody as the Jordanians filed a formal complaint with the United Nations. The hero of Petra and of Unit 101 was too much of a hero to be punished for his private revenge spree in Jordanian territory. Protected by their army colleagues, Har-Zion and his three companions were released without charge after twenty days and soon rejoined their unit.

Prime minister Moshe Sharett, who deplored such actions but suspected that Moshe Dayan had advance knowledge of the raid, noted critically in his diary that the "dark soul of the Bible has come alive among the sons of Nahalal and 'Ein Harod."[8]

---

8. See Sharrett 1978, 3:834. Seckbach 2014: 66–71.

Moshele and the Aftermath of the Har-Zion Affair

Given the international dimension of the Har-Zion affair, it is possible that it had repercussions at Yizreel, though we only have evidence for it in the form of a current
oral tradition, which associates Moshele's murder in March 19, 1955 with Har-Zion's
private revenge killings of the Bedouin at Wadi al-Ghar in March 4, a fortnight earlier.
Since Moshele's killers were never identified, their motives will never be established.
To be sure, Moshele was one casualty in the tit for tat cycle of revenge killings, which
plagued Sharrett's tenure and his relations with David Ben Gurion (Rabinovich and
Reinharz 2008: 130–32).

Moshele's murder could also be related to Har-Zion's activities in Unit 101 in the
previous year; for example, the attack of two Jordanian policemen near Jenin, taking one
of them prisoner (31 July–1 August 1954). On its way back from Jenin, the ten-raider
squad led by Har-Zion killed a farmer watching his fields.[9] If the squad was heading
back to 'Ein Harod where Har-Zion lived, the farmer they killed must have been watching his field somewhere near Yizreel. Geographic proximity favors viewing Moshele's
murder as retaliation for the blood of that farmer. But this entails a gap of almost nine
months between the two killings. Chronology favors retaliation for the Bedouin Har-
Zion killed near 'Ein Gedi on March 4, only two weeks before Moshele was shot.

According to the current oral tradition at Yizreel, the aim of the infiltrators who
shot Moshele was to kill a member of 'Ein Harod, the kibbutz immediately east of Yizreel. Either the infiltrators decided to cut their mission short by shooting someone
from Yizreel, or they mistook Yizreel for 'Ein Harod. Coming at night from Jenin to
reach 'Ein Harod, the infiltrators would pass by Yizreel to skirt the Gilboa range.

On March 19, the waning crescent was 24 percent visible and the new moon occurred on the 24th. There was probably still just enough light to walk across the fields
and it is likely that the murderers chose such a night for their revenge spree. March 19
was also a Sabbath. A more relaxed guard could be expected. Therefore, the operation
was well planned and the notion that Yizreel was mistaken for 'Ein Harod is hardly
convincing. Rather than a mistake, Yizreel may well have been deliberately targeted.
A reinforced guard could be expected in 'Ein Harod in the weeks following Har-Zion's
raid. In these conditions, Yizreel was a softer target, and a closer one for infiltrators
coming from Jenin.

Har-Zion's blood or the blood of other members of 'Ein Harod would have best
restored the honor of the Bedouin clans targeted by Har-Zion. Revenge requires "a life
for a life, an eye for an eye" (Deut 19:21), but that it is the blood of the actual perpetrator that must be shed is not absolutely necessary. Someone more or less associated with
the perpetrator is good enough. From the point of view of the infiltrators, any members
of the kibbutz established next to the ruins of Zer'in were legitimate expiatory victims

---

9. Teveth 1974: 253 describes the prisoner as a Jordanian soldier. See also Burns 1962: 36–37.

to atone for their dead. As a founding member of Yizreel who had first lived in the deserted houses of Zerʻin after the Palmaḥ's decisive victory in August 1948, Moshele became another entry on the ledger of victims of the Israeli-Palestinian struggle for survival. For Kvutzat Yizreel, however, Moshele was its first martyr.

Remembering Har-Zion

In the wake of the disastrous Lavon affair in 1955, Har-Zion's official activities in Unit 101 and his private revenge of Shoshanah's death were already controversial (Seckbach 2014: 72–75). For dovish-minded people, such as the Heber ha-Kvutzot to which Kvutzat Yizreel belonged, being a strong supporter of Sharrett's Mapai party, the Har-Zion legend was countered by stating that his activities were tainted by killings of "Arab soldiers, farmers and city-dwellers, with a rage deprived of hate, always cool and completely efficient, just doing a job and doing it well, three or four times a week, for months" (Elon 1971: 234–35). At the time of his death, these words were published again as a critique of the Har-Zion legend.[10]

The debate over Har-Zion's activities and the resulting ambivalence in the Israeli public opinion could add another potential layer to the memory of Moshele. Moshele the victim of infiltrators could become Moshele the collateral victim of Har-Zion. The present context of heightened tensions with Syria is not conducive to the integration of this additional facet of Moshele's fate into the community's shared memory. The integration of Kvutzat Yizreel into the United Kibbutz Movement in the 1980s placed the requirements of the national agenda above local rivalries, previously expressed as ideological differences with the hawkish Ahdut ha-Avodah of ʻEin Harod. Moshele and Har-Zion could thus serve as archetypical figures of the two breeds of Israelis at the inception of the State. The more social one, remembered by his contemporaries for his humor and his social skills, died at age 24, seven years after the birth of the State of Israel. The other died of natural causes at age 80, sixty-six years after the birth of the State. Both were sabras, soldiers, and farmers, but their fates could hardly have been more divergent.

Reading Naboth in Light of Moshele and Har-Zion

Having identified the formation and evolution of the memory of Moshele at Yizreel, similar patterns can be expected at work in ancient Israel before the biblical story entered the canon and Naboth became the parade victim of royal villains.

Because memory is both fallible and inventive, "emphasis must lie on the historical significance of the "remembering" rather than the reliability of the memory" (Da-

---

10. Sheizaf 2014. Most of this article has now been incorporated in the Wikipedia article on Meir Har-Zion. For another critical piece, see Sarid 2014.

vies 2017: 72). Three circles were identified above, corresponding to distinctive phases in the memory of Moshele: the original members of Kvutzat Yizreel whose memories of Moshele are based on personal interactions with him, members who joined the kvutzah later, and those born in or who arrived at Yizreel around the year 2000. For the last two, Moshele's memory is the fruit of yearly commemorations. So far, the youngest are the least likely to balance their memory of Moshele with their take on the activities of Har-Zion.

Obviously, Naboth's case is vastly different. Whether there ever were Jezreelites who remembered Naboth because they had rubbed shoulders with him is debatable because there is no evidence that Naboth is anything else than a literary figure created centuries after the days of King Ahab. Yet, it is precisely because Naboth is a biblical figure that he is a hero the world over for anyone who has received a basic biblical education. Though Moshele was a flesh-and-blood Yizreelite, so far he is a local figure only and a hero only as long as his name remains inscribed on stones in front of which the Yizreel community gathers to venerate the shared memory that keeps the community together. Moshele's memory remains under the threat of forgetfulness, until Moshele of Yizreel and Meir of 'Ein Harod become central figures in an internationally acclaimed novel yet to be written, or a yet-to-be-hewed basalt statue of Moshele is erected at a prominent location in Jerusalem or Tel Aviv.

Naboth, Ahab, and Jezebel as Sterotypical Figures

Of the three protagonists of the Naboth story, only King Ahab's existence is confirmed by extra-biblical evidence.[11] Ahab is mentioned as "the Israelite" in a royal inscription of Shalmaneser III and presented as the most powerful ruler across the Euphrates besides his Damascene colleague (Knauf and Guillaume 2015: 89). That such a favorable portrait of Ahab comes from his best enemy is a guarantee of its historical reliability. The contrast with biblical Ahab could not be greater. The ultimate coward, Ahab in 1 Kgs 21 submits to Jezebel, his femme fatale, who is all too happy to satisfy his greed. The epitome of the foreign woman popularized by the book of Proverbs, biblical Jezebel is a reflex of Solomon's wives who enticed Judah's fabled king to worship Astarte and Milcom (1 Kgs 11:4–7). As a one-dimensional figure, Jezebel is set beside Naboth to produce a sharp black-and-white contrast between the two central characters of the tale. The name "Naboth" itself was probably crafted to illustrate the story on the basis of the vineyard that stands at the center of the plot.[12] Naboth's vineyard echoes the vine-

---

11. An unprovenenced hieroglyphic seal simply reads "*yzbl*," with no patronym or title. See Avigad 1964. For the precarious identification of the owner of the seal as Jezebel daughter of King Ethbaal of the Sidonians, see Korpel 2006.

12. See Guillaume 2015: 179. The root *nabata*, "to grow," attested in Old Arabic (HALOT 2:660), suggests that Naboth was named after the vineyard, "Naboth" meaning something like a "shoot" or "scion."

yards and olive orchards which, Samuel foretold, the Israelite monarchs would take to give to his courtiers (1 Sam 8:14). Ahab is the worst of the lot. Instead of taking the best vineyards for his courtiers, Ahab wants Jezreel's best vineyard—as its location besides the palace suggests (1 Kgs 21:1)—for himself and lets his foreign wife do the dirty job to obtain it. Ever since the story was translated into Greek, many readers have implied that the vineyard was Naboth's only one (3 Kgdms 20:1; Rofé 1988: 90–91). As young Yizreelites only remember Moshele as a hero of their country's wars in general, biblical Israel only remembers Naboth as the parade victim of the rulers of the Kingdom of Israel.

If a man named Naboth ever owed a vineyard at Jezreel, which is doubtful because Naboth is given no patronym, no one has made the effort to recall anything else about Naboth because that sole recollection sufficed to construct Ahab as the parade ruler of the evil Israelite kingdom. The construction must be significantly late because the standard designation of that evil is systematically ascribed to Jeroboam son of Nebat (1 Kgs 16:26.31; 21:22.52; 2 Kgs 3:3; 10:29; 13:2.11; 14:24; 15:9.18.24.28), never to Ahab. The secondary nature of the elaboration of the figures of Naboth and Jezebel in Kings is supported by the silence of Chronicles.[13] Unless one could demonstrate that the Chronicler purposely ignored Naboth and Jezebel as he ignored Elijah and Elisha because they did not fit his agenda, the best explanation for the absence of any mention of Naboth and Jezebel in Chronicles is that they are later innovations in Kings.[14] Athaliah is presented as daughter of Omri (2 Kgs 8:26 // 2 Chron 22:2), never as Ahab's or Jezebel's. Jezebel is never mentioned in relation to the worship of Baal by Ahab (1 Kgs 16:31) and Manasseh (2 Kgs 21:3), though she supposedly had 450 prophets of Baal and 400 prophets of Asherah at her table (1 Kgs 18:19).

As for Naboth, he is portrayed as a silent victim, a sheep led to the slaughter without raising a sound (Isa 53:7), the victim without blemish that the story needs to inspire trust in YHWH's ability to avenge people wronged by the authorities.

Shifting Place: Samaria or Jezreel

As discussed above, the main physical site of Moshele's memory shifted to the west of Yizreel. In a similar fashion, the location of Naboth's vineyard has shifted from Jezreel to Samaria or vice versa. The words "in Jezreel" (אשר ביזרעאל) in 1 Kgs 21:1 are not attested in the Septuagint (3 Kgdms 20:1), which suggests that the vineyard is beside the royal palace at Samaria, even though Naboth is a member of the Jezreel gentry.[15]

---

13. On memory studies and Chronicles, see Ben Zvi 2011, 2017.

14. Of these four, only Elijah is mentioned once in 2 Chr 21:12, as the author of a letter written to King Jehoram. For the significance of the Chronicler's silence on the formation of the Book of Kings, see Auld 2017: 11–19.

15. In the Greek version (3 Kgdms 20:18), Elijah is to meet Ahab the king of Israel who is at

Shifting Times

The inventiveness of memory also involves shifts in time. Like young Yizreelites who package Moshele with other war casualties rather than associate him with a particular crisis in their country's history, Naboth is remembered as *the* victim of Jezebel, although the queen is also twice accused of having killed many prophets of YHWH (1 Kgs 18:4.13). The circumstances in which these prophets were killed is never narrated. It merely serves as a springboard for Obadiah's saving of a hundred prophets of YHWH. Though there is no hint that Naboth was a prophet, he is remembered as the parade victim of the evil queen of an evil king.

Shifting Sequence: After Elisha or after Death Oracle

The Greek version places the story of Naboth's vineyard a chapter earlier than is the case in the Hebrew text. Either the Alexandrian translators worked on a Hebrew text with a different sequence, or they are the ones who first inserted the Naboth episode into the Elijah cycle, placing it immediately after the call of Elisha (1 Kgs 19:19–21 and 3 Kgdms 19:19–21). The Hebrew placement of the Naboth story immediately after the king's return to Samaria produces a smoother transition. Having been tricked by a prophet who announced that he would die for having struck a deal with the king of Damascus (1 Kgs 20:43 // 3 Kgdms 21:43), the king of Israel goes back home "resentful and sullen." Naboth's refusal worsens the royal mood, which explains Ahab's subsequent passivity in letting Jezebel take over. A better sequence, however, is no proof of anteriority or posteriority. It is certainly more economical to view the Hebrew text as improving an earlier sequence transmitted by the Septuagint. Apart from that, we have no access to an earlier version of the Naboth story. The different sequences have more to do with the particular needs of the editors and translators than with the shape of the original story. Stories need literary figures, not flesh-and-blood individuals.

Fitting Figures into Patterns

Naboth belongs to the biblical metanarrative as much as Moshele belongs to Yizreel's social memory. In less than a century, Moshele's short life has been configured according to the template Yizreel needed to remember for its survival, that is, his death as a martyr. Moshele the man, the lover, the soldier, the farmer, the entertainer is about to be entirely forgotten. For young Yizreelites, Moshele is already a figure of the past like biblical Naboth, two characters in a gallery of martyrs of bygone days, a past in which fifty years are like two thousand and fifty. Young Yizreelites did not forget the actual circumstances of Moshele's murder. They never knew them and have no need—or feel

---

Samaria in the vineyard of Naboth. Hence, in some Greek manuscripts Naboth is an Israelite rather than a Jezreelite; see Seidel 2012: 53.

no need—to know them. All they know is what their community considers they need
to know: "You belong here thanks to Moshele's ultimate dedication to the kvutza."

The pattern is not complete until the last protagonists are considered. So far, we
have recovered four categories of actors in the crime:

- the victims: Moshele and Naboth
- the perpetrators: Har-Zion and the Jezreel council
- the instigators: Moshe Dayan and Jezebel
- the apparent authorities: Ben Gurion and Ahab

To complete the pattern, the figures of Moshe Sharrett and Elijah represent the
moral authority in the two stories. Elijah is YHWH's mouthpiece in the Naboth story,
the voice of justice. Sharrett was the Prime Minister when the crime was committed.
He favored diplomacy and restraint but had little control over the ruthless retaliations
of Dayan and the manipulations of Lavon. Obviously, this is an oversimplification of
the intricacies of Israeli politics at the time. Yet, patterns are exactly that. Patterns are
artificial constructions. They are simplifications of the complexities of real life.

Yizreel survived Moshele because Yizreel turned Moshele into its first martyr, a
founding father who overshadows the contribution of the others, in the same way that
the figure of Naboth has erased his colleagues of the Jezreel council who have neither
number nor names. Naboth occupies the entire Jezreel slot of the biblical metanarrative, at the expense of yet another biblical Jezreelite, Ahinoam, one of King David's
wives (1 Sam 25:43). Societies function because they make complex individuals play
a limited number of predefined roles. These roles impose the behavioral modes that
the system needs to be able to function, modes that are rarely in adequation with the
potential of the individual player who must play the role accordingly or be ostracized.

There was more to Meir Har-Zion, Ariel Sharon and Moshe Dayan than the roles
they played in the politics of their time, but what is remembered is what they did for
their country as a whole. Yet, this metanarrative is not fixed once and for all. It can
change according to the needs of their country at different times.

Potentialities: Har-Zion as Ahab or Moshele and Har-Zion as Heroes

The deaths of Moshele and of Naboth as martyrs is what the remembering communities—biblical Israel for Naboth and Yizreel for Moshele—needed to maintain their cohesion. Biblical Israel was conceived as an entity forever in tension between Jerusalem
and Samaria and between Judah and Benjamin (Davies 2007). The modern State of
Israel is built on the tension between dovish and hawkish approaches to its relations
with its neighbors. The tension results in a constant state of imbalance, which renders
any once-and-for-all solution inapplicable but fosters potential adaptation to new situ-
ations.

The canonization of the Naboth story froze the way the two different versions of the story are written, but not the way it is read. For instance, feminist readings can challenge readings of the figure of Jezebel that blame her for the crime.

The figure of Moshele holds a similar potential for alternative readings. Instead of simply remembering Moshele as a victim of infiltrators, Moshele's death holds the potential of being remembered as a collateral victim of Har-Zion in the overall cycle of reprisals and revenge following the foundation of the State.

So far, there are no signs that this change is happening. The memory of Moshele as it is honored at Yizreel seems incompatible with the way the memory of Har-Zion is to be honored at the Belvoir Park, if the Jewish National Fund proceeds with its plan for a grove of 101 trees planted in memory of Unit 101.[16] Though the evocation of the Har-Zion affair at Yizreel in the context of Moshele's death shows that Har-Zion has a place in the mindscape of the people of Yizreel, none of the interviewed Yizreelites gave the impression that they viewed Har-Zion as a hero.

Memory, however, is no basalt stele. It changes. Depending on the circumstances, the memory of Har-Zion could evolve at Yizreel toward the role that the figure of Ahab plays in the Naboth story. Remembering Moshele as a victim of infiltrators *and* of Har-Zion's killings could eventually lead one to regard Har-Zion himself as a victim of Sharon and Dayan's machinations.

In any case, Har-Zion's memory as much as Moshele's will evolve according to the needs of Israeli society, whereas the memory of Naboth has been fossilized according to the needs of those who canonized the biblical book of Kings. The canonical Naboth is what that particular change to "community chose to remember at a particular time about Naboth, that is, as a victim of Jezebel's machinations. Needless to say, a quest for the historical Naboth would be in vain, contrary to a quest for the memory of Naboth. It is likely that another remembering community, for instance the Samaritans, would have remembered Jezebel more positively. The Samaritans' Naboth would have been very different from the Naboth of our Bible. While Naboth and the book of Kings did not make it into the Samaritan canon, the Naboth story entered the mindscape of Bible-reading communities across the world.

Yet, canonization did not freeze the way these communities read the Naboth story. For instance, new meanings arise when feminist readings shift the focus away from the victimization of Naboth onto the portrayal of Jezebel viewed as the product of a patriarchal society, which views women as the origin of evil—a society held together by slurring its neighbors, that is, any group filling the slot of Israelites and Phoenicians in the biblical story.

---

16. "Following in the Footsteps of Meir Har-Zion," Keren Kayemeth LeIsrael Jewish National Fund, Tuesday, March 24, 2015, http://www.kkl-jnf.org/about-kkl-jnf/green-israel-news/march-2015/meir-har-zion-memorial/.

Timeline

1921		Arrival of the founders of 'Ein Harod
1931		Birth of Moshele in Tel Aviv
1934		Birth of Har-Zion in Herzliya
1948	?	Move of Har-Zion to 'Ein Harod
1948	May 14	Foundation of the State of Israel
1948	June	Conquest of Zer'in
1950		Increasing armed infiltrations
1953	August	Formation of Unit 101
1953	October 13	Qibya massacre
1954	January	Unit 101 disbanded. Sharrett replaces Ben Gurion as Prime Minister
1955	February	Lavon resigns as Defense Minister
1955	February	Shoshana's body discovered near Nahal Arugot
1955	March 4	Har-Zion kills Bedouin at Wadi el-Ghar
1955	March 19	Moshele is shot dead at Yizreel
1955	ca. March 24	Har-Zion and his companions are released
1955	November	Ben Gurion replaces Sharrett as Prime Minister
1956	October–December	Suez crisis
1967	June	Six-Day War
1973	October	Yom Kippur War
2008		Publication of booklet on Moshele
2014	March 14	Death of Har-Zion at age 80

References

Anonymous. 1985. "Artist Wins International Acclaim." TelFed II/1: 5–7, https://tel fedhistory.com/wp-content/uploads/2018/01/1985_jan.pdf.

Auld, A. Graeme. 2017. *Life in Kings: Reshaping the Royal Story in the Hebrew Bible.* AIL 30. Atlanta: SBL Press.

Avigad, Nahman. 1964. "The Seal of Jezebel." *IEJ* 14: 274–76.

Ben Zvi, Ehud. 2011. "On Social Memory and Identity Formation in Late Persian Yehud: A Historian's Viewpoint with a Focus on Prophetic Literature, Chronicles and the Dtr. Historical Collection." Pages 95–148 in *Texts, Contexts and Readings in Postexilic Literature: Explorations into Historiography and Identity Negotiation in Hebrew Bible and Related Texts.* Edited by Louis Jonker. Tübingen: Mohr Siebeck.

———. 2017. "Chronicles and Social Memory." *Studia Theologica–Nordic Journal of Theology* 71: 69–90, http://dx.doi.org/10.1080/0039338X.2017.1308718.

Burns, E. L. M. 1962. *Between Arab and Israeli.* London: Harrap.

Davies, Philip R. 2007. *The Origins of Biblical Israel*. London: T&T Clark.

———. 2017. "With a Bible in One Hand." Pages 71–86 in *Rethinking Israel: Studies in the History and Archaeology of Ancient Israel in Honor of Israel Finkelstein*. Edited by Oded Lipschits, Yuval Gadot and Matthew J. Adams. Winona Lake, IN: Eisenbrauns.

Elon, Amos. 1971. *The Israelis: Founders and Sons*. New York: Holt, Rinehart & Winston.

Guillaume, Philippe. 2015. "Naboth the Nabob." *UF* 46:161–82.

Knauf, Ernst Axel, and Philippe Guillaume. 2015. *A History of Israel's Tribes from Merneptah to Bar-Kokhba*. Sheffield: Equinox.

Korpel, Marjo C. A. 2006. "Queen Jezebel's Seal." *UF* 38:378.

Morris, Benny. 2001. *Righteous Victims: A History of the Zionist–Arab Conflict, 1881–2001*. New York: Vintage.

Peters, Dominik. 2015. "Melody of a Myth: The Legacy of Haim Hefers Red Rock Song." *De Gruyter Open* 13:103–13; DOI: 10.1515/tra-2015-0011.

Rabinovich, Itamar, and Yehuda Reinharz. 2008. *Israel in the Middle East: Documents and Readings on Society, Politics and Foreign Relations, Pre-1948 to the Present*. Waltham, MA: Brandeis University.

Rofé, Alexander. 1988. "The Vineyard of Naboth: The Origin and Message of the Story." *VT* 38:89–104.

Sarid, Yossi. 2014. "We Should Find Better Heroes Than Meir Har-Zion." March 21, 2014, https://www.haaretz.com/opinion/.premium-meir-har-zion-dont-follow-him-1.5337278.

Seckbach, Efrat. 2014. "Meir Har-Zion's Act of Reprisal: Reality and Memory." *Journal of Israeli History* 33:63–84.

Seidel, Hans-Joachim. 2012. *Nabots Weinberg, Ahabs Haus, Israels Thron: Textpragmatisch fundierte Untersuchung von 1 Kön 21 und seinen Bezugstexten*. Berlin: LIT.

Sharett, Moshe. 1978. *Yoman ishi [Personal diary, 1953–1957]*. Tel Aviv: Ma'ariv.

Shavit, Ari. 2015. *My Promised Land: The Triumph and Tragedy of Israel*. New York: Spiegel & Grau.

Sheizaf, Noam. 2014. "The Death of an Israeli War Hero and Palestinian Incitement," March 17, http://972mag.com/death-of-an-israeli-war-hero-and-palestinian-incitement/88499/

Teveth, Shabtai. 1974. *Moshe Dayan: The Soldier, the Man, the Legend*. London: Quartet.

PART TWO

THE JEZREEL VALLEY

The Rural Hinterland of the Jezreel Valley in the Late Bronze Age III and Iron Age I: A Petrographic Perspective

Eran Arie, Karen Covello-Paran,
and Anastasia Shapiro

Abstract: Most provenance studies carried out in the southern Levant are based on pottery uncovered in urban sites. Hinterland settlements are almost completely neglected as excavations and publications of countryside sites are relatively rare in the archaeology of the Bronze and the Iron Ages in this region. This article presents the result of a petrographic study of Late Bronze Age III and Iron Age I pottery assemblages at four rural sites from the Jezreel Valley.

Keywords: Jezreel Valley, rural hinterland, petrography, collared-rim pithoi, Philistine pottery.

To make up for the neglect of settlements located in rural hinterlands, we present the results of a petrographic study of Late Bronze Age III and Iron Age I pottery assemblages at four sites from the Jezreel Valley (fig. 1).

A total of seventy-seven ceramic vessels of different types were sampled for petrographic examination (tables 2–12): eight samples from Tel Kedesh, twenty-three from Tell Qiri, twenty-six from 'Ein el-Hilu and twenty from Tel Shunem. The selected sites are located in four distinct areas in the Jezreel Valley to include different geological settings. Table 1 presents the relative chronology of these sites during the research period in comparison to the well-known stratigraphy of Megiddo.

While the vessels from Tell Qiri and Tel Kedesh were sampled exclusively for this study, the samples from Tel Shunem and 'Ein el-Hilu were researched separately (Shapiro 2016; Goren and Shapiro forthcoming) and added to the current database to enhance the rural understanding of the valley. Thirty additional vessels (collared-rim pithoi and Philistine-style vessels) that were sampled from Tell Qiri in the past

---

Most of Norma Franklin's archaeological fieldwork was carried out in the Jezreel Valley—Megiddo and Jezreel. We dedicate this article to her, as an additional step in the investigation of the largest valley in Israel. We wish Norma many more years of fruitful research in the valley and far beyond.

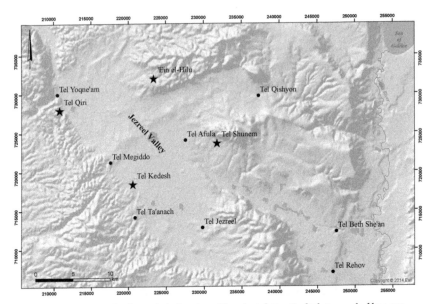

Figure 1. Map of the Jezreel Valley with the location of the selected sites. Studied sites marked by a star.

Table 1. Relative chronology of the four sampled sites with a comparison to Megiddo

	LB IIB	LB III	Early Iron I	Late Iron I	Early Iron IIA	Late Iron IIA
Megiddo	VIIB	VIIA	VIB	VIA	VB	VA–IVB
Tel Kedesh	VIII	VII	gap	gap	VI–V	IV
Tell Qiri	gap	gap	D-IX	D-VIII	D-VII	
'Ein el-Hilu	gap	gap	II		gap	gap
Tel Shunem	?	V	IV	III	IIc	IIb

(Cohen-Weinberger and Wolff 2001: table 32.3:76–80; Martin 2017: table 11:4–29) are not part of the current petrographic database, but their provenance is mentioned in our conclusions.

All vessels discussed in this article were classified according to the well-established typological system of Late Bronze Age III/Iron Age I Tel Megiddo assemblages (Arie 2006, 2013, forthcoming). Half of the sampled specimens were storage vessels (amph-oriskoi, storage jars and pithoi), of which thirty-seven vessels were examined. The rest were taken from open vessels (bowls, kraters, chalices and cup and saucers) and small containers (jugs, juglets, pyxides and flasks), twenty samples were tested from each group. Cooking vessels were not sampled, since they are almost always considered to be local to the sites in which they were found.

Prior to the petrographic study, the samples were examined under a stereoscopic microscope at magnifications ×20 to ×40. Then, thin-sections were prepared and examined under a petrographic (polarizing) microscope at magnifications of ×20 to ×200, and sorted into petrographic groups according to their lithological and technological properties. Description of the thin-sections was made with the aid of charts and tables (Whitbread 1986; Orton, Tyers, and Vince 1993). The observed data were compared to the geologic and pedologic settings of the discussed area (Blake and Goldschmidt 1947; Bentor 1966; Ravikovitch 1969; Sneh, Bartov, and Rosensaft 1998).

Geological and Pedological Background

Covered with brown alluvial calcareous soil, the Jezreel Valley is bounded by Alonim-Shefaram Hills and Nazareth Mountains at the north; Givat Ha-More and Mount Tabor at the east; Samaria Highlands and the western flank of Mount Gilboa on the south; and by the Carmel range at the west. Miocene basalt rocks are cropping in the center of the Jezreel Valley and at some points all around it. Pliocene-Pleistocene cover basalt is found at the hilly areas bounding the valley from the east, and these areas are covered with brown basaltic Mediterranean soils (Ravikovitch 1969). The hills and mountains surrounding the valley are composed of a number of geological formations. Cenomanian and Turonian limestone and dolomite and Senonian chalk and marl are cropping at Carmel and Umm el-Fahm areas of Mount Carmel range and southern flank of the Nazareth Mountains. Above these, *terra rossa* soil develops. The rests of the highlands surrounding the Jezreel Valley are composed of Lower-Middle Eocene chalk formations, covered by Rendzina mountainous soil (Ravikovitch 1969; Sneh, Bartov, and Rosensaft 1998).

Each of the four researched sites has its own geological micro-environment, which were defined by Arie, Buzaglo, and Goren (2006: 558) for Tel Kedesh; Buzaglo (2004: 101–3) for Tel Qiri; Covello-Paran (1999: 12–14) for 'Ein el-Hilu; and Shapiro (2016: 63) for Tel Shunem.

Sampled Sites

Tel Kedesh

Tel Kedesh is a 1 ha site in the western Jezreel Valley, some 4 km southeast of Megiddo. Limited excavations were conducted at the site in 1968 (Stern and Beit Arieh 1979). All of the finds from the excavations were critically restudied by one of us (Arie 2011: 294–303). Stratum VII, dated to LB III, was destroyed by a conflagration. Despite the conclusions reached by the excavators, the tell was abandoned during Iron I and was resettled only during the initial phase of Iron II. The area to the north of the tell was already used for burial during the LB III. Hence, contrary to the view of the excavators, the tombs unearthed around the site cannot all be dated to Iron II.

Since only stratum VII (dated to the LB III) is relevant to the current research, we compensated the very few finds from this stratum by sampling vessels from unclean contexts that according to typology are related to this phase. All in all, eight vessels were sampled from Tel Kedesh: mostly storage vessels (n=4), but also open vessels (n=2) and small containers (n=2).

Tell Qiri

Tell Qiri is located in Kibbutz Hazorea, about 2 km south of Tel Yoqneam, in the north-western part of the Jezreel Valley. Ein Qira and Nahal Hashofet, located at the foot of the site, provide its water. The site covers approximately 1 ha. The thickness of the Iron Age strata reached 4 m (Ben-Tor and Portugali 1987a: 3). Tell Qiri was excavated be-tween 1975 and 1977 in the framework of the regional study of Tel Yoqneam. After an occupational gap during the LB III, Tell Qiri yielded architectural remains from Iron Age I and Age II.

The two relevant strata for the current research are Strata IX–VIII, dating to Iron Age I (Ben-Tor and Portugali 1987b: 80–103). Area D provided the best stratigra-phy with each stratum divided into three subphases for a total of six phases; none of them was destroyed by fire. The rural nature of the architecture showed little change throughout Iron Age I. It mostly includes poorly preserved domestic structures with many silos, winepresses, everyday pottery vessels and numerous stone implements for grinding and crushing.

Twenty-three vessels were sampled for this petrographic study, almost equally divided between storage vessels (n=9), open vessels (n=7), and small containers (n=7).

'Ein el-Hilu

'Ein el-Hilu is situated in the northern Jezreel Valley, in the industrial area to the north of Migdal Ha'Emeq. The site spans the lower slopes of a hill and part of the valley floor; its total area is estimated as ca. 0.5 ha (Covello-Paran 2008, forthcoming). Stratum II, dated to Iron Age I, includes three structures scattered over the site (Arie and Covello-Paran forthcoming). Apparently, the inhabitants preferred to erect their buildings on the higher part of the site. It is possible that one or two additional buildings existed in the unexcavated area. Besides the buildings, a tabun and an oil press were uncovered as well as numerous refuse pits throughout the site. At the eastern boundary of the site, above the bedrock, a variety of agricultural activities and cultic ceremonies were performed.

The character of the buildings, the limited variety of pottery types, the simple stone tools and the kill-off patterns of the animals that were consumed at the site, indi-cate that this settlement existed on a minimal subsistence level.

Twenty-six vessels were sampled: half of them were taken from storage vessels (n=13), while open vessels (n=6) and small containers were also examined (n=7).

Tel Shunem

Tel Shunem (Sulam) is located at the foot of Givat Ha-More in the eastern Jezreel Valley, and it extends over ca. 2.5 ha. The references to Shunem in the historical and biblical sources have rendered it a key site toward understanding the Jezreel Valley in the Late Bronze and Iron Ages (Na'aman 2006: 232–41). While the limited excavations in the northern part of the site provided decisive evidence of occupation during the LB II until the end of Iron IIA (Covello-Paran and Arie 2016), the accumulated data for each individual settlement phase remains relatively small.

The sequence of events that took place at the site during the LB and Iron Ages can be reconstructed as follows: a settlement existed on the tell in LB II, which was apparently not destroyed at the end of the period, but continued into LB III (Stratum V). At the end of this period, the settlement was completely razed in a conflagration. After a certain time, the site was resettled in Iron I (Stratum IV) and, as opposed to other sites in the area, it did not suffer heavy destruction; it was probably abandoned at the end of Iron I (Stratum III). It seems that in the early Iron IIA, occupation on the tell was renewed and continued until the Aramean destruction.

Twenty vessels were sampled from the excavations of Tel Shunem for this petrographic research. More than half were storage vessels (n=11); the rest were open vessels (n=5) and small containers (n=4).

Petrographic Groups

Eleven petrographic groups (PG) were identified in this study. Their provenance and distribution are briefly presented in tables 13–14.

Petrographic Group 1

This petrographic group (PG 1) includes twenty-three vessels of diverse types (table 2). They are characterized by foraminiferous marl matrix containing rare silty grains of minerals derived from basalt (i.e., plagioclase and olivine) and small amount of silty quartz. Identifiable foraminifers *Parasubbotina* and *Subbotina* date to Eocene-Paleocene Age.

Nonplastics are badly sorted, their grain size range between 0.1-0.2 mm and 1.5–2.0 mm, compose 3–7 percent of the sherds' volume and could have been either naturally present in the marl or could have entered the ceramic paste by chance. They are represented by a number of rocks and minerals. Carbonate rocks include subrounded to rounded grains of foraminiferous and crystalline limestone, chalk balls, subrounded travertine pieces with skeletal voids of disintegrated vegetal matter and subangular to angular calcite crystals. Some sections have rounded to subangular grains of chert and eroded olivine basalt, where olivine is partially (when the olivine nucleus is visible under the microscope) or completely altered to iddingsite; mollusk shells fragments with clear lamellar inner structure; and nodules of ferruginous silty clay, where silt is angular

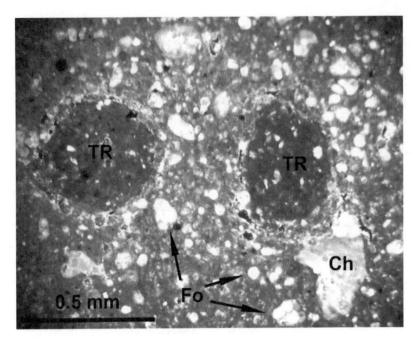

Figure 2. Microscopic view of thin-section of a chalice from Tel Kedesh (table 2:2). Petrographic
Group 1. TR=terra rossa; Ch=chalk; Fo=foraminifers.

quartz and can be *terra rossa* soil (fig. 2). Considering the small amounts of these nodules, it is possible that they originated from dry powder dust moved by wind into the
paste. Unidentified organic material mixed in the paste disappeared during the firing,
and some of the resultant voids are surrounded by charred aureoles.

    Firing temperature for most of the vessels of PG 1 was estimated ca. 700°C due
to the anisotropic crystalline carbonate materials and the clay minerals of the matrix.
However, higher firing temperature was noted on a number of samples and range from
750–800° C (table 2:23) to 800–850° C (table 2:13 and 21).

    All the components of this petrographic group may be found in the Jezreel Valley
(Ravikovitch 1969; Sneh, Bartov, and Rosensaft 1998). Thus, the vessels of Petrographic
Group 1 were manufactured in the valley, in close proximity to the researched sites.

Table 2. Inventory of the vessels attributed to Petrographic Group 1

	Slide	Site	Strat.	Type	Meg. Type	Publication	Reg. No.
1	P1	Kedesh	VII	Juglet	JT1	Stern and Beit Arieh 1979: fig. 10:19	62/5
2	P2	Kedesh	VII	Chalice	CH3	Stern and Beit Arieh 1979: fig. 9:20	62/2

	Slide	Site	Strat.	Type	Meg. Type	Publication	Reg. No.
3	P3	Kedesh	VII	Storage jar	SJ1b	Unpublished	62/12
4	P8	Kedesh	VII	Storage jar	SJ1b	Unpublished	62/8
5	P4	Kedesh	Unclean	Krater, decorated	K2?	Stern and Beit Arieh 1979: fig. 11:4	101b/3
6	P5	Kedesh	Unclean	Flask, decorated	F1b	Stern and Beit Arieh 1979: pl. 2:15	210/11
7	P30	Qiri	VIIIB	Storage jar handle with 3 pre-firing finger impressions	-	Unpublished	Area D; L.1107; B.2626
8	P38	Qiri	VIIIB	Cup and saucer	CS1	Hunt 1987: fig. 44: 13	Area D
9	P44	Qiri	VIII	Storage jar	SJ1a	Ben-Tor & Portugali 1987b: fig. 17: 6	Area D
10	P12	el-Hilu	II	Storage jar	SJ1	Arie 2011: fig. 9.2.5: 10	2559
11	P14	el-Hilu	II	Chalice	CH1	Arie 2011: fig. 9.2.3: 8	1019/9
12	P15	el-Hilu	II	Storage Jar	SJ2	Arie 2011: fig. 9.2.11: 4	12797/4
13	P20	el-Hilu	II	Storage jar	SJ1a	Arie 2011: fig. 9.2.8: 20	6690
14	S1.2	Shunem	V	Bowl	BL11	Covello-Paran and Arie 2016: fig. 20: 6	1045
15	S3.5	Shunem	V	Duck-bowl	-	Covello-Paran and Arie 2016: fig. 20: 7	1036
16	S3.6	Shunem	V	Storage Jar	SJ1a	Covello-Paran and Arie 2016: fig. 23: 1	1043
17	S2.5	Shunem	IV	Chalice	CH1	Covello-Paran and Arie 2016: fig. 25: 7	1023/3
18	S3.4	Shunem	IV	Chalice	CH1?	Covello-Paran and Arie 2016: fig. 25: 8	1015/1
19	S3.3	Shunem	IV	Amphoriskos (spout)	AM2	Covello-Paran and Arie 2016: fig. 25: 15	1016/3

Table 2, *cont'd.*

	Slide	Site	Strat.	Type	Meg. Type	Publication	Reg. No.
20	S3.7	Shunem	III	Jug base	J7b?	Covello-Paran and Arie 2016: fig. 27: 10	1003/2
21	S1.3	Shunem	III	Pithos	P1	Covello-Paran and Arie 2016: fig. 27: 16	1005/1
22	S3.1	Shunem	III	Amphoriskos	AM1	Covello-Paran and Arie 2016: fig. 27: 13	1009/1
23	S3.2	Shunem	III	Storage Jar	SJ1a	Covello-Paran and Arie 2016: fig. 27: 15	1010/2

Petrographic Group 2

Petrographic group 2 includes seventeen vessels (table 3). They are characterized by a calcareous fine textured clay matrix, which, when well fired, looks clean under the microscope. It contains small amounts of silty plagioclase and lesser olivine and or iddingsite, and infrequent tiny opaque specs. Some fine 0.1–0.3 mm round cryptocrystalline carbonate inclusions (possibly microfossils) are present in the samples.

Sand-size inclusions compose 2–5 percent of the sherds' volume for smaller vessels, like jugs and flasks, and 12–17 percent for storage jars. Foraminiferous chalk and limestone grains are rounded, subrounded or elongated cryptocrystalline or milky nodules of clay resemble the matrix or ferruginous and silty rounded and subrounded grains of fresh and/or eroded holocrystalline and microcrystalline alkali-olivine basalt. Aquatic shells fragments have a notable lamellar inner structure (present in some of the samples only). All inclusions range between 0.2–0.8 mm for small vessels and 0.7–2.0 mm for storage jars.

Firing temperature for most of the samples of this petrographic group was 700–750ºC, due to the optical activity of the clay minerals of the matrix and stage of decomposition of carbonate materials.

Most of the components of this petrographic group can be found within the Jezreel Valley. However, the presence of fresh basalt leads to the slopes of hilly areas bounding the northwestern Jezreel Valley where Pliocene-Pleistocene Cover basalt is cropping out (Sneh, Bartov and Rosensaft 1998). Rendzina mountainous soil from this same area partially mixed with brown basaltic Mediterranean soil is identified as raw material for the matrix (Dan, Yaalon, and Koyumdjisky 1975).

It should be mentioned, that petrographic affinities of the samples composing this petrographic group are identical to samples from the Middle Bronze Age kiln at 'Ein el-Hilu (Goren and Shapiro forthcoming). It is therefore suggested that the vessels of PG 2 were manufactured at a site in the northwestern Jezreel Valley. Moreover, it is probable that the vessels of PG 2 retrieved at 'Ein el-Hilu were manufactured on site.

Table 3. Inventory of the vessels attributed to Petrographic Group 2

	Slide	Site	Strat.	Type	Meg. Type	Publication	Reg. No.
1	P6	Kedesh	Unclean	Pithos	P1	Stern and Beit Arieh 1979: pl. 2:1	59b/1
2	P36	Qiri	IXB	Storage jar	SJ1a	Unpublished	Area D L.1098 B.2540
3	A5.7	el-Hilu	II	Bowl	BL8	Unpublished	12189/5
4	P9	el-Hilu	II	Jug	J1b	Stern and Beit Arieh 1979: fig. 9.2.2: 4	1943
5	P10	el-Hilu	II	Jug	J11	Stern and Beit Arieh 1979: fig. 9.2.9: 2	1151
6	A5.8	el-Hilu	II	Storage jar	SJ1a	Arie 2011: fig. 9.2.5: 8	1866
7	A5.9	el-Hilu	II	Storage jar	SJ1a	Arie 2011: fig. 9.2.5: 7	2586
8	P11	el-Hilu	II	Storage jar	SJ1a	Arie 2011: fig. 9.2.9: 3	1180/1
9	P13	el-Hilu	II	Juglet	JT1	Arie 2011: fig. 9.2.10: 7	8832
10	P16	el-Hilu	Unclean	Jug	J7a	Arie 2011: fig. 9.2.11: 9	2644/4
11	P17	el-Hilu	II	Jug	J1b	Arie 2011: fig. 9.2.9: 1	1131/1
12	P18	el-Hilu	II	Storage jar	SJ1a	Arie 2011: fig. 9.2.5: 6	2593
13	P19	el-Hilu	II	Chalice	CH1	Arie 2011: fig. 9.2.3: 9	1030/1
14	P21	el-Hilu	II	Storage jar	SJ2	Arie 2011: fig. 9.2.9: 4	1153/6
15	P22	el-Hilu	II	Storage jar	SJ1a	Arie 2011: fig. 9.2.5: 11	2621/1
16	S1.6	Shunem	V	Storage jar	SJ1b	Covello-Paran & Arie 2016: fig. 23: 5	1018/1
17	S3.8	Shunem	IV	Storage jar	SJ1a	Arie 2011: fig. 26: 2	1015/4

Petrographic Group 3

Petrographic group 3 is composed of nine samples (table 4), seven of which are storage vessels. They are characterized by ferruginous and slightly calcareous matrix containing silt size plagioclase, rare olivine, iddingsite, quartz (angular to subrounded grains), and rare foraminifers and their debris. Small quantities of nummulites and silt size grains of hornblende are present in some samples. Silt composes about 7 percent of the volume of the matrix.

Sand-size materials are represented by rounded grains of foraminiferous lime-stone; subrounded grains of crystalline limestone; subrounded to subangular grains

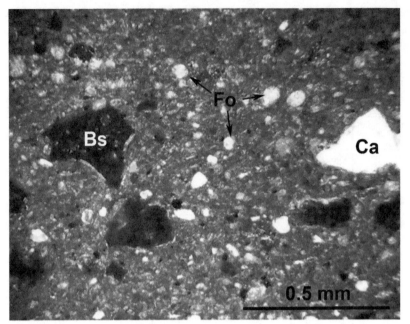

Figure 3. Microscopic view of thin-section of a storage jar from Tel Shunem (table 4:9). Petrographic Group 3. Ca=calcite; Fo=foraminifers; Bs=basic vulcanite.

of vesicular basic vulcanite, which consists of dark-brown volcanic glass, olivine and augite grains, and chlorite inclusions (fig. 3). There are also shell fragments, some crystalline; rare nodules of silty ferruginous clay (possibly *terra rossa*); and very rare small grits of crystalline calcite. The nonplastics are less than 5 percent of the volume of the sherds. Some organic material was mixed to the ceramic paste, indicated by voids with a gray to dark gray aureole.

Firing temperature was ca. 700–750°C (closer to 700°C) because clay minerals of the matrix are optically active and carbonate materials preserved their crystalline structure.

The most possible source of raw material for the matrix of the vessels of PG 3 is brown basaltic soil, and the tempers represent wadi sediments of a stream draining an area where chalk, crystalline limestone, and basalt are exposed (Ravikovitch 1969; Sneh, Bartov, and Rosensaft 1998). The above components are found in the Jezreel Valley; thus, a local provenance is suggested for PG 3.

Table 4. Inventory of the vessels attributed to Petrographic Group 3

	Slide	Site	Stratum	Type	Meg. Type	Publication	Reg. No.
1	P23	el-Hilu	Mixed	Pithos	P1	Arie 2011: fig. 9.2.11: 10	6532/1

	Slide	Site	Stratum	Type	Meg. Type	Publication	Reg. No.
2	P24	el-Hilu	II	Storage jar	SJ2	Arie 2011: fig. 9.2.1: 6	8874
3	P25	el-Hilu	II	Bowl	BL8	Arie 2011: fig. 9.2.5: 2	2002/20
4	P28	el-Hilu	II	Storage jar	SJ1b	Arie 2011: fig. 9.2.3: 4	5327/2
5	S1.4	Shunem	V	Krater with spout	K2a	Covello-Paran and Arie 2016: fig. 21: 1	1049
6	S1.5	Shunem	V	Storage jar	SJ1	Covello-Paran and Arie 2016: fig. 23: 3	1046/1
7	S2.2	Shunem	V	Storage jar	SJ2	Covello-Paran and Arie 2016: fig. 23: 4	1050
8	S2.3	Shunem	V	Storage jar	SJ1a	Covello-Paran and Arie 2016: fig. 23: 2	1039
9	S1.1	Shunem	IV	Storage jar	SJ1a	Covello-Paran and Arie 2016: fig. 26: 1	1026/2

Petrographic Group 4

Two vessels compose petrographic group 4 (table 5). They are characterized by homogeneous ferruginous and slightly calcareous matrix with tiny dark brown specks of iron oxides. Silt-size grains of minerals derived from basalt and quartz compose about 2 percent of the volume of the matrix.

Table 5. Inventory of the vessels attributed to Petrographic Group 4

	Slide	Site	Stratum	Type	Meg. Type	Publication	Reg. No.
1	S2.1	Shunem	V	Flask	F2	Covello-Paran and Arie 2016: fig. 22: 2	1035
2	S2.4	Shunem	IV	Jug (decorated body sherd)	-	Covello-Paran and Arie 2016: fig. 25: 14	1023/1

The polymineral sand temper (0.2–0.8 mm) comprises 14–16 percent of the sample in table 5:1 and 10 percent for sample in table 5:2. The rocks and minerals composing this sand include rounded to subrounded grains of limestone that turned cryptocrystalline while firing, but some of them bear traces of its biogenic origin. There are also elongated cryptocrystalline fragments, which may be shell remains from the same biogenic limestone and travertine fragments. Rounded to subrounded, sometimes elongated, grains of olivine basalt, where olivine partially altered to iddingsite, are present in lesser quantities. There are also rounded to angular grains of chert, phenocrysts of plagioclase and olivine, and rounded quartz grains. In each sample there was a single large limestone inclusion (2–3 mm).

Firing temperature was estimated at ca. 800°–850°C because clay minerals of the matrix are optically passive (and even show signs of vitrification in the sample in table 5:2) and carbonate materials are cryptocrystalline.

The rocks and minerals found in PG 4 and their preservation patterns (especially the basalt) are similar to those in Goren, Finkelstein, and Na'aman (2004: 234–37). The vessels from PG 4 were produced in the Central Jordan Valley near or at Beth-Shean (see Schulmann 1962; Shaliv, Mimran, and Hatzor 1992).

Petrographic Group 5

Petrographic group 5 is represented by only a single sample of a three-handled jug from Tell Qiri (table 6). The matrix is ferruginous clayey marl with ca. 2 percent of silty angular quartz of aeolian origin. Nonplastics, which compose not more than 4 percent of the sherd's volume, are badly sorted (0.3 and 1.5 mm) and could be naturally present in the marl. Fragments of pure clay, same as matrix, and rounded grains of chalk or limestone are dominant. Rounded grains of ferruginous quartz sandstone and quartz grains derived from it (with ferroxide coating), ferruginous shale, and shells fragments are present in lesser quantities.

Firing temperature is estimated at close to 800°C because the matrix is isotropic. The vessel was fired for a relatively short time since vitrification is present only along the sherd's outside surface.

Ferruginous sandstone is characteristic of the Lower Cretaceous lithological section. It appears frequently in southern Lebanon, in Transjordan (from Wadi Zarqa southward), and in all the Negev craters (Picard and Golani 1965; Bentor, Vroman, and Zak 1965). The closest outcrops of the Lower Cretaceous in the Jezreel Valley appear in eastern Samaria both in Wadi Far'ah and in Wadi Malih. Moreover, the three-handled jug sampled from Tell Qiri is a rare type, only two parallels were found at Mount Ebal (Zertal 1986–1987, 140; fig. 17: 2) and Tell Far'ah North (Chambon 1984: pl. 46: 13). Therefore, it is more conceivable that the jar from Tell Qiri originates from eastern Samaria and not from far-reaching areas.

Table 6. Inventory of the vessels attributed to Petrographic Group 5

	Slide	Site	Stratum	Type	Meg. Type	Publication	Reg. No.
1	P45	Qiri	VIII	Three-handled jug	-	Hunt 1987: fig. 45: 9	Area G

Petrographic Group 6

This petrographic group (PG 6) includes only one sample of a small, decorated flask from Tel Shunem (table 7). The matrix is characterized by a homogeneous calcareous and slightly ferruginous marl containing some foraminifers, rare silty quartz, and sporadic plagioclase.

Nonplastics compose less than 3 percent of the sherd's volume, possibly naturally present in the clay. They are fine-grained (0.1–0.3 mm) and are represented by sub angular to subrounded grains of limestone, few fine-sand-size foraminifers, quartz, chert, and aquatic shell fragments. Iron oxide fills the chambers of some foraminifers and/or covers these microfossils (fig. 4). The identifiable specimens are dated to Eocene-Paleocene age. Fragments of *Amphiroa sp.* (coralline algae fossil) and one rounded 0.5 mm grain of biogenic chalk are present in the section.

Firing temperature is estimated at ca. 750°C, because the clay minerals partially lost their optical properties and carbonate material is cryptocrystalline.

The outlook of the foraminifers under the microscope (i.e., iron oxide filling) is rather different from the microfauna of the rest of the petrographic groups. The clay used as raw material for this vessel might originate on top of Eocene chalk formations, and quartz sand, aquatic shells, and especially the presence of *Amphiroa sp.* point to a coastal provenance. The coastal area where Eocene chalk formations are close to the seashore are located in southern Lebanon, pointing to a provenance of this vessel in the

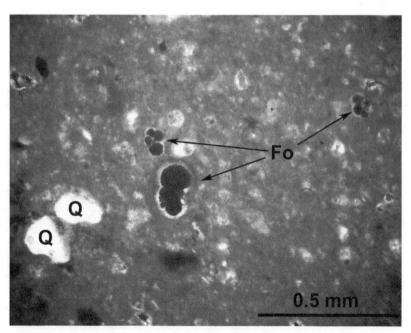

Figure 4. Microscopic view of thin-section of a flask from Tel Shunem (table 7:1). Petrographic Group 6. Q=quartz; Fo=foraminifers with iron oxide filling/coating.

vicinity of Tyre and Sidon (Sneh, Bartov, and Rosensaft 1998; Goren, Finkelstein, and
Na'aman 2004: 166–69).

Table 7. Inventory of the vessels attributed to Petrographic Group 6

	Slide	Site	Stratum	Type	Meg. Type	Publication	Reg. No.
1	S2.6	Shunem	III	Flask	F1b	Covello-Paran & Arie 2016: fig. 27:11	1001/2

Petrographic Group 7

Petrographic group 7 includes four samples (table 8). Their matrix is marly, with about
2 percent of quartz silt and abundant silt-size calcareous bodies and opaque minerals.
The silt contains accessory heavy minerals including hornblende, zircon and epidote.

The tempers compose 15–25 percent of the sherds' volume and are represented by
rounded to subangular well sorted quartz grains (0.2–0.5 mm) with accessory plagioclase. There are also some quantities of badly sorted rounded grains of foraminiferous
chalk (0.1–0.6 mm), often with glauconite concentrations. In each sample there is one
to few fragments of the following: *kurkar*, chert, glauconite bodies, aquatic shells and
Amphiroa sp.; nodules of silty ferruginous clay (0.5–1.0 mm). The pyxis (table 8:3)
is hardly cracked inside, which may be a result of over-tempering (at least 25% of the
sher''s volume).

Firing temperatures varied from ca. 700°C (table 8:2) to ca. 800°C (table 8:4),
with a middle range of ca. 700°–750°C for the other two samples.

This petrographic group has previously been identified in the Achshaph correspondence in the Amarna archive (Goren, Finkelstein, and Na'aman 2004: 232–33).
The petrographic affinities of the pottery of this group clearly point to a coastal origin
that can be pinned down to the western Galilee only (Baida 1963), from the Qiryat Ata
line northwards to the northern border of Israel, where Senonian chalk is exposed near
the Coastal Plain.

Table 8. Inventory of the vessels attributed to Petrographic Group 7

	Slide	Site	Stratum	Type	Meg. Type	Publication	Reg. No.
1	P29	Qiri	IX	Storage jar	SJ3	Ben-Tor and Portugali 1987b: fig. 20:5	Area D
2	P51	Qiri	VIII	Storage jar	SJ1b	Ben-Tor and Portugali 1987b: fig. 31: 2	Area F
3	P53	Qiri	IX	Pyxis	PX1	Ben-Tor and Portugali 1987b: fig. 20: 8	Area D
4	A5.10	el-Hilu	II	Storage jar	SJ3	Arie 2011: fig. 9.2.5: 11	2589/1

Petrographic Group 8

Petrographic group 8 includes six samples (table 9) characterized by calcareous homogeneous matrix, with less than 3 percent of angular silty quartz and accessory plagioclase of aeolian origin, some microfossils, sometimes silicified, and many very darkbrown to black tiny opaque specs.

Sand-size inclusions are rare and compose not more than 3–5 percent of the volume of the sherds. They are represented mostly by carbonate material—limestone and chalk with traces of biogenic origin (0.8–2.0 mm), crystalline limestone, aquatic shells, and *Amphiroa* sp. fragments. Two *Echinoidea* (sea urchin) spine cross-sections are present in one sample (table 9:4). There are some nodules of silty ferruginous clay (0.4–1.0 mm) and rare grains of subrounded quartz and rounded basalt (0.3–0.8 mm).

Firing temperature is estimated at 700–750°C. A single vessel (table 9:5) was fired above 800°C.

The origin of this petrographic group is a coastal area. Yet the presence of calcareous and basaltic sands suggests a location along the coast where they were washed down in a wadi. The Mount Carmel coast is the only area matching these conditions (Sneh, Bartov, and Rosensaft 1998), which is thus the origin of the vessels of PG 8. Most of the local ware from Tel Dor was made from this petrographic group (Golding-Meir 2010: 111–12).

Table 9. Inventory of the vessels attributed to Petrographic Group 8

	Slide	Site	Stratum	Type	Meg. Type	Publication	Reg. No.
1	P31	Qiri	IXB	Krater, decorated	K2?	Hunt 1987: fig. 39:8	Area D
2	P33	Qiri	IX	Juglet	JT1	Hunt 1987: fig. 20:6	Area D
3	P35	Qiri	IX	Flask	F1a	Hunt 1987: fig. 20:9	Area D
4	P32	Qiri	VIII	Storage jar	SJ1a	Ben-Tor and Portugali 1987b: fig. 32	Area F
5	P52	Qiri	VIII	Jug	J11	Ben-Tor and Portugali 1987b: fig. 25: 11	Area C
6	P34	Qiri	Unclean	Storage jar, decorated	SJ2	Hunt 1987: fig. 40: 6	Unknown

Petrographic Group 9

Petrographic group 9 is represented by four vessels (table 10), which are characterized by silty ferruginous clay matrix where silt is represented by angular quartz grains (aeolian dust).

Tempers compose 12–20 percent of the sherds' volume and are represented by rounded and subrounded quartz grains (0.3–0.5 mm), elongated bodies of gray and brown shale (1–2 mm), subrounded fragments of light brown and light gray limestone (1.5–2 mm), *kurkar* grains, silty shale, organic matter, which vanished while firing and left negatives. Coarse (3–4 mm) biogenic chalk inclusions are rare. *Hamra* soil was possibly used for matrix and sea sand for temper. Firing temperature is estimated at ca. 750°C.

The origin of this petrographic group is located at a coastal area, because *Hamra* soil appears most frequently along the central Israeli coast from the Ashdod area in the south to the Carmel coast in the north (Dan, Yaalon, and Koyumdjisky 1976). The two letters from the Amarna archive with a similar mineralogical profile were sent from Ashdod (Goren, Finkelstein, and Na'aman 2004: 292–94). Since three out of the four sampled vessels are collared-rim pithoi, a type never found in Philistia, we assume that the origin of these vessels and of this petrographic group can be confined to the northern part of this defined area, to the northern Sharon coast.

Table 10. Inventory of the vessels attributed to Petrographic Group 9

	Slide	Site	Stratum	Type	Meg. Type	Publication	Reg. No.
1	P7	Kedesh	Unclean	Prefiring marked pithos handle	P1?	Stern and Beit Arieh 1979: fig. 11:8	28/9
2	P37	Qiri	IX	Juglet	JT1	Ben-Tor and Portugali 1987b: fig. 20:7	Area D
3	P48	Qiri	Unclean	Pithos	P1	Unpublished	296/24
4	P49	Qiri	Unclean	Pithos	P1	Unpublished	573/6

Petrographic Group 10

Petrographic group 10 includes six samples (table 11), the matrix of which is silty marl represented by angular quartz and accessory olivine, iddingsite, augite and plagioclase, all apparently from aeolian dust.

Tempers compose 7–17 percent of the sherds' volume, except one sample (table 11:3), where sand size inclusions are almost absent (less than 2% of the volume). The tempers are represented mostly by rounded and subrounded grains of quartz. There are also rare grains of angular to subangular chert, nodules of silty ferruginous clay (*Hamra* soil; up to 0.8 mm) and rounded inclusions of biogenic chalk (1–5 mm). Firing temperature was 700–750°C.

Pararendzina soil of the coastal plain (Singer 2007: 40–42) could serve as raw material for the matrix and sea sand for temper. Pararendzina appears on the central and southern Israeli coast between Atlit and Gaza (Ravikovitch 1969). Since almost all of the vessels related to this group are of Philistine style, it is logical to assume that the origin of this group is from the southern coastal plain (Philistia).

Table 11. Inventory of the vessels attributed to Petrographic Group 10

	Slide	Site	Stratum	Type	Meg. Type	Publication	Reg. No.
1	P39	Qiri	VIII	"Philistine" krater	K8	Ben-Tor and Portugali 1987b: fig. 18:3	Area D
2	P40	Qiri	VIII/ IX	"Philistine" krater. Inaccurate drawing. Regular horizontal handles	K8	Ben-Tor and Portugali 1987b: fig. 19:3	Area D
3	P41	Qiri	VIII/ IX	Jug, decorated	J7c?	Ben-Tor and Portugali 1987b: fig. 19:7	Area D
4	P42	Qiri	VIII/ IX	"Philistine" bowl	BL8	Ben-Tor and Portugali 1987b: fig. 29:14	Area A
5	P43	Qiri	VIII/ IX	"Philistine" krater	K8	Ben-Tor and Portugali 1987b: fig. 19:2	Area D
6	P46	Qiri	VIII	Chalice	CH1?	Ben-Tor and Portugali 1987b: fig. 15:6	Area D

Petrographic Group 11

Petrographic group 11 includes four typologically Philistine-style vessels (table 12). They are characterized by ferruginous calcareous and very silty matrix with 25 percent silt represented mostly by quartz and lesser amounts of feldspar, hornblende, biotite, and opaque specs.

Inclusions compose 3–4 percent of the sherds' volume and are represented by well sorted rounded to subangular grains of quartz sand (0.2–0.5 mm). Firing temperature was 750–800°C.

The clay used as raw material for the matrix of this petrographic group can be identified as loess. It extensively covers parts of the northern Negev and the Shefela in the area between Gaza, Beersheba, Lachish, and Ashkelon (Dan, Yaalon, and Koyum-djisky 1975; Engstrom 2004) but does not appear north of Ashkelon. Small amounts of quartz sand, chalk, and shells fragments could be naturally present within the loess, and they strictly point to a southern coastal plain origin (Philistia).

Table 12. Inventory of the vessels attributed to Petrographic Group 11

	Slide	Site	Stratum	Type	Meg. Type	Publication	Reg. No.
1	P26	el-Hilu	II	Bowl	BL8	Arie 2011: fig. 9.2.6: 9	1382
2	P27	el-Hilu	II	Beer jug	J7c	Arie 2011: fig. 9.2.4: 4	7030/4
3	A5.5	el-Hilu	Unclean	Bowl	BL8	Arie 2011: fig. 9.2.11: 8	12314/18
4	A5.6	el-Hilu	Unclean	Beer jug?	J7c?	Arie 2011: fig. 9.2.11: 12	5627/6

Results: Summary Tables

Tables 13–16 summarize the results of the current petrographic research. Table 13 presents the provenance and distribution of the eleven petrographic groups. All in all, three petrographic groups were found within the Jezreel Valley (PG 1–3). The other eight groups reflect the commercial ties of the rural hinterland of the valley with Phoenicia (PG 6–9) and Philistia (PG 10–11). The pottery vessels from the last two groups were manufactured in the central Jordan Valley (PG 4) and in eastern Samaria (PG 5).

Tables 14–15 present the distribution of pottery types according to sites and according the petrographic groups to correlate these two variables. Table 16 compares the percentages of local and imported vessels in the four researched sites.

Table 13. Provenance and distribution of the eleven petrographic groups

PG	Provenance	Kedesh	Qiri	el-Hilu	Shunem	Total
1	Jezreel Valley	6	3	4	10	23
2	northwestern Jez. Valley (el-Hilu)	1	1	13	2	17
3	Jezreel Valley	-	-	4	5	9
4	Beth-Shean Valley	-	-	-	2	2
5	Wadi Far'ah/ Wadi Malih	-	1	-	-	1
6	southern Lebanese coast	-	-	-	1	1
7	western Galilee coast	-	3	1	-	4
8	Mount Carmel coast	-	6	-	-	6
9	northern Sharon coast	1	3	-	-	4
10	Philistia (Pararendzina)	-	6	-	-	6
11	Philistia (Loess)	-	-	4	-	4
Total		8	23	26	20	77

Table 14. Distribution of pottery types according to site

Type/ Site	Kedesh	Qiri	el-Hilu	Shunem	Total
Bowl		1	4	2	7
Krater	1	4		2	6
Chalice	1	1	2	2	6
Cup & saucer		1			1
Jug		3	6	2	11
Juglet	1	2	1		4
Pyxis		1			1
Flask	1	1		2	4
Amphoriskos				2	2
Storage jar	2	7	12	8	29
Pithos	2	2	1	1	6
Total	8	23	26	20	77

Table 15. Distribution of pottery types according to Petrographic Groups

Type/ PG	1	2	3	4	5	6	7	8	9	10	11	Total
Bowl	2	1	1							1	2	7
Krater	1		1					1		3		6
Chalice	4	1								1		6
Cup & saucer	1											1
Jug	1	4		1	1			1		1	2	11
Juglet	1	1						1	1			4
Pyxis							1					1
Flask	1			1		1		1				4
Amphoriskos	2											2
Storage jar	9	9	6				3	2				29
Pithos	1	1	1						3			6
Total	23	17	9	2	1	1	4	6	4	6	4	77

Table 16. Local vs. imported vessels (in %)

Site	Local Production	Imported Vessels
Kedesh	75	25
Qiri	17	83
'Ein el-Hilu	81	19
Tel Shunem	85	15

The Common Assemblage

About 80 percent of the petrographic samples from three out of the four rural sites under discussion (Tel Kedesh, 'Ein el-Hilu, and Tel Shunem) were found to be local to the Jezreel Valley (PG 1–3). Such a wide variety of locally made vessels of all sampled types (bowls, kraters, chalices, cup and saucers, jugs, juglets, flasks, jars, and pithoi) attests to the fact that most of the everyday pottery vessels during the research period were produced at sites in the valley and traded only locally.

Moreover, these results possibly reflect the high quality of ceramic production that existed in the Jezreel Valley, since the potters succeeded in producing many and varied vessels, including both local traditions and imitations of Philistine-style vessels. Local production and consumption modes provide proxy evidence for the self-sufficient economy of the sites in the valley, characterized by short-distance distribution and trade.

This situation seems to be the same in the urban center of Megiddo. Thorough petrographic analyses on vessels from Megiddo (Arie, Buzaglo, and Goren 2006; Arie 2011: table 12.2) demonstrate that during the LB III and the Iron I about 80 percent of the sampled vessels from Megiddo (N=82) were produced in the immediate vicinity of the site. At urban Megiddo as much as at rural Tell Kedesh, 'Ein el-Hilu, and Tel Shunem there was little flow of goods between the sites. The economy of the Canaanite Jezreel Valley was rather closed and self-supplied.

A Case Study for Regional Variation: Tell Qiri

The sampled pottery from Tell Qiri is outstanding with a greater variety of provenance of pottery vessels: only 4 out of the 23 samples (ca. 20%) were found to be of local production. This pattern is reinforced when the thirty vessels that were previously researched are added: collared-rim pithoi and Philistine-style vessels (Cohen-Weinberger and Wolff 2001: table 32.3: 76–80; Martin 2017: table 11: 4–29).

It can be assumed that the most influential factor (apart from a statistical deviation, which could result from the potentially nonrepresentative nature of the sample) is the location of Tell Qiri in the western part of the Jezreel Valley, on the edge of the Phoenician trade systems. This hypothesis is strengthened by the distribution of imports in the nearest urban center—Yoqneam. During the Iron I ca. 55 percent of the sampled pottery (21 vessels out of 38) from Yoqneam was produced in the Jezreel Valley (Buzaglo 2004: table 11; Arie 2011: table 12.4). The other vessels were imported from the western Galilee coast and the Carmel coast, both regions under Phoenician domination.

It is significant that Tell Qiri's imports are even more varied than those at Yoqneam, both in quality and quantity. In addition to the western Galilee coast and the Carmel coast, the sampled vessels from Tell Qiri originated from the central and southern coasts of Israel (PG 9-10) and from central Samaria (PG 5). None of the other rural sites revealed vessels from such a wide geographic distribution. Furthermore, many types that were defined as imports at Tell Qiri (and some from Yoqneam) are always typologically considered local vessels, for example, storage jars with a thickened rim (Type SJ1b) and decorated jars (Type SJ2), a dipper juglet and a flask (table 9).

The tight connection between Tell Qiri and Yoqneam, in regard to their ceramic imports distribution, is also significant for the understanding of the relation between urban centers and their rural hinterland in the Late Bronze III and Iron Age I. It appears that the city of Yoqneam drew much of its power from its location on the northwestern gate of the Jezreel Valley nearest to the Phoenician coast. As opposed to the inner sites of the valley, the economy of the western sites was more open to markets. As a "daughter" of Yoqneam, Tell Qiri achieved a significant flow of commerce that enriched its population.

Tel Shunem and the Beth-Shean Valley

Despite the proximity and continuity between the Jezreel Valley and the Beth-Shean Valley, almost no vessels were found in the Jezreel Valley that originated from the Beth-Shean area. Only two vessels from Tel Shunem were petrographically identified as imports from the region of the Central Jordan Valley (PG 4). The location of Tel Shunem in the eastern Jezreel Valley on the road toward Beth-Shean is probably the reason for the appearance of these two examples.

In addition to these two vessels, excavations in the entire Jezreel Valley found only a single vessel of the Late Bronze III produced in a workshop from the Beth-Shean Valley: a strainer jug from Level K-6 in Megiddo (Arie 2013: fig. 12.62: 8). The first Tel Shumen example (table 5:1) and the specimen from Megiddo are dated to the LB III, and reflect the connection between the Jezreel Valley and the Egyptian stronghold of Beth-Shean. The second Tel Shunem example (table 5:2) comes from Stratum IV (dated to the Iron I) and is rather small. It is either a residual sherd, or it might reflect the continuity of ties between these two regions during the Early Iron Age.

Trade in Jars?

It is commonly accepted that jars were the most frequent functional pottery vessels in ancient commerce. This is evident in Canaanite and Phoenician *maritime* trade, as reflected by the shipwrecks of Uluburun and the two wrecks off the shore of Ashkelon (Pulak 2008; Ballard et al. 2002), all containing hundreds of commercial jars.

The provenance of two sampled jars with a carinated shoulder (Types SJ3) from Tell Qiri and Ein el-Hilu was found to be in the western Galilee coast (PG 7). This demonstrates that they were a central component of the Phoenician trade, which is usually represented only by the Phoenician Bichrome vessels (these were not sampled in the current research). These Phoenician jars were found in impressive quantities along the coast, for example at Tell Qasile (Mazar 1985: 54–56) and Dor (Gilboa 2018: 115–16), and might be considered the successors of the traditional Canaanite jar of the Late Bronze Age that ceased to be produced at the end of this period.

Three additional storage jars—typologically identified by the present research as local to the Jezreel Valley—were also manufactured on the Phoenician coast and brought to Tell Qiri (tables 8:2; 9:4, 6).

Apart from these Phoenician jars, the other sampled one for the present research (over 80 percent) were found to be local to the Jezreel Valley. The attempt to elucidate intraregional trade in pottery vessels in the Jezreel Valley is almost impossible, due to the geological setting of the valley, which is almost similar throughout its territory. Yet, one may assume that some of the local jars identified in our research reflect an intraregional trade system from urban to rural sites and vice versa.

Moreover, our research reveals that most of the trade of the Jezreel Valley during the LB III and Iron Age I involved small containers rather than heavy jars. These included jugs, juglets, flasks, and pyxides originating from Phoenicia, Philistia, the central Jordan Valley, and eastern Samaria. Only high-value items were worth transporting and circulating.

Collared-Rim Pithoi

Collared-rim pithoi have been thoroughly studied throughout the years (summary and bibliography in Killebrew 2001). This type of vessel underwent the most intensive provenance studies, both petrography and neutron activation analysis (Yellin and Gunneweg 1989; Glass et al. 1993; Cohen-Weinberger and Wolff 2001; Arie, Buzaglo, and Goren 2006).

Six sherds of collared-rim pithoi were sampled in the current research. While three were found to be manufactured in the Jezreel Valley (PG 1–3; tables: 2:21; 3:1; 4:1), the other three samples all originated in the northern Sharon coast (PG 9; table 10:1, 3–4). Contrary to Faust 2006: 217–18, it must be stated that collared-rim pithoi do appear in all rural sites in the Jezreel Valley (Arie 2011: 307) and cannot be used as an indicator to distinguish urban from rural populations.

According to previous provenance studies (Glass et al. 1993: 279–82; Cohen-Weinberger and Wolff 2001: 654; Arie, Buzaglo, and Goren 2006: 561–62) collared-rim pithoi were almost never produced in the immediate vicinity of the site in which they were found, but were brought from elsewhere, usually somewhere nearby. Thus, it was concluded that they were made in local production centers due to the high level of specialization required in their manufacture.

At least half of the pithoi sampled here reinforce this conclusion. They were all manufactured near the coast—where pithos production has been observed in the past (Cohen-Weinberger and Wolff 2001: 654)—and later transported to Tell Qiri (two examples) and Tel Kedesh (one example). Moreover, the other three samples that were found to be local to the Jezreel Valley might have come from production centers in the valley itself, as was recognized in the petrographic research on fifteen pithoi from Megiddo (Arie, Buzaglo, and Goren 2006: table 30.1: 49–63). Previously published petrographic samples of collared-rim pithoi from Tell Qiri testify that three pithoi were manufactured in eastern Samaria (Lower Cretaceous outcrops; Cohen-Weinberger and Wolff 2001: table 32.3: 76–78), while two additional pithoi were made in the vicinity of the site (table 32.3: 79-80). Hence, these samples also fit the same conclusions.

The pithoi both in the urban and rural centers of the Jezreel Valley were the most-traded pottery vessel. Their distribution resulted from economic and social needs. Used for immobile storage, it is reasonable to assume that they were traded as empty containers and arrived empty at the various sites where they were uncovered. Cities might have functioned as distribution centers of pithoi to their rural hinterland, but this assumption deserves more study.

The Philistine-Style Vessels

The Philistine-style pottery vessels from northern Israel in general, and the ones from the Jezreel Valley in particular, have been the subject of in-depth studies (Raban 1991; Arie 2006: 222–24; Stern 2013). Martin (2017) published a vast petrographic study that included more than a hundred new samples of Philistine-style vessels from northern Israel, including twenty-five additional examples from Tell Qiri (2007: table 11: 4–29).

Eleven Philistine-style vessels were part of the current study. They fit the general conclusions from past research (Arie, Buzaglo, and Goren 2006: 563–64; Martin 2017: 224–26). While all the Philistine-style kraters (three examples of Type K8) and strainer jugs (three examples of Type J7c) originate from the coast of Philistia (PG 10–11), only about half of the bell-shaped bowls (Type BL8) were made in Philistia (three examples). The other half originated in the Jezreel Valley (two examples of PG 2–3).

Philistine-style ware stands out prominently in its "foreignness" within the pottery assemblages of the valley. Yet, due to their small number (Arie 2006: 222–24) and their varied sources (from Philistia as well as from the Jezreel Valley), Philistine-style vessels found in the Jezreel Valley should not be viewed as evidence of a Philistine population in the valley or in the north. They should rather be viewed as a testimony to trade with the Canaanite population of the northern valleys.

The discovery of Philistine-style bowls made in the valley can be understood within the context of a demand for luxury vessels and their contents, and the adoption of western drinking customs by the valley inhabitants. The Philistine vessels found in the rural hinterland of the Jezreel Valley are the products brought in from the furthest locations. Since they are also attested in the valley's urban center of Megiddo (Martin 2017), the latter could have served as a distribution center for the rural hinterland.

A chalice from Tel Qiri, probably of Type CH1 (table 11:6) also originated from the southern coastal plain. If this identification is correct, this is the first non-Philistine-style vessel from the Jezreel Valley that was made in Philistia and transported northward during the Late Bronze III and the Iron Age I. The implications to be drawn from this special find are yet unknown. Significantly, this vessel was excavated in Tell Qiri, which testifies again to the special nature of this site.

Acknowledgments

This study was supported by an Early Israel grant (New Horizons project), Tel Aviv University. We would like to thank Debi Ben-Ami and Dr. Michael Sebbane from the Israel Antiquities Authority, and Prof. Israel Finkelstein and Dr. Mario A. S. Martin from Tel Aviv University for their kind help and support.

References

Arie, Eran. 2006. "The Iron Age I Pottery: Levels K-5 and K-4 and an Intra-site Spatial Analysis of the Pottery from Stratum VIA." Pages 191–298 in *Megiddo IV: The 1998–2002 Seasons*. Edited by Israel Finkelstein, David Ussishkin, and Baruch Halpern. Tel Aviv: Emery and Claire Yass Publications in Archaeology.

———. 2011. "'In the Land of the Valley': Settlement, Social and Cultural Processes in the Jezreel Valley from the End of the Late Bronze Age to the Formation of the Monarchy." PhD diss., Tel Aviv University.

———. 2013. "The Late Bronze III and Iron I Pottery: Levels K-6, M-6, M-5, M-4 and H-9." Pages 475–667 in *Megiddo V: The 2004–2008 Seasons*. Edited by Israel Finkelstein, David Ussishkin, and Eric H. Cline. Tel Aviv: Emery and Claire Yass Publications in Archaeology.

———. Forthcoming. "The Late Bronze III and Early Iron I Pottery: Levels H-12 to H-10." In *Megiddo VI: The 2010–2014 Seasons*. Edited by Israel Finkelstein and M. A. S. Martin. Tel Aviv: Emery and Claire Yass Publications in Archaeology.

Arie, Eran, Eyal Buzaglo, and Yuval Goren. 2006. "Petrographic Analysis of Iron Age I Pottery." Pages 558–67 in *Megiddo IV: The 1998–2002 Seasons*. Edited by Israel Finkelstein, David Ussishkin, and Baruch Halpern. Tel Aviv: Emery and Claire Yass Publications in Archaeology.

Arie, Eran, and Karen Covello-Paran. Forthcoming. "Stratum II: The Iron Age Occupation." In *'Ein el-Hilu: Excavations at a Bronze and Iron Age Site in the Jezreel Valley*. Edited by K. Covello-Paran. Jerusalem: Israel Antiquities Authority.

Baida, U. 1963. "On the Geology of the Ga'aton-Hilazon Area, Western Galilee, Israel." *Israel Journal of Earth-Sciences* 13:1–15.

Ballard, Robert D., Lawrence E. Stager, Daniel Master, Dana Yoerger, David Mindell, Louis L. Whitcomb, Hanumant Singh, and Dennis Piechota. 2002. "Iron Age Shipwrecks in Deep Water off Ashkelon, Israel." *AJA* 106:151–68.

Ben-Tor, Amnon, and Yuval Portugali., eds. 1987a. *Tell Qiri: A Village in the Jezreel Valley*. Qedem 24. Jerusalem: Institute of Archaeology, Hebrew University.

———. 1987b. "The Iron Age: Stratigraphy, Architecture and Key Loci." Pages 53–131 in *Tell Qiri: A Village in the Jezreel Valley*. Edited by Amnon Ben Tor and Yuval Portugali. Qedem 24. Jerusalem: Institute of Archaeology, Hebrew University.

Bentor, Yaakov K. 1966. *The Clays of Israel: Guide-Book to the Excursions*. Jerusalem: Israel Program for Scientific Translations.

Bentor, Yaakov K., Akiva Vroman, and Israel Zak. 1965. *Geological Map of Israel 1:250000 (Southern sheet)*. Survey of Israel, reprinted 1987.

Blake, G. S., and M. J. Goldschmidt. 1947. *Geology and Water Resources of Palestine: Government of Palestine, Department of Land Settlement and Water Commissioner.* Jerusalem: Department of Land Settlement.

Buzaglo, Eyal. 2004. "The Technology and Origin of Pottery Assemblages from the Iron Age in Megiddo and the Northern Valleys." MA thesis, Tel Aviv University. (Hebrew with English abstract)

Chambon, Alain. 1984. *Tell el-Far'ah I: L'Âge du Fer.* Paris: Recherche sur les civilisations.

Cohen-Weinberger, Anat, and Samuel. R. Wolff. 2001. "Production Centers of Collared-Rim Pithoi from Sites in the Carmel Coast and Ramat Menashe Regions." Pages 639–57 in *Studies in the Archaeology of Israel and Neighboring Lands in Memory of Douglas L. Esse.* Edited by Samuel R. Wolff. SAOC 59. Chicago: The Oriental Institute of the University of Chicago.

Covello-Paran, Karen. 1999. "The Rural Aspect of the Jezreel Valley during the Intermediate Bronze Age in Light of the Excavations at 'Ein Helu (Migdal Ha'Emeq)." MA thesis, Tel Aviv University.

———. 2008. "'Ein el-Ḥilu (Migdal Ha-'Emeq)." *NEAEHL* 5:1711–12.

———. Forthcoming. *'Ein el-Hilu: Excavations at a Bronze and Iron Age Site in the Jezreel Valley.* Jerusalem: Israel Antiquities Authority.

Covello-Paran, Karen, and Eran Arie. 2016. "Excavations at Tel Shunem (Sulam): Areas G and G1." *'Atiqot* 84:25–62.

Dan, Yoel, Zvi Raz, Dan H. Yaalon, and Hanna Koyumdjisky. 1975. *Soil Map of Israel 1:500000.* Jerusalem: Survey of Israel.

Engstrom, Christin M. A. 2004. "The Neo-Assyrians at Tell el-Hesi: A Petrographic Study of Imitation Assyrian Palace Ware." *BASOR* 333:69–81.

Faust, Avraham. 2006. *Israel's Ethnogenesis: Settlement, Interaction, Expansion and Resistance.* London: Equinox.

Gilboa, Ayelet. 2018. "The Iron Age Pottery from Phases 10-5: Sequence, Contexts, Typology, Cultural Affinities and Chronology." Pages 97–172 in *Excavations at Dor, Final Report.* Volume IIB: *Area G, The Late Bronze and Iron Ages: Pottery, Artifacts, Ecofacts and Other Studies.* Edited by Ayelet Gilboa, Ilan Sharon, Jeffrey R. Zorn, and Sveta Matskevich. Qedem 11. Jerusalem: Institute of Archaeology, Hebrew University.

Glass, Jonathan, Yuval Goren, Shlomo Bunimovitz, and Israel Finkelstein. 1993. "Petrographic Analyses of Middle Bronze Age III, Late Bronze Age and Iron Age I Pottery Assemblages." Pages 271–86 in *Shiloh: The Archaeology of a Biblical Site.* Edited by Israel Finkelstein. Tel Aviv: Institute of Archaeology, Hebrew University.

Golding-Meir, Nissim. 2010. "Marine and Overland Interactions in the Eastern Mediterranean Area during the Late Bronze Age." MA thesis, Tel Aviv University.

Goren, Yuval, Israel Finkelstein, and Nadav Na'aman. 2004. *Inscribed in Clay: Provenance Study of the Amarna Tablets and Other Ancient Near Eastern Texts.* Tel Aviv: Emery and Claire Yass Publications in Archaeology.

Goren, Yuval, and Anastasia Shapiro. Forthcoming. "Petrographic Analysis of Intermediate Bronze Age, Middle Bronze Age, and Iron Age Pottery Assemblages." In *'Ein el-Hilu: Excavations at a Bronze and Iron Age Site in the Jezreel Valley.* Edited by Karen Covello-Paran. Jerusalem: Israel Antiquities Authority.

Hunt, Melvin. 1987. "The Tell Qiri Pottery." Pages 139–223 in *Tell Qiri: A Village in the Jezreel Valley.* Edited by Amnon Ben Tor and Y. Portugali. Qedem 24. Jerusalem: Hebrew University Institute of Archaeology.

Killebrew, Ann E. 2001. "The Collared Pithos in Context: A Typological, Technological, and Functional Reassessment." Pages 377–98 in *Studies in the Archaeology of Israel and Neigh-*

boring Lands: In Memory of Douglas L. Esse. Edited by Samuel R. Wolff. SAOC 59. Chicago: The Oriental Institute of the University of Chicago.

Martin, M. A. S. 2017. "The Provenance of Philistine Pottery in Northern Canaan, with a Focus
on the Jezreel Valley." *TA* 44:193–231.

Mazar, Amihai. 1985. *Excavations at Tell Qasile, Part 2.* Jerusalem: Institute of Archaeology, Hebrew University.

Na'aman, Nadav. 2006. *Canaan in the Second Millennium B.C.E.* Winona Lake, IN: Eisenbrauns.

Orton, Clive, Paul Tyers, and Alan Vince. 1993. *Pottery in Archaeology.* Cambridge: Cambridge
University.

Picard, Leo Y., and Uri Golani. 1965. *Geological Map of Israel 1:250000 (Northern Sheet).* Survey
of Israel, repr. 1987.

Pulak, Cemal. 2008. "The Uluburun Shipwreck and Late Bronze Age Trade." Pages 289–305 in
Beyond Babylon: Art, Trade, and Diplomacy in the Second Millennium B.C. Edited by Joan
Aruz, K. Benzel, and J. M. Evans. New York: Metropolitan Museum of Art.

Raban, Avner. 1991. "'The Philistines in the Western Jezreel Valley." *BASOR* 284:17–27.

Ravikovitch, Shlomo. 1969. *Soil Map 1:250000, North.* Jerusalem: Survey of Israel.

Schulmann, Nahman. 1962. "The Geology of the Central Jordan Valley." PhD diss., The Hebrew
University, Jerusalem. (Hebrew with English abstract)

Shaliv, Gabriel, Yaakov Mimran, and Yosef Hatzor. 1992. "The Sedimentology and Structural
History of the Bet She'an Area." *Israel Journal of Earth-Sciences* 40:161–79.

Shapiro, Anastasia. 2016. "Petrographic Examination of the Ceramic Vessels from Tel Shunem
(Sulam)." *'Atiqot* 84:63–68.

Singer, Arieh. 2007. *The Soils of Israel.* Berlin: Springer.

Sneh, Amihai, Yossi Bartov, and Marcello Rosensaft. 1998. *Geological Map of Israel 1:200000,
Sheet 1.* GSI, Jerusalem: Survey of Israel.

Stern, Ephraim. 2013. *The Material Culture of the Northern Sea Peoples in Israel.* Winona Lake, IN:
Eisenbrauns.

Stern, Ephraim, and Itzhaq Beit Arieh. 1979. "Excavations at Tel Kedesh (Tell Abu Qudeis)." *TA*
6:1–28.

Whitbread, Ian K. 1986. "The Characterization of Argillaceous Inclusions in Ceramic Thin Sections." *Archaeometry* 28:79–88, https://doi.org/10.1111/j.1475-4754.1986.tb00376.x

Yellin, Joseph, and Jan Gunneweg. 1989. "Instrumental Neutron Activation Analysis and the
Origin of Iron Age I Collared-Rim Jars and Pithoi from Tel Dan." *AASOR* 49:133–41.

Zertal, Adam. 1986–1987. "An Early Iron Age Cultic Site on Mount Ebal: Excavation Seasons
1982–1987." *TA* 13–14:105–65.

Gottlieb Schumacher,
First Excavator of Armageddon

Eric H. Cline

Abstract: There have been four expeditions to Megiddo during the course of the past century: Gottlieb Schumacher from 1903–1905, sponsored in part by the German Oriental Society and the German Society for the Exploration of Palestine; the team sent by James Henry Breasted from the Oriental Institute at the University of Chicago from 1925 to 1939; Yigael Yadin and his students from the Hebrew University of Jerusalem in the 1960s and 1970s; and the Tel Aviv University Expedition, primarily under the direction of Israel Finkelstein and David Ussishkin, from 1992 onward. This detailed look at Schumacher's excavation seasons is dedicated with great respect to Norma Franklin, who undoubtedly knows all of it already.

Keywords: Tell el-Mutesellim, Megiddo, excavations, Gottlieb Schumacher, Ottoman Palestine

G ottlieb Schumacher excavated at Tell el-Mutesellim, now more commonly known as Megiddo (biblical Armageddon), from 1903 to 1905.[1] He was the first archaeologist to actually begin digging at the site (fig. 1). He was sponsored in part by the German Oriental Society (*Deutsche Orient-Gesellschaft*), which had been founded in Berlin just five years earlier and was funded by Kaiser Wilhelm II. He was also sponsored

---

1. This brief contribution on Schumacher is dedicated with much affection to Norma Franklin. It stems from research originally conducted for my book *Digging Up Armageddon: The Search for the Lost City of Solomon* (Princeton University Press, 2020); portions of the following appear as snippets here and there in that volume, but not as the cohesive whole presented here. My debt of gratitude to Norma regarding Megiddo can never be repaid; I treasure the innumerable conversations that I have had with her, beginning at the site itself in 1994 and through the years that we were members of the Tel Aviv Expedition, and I look forward to many more to come. Undoubtedly, she will find errors and points of disagreement in this contribution, as always, and I look forward to discussing those with her as well. I would also like to thank again all those who helped with the specific material, which is presented here with their permission, especially Felicity Cobbing, Executive Director at the Palestine Exploration Fund; John Larson and Anne Flannery, successive Archivists at the Oriental Institute of the University of Chicago; Sabine Böhme of the Vorderasiatische Museum in Berlin; and Edhem Eldem of Bosphorus University, among others; additional relevant acknowledgements can be found in Cline 2020.

Figure 1. Gottlieb Schumacher. Wikimedia Commons, public domain.

by the "German Society for the Exploration of Palestine," which is sometimes simply called the "German Palestine Exploration Society" (*Deutscher Verein zur Erforschung von Palästina,* usually abbreviated *Deutsche Palästina Verein*). This society was based in Leipzig and had been founded even earlier, back in 1877.[2]

Although he had studied archaeology, Schumacher's principal occupation was as an engineer and surveyor. The few photographs available show him as a friendly looking man with a large mustache; a visitor to Megiddo in March 1904 noted in his diary that Schumacher was "an extremely pleasant companion with whom to share a hut."[3]

Schumacher was not highly trained in archaeology by any stretch of the imagination. However, he was not bad for his day and he had led his own surveys and mapping campaigns in northern Transjordan in the 1880s. He had also surveyed with Frederick

---

2. Silberman 1982: 167–69; Böhme 2014: 41–43; see also Niemann and Lehmann 2006a, 2006b; Daubner 2012–2013: 84–85. See now the useful discussion on Schumacher and his excavations in Ussishkin 2018: 29–41, which also covers some of the following material.

3. Niemann and Lehmann 2006a: 695; see also previously, in German, Niemann and Lehmann 2006b.

Bliss in 1893, including taking him to Tell el-Mutesellim, and had excavated with Ernst
Sellin at the site of Ta'anach, just down the valley from Megiddo, in the late 1890s.[4]

Although he was of German ancestry, Schumacher was an American, born in
Zanesville, Ohio. His father Jacob had become a naturalized U.S. citizen in 1856, but
in 1869 they all moved to Haifa, when Gottlieb was twelve years old. They belonged to
The Temple Society, a Christian religious movement that had been founded in Stuttgart in 1861 and which advocated that its members live in Palestine if possible. The
Templers, as they are called, had communities in Haifa, Jerusalem, Jaffa, and Sarona;
the colony in Haifa was the first one to be established and the Schumacher family was
among its founding members, since Jacob had been asked specifically to come help
with its planning and construction.[5]

In one of those odd coincidences that happen from time to time and sometimes
impact career decisions, when he was sixteen years old, Schumacher's family hosted
Lieutenants Claude Conder and Horatio Kitchener, as well as the other Royal Engineer surveyors at some point in 1874, while those men were conducting their survey of
western Palestine, including at what is now known to be the site of Megiddo. In return
for their hospitality, Kitchener gave the family a sundial before he left for England the
following year, which is still on the property today.[6] Although there is no way to prove
it, this chance meeting may explain why, after completing high school in Haifa, Schumacher went to Germany from 1876 to 1881 for additional education and received training in engineering, architecture, cartography, and archaeology at the Stuttgart Higher
Technical Institute, eventually receiving a PhD.

When Schumacher returned to Haifa, he first helped his father and then was appointed Chief Engineer for the nearby city of Akko. He also surveyed for a proposed
Haifa-Damascus railway line, as part of a project concocted by his next-door neighbor
in Haifa, the Scottish author and traveler Laurence Oliphant—another chance occurrence that greatly impacted Schumacher's career. In addition, he designed the wine
cellars for the Rothschild winery at Rishon Lezion, as well as the Scottish hostels in
Tiberias, and Safed and the Russian hostel in Nazareth. He also succeeded his father in
1891 as the consular agent in Haifa, although he resigned in 1904 while he was involved

4. Details from Clara Klingemann's letter to Gretel Braidwood dated 27 April 1987, now in the
archives of the Oriental Institute at the University of Chicago, as well as the PEF biography of Schumacher (http://www.pef.org.uk/profiles/gottlieb-schumacher), in addition to Hallote 2006: 122–24;
Niemann and Lehmann 2006a: 688–89.

5. Hallote 2006: 122, plus details from a letter from Clara Klingemann to Gretel Braidwood dated
27 April 1987, as well as the PEF biography of Schumacher (http://www.pef.org.uk/profiles/gottlieb-
schumacher). On the Temple Society and the Templers in Haifa, see Kark and Frantzman 2010; also
http://www.templesociety.org.au/about-temple-society.html. An excellent recent overview in German of Schumacher's life can be found in Daubner 2012–2013.

6. Conder 1873, 1877, 1879; Conder and Kitchener 1882; Grossberger, Freundlich, and Davis
2015: 20; 2016: 3.

in the excavations at Megiddo. Along the way he had nine sons and daughters with his wife, Mary Lange.[7]

Schumacher first received official permission from the Ottoman Turkish authorities in Constantinople, who controlled the region at the time, to survey Megiddo and the surrounding area. He created the first topographic map of the site as well as locating later Roman ruins in the vicinity. Then, despite his relative lack of excavation experience, Schumacher obtained a permit from the Ottoman authorities to begin digging at the site in 1903.[8]

It is not clear at all why Schumacher decided to dig at Tell el-Mutesellim, since he does not address it in any of his publications and we are missing much of his private correspondence. It may be that he too wondered what lay within the mound of Armageddon, since George Adam Smith had finally properly identified it just a few years before. It may simply be because it was partially owned by his good friend and next-door neighbor Laurence Oliphant, who had first written about it back in 1884, just two years after Oliphant had moved to Haifa (Oliphant 1887). Had they talked about it back in the day, when Schumacher was conducting the survey for the Haifa-Damascus railroad line that Oliphant had proposed in the mid-1880s? We may never know, but it is surely not a coincidence that Schumacher chose to dig at this specific site, for we do know that he had specifically dissuaded Bliss from digging there ten years earlier, back when they were surveying together in 1893, at a time when Bliss was actively looking for a site on behalf of the Palestine Exploration Society (Hallote 2006: 122–23).

Not everyone was in favor of this appointment, however. In 1889, almost fifteen years before Schumacher began digging at Megiddo, Charles Wilson—a noted explorer in his own right after whom "Wilson's Arch" by the Western Wall of the Temple Mount in Jerusalem is named and who had known Schumacher since the days of the Western Palestine survey—wrote: "Schumacher is no scholar in any sense; his copies of inscriptions are the despair of everyone I have spoken to on the subject.... He is, however, a shrewd observer and has done excellent work for the Fund east of Jordan." In fact, Schumacher kept quite good records, although most of them are now lost, and

---

7. See the PEF biography of Schumacher (http://www.pef.org.uk/profiles/gottlieb-schumacher); Taylor 1982: 226; Carmel 2006: 164–73; Hallote 2006: 122; Kreuzer 2010: 139–43; Kark and Frantzman 2010: 155–57, 160; Daubner 2012–2013: 76–89; Casey 2015: 230. Additional details come from the letter written by Clara Klingemann and sent to Gretel Braidwood, dated 27 April 1987.

8. See, among others, Silberman 1982: 167–68; Hallote 2006: 122–24. There are a number of documents in the Ottoman archives in Istanbul regarding Schumacher, including permit requests and permissions granted, for digging at Tell el-Mutesellim; these include File #2421 in Folder #181539 (Group Code: BEO); File #219 in Folder #69 (Group Code; SD); File #791 in Folder #52 (Group Code: MF.MKT); File #801 in Folder #44 (Group Code DH.MKT); and others. I am greatly indebted to Edhem Eldem of Bosphorus University for locating these and corresponding with me about them.

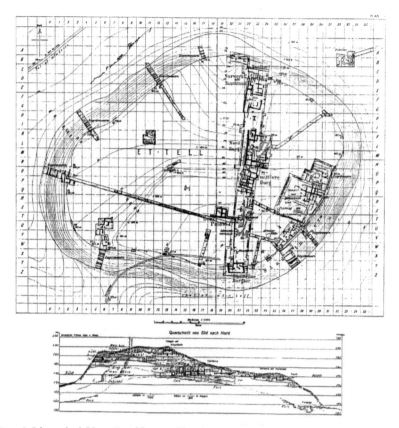

Figure 2. Schumacher's "Great Trench" at Megiddo. After Schumacher 1908: Taf. I.

executed beautiful drawings and plans of the buildings and architecture that he found at Megiddo.[9]

Schumacher's excavations at Megiddo took place over the course of three years, from 1903 to 1905, with two excavation seasons each year, usually in the Spring and then in the Fall (or, in one case, late Summer and Fall). To begin with, he hired as many as two hundred workmen and had them begin digging a huge trench from north to south across the entire mound, as well as several smaller secondary trenches. Later dubbed the "Great Trench," it wound up being more than 60 feet (20 m) wide,

9. PEF-DA-SCHUM-11, now in the archives of the PEF in London, is a letter sent from Sir Charles W. Wilson to Sir Walter Besant on 5 December 1889. Wilson later became the Chairman of the PEF, from 1901–1906; Besant had just ended a nearly twenty-year period as the Executive Secretary of the PEF, from 1868–1885. See also the PEF biography of Schumacher (http://www.pef.org.uk/profiles/gottlieb-schumacher) and Niemann and Lehmann 2006a: 688–90.

expanding to 90 feet (30 m) in at least one area, more than 750 feet (250 meters) long, and 36 feet (12 m) deep in places (fig. 2).[10]

In employing this strategy, he was following that used by Heinrich Schliemann at the site of Troy just a few decades earlier. There were problems, of course, including workmen not noticing and then throwing out many smaller objects, and Schumacher may have done as much damage at Megiddo as Schliemann did at Troy (Cline 2013). However, like Schliemann, Schumacher did publish the stratigraphic results of his excavations promptly, in 1908, although it took another twenty years and another scholar (Carl Watzinger) to publish the objects, which he did in 1929, four years after Schumacher's death.[11]

Schumacher published detailed preliminary reports each year and then a final report in 1908, all in German, as well as sending more concise letters written in English to the Palestine Exploration Fund (PEF) in London.[12] The German archaeologist Immanuel Benzinger served as his deputy upon occasion, including overseeing the excavations in Autumn 1903 and publishing the results under his own name, with Schumacher's blessing and permission. Most people who discuss Schumacher's work at Megiddo overlook Benzinger, but he had published a book on the archaeology of Palestine (entitled *Hebräische Archäeologie*) back in 1894, with updated editions appearing thereafter, incorporating new finds as they appeared, including from Megiddo (Silberman 1982: 167–68; Moorey 1991: 34; see Benzinger 1904: 65–74).

Schumacher's team stayed in rather primitive accommodations right at the site itself (fig. 3). He explained their living situation as follows:

> The camp, on a hill 95 m[eters] to the south of the edge of the tell, consisted of 3 wooden huts and one to two tents ... The first hut was divided into a kitchen and sleeping quarters for the foremen ... The second hut doubled as the commissioner's and the supervisor's sleeping quarters and as the common dining room. My son and I lived in the third hut, a part of which was reserved for my drawing table and the instruments ... The German flag waved on top of my hut, the Turkish flag on the commissioner's hut, and a white flag with the name Tell el-Mutesellim waved above the workers' hut. (Schumacher 1908: 3–4; see 1904a: 15)

---

10. Schumacher 1908: 7, Tafel 1; Harrison 2004: 1; Tepper and Di Segni 2006: 11–12; Fisher 1929: 26. See also the PEF biography of Schumacher (http://www.pef.org.uk/profiles/gottlieb-schumacher).

11. Schumacher 1908; Watzinger 1929. According to Ussishkin (2018: 32), Schumacher suffered a stroke and was partially paralyzed in 1922, before passing away in 1925; he is buried in the Templer cemetery in Haifa.

12. Schumacher 1904a, 1904b, 1905a, 1905b, 1905c, 1906a, 1906b, 1906c, 1906d, 1908; Benzinger 1904.

Figure 3. Schumacher's huts with flags. After Schumacher 1908: fig. 3.

Emil Kautzsch, a prominent German biblical scholar and founding member of the academic society that was co-sponsoring Schumacher's excavations, came to visit during the second year of excavations, in the Spring of 1904, and described some of Schumacher's team members whom he got to know. Regarding Schumacher himself, Kautzsch noted his "flawless command of Arabic (in addition to which he speaks German, English and French equally fluently) ... The whole day he is up on the tell surveying, sketching and taking photographs, and then he records the descriptions in the hut" (Niemann and Lehmann 2006a: 695).

There was also Johannes Bez, Schumacher's long-time friend and fellow Templer who eventually had to leave the dig after Easter 1904, perhaps because of malaria attacks which Kautzsch observed. When Bez left, a local teacher named Herr Dietrich Lange took his place, assisting Schumacher by taking photographs and drawing the finds. And there was Nicola Datodi, who was a trained clockmaker fluent in Italian, German, French, and Arabic. Datodi was only twenty-three years old at the time, but he eventually served as the overseer and was responsible for keeping all of the attendance and wage accounts. As a result, he knew all of the workers personally, as both Kautzsch and Schumacher attested. Schumacher noted, "He soon came to know all the sorrows and the joys of almost everyone of his 180 workmen and women, trying to cheer them up and to assist them in every possible way."[13]

Kautzsch also confirmed the basic and rather crowded living arrangements that Schumacher had described. He wrote, "Schumacher and I slept in the first hut, Bez and Datodi in the second one, in the third, the kitchen hut, the cook, the servant and the

---

13. Niemann and Lehmann 2006a: 694; Schumacher, p. 2 in the 1904 PEF notebook entitled "The Excavations on the Tell el-Mutesellim 1904," now in the archives of the PEF in London (PEF-DA-SCHUM-90); see also Schumacher 1904a: 14–15, 1908: 2–3.

Figure 4. Schumacher's early days of work at Megiddo. After Schumacher 1904b: 42.

5 foremen, in the tent the soldier, a Kurd with poor Arabic." (Niemann and Lehmann 2006a: 694)

Schumacher also recorded the fact, not mentioned by Kautzsch, that there was always a Turkish commissioner at the site during the excavation season. This is the man whom Schumacher described as sleeping in their second hut, with the Turkish flag waving above. At the end of each season, this commissioner "took charge of the finds, which had been recorded in a list, and packed them in preparation for transfer to the museums at Constantinople." There were four such local representatives who worked with Schumacher over the course of the three years of excavations.[14]

In addition, Schumacher's own son Alfred took part for almost a full year, from October 1904 through September 1905. During that time, as Schumacher said, Alfred became nearly indispensable, doing all of the measuring and drawing of the ruins, photographing the finds, and drawing the rock tombs that they found (Schumacher 1908: 1–3).

When their first excavation season started on 1 April 1903, they began with just twenty-four workmen, but within a week, they had more than a hundred, with five overseers (fig. 4). Upon occasion during the season, the number rose as high as two hundred, with the workers coming from several nearby villages, including Lajjun and Umm el-Fahm. About one-third were men and young boys, who dug with pickaxes and shovels, filled the baskets with earth, and pushed the wheelbarrows. The other two-thirds were local women and girls, who carried the dirt away in baskets and discarded it at the edge of the tell or in specific areas. Schumacher stated specifically that "Each unit

14. Böhme 2014: 41–43 also notes that Schumacher sent fourteen crates of material from his Megiddo excavations to Berlin in 1908.

of 20 workers consisted of about three men to loosen the soil, two to fill the baskets, and 15–18 women. Experience has shown that this ratio is the best." He also noted that the boys and young men were the "most worthwhile," while the young girls "were the most tireless." When they were digging in areas where they thought they would come across small precious objects, such as in tombs, he had women sieve all of the earth.[15]

Work began each day at 5:30 am, with a half-hour break at 8:00 am and a one-hour break at noon. They also had breaks of fifteen minutes once every four hours. The workday ended twelve and a half hours later, at 6:00 pm. Schumacher was well aware that this was a very long day, especially for the youngest workers, some of whom were only twelve years old. However, as he noted, the harvest was approaching, and they needed to get as much done as possible before their best workmen left (Schumacher 1904a: 16–17).

In his 1904 notebook, Schumacher also described several of the foremen who oversaw the rest of the workers. One, named Asfur, was known as "the doctor"—his knowledge of the Canaanite region was unrivaled, according to Schumacher. Another, Rashid, was called the "youngster" or "new hand." A third, Musa Deshirius, was the group's funny man, always ready with a joke to cheer up the men after a long day. As Schumacher noted, "They all did their duty patiently, even merrily, in spite of the rain and the great heat and the dust."[16]

Kautzsch recounted in detail how the foremen oversaw all of the workers, which allowed Schumacher time to roam the mound. His account corroborates what Schumacher said, so it is worth quoting in full:

> The work was divided up into 5 divisions; every foreman stood so that he could clearly see his 20 or so people. One constantly heard the admonishing yalla, yalla (onwards!), often with the addition of the name of the person who was falling behind, and often extremely vigorous curses as well. Everything happened silently: no chattering whatsoever was allowed. The digging was handled by men only, while only women and girls carried away the dirt and stones, often in a long procession. Under no circumstances would a man carry anything, let alone put a basket on his head. A female always stood next to the digger to lift the heavy baskets onto the heads of the approaching porters, on which there was a thick pad. It took something like 2 to 2 ½ minutes until a woman appeared again with the empty bucket. As soon as the foreman noticed that finer and more careful work was required, he was immediately at hand with his long, pointed chisel and did the digging himself. In special cases Schumacher only let the foremen work. (Niemann and Lehmann 2006a: 697)

---

15. Schumacher 1904a: 14; 1908: 2 (English translation here and elsewhere for the 1908 volume is courtesy of Mario Martin). The preliminary reports for this season were published as Schumacher 1904a: 14–20 and 1904b: 33–56. See also Silberman 1982: 167–69.

16. Schumacher, p. 2 in the 1904 PEF notebook entitled "The Excavations on the Tell el-Mutesellim 1904," now in the archives of the PEF in London (PEF-DA-SCHUM-90).

Kautzsch confirmed that the women and girls outnumbered the men by a wide margin, making up about two-thirds of the workforce since, as he put it, "a hard-working digger could easily keep 4–5 female porters busy." The men were each paid about 6 piasters (the equivalent of about 25 cents) per day, which was considered a good wage at the time, but the women were only paid half that, in return for working from dawn to dusk (Niemann and Lehmann 2006a: 697). The foremen, on the other hand, received between 12 and 17 piasters for each day's work (about 50 to 75 cents per day). Schumacher noted that everyone was paid once every two weeks and that salaries were raised by 10–20 percent at harvest time, in an attempt to keep the workers rather than losing them to the fields.[17]

That initial Spring 1903 season ended on 1 May, after just four weeks of excavation on the actual mound.[18] Schumacher said that they began excavating at the eastern edge of the tell, in what he called Square O31, and explained that the reason for starting there was that "the tell reached its highest elevation at this point, which led us to assume the existence of a cultic place." Sure enough, he found what he called a "tower" and a "sanctuary" in this area; the accompanying illustration in his 1904 preliminary report labels one of the buildings as the "Massebot Tempel" and it appears that these remains were part of what he later came to call the "Tempelburg," which roughly translates as "Temple Castle."[19] Meanwhile, at the southern edge of the mound, Schumacher's workmen found upright-standing monoliths and the remains of massive walls, while at the northern edge they began to dig what would become Schumacher's Great Trench, "20 m wide and quite exactly orientated from north to south" (Schumacher 1908: 7; 1904b: 42–53).

In late September, the Fall 1903 excavation season began. It lasted for ten weeks, until the end of November. It was overseen and then published in a brief report by Benzinger, because Schumacher was working elsewhere at the time. The report doesn't say much, although it does record that they began extending the Great Trench, heading south from the northern edge of the mound.[20]

By this point, the excavations were underwritten by a grant of £1,300 (British pounds) from the German Emperor.[21] While £1,300 might not sound like much, it

17. Niemann and Lehmann 2006a: 697; Schumacher 1908: 3. See http://www.history.ucsb.edu/faculty/marcuse/projects/currency.htm for the conversion rate.

18. Schumacher 1908: 1; Schumacher 1904b: 42–53. Note that Wilson 1905: 78 says that Schumacher dug until 29 May, but this is probably because, as Schumacher noted in his preliminary report (1904b: 54–56), additional work was both carried out elsewhere and on the finds that they had made during April.

19. Schumacher 1904b: abb. 10; Schumacher 1908: 110–24. For a concise description of the history of excavations in this area, see now Ussishkin 2018: 363–79.

20. Published as Benzinger 1904: 65–74. Schumacher 1908: 1 says they concluded the season at the end of November; Wilson 1905: 79 says, "On December 1st the work was closed for the winter."

21. As reported in the "Notes and News" section of the Palestine Exploration Fund Quarterly Statement in July 1904 (no. 36.3: 188).

Figure 5. Jasper seal with inscription "Shema, servant of Jeroboam." After Schumacher 1908: fig. 147.

is the equivalent of £143,000, or just over $206,000, in terms of today's money.[22] Interestingly, this is almost the exact same amount that it costs to dig at Megiddo today, for a seven-week season. Back then, that amount paid for two seasons—Benzinger's excavations in the Fall of 1903, including the beginning of the Great Trench, as well as Schumacher's subsequent Spring 1904 excavations.

R. A. S. Macalister, who was excavating at the biblical site of Gezer on behalf of the PEF at the same time that Schumacher was digging at Megiddo, noted rather bitterly that "the one donation of the German Emperor was considerably greater than the total possible annual outlay of our Society [PEF] ... In consequence, while the Gezer works could never employ more than eighty labourers ... the Megiddo staff was almost always over a hundred, and sometimes numbered as many as a hundred and eighty-five." (Macalister 1906: 62)

After a layoff of three months, the Spring 1904 season began at the beginning of March. Schumacher only had 20 workmen on the first day, but within less than a week there were 167 workers, finally increasing to 182 by the middle of the month.[23] Work progressed extremely well and already by mid-April, just six weeks into the dig season, Schumacher sent a letter full of news and speculation to George Armstrong, who was at one time the Secretary of the PEF and a former surveyor and cartographer himself. He described the excavations as "becoming daily more interesting," noting that they had found "an underground building, built up in huge blocks one projecting over the other, without any chisel ever having touched them," which he dated to the time of Solomon. Underneath it were a number of graves and bodies that he thought might have been sacrifices made at the time of the building's construction. Elsewhere, another large building was similarly described as perhaps being "the government building or

---

22. Conversion based on http://inflation.stephenmorley.org. See also Silberman 1982: 168, who gives the figure as 40,000 German marks, which was the equivalent of 2,000 British pounds. The grant was given in June 1903, after the initial Spring season had concluded.

23. Schumacher 1905a: 1; see also Schumacher, pages 1–2 in the 1904 PEF notebook entitled "The Excavations on the Tell el-Mutesellim 1904," now in the archives of the PEF in London (PEF-DA-SCHUM-90).

castle of Solomon's Governor of Megiddo."[24] It is not entirely clear why he dated both of them to the time of Solomon.

Schumacher also mentioned in this letter to Armstrong an item that he had found a few weeks earlier, just after the beginning of the season. This turned out to be one of the most famous artifacts ever to be excavated at Megiddo: a small oval seal made of green jasper. Carved into the face of the seal is a roaring lion and the words "[Belonging] to Shema, servant of Jeroboam." It is not clear which Jeroboam is meant in the inscription, but most likely it was one of the two kings who ruled over Israel in the early first millennium BCE—either Jeroboam I, the son of King Solomon, who ruled after Solomon's death in the late tenth century (ca. 922–901 BCE), or Jeroboam II, who ruled in the eighth century BCE (ca. 786–746 BCE); most scholars believe it was the latter.[25]

In a handwritten report for that season, now in the archives of the PEF in London, Schumacher wrote: "…we found a beautifully cut sealing stone, a Jasper, according to the statement of Herr Dr. Blanckenhorn. It showed a lion "passant" and roaring after the Babylonian fashion, and an old Hebrew inscription."[26] Later, in the final publication, Schumacher wrote: "It was found … inside the courtyard, only 4 m west of the southwestern corner of the Palastwohnung, very close to the northern courtyard wall."[27]

This is the same area where Schumacher found a scaraboid (similar to an Egyptian scarab) made of lapis lazuli about a year later, which has a depiction of a winged griffin wearing the double crown of Egypt and an inscription in Hebrew that reads (in translation), "[belonging] to Asaph." It has been suggested that the scaraboid of Asaph

24. Letter from Schumacher to George Armstrong dated 20 April 1904, now in the archives of the PEF in London (PEF-DA-SCHUM-79).

25. The literature on this seal is enormous; for the most recent, with previous references, see Ussishkin 1994: 410, 419–22, figs. 24-1, 24-2, and 24-6a, 2018: 40, 415–18, fig. 18:26; Shanks 2000: 4; Strawn 2005: 102–4; Niemann and Lehmann 2006a: 700; also previously Yeivin 1960. Schumacher describes its findspot on p. 28 in the 1904 PEF notebook entitled "The Excavations on the Tell el-Mutesellim 1904," now in the archives of the PEF in London (PEF-DA-SCHUM-90). See also Cook 1904: 287–91 and fig. 3; Kautzsch 1904; Erman and Kautzsch 1906; Schumacher 1908: 99–101, fig. 147; Watzinger 1929: 64–67; and the PEF biography of Schumacher (http://www.pef.org.uk/profiles/gottlieb-schumacher). The other most famous artifact uncovered during Schumacher's excavations, a stone fragment inscribed with the cartouche of the Egyptian pharaoh Sheshonq, was actually missed by his workmen and was only recovered later, by the Chicago team, during Fall 1925; for a full discussion of this item, see now Cline 2020, with further references.

26. Schumacher, p. 28 in the 1904 PEF notebook entitled "The Excavations on the Tell el-Mutesellim 1904," now in the archives of the PEF in London (PEF-DA-SCHUM-90). See also Cook 1904: 287–91; and the PEF biography of Schumacher (http://www.pef.org.uk/profiles/gottlieb-schumacher).

27. Schumacher 1908: 99–100, fig. 147 (translation courtesy of Mario Martin); Ussishkin 1994: 410, 419–22, figs. 24-1, 24-2, and 24-6a; see also Strawn 2005: 103.

belonged to an official comparable to Shema, that both objects should be considered and discussed together, and that government officials probably used them.[28]

The Shema seal was found during Kautzsch's visit to the dig and, in his journal entry for 22 March, the same day that the seal was found, Kautzsch said that he would "spare no effort to hand it over personally in Stamboul," which indicates that he was planning to take it to Beirut and then on to Istanbul, where it would be presented to the Ottoman sultan, Abdul Hamid II.[29] However, documents now in the Ottoman archive in Istanbul indicate that the seal was actually brought to Beirut by the Turkish excavation commissioner. These, written in Turkish and dating to 21 and 23 April 1904, specifically state that Schumacher had discovered a jasper seal inscribed with the name "Yeshmu' son of Jeroboam son of King Solomon" in the excavations at Tell el-Mutesellim, and that the excavation commissioner was bringing it in person to Beirut.[30]

The last official mention that we have of the seal is a report in the *Palestine Exploration Fund Quarterly Statement* for 1904, stating that the seal was sent to the Turkish Governor of Beirut to be presented to the Sultan, which is when the journal's correspondent, Dr. A. N. Baroody, was able to study it and take photographs (Cook 1904: 287–91 and fig. 3). Schumacher later wrote that "the seal was brought to Constantinople through the intervention of a high official and was not added to the precious collection of the imperial Ottoman museum but to the private collection of His Majesty the Sultan [Abdul Hamid II]" (Schumacher 1908: 100).

Alas, even if it ever arrived, the seal is now nowhere to be found. It should be in the Istanbul Archaeological Museum, since after the Sultan's death in 1909 the archaeological material kept in the palaces was transferred there. However, it does not seem to be in the present collections of the museum.[31] On the other hand, it is quite possible that the seal was viewed as jewelry rather than an archaeological artifact, and perhaps even set into a ring or other large piece of jewelry, and so was not transferred from the private collection of the Sultan. In that case, it may still be in a collection at Beylerbeyi Palace or elsewhere in Istanbul, but for the moment it remains lost, although persistent unconfirmed rumors say that it is now in Switzerland (Shanks 2000: 4; Ussishkin 2018: 40).

---

28. Erman and Kautzsch 1906; Schumacher 1908: 99–101, fig. 148; and Watzinger 1929: 64–67; Ussishkin 1994: 410, 421–22, fig. 24-6b, 2018: 415–18, figs. 18:26–27.

29. Translation following Niemann and Lehmann 2006a: 700. Kautzsch was subsequently responsible for publishing the Shema seal. See Kautzsch 1904; Erman and Kautzsch 1906; Schumacher 1908: 99–100, fig. 147; Watzinger 1929: 64–67.

30. These include 1904 04 21 DH.MKT 844/25-1; 1904 04 21 Y.PRK.DH 13/3-2; 1904 04 21 Y.PRK.DH 13/3-3; 1904 04 23 DH.MKT 844/25-2; and 1904 04 23 Y.PRK.MKT 13/3-1. I am indebted to Edhem Eldem of Bosphorus University for his assistance in this matter (pers. comm., 4 March and 20 April 2016), which we are hoping to investigate further at some point.

31. Pers. comm., 1 March 2016, from Dr. Zeynep S. Kiziltan, Director of the Istanbul Archaeological Museums; pers. comm. from Professor Dr. Yasar Ersoy, 22 February 2016, citing information from the Museum Director of the Yildiz Palace Museum in Istanbul concerning the transfer of material from the palace collections to the Istanbul Archaeological Museum after the death of the Sultan.

Schumacher's Fall 1904 season began in early October and lasted almost two months, until the beginning of December. Digging was almost impossible at times, especially when the temperature reached 104 degrees, as it did during the first few weeks, but cooling winds soon brought the temperature to temperate ranges before ushering in Fall rains in October and then November.[32]

During this season, Schumacher continued to excavate in what he called the "Tempelburg" and the "Treasury." The latter is now simply known as "Chamber F"; during the Tel Aviv excavations, it was reinvestigated by Norma Franklin as part of Area M. It is probably of Late Bronze Age date, perhaps with influences from the Aegean region, but it is still debated as to whether it was a tomb or instead served some sort of cultic function.[33]

Schumacher also extended the Great Trench and opened smaller trenches on the eastern edge of the tell and elsewhere on the mound. By this point, his men were excavating 10 m (30 feet) below the surface in some parts, reaching deep into what Schumacher was then calling the third, fourth, and fifth levels of the tell.[34] He also began investigating nearby ruins, in eight separate locations off the mound.[35]

During the Spring of 1905, they only dug for six weeks, from mid-March through the end of April, because of the harvest season.[36] However, even in the shortened season, they made some unique discoveries. Graves with "all sorts of pottery and Egyptian scarabs, all very well preserved" were uncovered, along with some tombs that had unusual vaulted roofs, in the general vicinity of Chamber F.[37] Schumacher later described them further:

> I discovered … 3 ancient tombs partly vaulted with unworked but conically shaped stones containing some 40 well preserved jars of all shapes and a number of scarabs partly lined with gold.… Every tomb contained from 6 to 9 human sceletons [sic], laid with their knees bent upwards. A number of

32. Although Wilson sent Schumacher a letter saying that he was "glad to hear that you are to be again at work at Tell Mutesellim on the 1st October," Schumacher's published preliminary report states that the excavations did not actually begin until 6 October. See the letter sent from Sir Charles W. Wilson to Schumacher on 18 December 1904, now in the archives of the PEF in London (PEF-DA-SCHUM-82). See also Schumacher 1905c: 81–82; Böhme 2014: 41–43.

33. See, e.g., Ussishkin 2018: 283–89. See full publication of Chamber F, with opposing viewpoints, in Franklin 2013; Pechuro 2013; Finkelstein 2013.

34. Schumacher seems not to have reversed the order in which he numbered the levels until his final report in 1908.

35. The report for the season was published as Schumacher 1905c: 81–82 and 1906a: 1–14.

36. A letter sent from Schumacher to Armstrong, the one-time Secretary of the PEF, a week before the end of the dig noted that the excavations were being halted "owing to the crops"; see Schumacher 1906b: 17–30.

37. Letter sent from Schumacher to George Armstrong dated 22 April 1905, now in the archives of the PEF in London (PEF-DA-SCHUM-84).

bronze implements was found with them and terra cotta idols and such of glass.[38]

Schumacher thought that these perhaps held the remains of the royal family who ruled at Megiddo during the Middle Bronze Age, although it is still a matter of some dispute (Ussishkin 2018: 194–97). The finds themselves were transported to Istanbul at the end of the season and, like the Shema seal, promptly disappeared. Their current whereabouts also remain unknown, despite recent efforts to locate them again.

In addition, Schumacher discovered a large gate and causeway made of huge unworked stone blocks on the southern edge of the tell. He also noted that they had found the corner of a large building made of similar huge stones, each up to seven feet long but with drafted margins on their edges, which he thought "dates from 1000 to 800 B.C." He described it as lying at "a depth of 14 feet below the surface" and thought that it was so important that it "may represent Solomon's *Burg*." Why this building had to be Solomon's palace is not clear, apart perhaps for wishful thinking, but Schumacher noted that in any event, "I have to remove great masses of earth yet until it is laid entirely free."[39]

In his final lengthy season, which spanned the summer and fall of 1905, Schumacher (1906c: 35–64; 1906d: 65–70) concentrated on expanding the great north-south trench as well as continuing to excavate the large buildings that he had found previously, which by now he was calling the "Nordburg" and the "Mittelburg." He also decided that *Solomon's Burg* just mentioned was indeed a *Palast*; he seems to have changed his terminology every time he changed his mind. They also had separately excavated a "large gate structure" that he called the "Südliches Burgtor," the southern castle gate.[40] Several of these structures were later reexamined and renamed by the Chicago excavators, such as the *Nordburg*, which seems to have been a large public building or perhaps even a palace, rather than a fortress, and the *Mittelburg*, which wasn't actually a separate building at all (Nigro 1994; Yasur-Landau and Samet 2017: 464–67; Ussishkin 2018: 267, 283).

By now, Schumacher was also suffering physically. He wrote in June 1905, "My health has not been well at Tell el Mutesellim, which is a feverish place."[41] Clearly, malaria had affected Schumacher and his team, as it would the later Chicago excavators. In fact, during Kautzsch's visit back in March 1904, he had remarked that Schumacher's

---

38. Letter sent from Schumacher to Sir Charles W. Wilson dated 5 June 1905, now in the archives of the PEF in London (PEF-DA-SCHUM-85).

39. Letter sent from Schumacher to Sir Charles W. Wilson dated 5 June 1905, now in the archives of the PEF in London (PEF-DA-SCHUM-85).

40. Schumacher 1908: 8. It is likely that these, i.e., the Palast and the Southern Gate, are the same structures that he had mentioned in his letter to Wilson earlier, following the Spring 1905 season.

41. Letter sent from Schumacher to Sir Charles W. Wilson dated 5 June 1905, now in the archives of the PEF in London (PEF-DA-SCHUM-85).

teammate, Johannes Bez, suffered from recurring attacks of malaria while at the site, as mentioned (Niemann and Lehmann 2006a: 695).

In his final report on the three years of excavation, published in 1908, Schumacher lamented that the work at Megiddo could in no way be considered complete. Only in a few areas had they excavated all the way down to bedrock—in one spot they dug a test trench that was more than sixty feet (22 m) deep. In most places, they had barely gone below the surface of the mound. Moreover, only half of the *Nordburg, Mittelburg,* and the *Palast* had been explored, and he had not been able to excavate underneath any of them (Schumacher 1908: 7–8).

Like Schliemann at Troy, the major mark that Schumacher left at Megiddo was his Great Trench, which stretched across the top of the mound. In the end, Schumacher determined that there were eight layers of occupation at the site, which he numbered from the bottom up, just as Schliemann had done earlier at Troy.[42] However, there was almost instant disagreement with "the counting and numbering of the strata" that he had proposed. An appendix was added to his 1908 final report, written by Professor Steuemagel of the University of Halle in Germany, who noted his various problems with both the suggested chronology and the assignation of various buildings and other monuments that Schumacher had excavated.[43] Partially as a result of these disagreements, Schumacher's numbering system, and the accompanying chronology, was soon abandoned in favor of the new terminology put into place during the Chicago excavations at the site.

It is true that, as an architect and engineer, Schumacher was far more interested in recording the buildings that he found, as was most common for a man of his time and his profession, and that he was not always successful in separating the pottery and other artifacts from the different layers, occasionally lumping them together. It was not until Watzinger was asked to publish the small finds, after Schumacher died in 1925, that some semblance of order was brought to these smaller objects and some of Schumacher's mistakes could be corrected. Some of these errors, including stratigraphy and identifications of buildings, were fairly major—for instance, Watzinger realized that Schumacher's "Templeburg" was simply a very elaborate building and had nothing to do with a temple, a palace, or anything of that sort. Watzinger was also able to assign a Late Bronze Age date to the abandonment of the *Mittelburg*, ca. 1400 BCE, and to the *Nordburg*, ca. 1300 BCE (Niemann and Lehmann 2006a: 690–91; Watzinger 1929).

In a brief reanalysis of Schumacher's work at Megiddo, Michael Niemann and Gunnar Lehmann (2006a: 693; also Kempinski 1989: 7–8) concluded that there were "clear consequences" because of his appointment. They described Schumacher as "a

---

42. See Schumacher 1908: passim; Niemann and Lehmann 2006a: 693, table 39.1. Ussishkin 2018: 39 says that Schumacher found only seven strata, but there were actually eight—"Schicht VIII" was the Ottoman period material that Schumacher found on the top of the mound when he first began digging.

43. Steuernagel, "Appendix to the Numbering of the Strata," in Schumacher 1908: 191–92.

man of great talent but untutored in the latest excavation methodology" and noted that "his methods of documentation were inadequate." Similarly, David Ussishkin has also recently suggested that Schumacher

> lacked the background, knowledge and practical experience essential for a proper direction of a complex stratigraphic excavation in a multi-leveled mound … He dealt alone with all the archaeological aspects of the dig, while the foremen and workers lacked any experience in archaeological field work. (Ussishkin 2018: 38–39)

In fact, Schumacher himself undoubtedly realized much of this. He stated in his final report of 1908,

> We … have to hope that a second, more exhaustive excavation might follow this first one on Tell el-Mutesellim. This would enable us to envision the layout of an entire city that existed in the most ancient periods of civilization of this country. It would also help us solve a fair number of the riddles regarding details we do not understand. For such an undertaking, long years of work and considerable financial resources would be necessary. (Schumacher 1908: 8)

That is exactly what the University of Chicago archaeologists were able to provide, in large part because they were endowed with "considerable financial resources," courtesy of John D. Rockefeller, Jr. However, that would not happen for nearly twenty years and unfortunately Schumacher did not live to see the start of their excavations, which began shortly after his death.

References

Benzinger, Immanuel. 1904. "Die Ausgrabungen auf dem Tell el-Mutesellim. VI. Die Ausgrabungen im Herbst 1903." *MNDPV* 1904:65–74.

Böhme, Sabine. 2014. "'Alltägliches' aus Megiddo: Die ersten Funde, ihr Ausgräber, und Berlin." *AntW* 45.5:41–43.

Carmel, Alex. 2006. "Die württembergische Familie Schumacher in Palästina." Pages 164–73 in *Palaestina exploranda: Studien zur Erforschung Palästinas im 19. Und 20. Jahrhundert anläßlich des 125jährigen Bestehens des Deutschen Vereins zur Erforschung Palästinas*. Edited by U. Hübner. Wiesbaden: Harrassowitz.

Casey, Bart. 2015. *The Double Life of Laurence Oliphant: Victorian Pilgrim and Prophet*. New York: Post Hill.

Cline, Eric H. 2013. *The Trojan War: A Very Short Introduction*. New York: Oxford University Press.

———. 2020. *Digging Up Armageddon: The Search for the Lost City of Solomon*. Princeton: Princeton University Press.

Conder, Claude R. 1873. "The Survey of Palestine. VII. The Plain of Esdraelon." *PEQ* 5–6:3–10.

———. 1877. "Megiddo." *PEQ* 9.1: 13–20.

———. 1879. *Tent Work in Palestine: A Record of Discovery and Adventure*. 2 vols. London: Bentley & Son.

Conder, Claude R., and Horatio H. Kitchener. 1882. *The Survey of Western Palestine: Memoirs of the Topography, Orography, Hydrography, and Archaeology*. Vol. 2: *Sheets VII.–XVI. Samaria*. London: Palestine Exploration Fund.

Cook, S. A. 1904. "Notes and Queries." *PEFQS* 36.3:285–92.

Daubner, Frank. 2012–2013. "Gottlieb Schumacher, ein Pionier der historisch-geographischen Erforschung Syriens." *Orbis Terrarum* 11:73–89.

Erman, A., and E. Kautzsch. 1906. "Ein Siegelstein mit hebräischer Unterschrift vom Tell el-Mutesellim." *MNDPV* 12:33–34.

Finkelstein, Israel. 2013. "Chapter 4, Pt. III: Area M: Another Interpretation of the Remains; The Nordburg and Chamber F." Pages 228–46 in *Megiddo V: The 2004–2008 Seasons*, vol. 1. Edited by Israel Finkelstein, David Ussishkin, and Eric H. Cline. Tel Aviv: Emery and Claire Yass Publications in Archaeology.

Fisher, Clarence Stanley. 1929. *The Excavation of Armageddon*. Chicago: The Oriental Institute of the University of Chicago.

Franklin, Norma. 2013. "Chapter 4, Pt. I: Area M: The Excavation." Pages 178–214 in *Megiddo V: The 2004–2008 Seasons*, vol. 1. Edited by Israel Finkelstein, David Ussishkin, and Eric H. Cline. 3 vols. Tel Aviv: Emery and Claire Yass Publications in Archaeology.

Grossberger, Tommer, Amir Freundlich, and John Davis. 2015. "Kitchener's Sundial in Palestine." *The Early Exploration of the Holy Land: University of Haifa, December 20–21, 2015*. Edited by A. Kidron and D. Gurvich. Haifa: Gottlieb Schumacher Institute and University of Haifa.

———. 2016. "Kitchener's Sundial in Palestine." *British Sundial Society Bulletin* 28:13–16.

Hallote, Rachel. 2006. *Bible, Map, and Spade: The American Palestine Exploration Society, Frederick Jones Bliss, and the Forgotten Story of Early American Biblical Archaeology*. Piscataway, NJ: Gorgias.

Harrison, Timothy P. 2004. *Megiddo 3: Final Report on the Stratum VI Excavations*. Chicago: The Oriental Institute of the University of Chicago.

Kark, Ruth, and Seth J. Frantzman. 2010. "Consuls, Demography and Land in Palestine: German-Americans in the Haifa Templer Colony." *ZDPV* 126.2:153–67.

Kautzsch, Emil. 1904. "Ein althebräisches Siegel vom Tell el-Mutesellim." *MNDPV* 10:1–14.

Kempinski, Aharon. 1989. *Megiddo: A City State and Royal Centre in North Israel*. Munich: Beck.

Kreuzer, Siegfried. 2010. "Ernst Sellin und Gottlieb Schumacher in Palästina." Pages 136–45 in *Das Grosse Spiel: Archäologie und Politik zur Zeit des Kolonialismus (1860–1940)*. Edited by C. Trümpler. Cologne: Dumont.

Macalister, R. A. S.. 1906. "Gezer and Megiddo." *PEFQS* 38.1:62–66.

Moorey, P. Roger S. 1991. *A Century of Biblical Archaeology*. Louisville, KY: Westminster John Knox.

Niemann, Hermann M., and Gunnar Lehmann. 2006a. "One Hundred Years After Gottlieb Schumacher, Carl Watzinger and Excavations at Megiddo with an Extract from Emil Kautzsch's Diary about his Visit to Megiddo in 1904." Pages 688–702 in *Megiddo IV: The 1998–2002 Seasons*, vol. 2. Edited by Israel Finkelstein, David Ussishkin, and Baruch Halpern. Tel Aviv: Emery and Claire Yass Publications in Archaeology.

———. 2006b. "Gottlieb Schumacher, Carl Watzinger und der Beginn der Ausgrabungen in Megiddo: Rückblick und Konsequenzen nach 100 Jahren." Pages 174–203 in *Palaestina Exploranda: Studien zur Erforschung Palästinas im 19. Und 20. Jahrhundert anläßlich des 125jährigen Bestehens des Deutschen Vereins zur Erforschung Palästinas*. Edited by Ulrich Hübner. Wiesbaden: Harrassowitz.

Nigro, Lorenzo. 1994. "The 'Nordburg' of Megiddo: A New Reconstruction on the Basis of Schumacher's Plan." *BASOR* 293:15–29.

Oliphant, Laurence. 1887. *Haifa; or, Life in Modern Palestine*. 2nd ed. London: Blackwood & Sons.

Pechuro, Alexander. 2013. "Chapter 4, Pt. II: Area M: An Architectural Study of Chamber F." Pages 215–27 in *Megiddo V: The 2004–2008 Seasons*, vol. 1. Edited by Israel Finkelstein, David Ussishkin, and Eric H. Cline. Tel Aviv: Emery and Claire Yass Publications in Archaeology.

Schumacher, Gottlieb B. 1904a. "Die Ausgrabungen auf dem Tell el-Mutesellim. I. Die Einrichtung der Arbeit." *MNDPV* 1904:14–20.

———. 1904b. "Die Ausgrabungen auf dem Tell el-Mutesellim. II. Der Tell el-Mutesellim und die Chirbet el-Leddschön." *MNDPV* 1904:33–56.

———. 1905a. "Die Ausgrabungen auf dem Tell el-Mutesellim. VII. Die Ausgrabungen im Frühjahr 1904." *MNDPV* 1905:1–16.

———. 1905b. "Die Ausgrabungen auf dem Tell el-Mutesellim. VII. Die Ausgrabungen im Frühjahr 1904 (Fortsetzung und Schluss)." *MNDPV* 1905:17–26.

———. 1905c. "Die Ausgrabungen auf dem Tell el-Mutesellim. VIII. Die Ausgrabungen im Herbst 1904." *MNDPV* 1905:81–82.

———. 1906a. "Die Ausgrabungen auf dem Tell el-Mutesellim. VIII. Die Ausgrabungen im Herbst 1904 (Fortsetzung und Schluss)." *MNDPV* 1906:1–14.

———. 1906b. "Die Ausgrabungen auf dem Tell el-Mutesellim. IX. Die Ausgrabungen im Frühjahr 1905." *MNDPV* 1906:17–30.

———. 1906c. "Die Ausgrabungen auf dem Tell el-Mutesellim. X. Die Ausgrabungen im Sommer und Herbst 1905." *MNDPV* 1906:35–64.

———. 1906d. "Die Ausgrabungen auf dem Tell el-Mutesellim. X. Die Ausgrabungen im Sommer und Herbst 1905 (Schluss)." *MNDPV* 1906:65–70.

———. 1908. *Tell el-Mutesellim: Bericht über die 1903 bis 1905 mit Unterstützung Sr. Majestät des Deutschen Kaisers und der Deutschen Orient-gesellschaft vom Deutschen Verein zur Erforschung Palästinas veranstalteten Ausgrabungen. Band I: Fundbericht*. Leipzig: Haupt.

Shanks, Hershel. 2000. "First Person: Have You Seen This Seal? Probably Not." *BAR* 26.1:4.

Silberman, Neil. A. 1982. *Digging for God and Country: Exploration, Archeology, and the Secret Struggle for the Holy Land 1799–1917*. New York: Knopf.

Strawn, Brent. A. 2005. *What Is Stronger Than a Lion? Leonine Image and Metaphor in the Hebrew Bible and the Ancient Near East*. OBO 212. Fribourg: Academic Press; Göttingen: Vandenhoeck & Ruprecht.

Taylor, Anne. 1982. *Laurence Oliphant: 1829–1888*. Oxford: Oxford University Press.

Tepper, Yotam, and L. Di Segni. 2006. *A Christian Prayer Hall of the Third Century CE at Kefar 'Othnay (Legio): Excavations at the Megiddo Prison 2005*. Jerusalem: Israel Antiquities Authority.

Ussishkin, David. 1994. "Gate 1567 at Megiddo and the Seal of Shema, Servant of Jeroboam." Pages 410–28 in *Scripture and Other Artifacts: Essays on the Bible and Archaeology in Honor of Philip J. King*. Edited by Michael D. Coogan, J. Cheryl Exum, and Lawrence E. Stager. Louisville: Westminster John Knox.

———. 2018. *Megiddo-Armageddon: The Story of the Canaanite and Israelite City*. Jerusalem: Israel Exploration Society/Biblical Archaeological Society.

Watzinger, Carl. 1929. *Tell el-Mutesellim: Bericht über die 1903 bis 1905 mit Unterstützung Sr. Majestät des Deutschen Kaisers und der Deutschen Orient-gesellschaft vom Deutschen Verein zur Erforschung Palästinas veranstalteten Ausgrabungen. Band II: Die Funde*. Leipzig: Hinrichs.

Wilson, Charles W. 1905. "Excavations of the German Palestine Exploration Society at Tell el-Mutesellim in 1903." *PEQ* 37.1:78–79.

Yasur-Landau, Assaf, and Inbal Samet. 2017. "Resilience and the Canaanite Palatial System: The Case of Megiddo." Pages 463–81 in *Rethinking Israel: Studies in the History and Archaeology of Ancient Israel in Honor of Israel Finkelstein*. Edited by Oded Lipschits, Yuval Gadot, and Matthew J. Adams. Winona Lake, IN: Eisenbrauns.

Yeivin, S. 1960. "The Date of the Seal 'Belonging to Shema' (the) Servant (of) Jeroboam." *JNES* 19:205–12.

The "Ta'anakh Winepress" Revisited: Further Evidence of the Middle Bronze Age Wine Industry in the Jezreel Valley

Karen Covello-Paran, Nimrod Getzov,
and Yotam Tepper

Abstract: In this article we examine a type of rock-hewn winepress initially exposed below the Tel Ta'anakh fortifications. Similar winepresses have been exposed in subsequent excavations and surveys in the Jezreel Valley. After reviewing the surveyed and excavated data, we set out the parameters for identifying the Ta'anakh winepresses type. Their uniformity, chronology, and geographic distribution are discussed. The work process and the implications for the intensification of wine production in the Jezreel Valley during the first half of the second millennium are reviewed.

Keywords: Ta'anakh, winepress, Jezreel Valley, treading, Shimron, Middle Bronze Age

A unique type of rockhewn winepress was exposed at Tel Ta'anakh (Taanach) in excavations directed by Paul Lapp during the 1960s (Lapp 1969: 13–14; fig. 1a). Similar winepresses exposed in subsequent excavations and surveys in the Jezreel Valley lead us to propose that this winepress type be coined the "Ta'anakh Winepress" (Getzov, Covello-Paran, and Tepper 2011).[1] In recent years a number of winepresses bearing affinities to the Ta'anakh winepress have been exposed in both excavations and surveys in regions bordering the Jezreel Valley.

Defining the Ta'anakh Winepress

Five features are characteristic of the Ta'anakh winepress (fig. 1a, b):

---

1. This article is an updated version of an article published in Hebrew (Getzov, Covello-Paran, and Tepper 2011). The photographs from Midrakh Oz, Yifat, and 'Ein el Hilu were taken during the excavations under the auspices of the Israel Antiquities Authority (IAA), which granted the permission to use them. The photographs from 'Ein el Hilu and Yifat were taken by H. Smithline (IAA), the rest were taken by the authors (IAA). We thank Edna Dalali Amos (IAA) for figures 15–17. We thank Rafi Frankel for discussions on this article.

1. An elongated treading floor and a rectangular collecting vat separated by a narrow partition wall. The treading floor is usually trapezoidal with the narrow end at the lowest point close to the collecting vat, which is rectangular and narrower than the treading floor.

2. A shallow sloping treading surface, of which the gradient increases with the length of the floor, especially when it is longer than 2.5 m.

3. Two conduits between the vat from the treading floor. There are two subtypes: (a) the conduits start vertically and bend toward the vat to pass under the partition; (b) the conduits are straight and slope under the partition wall toward the vat (see fig. 1). Most of the winepresses are of the subtype b.

4. Two deep rock-hewn circular depressions flank the treading floor, though the winepress from Ta'anakh had no such depressions (see below). The distance between the depressions and the collecting vat is constant (1.1 m average), regardless of the length of the treading surface.

5. Treading floor and vat have rounded corners. Not all of the winepresses we ascribe to the Ta'anakh type display these five components. Therefore, a winepress would need to display at least three of the above features to qualify as a Ta'anakh winepress. Among these three features, the two conduits (no. 3 above), would need to be present as they constitute the most distinctive feature of this type.

The Data

Ta'anakh winepresses are presented from north to south. The site number corresponds to the number on the accompanying map (fig. 2).

1. Nahal Hanita. North of Nahal Hanita, at the base of Rekhes ha-Sullam, a Ta'anakh type winepress was surveyed (Frankel and Getzov 1997: 75*, site 2.28; fig. 2.28.2) and excavated (J. Gosker, pers. comm., whom we thank for providing metric data). Winepress L800 is hewn into the nari outcrop. It comprises a trapezoidal shallow treading floor with rounded corners and a rectangular collecting vat. The treading floor slopes southwards toward the collecting vat to which it is connected by two conduits. Two circular depressions flank the treading floor and two additional ones flank the separation between the treading floor and the vat. This single winepress is located at the eastern periphery of the Byzantine Bat el Jebel site, near numerous Byzantine-period winepresses.

2. Nahal Hilazon. A winepress (site 27) was documented within a development survey near the Ahihud junction in 2011 (Lerer 2012: fig. 8). The hills of this site are an integral part of the Western Lower Galilee and overlook Nahal Hilazon.

3. Horbat Tirat Tamra. Along the hills encompassing the Acco Plain, two winepresses (nos. 2,3) were excavated at the outskirts of Horbat Tirat Tamra (Dalali-Amos 2007: fig.1:2–3). The winepresses are poorly preserved. Nevertheless, they feature a shallow treading floor, rounded walls and corners, adaptation to the rock outcrop contours and two tunnels leading from the treading floor to a collecting vat. Therefore, they qualify as Ta'anakh presses.

4. Lavie. Seven winepresses were identified in a survey near Horvat Nimrin in the eastern Lower Galilee (Abarbanel 2009). A particular feature of all these winepresses are the elongated rock-hewn depressions flanking winepress 192404-13 (Abarbanel 2009: 66), which is characteristic of this group. Contrary to Abarbanel, we identify only seven of the numerous winepresses at the site as Ta'anakh presses on the basis of the trapeze shallow treading floors, the rounded walls, and in particular the two conduits.[2]

5. Allonei Aba. A single winepress was discovered in the Jezreel Valley margins southwest of Allonei Aba during the course of salvage excavations (Porat 2009). This winepress in Area B had a squarish treading floor (2.17 × 2.20 m) and a rectangular collecting vat (0.65 × 1.04 m, depth 0.27 m), with two tunnels connecting them. There are no circular depressions flanking the treading floor; possibly the presence of a rocky outcrop did not allow the hewers to make such depressions (Porat 2009: fig. 1).

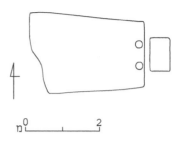

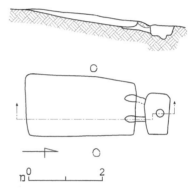

Figure 1. Ta'anakh winepress type schematic drawing: (a) winepress from Ta'anakh, (b) winepress from 'Ein el Hilu.

6. Alonim. A poorly preserved winepress was documented 700 m north of Tel Beer Tabun (Kapul 2018) on the hills above which Kibbutz Alonim is located. Distinguishable are the shallow trapezoid treading floor (3.5 × 4.5 m), a rectangular collecting vat with a sump and circular rock-hewn depressions (Kapul 2018: fig. 11; personal observation). The bedrock surfaces adjacent to the winepress were neither surveyed nor excavated and it is probable that there are additional rock-hewn installations.[3]

---

2. They are: 192403-11, 19504-07, 192404-13, 192415-07, 192415-09, 192415-11, 192415-13, 192426-03.

3. Small-scale salvage excavations in Kibbutz Alonim ca. 150 m north of the winepress exposed Roman and Byzantine rock-hewn storage installations (Atrash 2015). The excavator noted that these installations cut an earlier rock-hewn installation, which we suggest could have been part of a Ta'anakh winepress (Atrash 2015: fig. 9).

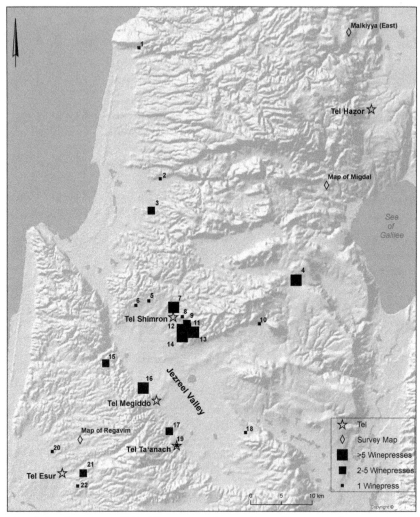

Figure 2. Distribution map of Ta'anakh winepresses (site numbers and name in text). Map prepared by A. Shapiro.

7. Tel Shimron North. The site Tel Shimron north was surveyed as part of the Na-halal survey map where the schematic plans of seven winepresses are published (Raban 1982: site 82, figs. a, b). The site is characterized by numerous winepresses, some of which are aligned in rows. During Raban's survey the winepresses were covered in veg-etation and the two tunnels from the treading floors to the collecting vat were invisible.[4]

_____

4. According to Shahar, there are at least nine winepresses related to the layout of the adjacent Roman road. We found no evidence for this claim. Given the poor preservation of the site and the thick vegetation covering it, the total number of winepresses is unknown.

Figure 3. Tel Shimron North, winepresses of Group b, facing west (Dr. Rafi Frankel standing).

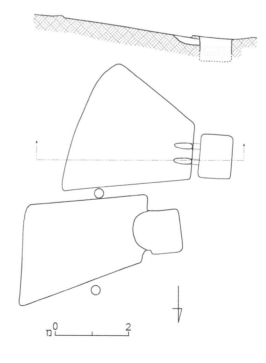

Figure 4. Tel Shimron North, plan of
Group b winepresses.

Figure 5. Timrat winepress, facing north.

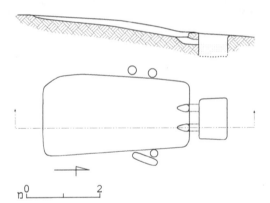

Figure 6. Timrat winepress, plan.

A later report described nine winepresses with two tunnels leading from the tread-ing floor to the collecting vat (Shahar 2007: 84–85). In preparation of this article, the authors revisited the site and cleaned the winepresses from Raban's group b for photog-raphy (figs. 3, 4) revealing that the southern winepress is also a Ta'anakh winepress. As is the case with the pair of winepresses at Yifat (see fig. 12), only one of the winepresses from the pair at Shimron North (fig. 4) has the two round depressions flanking the treading floor.

   8. Timrat. A single winepress was documented by the authors close to the sum-mit of the hill above the modern village of Timrat. This press displays a unique pair of rock-hewn depressions on one side of the treading floor and an oval shaped depression on the other side (figs. 5, 6).

9. Nahal Zvi 3. Numerous winepresses were surveyed and excavated along the northwestern hills of Migdal Haemeq along the riverbed of Nahal Zvi. As they are over 1 km away from the MBA site of 'Ein el Hilu, they are listed separately here, though this may not reflect any ancient reality. There are four Ta'anakh winepresses in site II of the survey, clustered at map coordinates NIG 2224/7332 (Tepper 2014).

10. Dabburiya. A single Ta'anakh winepress was excavated at the southeastern fringes of Mount Tabor, adjacent to the village of Dabburiya (A. Moqari, pers. comm.). The winepress has a shallow treading floor (1 × 1.8 m), rounded corners and two conduits connecting the treading floor with the collecting vat (0.60 × 1.10 m) which has a sump at its base. Next to the collecting vat is a tethering-hole. The back of the treading floor connects to the natural slope of the bedrock without high margins.

11. Nahal Zvi 2. This site represents an isolated cluster of four Ta'anakh winepresses (map coordinates NIG 2225/7327) in site V of Tepper's survey (Tepper 2014).

12. Nahal Zvi 1. Tepper surveyed thirteen Ta'anakh winepresses, four of which were later partially excavated (A. Moqari, pers. comm.) in the area designated as site IV (map coordinates NIG 2217/7323). Though the treading floors of the excavated winepresses follow the contours of the rocky outcrop, all their collecting vats have the same dimensions and are connected to the treading floor by two conduits (Tepper 2014: fig. 30). The Ta'anakh winepresses were later altered to screw presses.

13. 'Ein el Hilu. 'Ein Hilu is a small spring that flows at the bottom of the slopes north of the ruins of Hirbet el-Mujeidel, today within the confines of the modern city Migdal Haemeq. The ancient site of 'Ein el Hilu is located in proximity to the spring, at the north-facing bank of Wad al-'Ein, one of the dendrites of Nahal Zvi. The occupation of the site spans the IB, MBII, LB and Iron I periods with later agricultural activities dating to the Roman Period (Covello-Paran 1997, 2008).

The slopes above the site are comprised mostly of Neogene sediments and continental conglomerates that lie above the Eocene formations consisting of chalky limestone and flint formations with a Nari cover. In small flattened areas of the Nari several winepresses have been exposed in four archaeological expeditions. Salvage excavations carried out in the 1980s and beginning of the 1990s exposed eleven Ta'anakh winepresses (Z. Gal, pers. comm.). Seven more were exposed in 1994 (Getzov, Avshalom-Gorni, and Moqari 1998; table 2), four in 1998 (excavations directed by K. Covello-Paran) and two more in 2006 (A. Moqari, personal communication). Three additional Ta'anakh winepresses were revealed at the location of the present archaeological park, two of which were cut by the shaft of an Early Roman Period tomb (fig. 7). Altogether there are twenty-seven winepresses on the slope between the ancient sites of 'Ein el Hilu and Hirbet el-Mujeidel.

The majority of these winepresses were abandoned and the sites made over to quarrying for building stone (fig. 8; e.g., Getzov, Avshalom-Gorni, and Muqari 1998:

Figure 7. 'Ein el Hilu, paired winepresses (nos. 2, 4) cut by the shaft of an early Roman period tomb, facing north (Dr. Rafi Frankel standing).

plan 1:26 west, plan 2:L14) or the hewing of tombs (fig. 8; e.g., Getzov, Avshalom-Gorni, and Muqari 1998: plan 1:33).

Of special interest is a winepress (no. 6) excavated in the 1998 excavations (fig. 9). The treading floor of the original Ta'anakh winepress had a 21 percent slope. When it was modified to a screw press, the new treading floor had a mere 9 percent slope. Additional alterations included deepening and enlarging the collecting vat and hewing out two additional vats. The screw press type winepresses are dated throughout the country to the Byzantine period (Frankel 1999: 140–48), therefore we date the transformation of the original Ta'anakh winepress into a screw press winepress to this period.

An additional five Ta'anakh winepresses in the park adjacent to 'Ein el Hilu were successively recut and altered. Each time the treading floor was leveled and in most cases the collecting vat was enlarged. Besides the twenty-seven Ta'anakh winepresses there were at least another eleven winepresses of various types, yet none of these winepresses showed any signs of modification, be it for quarries or tombs.

The excavations at 'Ein el Hilu uncovered two kilns (fig. 10) and additional installations associated with potters' workshops from the later of the two MB strata (Stratum IV; Covello-Paran forthcoming). Specialized production of jars for wine transport was indicated by the dominance of storage jar handles among the ceramic wasters. The Stratum IV farmstead was interpreted by the excavator as a single complex that was erected

Figure 8. 'Ein el Hilu, two Ta'anakh winepresses cut by quarrying activities.

Figure 9. 'Ein el Hilu, Ta'anakh winepress (no. 6) recut into screw press winepress.

for the purpose of producing and transporting wine. The farmstead was probably built in direct proximity to the vineyards as well as to the roads that most likely led to Tel Shimron, located ca. 4 km west of the site.

Albeit later in date, the pairing of a winepress and adjacent kiln for production of storage jars is known from the Byzantine period near Ashkelon (Israel 1994).

14. Yifat. Kibbutz Yifat, located on the limestone hills south of Migdal Haemeq, is the location of one of the largest clusters of Ta'anakh winepresses in the Jezreel Valley.

Figure 10. ʿEin el Hilu potters kilns, facing west.

The survey was directed by the late Prof. Avner Raban (z"l) during the Migdal Ha-emeq excavations. The measurements presented in the table are based on his sketches and plans. Two winepresses were documented within the grounds of the regional high school—one is a complex winepress dated to the Byzantine period and the second is a Ta'anakh winepress. Salvage excavations at the site in summer 2008 southeast of the kibbutz revealed an additional ten winepresses (Covello-Paran 2009; table 1). Moshe Barak surveyed ca. 70 winepresses within the limits of Kibbutz Yifat, of which the majority are Ta'anakh winepresses (pers. comm.; see also Shahar 2007: 85).[5] Access to the full metric data for these winepresses was not granted to the authors, therefore only the other eleven Ta'anakh winepresses are included in the present study.

Four of the Yifat winepresses, nos. I, XI, XII, and XIII are of special interest. Number I is a typical Ta'anakh winepress put out of use when ashlars were quarried out of the rocky outcrop. Winepress XI (fig. 11) illustrates adaptations required by the presence of a narrow bedrock outcrop. The treading floor has an irregular rectangular form with a collecting vat located at its corner. The conduits are each hewn on different sides of the vat. A well-hewn deep circular depression in the center of the treading floor was aligned with another deep circular depression cut to the east of the treading floor. The placement of the depression in the treading floor enabled the hewers to maintain the preset distance between circular depressions.

Winepresses XII and XIII (fig. 12) exhibit high similarity and it is likely they were planned and hewn together, otherwise the earlier winepress would have been placed in the center of the bedrock platform leaving no room for the second winepress. The intent was to maximize bedrock use, which led to adapting the components of this type to the actual bedrock contours. Two main differences are noted: winepress XII has a shorter treading floor and only this winepress has two circular depressions flanking the floor.

The dimensions of the various components of the winepresses exhibit a high degree of similarity between them, such as the distance between the two circular depressions and the distance from the depressions or cupholes to the edge of the treading floor, despite certain deviations, such as the depth of Winepress XI's collecting vat (see table 1). An additional circular cupmark in the treading floor was found in a number of the Yif'at winepresses, which can also be characterized as adaptations to local topography that somewhat altered the traditional shape of the installation while retaining most of the features of this type, in particular the preset distance between the circular depressions (2.35 m).

---

5. Excavations at 'Ein Hakhlil, southeast of Yifat, on the spurs directly south of Migdal Haemeq exposed three simple but poorly preserved winepresses (nos. 7–9), which cannot be conclusively identified as Ta'anakh presses (Shalev 2017: figs. 14–18). It is possible that winepress X was originally a Ta'anakh winepress, damaged following the hewing and expansion of winepress XI: it is not preserved well enough to determine its type (see also Shalev 2017). Whatever their types, this group belongs to the Yifat cluster.

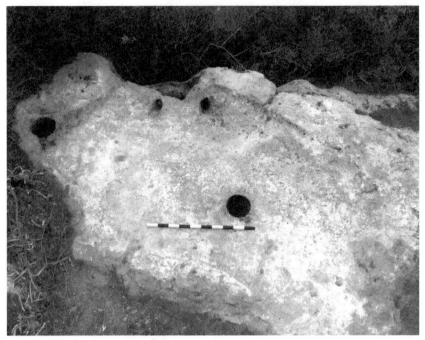

Figure 11. Yifat Winepress XI, facing south.

Figure 12. Yifat paired Winepresses XII–XIII, facing north.

Figure 13. Midrakh Oz winepress, facing west.

Figure 14. Gan Ner winepress, facing south.

15. Yoqneam. Three documented winepresses at site no. 44 of the Daliya Survey, are located on the hills above Nahal Hashofet, south of modern Yoqneam (Olami 1981: 31). Of the three installations, winepresses B and C have features characteristic of the Ta'anakh type such as the rounded walls and the two conduits. The short length of the treading floor is representative of the diversity of this type feature (see Yifat below). The site was surveyed again by Tepper who clarified the identification of two Ta'anakh winepresses at Olami's site 44 (Tepper 2012: site 16, fig. 4).

16. Khirbat el-Hashah (Midrakh ʿOz). Surface reconnaissance and salvage excavations at the site of Khirbat el-Hashash, at the modern moshav Midrakh ʿOz at the western border of the Jezreel Valley, exposed installations, quarries, and caves (Tepper 2009; Getzov, Tepper, and Tepper 2017; Getzov, Tepper, and Katlav 2008). Among the rock-hewn agricultural installations are four complex winepresses dating to the Roman and Byzantine periods, three simple winepresses and a total of six Ta'anakh winepresses (nos. 6, 8, 10, 12, 27, 31; fig. 13). The Ta'anakh winepresses were cut by later installations at the site and are therefore the earliest at the site.

17. Salim. Salvage excavations adjacent to Kafr Salim exposed numerous rock-hewn winepresses in use apparently until the end of the Byzantine period (Cohen and Haiman 2008). Three winepresses can be attributed to the Ta'anakh type: 31/3, 33/4, 48/1. The authors thank M. Cohen for sharing additional photographs of winepress 31/3, which enabled the identification of this winepress as a Ta'anakh type, despite it missing two depressions flanking the treading floor (Cohen and Haiman 2008: fig. 2). The original hewing of winepress 33/4 exhibits some characteristics of the Ta'anakh winepress, though modifications during the Byzantine period do not enable us to uphold this securely. Winepress 48/1 comprises two adjacent winepresses whose irregular treading floors are shallow. The vat of these winepresses is narrower than the treading floor, a characteristic of the Ta'anakh type.

18. Gan Ner. East of Gan Ner, on the lower slopes of the Gilboa mountains, two winepresses were exposed in salvage excavations (Porat 2008). The eastern winepress was dated to the Roman period according to the mosaic floor and potsherds in the plaster of the collecting vat. The western winepress (fig. 14) is a typical Ta'anakh winepress with the two circular conduits. One of these winepresses was transferred to the KKL-JNF Kabri Archaeological Forest Garden in Western Galilee.

19. Tel Ta'anakh (Taanach). The winepress was hewn into the bedrock at the southern slope of the tell (squares SW 29-2) and was covered and sealed by fortifications dating to the Middle Bronze Age III (Lapp 1969: 12–14, fig. 8). The excavators of Tel Ta'anakh assumed that the winepress was in use during the Early Bronze II–III (phases II–IV of the fortifications) while proposing that the winepress was aligned with Wall 36 in Square SW 28-1. We suggest that the winepress was hewn following the abandonment of the Early Bronze Age city, during the Middle Bronze Age I or II.

Of all the winepresses presented here, only the Tel Ta'anakh winepress can be securely dated to the Middle Bronze Age or earlier. The conduits are of subtype a and the winepress is different from most of the winepresses presented here: the walls are straight with square corners, and there are no depressions flanking the treading floor. A tethering hole was found close to the collecting vat.

20. Alloné Yizhaq West. Eight winepresses were documented in the survey of the Regavim Map of the Archaeological Survey of Israel that have the characteristic two conduits (Gadot and Tepper 2008: introduction). Of these, only the press at Allone Yizhaq west (Gadot and Tepper 2009: site 188) should be ascribed to the Ta'anakh type. The others are later complex winepresses. This cluster of winepresses and those from sites 21 and 22 (below) are in close proximity to a number of tells, including Tel Esur.

21. Nahal Samtar. During the course of salvage excavations prior to the expansion of the Vered Quarry (Oren 2009) two winepresses (A and B) were exposed. The original winepress A was later transformed into a complex winepress with a screw press; the only remaining components of the original press are the two conduits. During the transformation, an additional drain was hewn to bypass the original conduits (Oren 2009: fig. 2). Winepress B (Oren 2009: figs. 5–6) has a treading floor and two collecting vats. Notable is the sump at the base of the upper collecting vat. The excavator suggests that the second vat was hewn following damage to the original one. Neither of the Samtar winepresses had rock-hewn depressions flanking the treading floor.

22. Harish. A single winepress of the Ta'anakh type was excavated in the low flat Samarian hills at Harish point 723 (Haddad 2015: figs. 8–9). The winepress had a shallow trapezoid sloping treading floor (L454) whose exact dimensions were not determinable as a result of the later cutting of the floor for two burial cave shafts. The must drained into the rectangular collecting vat (L484A) through the standard two conduits (see Hadad 2015: fig 10).

Working the Ta'anakh Winepress

We reconstruct the work process in the Ta'anakh winepress as follows. A wooden frame was erected by the insertion of two vertical beams or poles in the depressions flanking the treading floor connected to the top with a horizontal wooden beam. This wooden frame spanning the width of the treading floor was used by the treaders as depicted in a scene from an Early Dynasty Egyptian tomb at Thebes (see figs. 15 [upper panel], 16). According to this interpretation, the grapes were piled at the upper part of the treading floor, which functioned as a holding area. The constant distance between the collecting vat and the rock-hewn depressions, despite variation in floor length, (see tables 1, 2) indicates that most of the treading occurred on the narrower part of the floor close to the collecting vat, while the grapes were piled at the wider back part of the treading floor. This is why some of the presses have an unfinished back part of the treading surface while the front of the floor closer to the vat is meticulously hewn. The two conduits were most likely plugged with plants such as thorny burnet

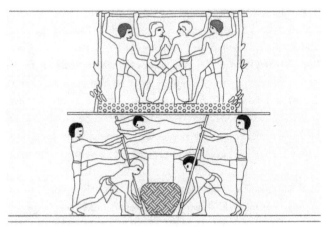

Figure 15. Treading grapes in a winepress (above) and wringing out the must in a sack-press (below), based on a wall painting in Tomb 1 at Saqqara, Dynasty 4 (based on Lepsius 1897, 4: Abt. 11.B1.96:s). Drawing by E. Dalali-Amos.

Figure 16. Treading grapes and collecting juice, on a wall painting in Nakht's tomb (TT52) in Sheikh Abd El-Qurna,Thebes, Dynasty XVIII (based on Davies 1917: pl. 26). Drawing by E. Dalali-Amos.

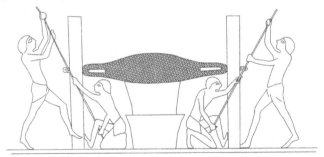

Figure 17. Employment of a sack-press based on wall painting in Intef's tomb (TT155) (based on Säve-Söderbergh 1957: pl. 15). Drawing by E. Dalali-Amos.

(*Sarcopoterium spinosum*), which functioned as a strainer for the must. Due to the small volume of the collecting vat, it is probable the must was extracted from the vat during the process and the fermentation occurred elsewhere. The sump at the bottom of the vats facilitated the collection of the last remains of the must.

As an alternate function of the rock-hewn depressions characteristic of the Taʿanakh winepress, the wooden frame could have supported a sack-press to wring the treaded remains to achieve additional extraction of the must. This wringing or pressing in a sack during the wine-making process is depicted in Egyptian tomb paintings (see figs. 15 [lower panel], 17). The current state of the evidence does not favor one interpretation over the other.

More revealing is the constant distance between the two depressions. It suggests that the sack-press was mobile and employed above numerous winepresses in a single location. In the two instances where paired winepresses were found (Yifat winepresses XII–XIII and Tel Shimron North group b), only one of the two winepresses had the depressions, indicating a division of labor between the winepresses with a single sack-press.

Uniformity

On the whole, simple winepresses have a high rate of size diversity (Frankel 1999: 51–52). On the contrary, the Taʿanakh winepresses exhibit a high rate of uniformity or standardization. We have been able to isolate standard measurements that were adhered to as far as possible while taking into account the limitations imposed by the presence of rocky outcrops. Table 1 presents the analysis of the dimensions of the winepress components from Yifat, and table 2 for ʿEin el Hilu. The last three columns present the average, standard deviation, and a percentage of the average.

The standard deviation presents the level of distribution of the sizes from the average and the calculation according to percentage, which enables us to compare the uniformity of dimensions where the average is different and if measurements are in differing measurement modes (for example comparison of meters against liters or slope).

According to the analysis, numerous components of the Taʿanakh winepresses exhibit a high attention to the width of the treading floor, the size of the depressions, the distance between depressions, the distance between the depressions and the base of the treading floor, and the length of the collecting vat. Diversity is greater with regard to the length of the treading floor and its gradient. The uniform distance between the circular depressions reflects the use of a mobile sack-press at different winepresses. A set distance is noted at Yifat Winepress XI, characterized by its adaptation to local topography that somewhat altered the traditional plan of the winepresses (Covello-Paran 2009: figs. 17–19). Regardless of the altered floor plan of the winepress, the rock hewers preserved the preset distance between the circular depressions by placing one depression outside of the treading floor with the second depression in the treading floor

Table 1. Metric data of Yifat winepresses (2008 excavations)

Winepress	I	V	VI	VII	VIII	IX	X	XI	XII	XIII	average	standard deviation	% standard deviation of average
Treading floor:L	5.55	2.2	2	2.2	7	2.5	2.4	3.75	3	4.5	3.51	1.69	48%
Width at top of floor	2.25	2.24	2	2.2		2.24	2		2.3	2.88	2.32	0.29	13%
Width at bottom of floor	1.5	1.7	1.15	2.2	2.6	1.9	1.8	2.25	1.93	1.6	1.86	0.42	22%
Treading floor area (sq,m)	10.41	4.33				5.18	4.56		6.35	10.08	6.82	2.75	40%
Flanking circ. depressions: diam.	0.26						0.25	0.25	0.27		0.26	0.01	4%
Flanking circ. depressions: D п	0.3						0.25	0.3	0.33		0.30	0.03	11%
Cuphole: distance between	2							2.24	2.37				
Cuphole : Distance from edge of pressing floor	1.4						1.1	0.96	0.75		1.05	0.27	26%
Treading floor circ. Depression: diam.	0.15		0.15			0.2		0.25	0.16	0.14	0.18	0.04	24%
Treading floor circ. Depression: D.	0.7		0.05			0.1		0.37	0.1	0.07	0.23	0.26	111%
Channels: diam.	0.15	0.15	0.21				0.2	0.15	0.15	0.16	0.17	0.03	16%
Collecting vat: L	1.2	0.97	0.97	1	1.35	1.11	1.14	1.15	1.06	1.14	1.11	0.12	11%
Collecting vat: W	0.58	0.58	0.63	0.65	0.8	0.53	0.58	0.6	0.73	0.65	0.63	0.08	13%
Collecting vat: D	0.35	0.35	0.35			0.3	0.38	0.6	0.35	0.35	0.38	0.09	24%
Collecting vat: volume (liters)		197	214			176	251	414	271	259	254.67	78.31	31%
Circ. of depression in collecting vat		0.24	0.19			0.2	0.2	0.2	0.3	0.3	0.23	0.05	21%
Treading floor: slope %	4.5	14.3	3.3			3.8	2	7	5	11.3	6.40	4.28	67%

Table 2. Metric data of 'Ein el Hilu winepresses (1994 excavations)

Winepress no.	15	16	20	25	26 west	26 east	33	average	standard deviation	% standard deviation of average
Pressing floor Length	3.15	?	3.1	3.1	2.35	2.4	5.8	3.32	1.16	35%
Width at top of floor	2.1	?	2	?	1.65	1.9	2.8	2.09	0.39	18%
Width at bottom of floor	1.6	1.5	1.75	1.4	1.4	1.6	1.7	1.56	0.13	8%
Treading floor area (sq.m)	5.83		5.81		3.58	4.20	13.05	6.06	3.40	56%
Circ. Depressions: diam.	0.2	0.3	0.17	0.25	0.18	0.2	0.3	0.23	0.05	22%
Circ. Depressions: D	0.2	0.4	?	0.3	0.2	0.25	0.3	0.28	0.07	25%
Cuphole: distance between	2.25	2.3	2	2.5	2.3	2.4	2.7	2.35	0.20	9%
Cuphole : Distance from edge of pressing floor	1.2	1	1.1	1.2	1.2	1.45	1.5	1.24	0.17	13%
Channels: diameter	0.12	0.13	0.8	0.15	0.14	0.17	0.11	0.23	0.23	101%
Collecting vat: L	1.3	1.06	1	1.05	1.1	1.15	?	1.11	0.10	9%
Collecting vat: W	0.7	0.56	0.8	0.6	0.56	0.84	?	0.68	0.11	17%
Collecting vat: D	?	0.35	?	0.4	0.3	0.6	?	0.41	0.11	28%
Collecting vat: volume (liters)		208		252	185	580		306	159.78	52%
Circ. of depression in collecting vat	0.25	0.17	?	?	0.2	0.6	0.2	0.28	0.16	56%
Treading floor: slope	20.0%			21.5%	5.2%	8.8%	13.6%	13.8%	6.3%	45%

itself (fig. 11). Among the winepresses reviewed above, a subtype devoid of circular depressions flanking the treading floor has been identified at Tel Ta'anakh, Nahal Samtar, Alloné Yizhaq West, Allonei Aba, Salim, and Harish. With the exception of Allonei Aba, these winepresses are all located in the Samaria Hills bordering the Jezreel Valley in the south.

Spatial Distribution

The distribution of the Ta'anakh type displays three characteristics:

1. Nearly all of the Ta'anakh winepresses are located in the limestone hills bordering the Jezreel Valley. The few exceptions are found in the Samarian Hills directly south of the Jezreel Valley (Nahal Samtar, Alloné Yizhaq, Harish) and in Lower Galilee (Ahihud, Horbat Tirat Tamra).

2. Most of the Ta'anakh winepresses are arranged in clusters. At twenty-two of the sites reviewed there are at least ninety-two winepresses, of which ten are single presses, seventeen are arranged in small clusters (2–5), though sixty-five of the winepresses are part of large clusters (>5) at three sites.

This clustering could be the prime reason for the lack of documented winepresses of this type in the archaeological surveys around the Jezreel Valley: Gazit Map (Gal 1991), Har Tavor and 'En Dor Maps (Gal 1998), Mishmar Haemeq Map (Raban 1993), Ahlstrom's surveys near Ta'anakh (Ahlström 1978), the regional research conducted by Safrai and Lin within Geva (1988) and the regional research conducted by Tepper at Legio (Tepper 2003). Numerous winepresses of other types were documented, but only in the Nahalal Map (Raban 1982) do we identify Ta'anakh type winepresses (see above site 7). Additional surveys bordering the Jezreel Valley such as the Dalia Map (Olami 1981) and the Regavim Map (Gadot and Tepper 2008) documented a single winepress of this type (see above, sites 15 and 20) in each map. There is the possibility that characteristics of the Ta'anakh type were missed in some cases (e.g., Tel Shimron North).

3. The updated study of the spatial distribution reinforces the previous observation that the Ta'anakh winepress is predominant in the Jezreel Valley. Although other winepress types exhibit a wider spatial distribution, the data show clearly the clustering of Ta'anakh winepresses around two of the largest tells in the Jezreel Valley: Megiddo (Midrakh Oz 3 km from Megiddo)[6] and Tel Shimron with five of the largest clusters— 'Ein el Hilu, Yifat, Tel Shimron North, and Migdal Haemeq—within 4 km of Tel Shimron. The highest concentration of clusters of Ta'anakh winepresses is centered around

---

6. In the survey of the Jezreel Valley (unpublished; Y. Tepper, pers. comm.), which was done on behalf of the JVRP (Homsher et. al. 2017), a few more Ta'anakh winepresses were reported in the Jezreel Valley near the two large sites of Megiddo and Tel Shimron.

Migdal Haemeq south of Tel Shimron. The clustering of winepresses next to the large tels is noted also near Tel Esur south of the Jezreel Valley.

Chronology

The evidence from Tell Ta'anakh points to the Early Bronze and Middle Bronze Age for the rise of the Ta'anakh type, a time span confirmed by the many cases in which Ta'anakh winepresses were cut by later winepresses, tombs, and quarries of the Roman and Byzantine periods.

It is conceivable that the Ta'anakh type continued after the Middle Bronze Age until the Hellenistic period. Their high rate of uniformity and unique spatial distribution argue, however, against such a long use. Had the Ta'anakh winepresses spanned a period of over 1500 years, we would expect greater changes in size and in components. Furthermore, it is not feasible that such a specifically unique type of winepress was only hewn in clusters at a limited number of sites during such a lengthy period.

The clusters around Tel Megiddo and Tell Ta'anakh could be dated already to the Early Bronze Age III, when these two sites were settled. This is, however, not the case for Tel Shimron—according to our research, we would suggest it constitutes the center of the largest cluster of Ta'anakh winepresses.

It is only in the Middle Bronze Age that the three sites—Megiddo, Ta'anakh, and Tel Shimron—were settled together for the first time. Therefore, we propose to date the hewing of the majority of the Ta'anakh type in the Middle Bronze Age. Nonetheless, we cannot rule out the possibility of their continued use in the Late Bronze Age.

Comparable Winepresses

Analogous rock-hewn winepresses are located at sites in other regions.

Tel Hazor: North and west of Tel Hazor, six winepresses were excavated. These bear analogies with the Ta'anakh winepress: sloping treading floor and circular depressions/cupmarks. Yet their dimensions are smaller and they have only a single drain (Stephansky 1994; Amos and Getzov 2011). Coined the "Hazor Winepress," the excavators date this press type to the Middle Bronze Age (Amos and Getzov 2011: 24*). The pair of winepresses 15b excavated west of the tell (Area B; Amos and Getzov 2011: 30, pl. 4, fig. 2) are comparable to the pair of presses at Yifat and Shimron North with circular depressions flanking only one of the winepresses.

Map of Migdal: Within the framework of the archeological survey of the Map of Migdal four clusters with over eighty winepresses were discovered. The majority of the presses have a single drain leading from the treading floor to the collecting vat. Therefore, they belong to the Hazor type. A few of these winepresses do have two rock-hewn conduits that would identify them as Ta'anakh winepresses. The lack of metric data, however, prevents any firm conclusion (Tor 2000).

The clustering of large numbers of Hazor winepresses in the vicinity of Tel Hazor and within the Migdal map indicate an economic system parallel to and contemporary with the network in the Jezreel Valley indicated by the Ta'anakh winepresses.

Malkiyya (East): East of Malkiyya, a large winepress displays a shallow sloping treading floor, three rock-hewn drains, and a rectangular collecting vat, all very similar to the Ta'anakh type (Stephansky 2004: fig. 1). The Makiyya winepress was reexamined by Rafi Frankel who cleaned the winepress together with members of Kibbutz Malkiyya. Frankel pointed to the similarity of the Malkiyya winepress with the Ta'anakh winepress.

Map of Regavim: The surveyors of the Regavim Map identified eight simple winepresses characterized by rock-hewn drains for the must (Gadot and Tepper 2009). One of these located at Alloné Yizhaq west is listed above as a Ta'anakh type winepress, while the others have square corners and conduits or opening places at the corners of the treading floor instead of conduits known from the Ta'anakh winepress. The question remains whether these altered features are indicative of adaptations of the Ta'anakh winepress over an extended period of time. The simple winepresses from this region together with the Ta'anakh-type winepresses indicate a cluster of installations near Tel Esur. The concentration of winepresses near the major tells in the Jezreel Valley is mirrored also at Tel Esur.

Horvat Hazan: A single winepress bearing affinities to the Ta'anakh type was exposed in salvage excavations at Horvat Hazan in the Lachish region (Peretz and Talis 2012: figs. 4–5). The sloping asymmetric treading floor with rounded corners, the rectangular collecting vat with sump on the floor, and the two conduits are features characteristic of the Ta'anakh type. The excavators recovered poorly preserved Iron Age potsherds from the winepress.

Conclusion

The Ta'anakh winepress is a well-defined type predominant in the hills bordering the Jezreel Valley where they are mostly found in large clusters. Other regions have clusters of presses that are sufficiently different to be classified as another type, such as the "Hazor winepress" for instance. Numerous salvage excavations in recent years have upheld this observation and have strengthened the identification of the main cluster of Ta'anakh winepresses in the hills in close vicinity to Tel Shimron, which provides evidence of the importance of viticulture in the local economy there. The sparse data for the chronological span of the Ta'anakh winepresses supports a likely date in the Middle Bronze Age, a period of extensive international trade, including wine. The excavations at 'Ein el Hilu, under the likely control of Shimron, exposed a Middle Bronze Age farmstead with an integrated system of wine production alongside the production of ceramic vessels for wine storage and transportation.

The discovery of a Middle Bronze Age wine cellar at the palace of Kabri provides additional data on the importance of wine in the palatial economy (see Koh, Yasur-Landau, and Cline 2014). Wine production at royal farms or estates is also known from the Late Bronze Age from a farmstead near Tel Ashdod (see Nahshoni 2013). Ugaritic texts mention potters sent to work in royal estates in rural areas (Heltzer 1982: 74). Considering the religious, social, and economic role of wine at Ugarit (Zamora 2000), it is conceivable that wine production in the Jezreel Valley was similarly organized. Future research should focus on the correlation of the archaeological evidence for production together with the consumption of wine in the Middle and Late Bronze Ages in Canaan.

In conclusion, the clustering of Ta'anakh winepresses provides evidence of farmsteads or royal estates controlled and organized by the elites or rulers of the Jezreel Valley city-states during the Middle Bronze Age, in particular the kings of Shimron. We suggest that the data on the distribution of the Ta'anakh winepresses can contribute to investigations into the economic relationship between the rulers of the Middle Bronze Age city-states and their intraregional dependencies in the Jezreel Valley. Moreover, from the distribution of the Hazor winepresses and those near Tel Esur, it is conceivable that contemporary schemes of wine production existed in other regions and polities.

References

Abarbanel, Moshe. 2009. "Documentation of Field Installations for Wine Production in the Eastern Lower Galilee in Relation to the Talmudic Literature." MA thesis, Ramat Gan.

Ahlström, G. W. 1978. "Wine Presses and Cup-Marks of the Jenin-Megiddo Survey." *BASOR* 231:19–49.

Amos, Edna, and Nimrod Getzov. 2011. "The Rural Hinterland West of Tel Hazor." *'Atiqot* 67:27–39. (Hebrew; English summary, pp. 84–85*)

Atrash, Walid. 2015. "Alonim." *HA-ESI* 127, http://www.hadashot-esi.org.il/Report_Detail_Eng.aspx?id=15724&mag_id=122.

Cohen, Michael, and Mordechai Haiman. 2008. "Salim." *HA-ESI* 120, http://www.hadashot-esi.org.il/report_detail_eng.aspx?id=796&mag_id=114.

Covello-Paran, Karen. 1997. "Migdal Ha'Emeq." *HA-ESI* 19:19*–20*.

———. 2008. "'Ein el-Ḥilu (Migdal Ha-'Emeq)." *NEAEHL* 5:1711–12.

———. 2009. "Yif'at (East)." *HA-ESI* 121, http://www.hadashot-esi.org.il/report_detail_eng.aspx?id=1027&mag_id=115.

———, ed. Forthcoming. *'Ein el-Hilu: Excavations at a Bronze and Iron Age Site in the Jezreel Valley.* IAA Reports. Jerusalem: Israel Antiquities Authority.

Dalali-Amos, Edna. 2007. "Horbat Tirat Tamra." *HA-ESI* 119: *A-4014, http://www.hadashot-esi.org.il/report_detail_eng.aspx?id=665&mag_id=112.

Frankel, Rafael 1999. *Wine and Oil Production in Antiquity in Israel and Other Mediterranean Countries.* Sheffield: Sheffield Academic.

Gal, Zvi. 1991. *Archaeological Survey of Israel Map of Gazit (46).* Jerusalem: Israel Antiquities Authority.

———. 1998. *Archaeological Survey of Israel Map of Har Tavor (41) Map of 'En Dor (45).* Jerusalem: Israel Antiquities Authority.

Gadot, Yuval, and Yotam Tepper. 2009. *Archaeological Survey of Israel Map of Regavim (49)*, http://survey.antiquities.org.il/index_Eng.html#/MapSurvey/1.

Getzov Nimrod, Dina Avshalom-Gorni, and Abdalla Muqari. 1998. "Installations and Tombs near el-Mujeidil (Migdal Ha-'Emeq)." *'Atiqot* 34: 195–207 (Hebrew; English summary, p. 12*).

Getzov Nimrod, Karen Covello-Paran, and Yotam Tepper. 2011. "The 'Ta'anakh Winepress'— Evidence of the Middle Bronze Age Wine Industry in the Jezreel Valley." *ErIsr* 30: 145–55 (Hebrew; English summary p. 149*).

Getzov, Nimrod, Yotam Tepper, and Inbar Katlav. 2008. "Midrakh 'Oz, Khirbat el-Khishash." *HA-ESI* 120, http://www.hadashot-esi.org.il/Report_Detail_Eng.aspx?print=all&id=905&mag_.

Getzov, Nimrod, Yotam Tepper, and Yigal Tepper. 2017. "Evidence of a Flourishing Ancient Viticulture in Light of the Excavations near Khirbat el-Hashash (Midrakh 'Oz) in the Rural Area between Geva' and Legio." *'Atiqot* 89:*75–*132 (Hebrew; English summary, pp. 119–22).

Haddad, Elie. 2015. "Harish." *HA-ESI* 127, http://www.hadashot-esi.org.il/report_detail_eng.aspx?id=24882&mag_id=122.

Heltzer, Michael. 1982. *The Internal Organization of the Kingdom of Ugarit.* Wiesbaden: Harrassowitz.

Israel, Yigal. 1994. "Ashkelon." *Hadashot Arkheologiyot* 100:86–91 (Hebrew).

Homsher, Robert S., Matthew J. Adams, Adam B. Prins, Ryan Gardner-Cook, Yotam Tepper. 2017. "New Directions with Digital Archaeology and Spatial Analysis in the Jezreel Valley." *Journal of Landscape Ecology* 10:153–64.

Kapul, Reuven. 2018. "Allonim." *HA-ESI* 130, http://www.hadashot-esi.org.il/Report_Detail_Eng.aspx?id=25430.

Koh, Andrew J., Assaf Yasur-Landau, and Eric H. Cline. 2014. "Characterizing a Middle Bronze Palatial Wine Cellar from Tel Kabri, Israel." *PLoS ONE* 9(8): e106406, https://doi.org/10.1371/journal.pone.0106406.

Lapp, Paul. 1969. "The 1968 Excavations at Tell Ta'annek." *BASOR* 195:2–52.

Lepsius, C. R. 1897. *Denkmäler aus Ägypten und Äthiopien.* Leipzig: Hinrichs.

Lerer, Yoav. 2012. "Ahihud, Bar Lev Industrial Zone, Survey." *HA-ESI* 124, http://www.hadashot-esi.org.il/report_detail_eng.aspx?id=2012&mag_id=119.

Nahshoni, Pirhiya. 2013. "A Thirteenth Century BCE Site on the Southern Beach of Ashdod." *'Atiqot* 74:59–122.

Olami, Ya'aqov. 1981. *Archaeological Survey of Israel: Daliya Map (31) 15–22.* Jerusalem: Israel Antiquities Authority.

Oren, Eliran. 2009. "Nahal Samtar." *HA-ESI* 121, http://www.hadashot-esi.org.il/Report_Detail_Eng.aspx?id=1104&mag_id=115.

Peretz, Ilan, and Svetlana Talis. 2012. "Horbat Hazzan and Horbat Avraq." *HA-ESI* 124, http://www.hadashot-esi.org.il/Report_Detail_Eng.aspx?id=2142&mag_id=119.

Porat, Leea. 1982. *Archaeological Survey of Israel. Nahalal Map (28) 16–23.* Jerusalem: Israel Antiquities Authority.

———. 1999. *Archaeological Survey of Israel. Mishmar Ha'Emeq (28) 16–22.* Jerusalem: Israel Antiquities Authority.

———. 2008. "Gan Ner." *HA-ESI* 120, http://www.hadashot-esi.org.il/report_detail_eng.aspx?id=987&mag_id=114.

———. 2009. "Alloney Abba." *HA-ESI* 120, http://www.hadashot-esi.org.il/Report_Detail_eng.aspx?print=all&id=1153&mag_id=115.

Safrai, Ze'ev, and Micha Lin. 1988. "Excavations and Surveys in the Mishmar Ha-'Emeq Area." Pages 167–214 in *Geva: Archaeological Discoveries at Tell Abu-Shusha, Mishmar Ha-*

'Emeq. Edited by Benjamin Mazar. Jerusalem: Israel Exploration Society.

Säve-Söderbergh, Torgny. 1957. *Four Eighteenth Dynasty Tombs: Private Tombs at Thebes*. Oxford: Oxford University Press.

Shahar, Yuval. 2007. "The Road to Sepphoris: Settlements, Tombs, Winepresses and Milestones." Pages 72–92 in *The Jezreel Valley and All Its Routes*. Edited by A. Zeltser. Jerusalem: Hebrew University.

Shalev, Yiftah. 2017. "Migdal Ha-'Emeq, 'En Hakhlil." *HA-ESI* 129, http://www.hadashot-esi.org.il/report_detail_eng.aspx?id=25297&mag_id=125.

Stephansky, Yosef. 1994. "Winepress near Tel Ḥaẓor." *Hadashot Arkheologiyot* 101–102: 117.

———. 2004. "Malkiyya (East)." *HA-ESI* 116, http://www.hadashot-esi.org.il/Report_Detail_Eng.aspx?id=50&mag_id=108.

Tepper, Yotam. 2009. "Midrakh 'Oz, Khirbat el-Khishash, Survey." *HA-ESI* 121, http://www.hadashot-esi.org.il/Report_Detail_Eng.aspx?id=1233&mag_id=115.

———. 2012. "Yoqne'am, Survey." *Excavations and Surveys in Israel*. 124, http://www.hadashot-esi.org.il/report_detail_eng.aspx?id=2189&mag_id=119.

———. 2014. "Migdal Ha-'Emeq (North), Survey." *HA-ESI* 126, http://www.hadashot-esi.org.il/report_detail_eng.aspx?id=9561&mag_id=121.

Tor, Yitzhak. 2000. "Survey of the Migdal Map." *Hadashot Arkheologiyot* 112:17* (Hebrew).

Zamora, José-Angel. 2000. *La vid y el vino en Ugarit*. Madrid: Consejo Superior de Investigaciones Científicas.

Traditionalism and Transformations in Canaanite Cultic Architecture: A View from Middle Bronze Age Megiddo

Matthew Susnow

Abstract: This paper explores the different types of cultic spaces that appear in the southern Levant during the Middle Bronze Age. The site of Megiddo provides a perfect case study for investigating the diversity attested within local Canaanite cultic architectural traditions, diachronic changes in temple types and forms, and the relationships between temples, their surrounding settlements and landscapes, and society at large. Megiddo's strategic location and high degree of connectivity to both the coast and the inland Jordan Valley make it a microcosm for the rich diversity of cultic traditions within Canaan at large.

Keywords: temples, Levant, Megiddo, Jezreel Valley, Middle Bronze Age

B eginning in the EB I, large cultic architecture was already an established hallmark of Megiddo's landscape.[1] By the earliest phases of the MB, no fewer than five strata of superimposed temples had been constructed in the settlement's cultic precinct, Area BB/J (Finkelstein and Ussishkin 2000: 38; Adams 2013: 94–100, 117–18; 2017; Adams, Finkelstein, and Ussishkin 2014). The awareness of earlier layers of sacred structures and the premeditated decision to use and reuse the same space continuously for cultic purposes is remarkable in its own right. This phenomenon was not unique to Megiddo; it is well attested at sites across the southern Levant. However, the span of two millennia during which Megiddo's Area BB was continuously dedicated to sacred purposes is unique, indicating the impressive resiliency and strength of continuity and traditionalism in cultic activities at the site. At the same time, many different architectural traditions are witnessed in the precinct over time, emphasizing the transforma-

---

1. It is with great pleasure that I dedicate this paper that deals with architecture, cult and the site of Megiddo to Dr. Franklin, whose career in archaeology has largely focused specifically on the site and its architecture, and who is deeply interested in and has written on cult on a number of occasions in the past. While I had visited and written about Megiddo before, it was only after my first time touring the site with Dr. Franklin that Megiddo of old, and all of its stories, came to life and have ever since captivated me. I owe a great deal of gratitude to Dr. Franklin for this.

tions in the form of cultic space, if not also the form of cultic practice, that took place at the site.

This article focuses specifically on Megiddo's MB cultic architecture. Throughout the Middle Bronze Age, architectural traditions and use of the sacred precinct changed. These changes are reflected in the different traditions of cultic architecture throughout the southern Levant at large. Accordingly, this paper first presents the different temple types extant in the region, followed by an analysis of Megiddo's MB temple sequence. The analysis of the temples will be further contextualized by the subsequent discussion of the changing nature and role of MB temples in the southern Levant and within the evolving landscape of Megiddo. The aim is to demonstrate and to underscore the uniqueness of Megiddo owing to its strategic location not only between north and south but also between east and west.

MB Cultic Architecture in the Southern Levant

During the MB, there were essentially two different forms of cultic spaces: open-air cultic precincts and roofed temples (A. Mazar 1992). Although these categories are not necessarily evolutionary—that is, earlier forms were open-aired and only later did they develop into constructed edifices—the current state of the data indicates that the earliest phases of the MB lacked standardized, built-up cultic precincts, with the exception of Tell el-Hayyat. Open-air precincts were typified by their lack of substantial architecture. The focal points of cultic activities were outdoor settings, making use of the natural landscape and at times, aniconic standing stones (*maṣṣebot*).[2] Examples of this form of cultic space are evident at Nahariya, Megiddo, Lachish (Area D), Hazor (the Complex of Standing Stones), Gezer, and Byblos. It is likely that the roots of this form of cultic space, and the religious traditions that were practiced therein, were already established in the Intermediate Bronze Age—evident at Tel 'Ashir—if not earlier.[3] While some cultic spaces of this type were extramural, others appeared in rural and even urban settings. Thus, there is a degree of diversity in terms of setting and location. These open-air cultic precincts were largely inclusive and highly accessible spaces in nature, stressing community, communal consumption, the use of special miniature votive vessels, and in general, few social or physical barriers separating the populous from the central focal point of cultic activity. At the same time, social and cultic hierarchy are at times evident, exemplified by the many metal figurines and objects of prestige found at a number of these sites, and in particular, the wealth of objects recovered from hoards

---

2. Although see Tel Kitan for an iconic standing stone in the form of a naked female (Eisenberg 1977).

3. On Tel 'Ashir, see Gophna and Ayalon 2004. Standing stones have been found in EB and earlier contexts as well (e.g., Mazar, de Miroschedji, and Porat 1996: 7–9, figs. 7–12; Avner 2001).

and favissae.[4] Further, open-air cultic spaces within urban settings, such as the Complex of Standing Stones in Area A at Hazor and the Temple of the Obelisks at Byblos, were comparatively more complex, and by nature more hierarchic, than the extramural and rural precincts. Thus, while open-air cultic precincts were the most inclusive of religious spaces in MB Canaan, there was a degree of diversity.

Within the category of roofed temples, one can differentiate between monumental symmetrical temples (migdal temples) and small shrines (A. Mazar 1992; Nakhai 1993; Susnow 2019). While small shrines were generally constructed in nonurban settings (Givat Sharett, Wallajeh, Naḥal Repha'im), the more monumental migdal temples were part of the elite sectors of urban landscapes (Megiddo, Hazor, Pella, Shechem, Tel Haror),[5] with a few constructed at rural sites in somewhat diminutive forms (Tell el-Hayyat, Tel Kitan). Migdal temples have been discussed extensively by scholars since the first of this type was identified in the region at Shechem (Sellin 1926; Campbell 2002; cf. B. Mazar 1968: 92–93). These temples share the following six features: (1) they were constructed on raised ground or within a walled temenos; (2) they had exceptionally thick walls, at least 2 m thick, perhaps to support upper stories and to create a towering sense of monumentality; (3) they had a single direct entrance along a longitudinal central axis; (4) they were composed of at least two architectural units—an entrance hall and a larger inner sanctum that was either of a long- or broad-room layout; (5) the innermost room was the focal point of cultic activity, marked by either a cultic niche or a raised platform against the back wall on a direct axis from the entrance; and (6) they often had two large antae flanking either side of the entrance, forming tower-like structures within which staircases might have led to upper stories (A. Mazar 1992: 166–67).

This architectural tradition likely originated in the north in Syria (hence the term Syrian temple), where many temples in antis appear there as early as the Early Bronze Age (Kempinski 1992: 197; A. Mazar 1992: 167–69; Matthiae 2007, 2010; Castel 2010; Yasur-Landau et al. 2012: 19–24). This temple form continued to be attested in the MB at sites such as Mari, Aleppo, Ebla, Alalakh, Ugarit, and possibly at Kamid el-Loz (Schaeffer 1935: 155–56; Woolley 1955: 43–59; Matthiae 1980; 1997: 381, 387–88; Margueron 2004; Kohlmeyer 2012; Metzger 2012). One further migdal temple was constructed at the Hyksos capital of Tell el-Dab'a (Avaris) in the Area A/II precinct during the MB II (Bietak 1997: 104–8). It is no surprise that the cultic architecture associated with the non-Egyptian Asiatic rulers of the Fifteenth Dynasty was the very temple type associated with the urban elites of the Levant.

How migdal temples became associated with Canaanite elites and why they were established as the standardized temple form of the southern Levant is still unclear.

---

4. Hoards and deposits were recovered from Nahariya, Byblos, Gezer, and Dan, for example (Philip 1988; Ilan 1992).

5. Recently, Ilan has suggested that a late MB I migdal temple stood at Dan (Ilan 2018).

Some have viewed the migdal temple as evidence of state cult (Burke 2014a: 361), while others have emphasized the temple type's conspicuous, towering, and fortified nature, leading to an interpretation whereby they are not simply religious structures but also symbols of power that indicate a competitive elite capable of procuring and controlling significant resources and manpower (Ilan 1995: 314; cf. Wright 1985: 233–34). Perhaps in some instances the temple type was associated with the worship of a specific deity, with certain militaristic aspects (e.g., Haddu/Ba'al) encapsulated by the imposing monumentality and fortress-like façades of the edifices. Although southward Amorite migrations are likely (Burke 2014b: 404–5), it seems more plausible to associate the rise of these temples in the southern Levant not with the arrival of a new population but rather with locals emulating Syrian elites by borrowing from northern urban architectural traditions (Yasur-Landau 2011: 61). However, as the entire Levant can be viewed as part of a cultural continuum (Schloen 2001: 201), perhaps these temples were just as much a part of a local indigenous tradition as they were of a northern one, which emerged somewhat later in the MB (Greenberg 2002; S. Cohen 2009; Burke 2014b). The one MB site where all temple types are attested is Megiddo.

Megiddo as a Case Study: Different Types
of Cultic Spaces through Time

Megiddo is the only MB site in the southern Levant with an open-air cultic precinct, a small shrine, and a monumental migdal temple. These temples were not contemporary, but were established in superimposed strata within the sacred precinct of Area BB. The following will discuss the different temples of the MB at Megiddo, taking into account not only the original suggested stratigraphy of the University of Chicago Expedition but also the subsequent reworked stratigraphy of the precinct by various scholars.

This survey begins in the second phase of Stratum XIV (J-8/J-9), when the nature of the cultic precinct was reoriented from standardized megaron temple forms to irregular architecture. The precise dating of this stratum—which was entirely removed by the University of Chicago excavators—is highly debated, and even among the directors of the renewed Tel Aviv University Expedition there is no consensus as to the exact chronology. While Ussishkin (2015: 98–100, table 2) and others have placed this stratum at the end of the Intermediate Bronze Age, Adams argues Stratum XIV belongs to the onset of the MB I (Adams and Bos 2013: 120–25, table 2.2). In either case, there is a significant shift in this stratum from the previous stratum's cultic infrastructure.

In Stratum XIVa, an irregularly shaped shrine was constructed within the remains of Stratum XV's Temple 4040, reusing the previous temple's interior space (Loud 1948: 84). The shrine was significantly smaller, measuring ca. 4 × 5.5 m. The space between the original walls of Temple 4040 and the new sanctuary was filled in with rubble. Part of Temple 4040's raised podium was reused as a raised niche within the new shrine. The entrance, situated opposite the niche, was essentially a narrow passage leading into the small interior space. A large stone (measuring 1.75 × 1.25 m) with a cup mark sat on the west side of the room, possibly having functioned as an offering table. This small cult chamber differed significantly from the site's previous temples. It was small, had very limited accessibility, and was not suitable for large groups. In fact, the narrow entrance could not have allowed more than a single ritual participant to enter the space at any given time. However, while there was a shift in the configuration and layout of Temple 4040 and likely in the types of rituals and activities performed within it, there still was an awareness of and effort to preserve the sacredness of the previous temple and its location. Significant effort was made to continue utilizing Temple 4040's central space in addition to the repurposing of the raised podium against the back wall.

In stratum XIII, the precinct appears to have been empty and set aside from the rest of the settlement. The University of Chicago excavators admitted uncertainty as to the nature of the Strata XIIIB and XIIIA cultic precinct. Due to continued preservation of cultic activity in the area, it was presumed that there was no reason to doubt the cultic nature of Area BB in Stratum XIII as well (Loud 1948: 84). At the same time, there was a lack of actual positive evidence. Private dwellings were erected in this stratum around the precinct, possibly an indication of efforts to enclose and preserve it (Dunayevsky and Kempinski 1973: 175–78; cf. Kempinski 1989: 178). While no monumental architecture was yet constructed in the sacred precinct, by the end of Stratum XIII, a city wall was built and large palatial architecture was erected in the following stratum.[6]

Until recently, the cultic precinct in Stratum XII was thought to have retained its open-air nature while featuring newly erected *maṣṣebot*, possibly in association with a small chamber (Loud 1948: figs. 206, 207; Dunayevsky and Kempinski 1973: 177–78). According to the original excavators, the cultic precinct was now composed of randomly spaced *maṣṣebot* of varying shapes and sizes. They were each about 1 m tall and most were found still upright in situ (Loud 1948: 87–92). A small, single-roomed chamber measuring 5.5 × 3 m was built at the southwestern corner of the temenos during this phase as well (Dunayevsky and Kempinski 1973: fig. 13, already indicated in Loud 1948: fig. 398; Kempinski 1989: 178). Thus, while open air in nature, the *maṣṣebot* were associated with a small shrine, all within an enclosed temenos.

Many stratigraphic issues and conundrums surround Strata XII–VIII. While it is clear that Temple 2048—a migdal temple measuring 21.5 × 16.5 m constructed according to a long-room layout—was later built above the precinct with the standing stones, the initial date of its construction has been debated. The University of Chicago excavation assigned the standing stone precinct to Stratum XII and Temple 2048 to Stratum VIII (Kempinksi 1989: 181–82). Epstein (1965) suggested that the earliest phase of construction of the migdal temple was in fact Stratum XII. Epstein, however, did not address the new issue that arose from this suggestion—that the standing stones

---

6. Locus 4009, which was considered an altar or *bammah*, was placed in Stratum XIII by Loud (1948: fig. 396) but has since been reconstructed as part of Stratum XIV (Ussishkin 2015: 99–100).

were purportedly also from Stratum XII. A few years later, Dunayevsky and Kempinski rejected Epstein's assessment, although they did agree that Loud's Stratum VIII dating was too late for the initial construction of the temple (Loud 1948: 102–5). They placed the temple's first phase in Stratum X, at the end of the MB, contemporary with the construction of Hazor's Area H Orthostat Temple and the migdal temple at Shechem (Dunayevsky and Kempinski 1973: 180–84), and the standing-stone precinct remained securely in Strata XII and XI. This was the general consensus until Adams suggested once again a possible Stratum XII date for the migdal temple, for reasons slightly different than those of Epstein (Adams 2017: 49–51). Adams's suggested reconstruction pushes back the phase with the *maṣṣebot* to Stratum XIII, which might have previously been misattributed to Stratum XII due to its raised height relative to its surroundings (Adams, pers. comm. 2019). Accordingly, the confusion and uncertainty expressed in Loud's report and notes, and further expressed by Dunayevsky and Kempinski, regarding the nature of Stratum XIII would be solved—the standing stones were erected in this stratum at a raised level, as one might suspect a high place to be.

Regardless of the correct reconstruction of the precinct, in addition to the temple/open-air *maṣṣebah* installations of Stratum XII, the city became fully fortified and urban in this stratum, and Area BB/J witnessed the construction of a large palace just west of the sacred precinct. As this part of the city was heavily built up, elites appear to have gained control over the cult, which is evident in the construction of the large palace (the "Nordburg") directly to its west. The boundaries of the newly formed temenos of the cultic precinct were dictated by the palace walls (Nigro 1994: 20–21). If Stratum XII was open air in nature, then as Megiddo's elites gained control over the cultic precinct, there was initially no attempt to construct monumental temple architecture. This underscores the extreme traditionalism and resiliency in the practice of traditional forms of cult at the site, even as a local ruler, family, or elite consolidated power and gained control over access to and use of the site's cultic precinct. While palatial architecture was monumental, religious architecture remained relatively nonmonumental, maintaining the older traditions of the local population. However, according to Adams's recent suggestion, during Megiddo's transformation into full-fledged urbanism, elites constructed Temple 2048 in tandem with the palace, thus not only transforming the site into a well-built urban landscape but forever altering Megiddo's religious landscape. For the duration of the Bronze Age, and into the earliest phases of the Iron I, Temple 2048 remained the focal point of cult, even as the elite focuses and palatial architecture shifted to the north end of the site (Area AA) in Stratum IX (LB I).

Thus, at least three different configurations of cultic space were extant during the MB at Megiddo—open air, small shrine, and monumental symmetrical temple. These shifts exhibited transformations and innovations within the local landscape. However, the superimposed cultic spaces also exhibited degrees of traditionalism. In addition to the maintenance of the sacredness of space, there was also an effort to preserve the same orientations of the temples. Throughout the longue durée of Bronze Age temples at the site, a consistent northern orientation is evident. It seems plausible that the 'Ein el-Qubbi spring, one of the site's two main water sources, which these temples faced, bore continual significance to the practice of cult at the site. Therefore, even as cultic architecture shifted in the MB, this northward-facing orientation was maintained.

The Settlement History and Interregional Interconnectivity of MB Canaan

In order to contextualize the phenomena evident at Megiddo, this section will elucidate the general settlement history of MB Canaan, the role of urban elites in the increasingly urban landscapes, and the southern Levant's general interconnectivity to the surrounding regions of the eastern Mediterranean littoral.

While the earliest settlements of the MB predate large-scale construction of monumental architecture and fortifications, by Phase 2 of the MB I, significantly more complex settlements with indications of political and social hierarchy began to emerge (S. Cohen 2016). This is visible in the implementation of large-scale construction projects that transformed settlement landscapes. While fortifications (ramparts, city walls, bastions), city gates, and large elite buildings or palaces were built during this period (Herzog 1997), large cultic architecture was not yet featured within the urban plan. In other words, elites were not yet concerned with setting aside public space for cultic activity. As the MB I progressed, more firmly established settlement networks were established, particularly along the rivers of the coastal region and in the Jezreel, Jordan, and Hula Valleys. By the MB II, a series of local settlement networks was extant within the region at large in which large core sites could rely on smaller surrounding sites in the hinterland, allowing the larger settlements to focus on other types of interactions with other sites and regions (S. Cohen 2016: 84–85, fig. 6.8). This consolidation of political power, the strengthening of settlement systems and networks, and the concentration of small sites around larger core sites, signifies the development of Canaanite city-states (Ilan 1995). In tandem with this process was, notably, increased social stratification, while at the same time, the solidification of both social and regional group identities which supported the urban centers and their elites. It was mainly during this latter phase of the MB when migdal temples were introduced by urban elites to the urban landscape of the southern Levant.

Developments in the southern Levant did not occur in isolation. This is not surprising, as the southern Levant in general functioned as a land bridge between Egypt and the rest of the ANE from time immemorial. Thus, there was a long history already in the EB of Egyptian involvement in the southern Levant (S. Cohen 2016: 5, 22–38), and during the MB in particular, the two were in close contact, with textual and archaeological evidence indicating trade and interactions between the two regions, although not actual Egyptian colonization of the southern Levant (Marcus 1991: 19–45; 1998). Cultural affinities with the northern Levantine coast, Syria and Mesopotamia are also well attested in ceramics, architecture, iconography, cuneiform writing, and burial types (Gerstenblith 1983: 59–87; Ziffer 1990: 14*–15*; Kempinski 1992: 166–67; Ilan 1995: 300–301, 309–14; Burke 2014b; Y. Cohen 2019). MB Canaan also had contact with the west, visible in the import of Cypriot pottery and Aegean foodstuffs and art traditions (Kislev, Artzy, and Marcus 1993; Marcus 1998: 207–8; Niemeier and Niemeier 2002).

As noted above, cultic sites during the early phases of the MB were generally non-urban and isolated. Most lacked architecture, a number featured *maṣṣebot*, and in general, there was ample evidence of consumption on site. These sites served as spaces for communal consumption and gatherings, aiming to forge and reinforce shared group identities and social cohesion through common religious experience. They were generally situated outside the bounds of the local hierarchic structures within the urban settlement spheres and although not undisputed, many scholars have connected outdoor cult and ritual to the worship of female deities—whether related to fertility, the sea, or some other function (Negbi 1976: 130–32, 140; Dothan 1981; Brody 1998: 9–38; Keel and Uehlinger 1998: 19–37, 47–48). These phenomena are quite reminiscent of the contemporary outdoor cultic spaces in Syria (Marchetti and Nigro 1997) and the form of cult sites and peak sanctuaries and the primary worship of a female goddess (or goddesses) elsewhere in the Mediterranean such as Middle Minoan Crete (Lupack 2010). As stated, these early MB cultic traditions had precursors in the earlier local practices of the indigenous population. The lack of built-up temple architecture during this period seems to indicate a strong local and, more broadly, eastern Mediterranean tradition of encountering the cult in the natural landscape and of resistance to monumental cultic architecture.

Megiddo: A Unique and Strategic Site Situated between North and South, East and West

Megiddo's strategic location in the Jezreel Valley and at the entrance of Wadi ʿAra placed it at the crossroad of two important trade and communication routes: the southwest–east running route that connected Egypt to Syria and Mesopotamia via the coastal plain of the southern Levant (the Via Maris); and the route running northwest–southeast connecting the Levantine coast north of Mount Carmel and the Acre plain to inland Canaan (Kempinski 1989: 3). As reflective of the region at the time, Megiddo displayed many international influences, both from the north and from the south. Heavy Egyptian influences were already attested at Megiddo in the EB (Ilan and Goren 2003; Blockman and Groman-Yeroslavski 2006: 315; Finkelstein, Ussishkin, and Halpern 2006: 843–47; Keinan 2007; Regev et al. 2014: 258–61). These Egyptian connections, evolving in nature, continued throughout the MB and LB. Northern influences are also evident at the site, for example, in ceramic forms, architectural traditions, burial types, and other small finds from the site. While Megiddo served as a prominent site internationally due to its location along the Via Maris, it also served as an important—if not the central—cult center within the Jezreel Valley region. As early as the EB Ib, the site was predominantly, if not solely, cultic in nature and served the religious needs of the populous from the surrounding hinterland (Adams, Finkelstein, and Ussishkin 2014). A similar phenomenon might account for the early MB phases as well.

MB urbanization at Megiddo appears to follow certain trajectories noticed along the coast, such as displaying urban phases and the construction of fortifications prior to the establishment of monumental religious architecture, while at the same time, the process was more gradual and chronologically later than the patterns of early settlement complexity noted along the coast (Loud 1948; Kempinski 1989; Yasur-Landau 2019: 228). For the first half of the MB, the site maintained its unfortified and non- (or pre-)urban status and its gradual rise to "city" probably included an intermediate phase as a fortified village, prior to the construction of monumental palatial and temple architecture (Kempinski 1989: 45).[7] In other words, by the time of the migdal temple's construction, the site had already been urban for some time.

Here, I would like to further suggest that Megiddo not only played an important role between north and south and within the Jezreel Valley, but it was also strategically situated between the east and west. Connectivity with the east—or more accurately with inland/noncoastal Canaan—is most apparent in the material culture and architectural traditions shared with the Jordan Valley, such as the construction of the migdal temple in the cultic precinct. The west, represented by the site's interconnectivity to coastal sites, to coastal settlement history and trade routes, and to coastal traditions more broadly, is possibly most apparent in the LB (Artzy 2006). However, already early in the MB, a number of "western" traditions—what could be referred to as eastern Mediterranean—already appear in the sacred precinct. This includes the double ax of likely Minoan origin from Locus 4009 (Loud 1948: pl. 182:7), the only one coming from a secure MB I context in the southern Levant (Yasur-Landau 2015: 146), as well as miniature vessels and three seven-cupped bowls (Loud 1948: pls. 16:21, 19:19, 47:9). In particular, seven-cupped bowls have a distribution mainly along the coast, between Ugarit and Byblos in the north down south through Bat Yam (Naeh 2012: 84–87). Further, the majority of metal figurines yielded from the southern Levant in the early phases of the MB were not only overwhelmingly coastal, but also female. This was similarly the case at Megiddo where the earlier MB figurines most closely resemble those from MB I cultic sites at Nahariya and Byblos (Kempinski 1989: 180–81).

Beyond the ritual objects at the site, the nonmonumental configuration of the space, and in particular, the open-air precinct with *maṣṣebot*, is reflective of local traditions that were already practiced in pre-Middle Bronze Age contexts in the region. Although there has been a scholarly propensity to connect open-air cultic sites, *bammot*

---

7. For a recent definition of a city in MB Canaan, see Yasur-Landau 2019: 225 and references therein.

and *maṣṣebot* to coastal phenomena (Dothan 1981: 77–78; Nakhai 1993: 196–97), I would suggest these are not reflective of coastal traditions but rather of more generally local and popular southern Levantine traditions. Arguing that sites with open-air or standing-stone precincts such as Megiddo, Gezer, or Lachish were coastal is untenable—they are not on the coast. Further, *maṣṣebot* were certainly not solely attested along the coast, but rather were distributed throughout the Levant, indicating a widespread and deeply imbedded popular Canaanite cultic tradition. This would better account for the many standing stones found at inland sites. Tell el-Hayyat, Tel Kitan, Shechem, possibly Pella, as well as the LB Orthostat Temple at Hazor all had standing stones as part of their temple complexes. However, the standing stones were located in the open-air temple courtyards. They were not featured as focal points of the temple interiors, which were more restricted and likely off limits to the majority of the population, but rather were situated in the open-air spaces as communal apparatuses for more accessible and vernacular use.

The one idiosyncratic facet that does appear to be coastal is the continued avoidance of monumental temple architecture. Migdal temples are attested in the Jordan Valley, the Jezreel Valley, the central highlands and the Negev, but not in the coastal region, perhaps indicative of an eastern Mediterranean religious ethos to experience cult in the natural landscape. That monumental temples were not constructed at coastal sites holds true for the LB and the Iron Age as well. Therefore, throughout the MB Megiddo demonstrated both western and eastern tendencies: on the one hand there was a long period during which nonmonumental temple architecture was constructed at the site, while on the other hand, Megiddo's interconnectivity with the eastern outlet of the valley—that is, the Jordan Valley where migdal temples were most heavily attested—led to the eventual construction of the temple type at the site. Once again, Megiddo stands unique in that it was the westernmost site at which a migdal temple was constructed.

Conclusions

During the MB, sites such as Hazor, Tell el- Dabʻa, Ashkelon, Kabri, and Pella functioned as "gateways" to trade and interactions with regions further afield. I suggest that Megiddo too functioned as such a site, not only in terms of its clear display of a mixture of local and cross-cultural affinities and interactions, but also, historically, as a "gateway" site for the modern scholar to engage a plethora of research topics on the Bronze and Iron Ages in the southern Levant. Megiddo has been the exemplary site for studies on early forms of local iconography (e.g., the incised stone slabs of the EB I Picture Pavement), later Canaanite art and the LB ivories, palatial architecture (of the EB, MB, LB, and Iron Ages), metal statuary, Canaanite rulership, and importantly for the MB, chronology and change in typology and morphology of ceramic forms.

In this article, the site has been established as unique in its expressing all types of MB cultic architecture. While a number of MB sites had cultic precincts with long sequences of superimposed temples, and sites like Hazor and Lachish had many different temple forms throughout the MB and LB located in different parts of the sites, Megiddo is the only site that not only continuously reused the same space for cultic purposes but that the form of the temple in that space changed over time. This was a reflection of the changing nature of the site, of its evolving role in the region between north and south and between west and east, and of the overarching evolution of the geopolitical and socioeconomic status of the southern Levant and its various microregions during the MB. In spite of all of these apparent shifting transformations, traditionalism was extant in the remarkable awareness of what previous generations maintained as sacred, in the continual preservation of a northern orientation, and in the retention of the sanctity of space for millennia even as the center of political life and elite rulership shifted away from the cultic precinct in the LB to Area AA in the north of the site.

References

Adams, Matthew J. 2013. "Area J, Part III: The Main Sector of Area J." Pages 47–118 in *Megiddo V: The 2004–2008 Seasons*. Edited by Israel Finkelstein, David Ussishkin, and Eric H. Cline. Tel Aviv: Emery and Claire Yass Publications in Archaeology.

———. 2017. "Djehutihotep and Megiddo in the Early Middle Bronze Age." *JAEI* 13:1–11.

Adams, Matthew J., and Bos, J. 2013. "Area J, Part IV: Sub-Area Upper J." Pages 111–33 in *Megiddo V: The 2004–2008 Seasons*. Edited by Israel Finkelstein, David Ussishkin, and Eric H. Cline. Tel Aviv: Emery and Claire Yass Publications in Archaeology.

Adams, Matthew J., Israel Finkelstein, and David Ussishkin. 2014. "The Great Temple of Early Bronze I Megiddo." *AJA* 118:285–305.

Artzy, Michal. 2006. "The Carmel Coast during the Second Part of the Late Bronze Age: A Center for Eastern Mediterranean Transshipping." *BASOR* 343:45–64.

Avner, Uzi. 2001. "Sacred Stones in the Desert." *BAR* 27:30–41.

Bietak, Manfred. 1997. "The Center of Hyksos Rule: Avaris (Tell el-Dabʿa)." Pages 89–139 in *The Hyksos: New Historical and Archaeological Perspectives*. Edited by Eliezer D. Oren. Philadelphia: University Museum, University of Pennsylvania.

Blockman, Noga, and Iris Groman-Yeroslavski. 2006. "The Early Bronze Age Flint Assemblage." Pages 315–42 in *Megiddo IV: The 1998–2002 Seasons*. Edited by Israel Finkelstein, David Ussishkin, and Baruch Halpern. Tel Aviv: Emery and Claire Yass Publications in Archaeology.

Brody, Aaron J. 1998. *"Each Man Cried out to His God": The Specialized Religion of Canaanite and Phoenician Seafarers*. Atlanta: Scholars Press.

Burke, Aaron. 2014a. "Entanglement, the Amorite Koiné, and Amorite Cultures in the Levant." *ARAM* 26:357–73.

———. 2014b. "Introduction to the Middle Bronze Age: Themes and Developments." Pages 403–13 in *The Oxford Handbook of the Archaeology of the Levant: c. 8000–332 BCE*. Edited by Margreet L. Steiner and Ann E. Killebrew. Oxford: Oxford University Press.

Campbell, Edward. 2002. *Shechem III*. Vol. I: *Text*. Boston: American Schools of Oriental Research.

Castel, Corinne. 2010. "The First Temples in antis: The Sanctuary of Tell Al-Rawda in the Context of 3rd Millennium Syria." Pages 123–64 in *Kulturlandschaft Syrien: Zentrum und Peripherie; Festschrift für Jan-Waalke Meyer*. Edited by Jörg Becker, Ralph Hempelmann, and Ellen Rehm. AOAT 371 Münster: Ugarit-Verlag.

Cohen, Susan L. 2009. "Continuities and Discontinuities: A Reexamination of the Intermediate Bronze Age-Middle Bronze Age Transition in Canaan." *BASOR* 354:1–13.

———. 2016. *Peripheral Concerns: Urban Development in the Bronze Age Southern Levant*. Sheffield: Equinox.

Cohen, Yoram. 2019. "Cuneiform Writing in Bronze Age Canaan." Pages 245–64 in *The Social Archaeology of the Levant: From Prehistory to the Present*. Edited by Assaf Yasur-Landau, Eric H. Cline, and Yorke Rowan. Cambridge: Cambridge University Press.

Dothan, M. 1981. "Sanctuaries along the Coast of Canaan in the MB Period: Nahariya." Pages 74–81 in *Temples and High Places in Biblical Times: Proceedings of the Colloquium in Honor of the Centennial of Hebrew Union College-Jewish Institute of Religion, Jerusalem, 14–16 March 1977*. Edited by A. Biran. Jerusalem: Hebrew Union College.

Dunayevsky, Immanuel, and Aharon Kempinski. 1973. "The Megiddo Temples." *ZDPV* 89:161–87.

Eisenberg, Emmanuel. 1977. "The Temples at Tell Kittan." *BA* 40:77–81.

Epstein, Claire. 1965. "An Interpretation of the Megiddo Sacred Area during Middle Bronze Age II." *IEJ* 15:204–21.

Finkelstein, Israel, and David Ussishkin. 2000. "Area J." Pages 25–74 in *Megiddo III: The 1992–1996 Seasons*, vol. 1. Edited by Israel Finkelstein, David Ussishkin, and Baruch Halpern. Tel Aviv: Emery and Claire Yass Publications in Archaeology.

Finkelstein, Israel, David Ussishkin, and Baruch Halpern. 2006. "Archaeological and Historical Conclusions." Pages 843–59 in *Megiddo IV: The 1998–2002 Seasons*. Edited by Israel Finkelstein, David Ussishkin, and Baruch Halpern. Tel Aviv: Emery and Claire Yass Publications in Archaeology.

Gerstenblith, Patty. 1983. *The Levant at the Beginning of the Middle Bronze Age*. Philadelphia: American Schools of Oriental Research.

Gophna, Ram, and Etan Ayalon. 2004. "Tel 'Ashir: An Open Cult Site of the Intermediate Bronze Age on the Bank of the Poleg Stream." *IEJ* 54:154–73.

Greenberg, Raphael. 2002. *Early Urbanizations in the Levant*. London: Leicester University Press.

Herzog, Ze'ev. 1997. *Archaeology of the City: Urban Planning in Ancient Israel and Its Social Implications*. Tel Aviv: Emery and Claire Yass Publications in Archaeology.

Ilan, David. 1992. "A Middle Bronze Age Offering Deposit from Tel Dan and the Politics of Cultic Gifting." *TA* 19:247–66.

———. 1995. "The Dawn of Internationalism—The Middle Bronze Age." Pages 297–319 in *The Archaeology of Society in the Holy Land*. Edited by Thomas E. Levy. New York: Facts on File.

———. 2018. "A 'Migdal' Temple from the Middle Bronze Age at Tel Dan?" Pages 25–37 in *Eretz Israel, Lawrence E. Stager Volume*. Edited by Joseph Aviram, Amnon Ben-Tor, and Jodi Magness. Eretz Israel 33. Jerusalem: Israel Exploration Society (Hebrew).

Ilan, Ornit, and Yuval Goren. 2003. "The Egyptianized Pottery Vessels of Early Bronze Age Megiddo." *TA* 30:42–53.

Keel, Othmar, and Christoph Uehlinger. 1998. *Gods, Goddesses and Images of God in Ancient Israel*. Minneapolis: Fortress.

Keinan, Adi. 2007. "The Megiddo Picture Pavement: Evidence for Egyptian Presence in Northern Israel during Early Bronze Age I." MA thesis, Tel Aviv University (Hebrew).

Kempinski, Aharon. 1989. *Megiddo, A City-State and Royal Center in North Israel*. Munich: Beck.

———. 1992. "The Middle Bronze Age." Pages 159–210 in *The Archaeology of Ancient Israel*. Edited by Amnon Ben-Tor. New Haven: Yale University Press.

Kislev, M., M. Artzy, and E. Marcus. 1993. "Import of an Aegean Food Plant to a Middle Bronze IIA Coastal Site in Israel." *Levant* 25:145–54, https://doi.org/10.1179/lev.1993.25.1.145.

Kohlmeyer, Kay. 2012. "Der Tempel des Wettergottes von Aleppo: Baugeschichte und Bautyp, räumliche Bezüge, Inventar und Bildliche Ausstattung." Pages 55–78 in *Temple Building and Temple Cult: Architecture and Cultic Paraphernalia of Temples in the Levant (2.–1. Mill. B.C.E.).* Edited by Jens Kamlah. Wiesbaden: Harrassowitz.

Loud, Gordon. 1948. *Megiddo II: Seasons of 1935–39; Text.* Chicago: University of Chicago.

Lupack, Susan. 2010. "Minoan Religion." Pages 251–62 in *The Oxford Handbook of the Bronze Age Aegean (ca. 3000-1000 BC).* Edited by Eric H. Cline.. Oxford: Oxford University Press.

Marchetti, Nicolò, and Lorenzo Nigro. 1997. "Cultic Activities in the Sacred Area of Ishtar at Ebla during the Old Syrian Period: The Favissa F.5327 and F.5238." *JCS* 49:1–44.

Marcus, Ezra. 1991. "Tel Nami: A Study of a Middle Bronze IIA Period Coastal Settlement." MA thesis, University of Haifa.

———. 1998. "Maritime Trade in the Southern Levant from Earliest Times through the Middle Bronze IIa Period." PhD diss., University of Oxford.

Margueron, Jean-Claude. 2004. *Mari: Métropole de l'Euphrate au IIIe et au début du IIe millénaire av J.-C.* Paris: Picard.

Matthiae, Paolo. 1980. *Ebla: An Empire Discovered.* Garden City, NY: Doubleday.

———. 1997. "Ebla and Syria in the Middle Bronze Age." Pages 279–314 in *The Hyksos: New Historical and Archaeological Perspectives.* Edited by Eliezer D. Oren. Philadelphia: University of Pennsylvania Museum.

———. 2007. "Nouvelles fouilles à Ébla en 2006: Le temple du rocher et ses successeurs protosyriens et paléosyriens (Communication)." *CRAI* 2007:481–525.

———. 2010. "Excavations at Ebla 2006–2007." Pages 3–26 in *Proceedings of the VIth International Congress on the Archaeology of the Ancient Near East, Rome 5–10 May 2008.* Wiesbaden: Harrassowitz.

Mazar, Amihai. 1992. "Temples of the Middle and Late Bronze Age and the Iron Age." Pages 161–87 in *The Architecture of Ancient Israel from the Prehistoric to the Persian Periods.* Edited by Ronnie Reich and Aharon Kempinski. Jerusalem: Israel Exploration Society.

Mazar, Amihai, Pierre de Miroschedji, and Naomi Porat. 1996. "Hartuv, An Aspect of the Early Bronze I Culture of Southern Israel." *BASOR* 302:1–40.

Mazar, Benjamin. 1968. "The Middle Bronze Age in Palestine." *IEJ* 18:65–97.

Metzger, Martin. 2012. *Kamid el-Loz. 17: Die Mittelbronzezeitlichen Tempelanlagen T4 und T5.* Bonn: Habelt.

Naeh, L. 2012. כלים זעירים ושבעתנים במקדש הברונזה התיכונה בנהריה תפקידים ומשמעותם לאור פולח מקומם של כלים זעירים ומורכבים בהקשרי (The Role and Importance of the Miniature Pottery Vessels in Nahariya: A Middle Bronze Age Temple in Northern Israel). MA thesis, The Hebrew University.

Nakhai, Beth Alpert. 1993. "Religion in Canaan and Israel: An Archaeological Perspective." PhD diss., The University of Arizona.

Negbi, Ora. 1976. *Canaanite Gods in Metal: An Archaeological Study of Ancient Syro-Palestinian Figurines.* Tel Aviv: Institute of Archaeology.

Niemeier, B. and Niemeier, W.-D. 2002. "The Frescoes in the Middle Bronze Age Palace." Pages 254–85 in *Tel Kabri: The 1986–1993 Excavation Seasons.* Edited by Aharon Kempinski, Na'ama Scheftelowitz, and Ronit Oren. Tel Aviv: Emery and Claire Yass Publications in Archaeology.

Nigro, Lorenzo. 1994. "The Nordburg of Megiddo: A New Reconstruction on the Basis of Schumacher's Plan." *BASOR* 293:15–29.

Philip, Graham. 1988. "Hoards of the Early and Middle Bronze Ages in the Levant." *World Archaeology* 20:190–208.

Regev, Johanna, Israel Finkelstein, Matthew J. Adams, and Elisabetta Boaretto. 2014. "Wiggle-Matched ^{14}C Chronology of Early Bronze Megiddo and the Synchronization of Egyptian and Levantine Chronologies." *Ä&L* 24:241–64.

Schaeffer, Claude F. A. 1935. "Les fouilles de Ras Shamra-Ugarit. Sixième campagne (Printemps 1934). Rapport sommaire." *Syria* 16:141–76.

Schloen, J. David. 2001. *The House of the Father as Fact and Symbol: Patrimonialism in Ugarit and the Ancient Near East.* Studies in the Archaeology and History of the Levant 2. Winona Lake, IN: Eisenbrauns.

Sellin, Ernst. 1926. "Die Ausgrabung von Sichem: Kurze vorläufige Mitteilung über die Arbeit im Sommer 1926." *ZDPV* 49:304–20.

Susnow, Matthew. 2019. "The Practice of Cult within Canaanite Temples: Space, Activities and Religious Ideologies." PhD diss., University of Haifa.

Ussishkin, David. 2015. "The Sacred Area of Early Bronze Megiddo: History and Interpretation." *BASOR* 373:69–104.

Woolley, Leonard. 1955. *Alalakh: An Account of the Excavations at Tell Atchana in the Hatay, 1937–1949.* London: Society of Antiquaries.

Wright, G. R. H. 1985. *Ancient Building in South Syria and Palestine*, vol. 1. Leiden: Brill.

Yasur-Landau, Assaf. 2011. "'The Kingdom Is His Brick Mould and the Dynasty Is His Wall': The Impact of Urbanization on Middle Bronze Age Households in the Southern Levant." Pages 55–84 in *Household Archaeology in Ancient Israel and Beyond.* Edited by Assaf Yasur-Landau, Jennie Ebeling, and Laura B. Mazow. CHANE 50. Leiden: Brill.

———. 2015. "From Byblos to Vapheio: Fenestrated Axes between the Aegean and the Levant." *BASOR* 373:139–50.

———. 2019. "The Middle Bronze Age Canaanite City as a Domesticating Apparatus." Pages 224–44 in *The Social Archaeology of the Levant: From Prehistory to the Present.* Edited by Assaf Yasur-Landau, Eric H. Cline, and Yorke Rowan. Cambridge: Cambridge University Press.

Yasur-Landau, Assaf, Eric H. Cline, Nurith Goshen, Nimrod Marom, and Inbal Samet. 2012. "An MB II Orthostat Building at Tel Kabri, Israel." *BASOR* 367:1–29.

Ziffer, Irit M. 1990. *At That Time the Canaanites Were in the Land.* Tel Aviv: The Land of Israel Museum (Hebrew).

PART THREE

BEYOND THE VALLEY

WOMEN REGULATE THEIR FERTILITY:
PROACTIVE AND REACTIVE ASPECTS

ATHALYA BRENNER-IDAN

Abstract: In modern Western cultures, the objection to female self-regulated reproduction, in whatever form, proactive or reactive, is claimed to be religiously and divinely ordained, certainly so in orthodox Judaism and orthodox Christianity. Furthermore, prioritizing the life of a fetus over its mother is an innovation compared to the ancient sources. It is therefore worth noting once again that the Hebrew Bible does not contain explicit prohibitions against either female or male birth control. It does, nevertheless, obliterate details of current practices, and their being largely a matter of female traditions; only traces remain. It is therefore also worth noting that women of the biblical worlds, like other women of antiquity, did understand the need for regulating their own reproduction, and were prepared and able to step out of the "Be Fruitful and Multiply" propaganda that could cost them their lives. And this, as well as the glory of parenthood, should be remembered.

Keywords: birth control, fertility; miscarriage, abortion, gynecological knowledge, Exodus 22, Numbers 5, Ezekiel 13, Ezekiel 16

That women should have control over their fertility seems obvious, does it not? That women have always, but always, cared about that control cannot be disputed. That they were always looking for ways to enhance fertility as well as to curb it, as the timely situation may be, is common-sense. It is reasonable to assume that those women who could, who were allowed to implicitly if not always explicitly by the societies they lived in to do so, always strove to exercise control in this regard. However, it can also not be disputed that religion and religious texts have regularly diminished the legitimacy of descriptions of women's agency in such matters, or of their judgment. And the Hebrew Bible is no exception. This basic women's right is still questioned, in the United States as well as in other western countries (Ireland is a recent exception, anno 2019!), as men still limit and control women's fertility or [choice of] lack thereof, ostensibly in the name of religion; so I feel that the subject should be discussed again, and again, at this time.

Some Assumptions

Birth control and abortion/planned miscarriage[1] are two sides of the same coin: the
one more proactive, the other more reactive. Attitudes to both hang on a society's fertility, food resources, strength, and general political condition. A rule of thumb: a society that feels its continuity is threatened would either advertise fertility as a normative
wished-for mode for women (and men), and/or will malign and suppress knowledge
and practice of either gender's birth control (and here I am not talking about twentieth-
century China or India). The societal need will be translated into religious instruction
("Be fruitful and multiply"!) and fetal viability may be moved backward, even to the
moment of conception. In a society such as this, which by and large views itself under
some kind of siege, women's fertility and life will not be controlled by them themselves.
It would be controlled by the real or imagined need to produce, thus literally keeping
their society alive at a great price to their own lives.

What Does the Hebrew Bible "Say"?

Much can be gleaned from the Hebrew Bible about the need for women to be fertile,
to give birth to viable children (especially sons), and about their presumed wish to become mothers. Not much can be gleaned from the Hebrew Bible about pregnancy termination and how women felt about it. However, some information about this can be
agreed upon by readers, even if their readerly position is sympathetic to the presumed
need of "biblical women" to value fecundity above all.

   Deliberate termination of unwanted pregnancy? Can this be done? Not implicitly,
in the Hebrew Bible, as if this was not within the gynecological knowledge of biblical
times. But this is not correct. I would think, together with many commentators on the
sôṭâh section (Num 5:12–28) that the sentence, "her belly shall distend and her thigh
shall sag" (v. 27; JPS 1985) after drinking the prescribed potion, does indicate an externally induced (by the officiating priest) abortion or miscarriage, if the woman has had
an illicit affair and has become pregnant by it. If this is the correct understanding, the
miscarriage/abortion is both proof of the woman's behavior, and punishment for it. In
this case, the line between abortion and miscarriage is fluid and somewhat blurred, for
the ceremony seems—albeit mysteriously so—to induce a deliberate termination of a
suspected illicit pregnancy.[2]

---

1. For the purpose of the present discussion, "abortion" will serve as an intended self-induced termination of pregnancy, whereas "miscarriage" will designate an accidental—externally induced—termination.

2. It is worth noting that in ancient rabbinic sources the punishment was changed into the accused
woman's dramatic public death, thus obliterating all possibilities of a public abortion/miscarriage (see
m. Soṭ. 3.4–5). The rabbis were perhaps averse to displays of public termination with a mythic element,
or to the sight of a woman giving (untimely) birth in public; or they disliked the thought that a human

Violent miscarriages? Yes. They did occur, even within regulated society. Damaged fetuses configure in Exod 21:22–24:

> When men fight, and one of them pushes a pregnant woman and a miscarriage results, but no other damage ensues, the one responsible shall be fined according as the woman's husband may exact from him, the payment to be based on reckoning. But if other damage ensues, the penalty shall be life for life, eye for eye, tooth for tooth, hand for hand, foot for foot, burn for burn, wound for wound, bruise for bruise (*JPS* 1985).

This is not a literal translation. Here is another try:

> When people who are fighting injure a pregnant woman so that there is a miscarriage, and yet no further harm follows, the one responsible shall be fined what the woman's husband demands, paying as much as the judges determine. If any harm follows, then you shall give life for life, eye for eye, tooth for tooth, hand for hand, foot for foot, burn for burn, wound for wound, stripe for stripe (*NRSV*).

The MT text translates it more precisely:

> If men fight, and they cause a pregnant woman to fall, and her children come out, and there will be no disaster, he [the one responsible] will pay as demanded by the woman's husband, according to criminal law. If there is a disaster... [then the principle of lex talionis is invoked]

The Hebrew text is not clear: what here is the "disaster" (Heb. *'āsôn*)—is it a miscarriage (death of fetuses), or the woman's death, or both, since the "disaster" is mentioned twice, and with different punishment for the perpetrator(s)? The *JPS* translation here obscures the two possible consequences; commentators, as well as medieval Jewish commentators, see two different cases here;[3] and the standard Aramaic Targum (Onqelos) makes it clear that the correct understanding of disaster here is "death," of either the fetus[es] or the woman. Another problem is whether the lex talionis principle is to be applied literally, as, for example, in other ancient Near Eastern cultures and Islam, or substituted by fines.[4]

---

messenger, even a cultic official, could do god's work. At any rate, the Mishna states that the ritual was discontinued after the destruction of Jerusalem's Second Temple, and with a peculiar reason: there were too many fornicators to enact the law (9.9). Since it is not clear whether it was ever enacted, this is a moot point; and we are left with a graphic miscarriage/abortion image in the biblical text. On Mishna Soṭah in general see Rosen Zvi 2012 and the copious literature mentioned there.

   3. See for instance Cassuto 1967: 273–75; Childs 1974 for this verse; also Rashi and other medieval Jewish commentators who wrestle with the different punishments for the two "disasters."

   4. Cassuto 1967: 276–77; b. Bab. Qam. 83a–84b; Rashi for the same verses; also Ibn Ezra, referencing Sa'adia Gaon and other Jewish sages.

Fertility propaganda for women abounds, which is worth mentioning again and again since it appears as a matter of natural course; and woman figures are presented as always wishing for sons, not simply "children."

No male is ever directly presented as infertile or sterile; only women are.

Females are midwives. This is mentioned distinctly in Exod 1:15–22 (the Hebrew midwives in Egypt) and implicitly in the case of the nameless daughter-in-law of Eli, Phinehas's wife, who dies while giving birth (the women attending her, 1 Sam 4:20) and the women present at Ruth's giving birth (Ruth 4:13–17).

Females know nothing about birth prevention; males do. So in the Onan episode, Gen 38; Onan refrains from fertile intercourse by resorting to coitus interruptus. Revisiting that chapter, and pondering the reason why Yhwh kills Onan, it is quite clear that not the act per se—a basic although not foolproof act of birth control—is the problem, but Onan's refusal to provide "seed" (offspring) for his dead brother's name. A question of male line inheritance no doubt.

Further, and I've written about it at some length (e.g., Brenner 1983), in the Song of Songs (ch. 4) a long list of aromatics and perfumes cited by a male lover finally seduces his female lover to have sex with him. As is well known, sexual contact in the Song somehow doesn't lead to pregnancy, wanted or otherwise. It is therefore logical that what the male is actually saying is, we can prevent pregnancy by using the substances I cite. And, as is well known, the same plants form many preparations and still do today: from spices to aromatics to medicine and beyond.

Furthermore, in postbiblical literature, there's much rabbinic (male) knowledge about both birth prevention and abortion. Lamech is famously controlling the fertility of his two wives by letting them have a "drink of sterility" (in Hebrew, literally: "a cup of barrenness") in turn, so that one produces and one can remain sexually active at any given time (m. Gen. Rab. 23:2). Such preparations are also available for men. Mechanical means such as cotton wads for females are mentioned. Abortion is recommended for cases of יוצא דופן, extra-uterine pregnancy, especially when the mother's life is threatened. The approach is, save her first; the fetus's life is secondary to the mother's, for obvious reasons.

Ultimately, as the Bible insists, the Hebrew god is the giver of pregnancy: as in the cases of Sarah (Gen 18), Rachel (Gen 30:1), Samson's nameless mother (Judg 13), Ruth (Ruth 4:13), and more.

This is a sketchy picture because the material is sketchy. Also, since most Bible readers for many centuries are under the spell of "Be fruitful and multiply," as are biblical writers, a discussion of these knowledge traces is important.

Additional Considerations

Some additional considerations can be added to these traces. If you have knowledge about antifertility drugs, you probably do also about inducing fertility (mandrake root, *duda'im*, Rachel and Leah, Gen 30). Much like other medications until today, for instance in the case of vaccinations, the two are two sides of the same coin in the sense that the same substances, in different quantities/proportion or mixtures, can be used for opposite purposes. It stands to reason that whoever knows about promoting pregnancy by chemical (mostly plant, in the ancient worlds) agents will know how to prevent it. And here, in contradistinction to the biblical silence, women's knowledge must have been broader than men's.

As stated, in the Bible birth-assisting personnel are presented exclusively as women, midwives. There are no male birth-assistants: although, it must be recognized, whoever composed the passage about the abandoned female newborn in Ezek 16:1–7, and "he" speaks in the first-person singular masculine mode, knew quite a lot about antenatal baby care (and we shall return to this passage later). I feel this needs emphasis in today's culture, where gynecology developed as a majority-male profession (and this is fast changing). If you have knowledge about assisting birth, as for instance the midwives in Egypt do (Exod 1), you probably also have knowledge about preventing or aborting it: gynecological knowledge exists on a continuous spectrum. Once more, as in other cultures and other times, it seems that such female knowledge is either suppressed or else attributed to males.

Why Does This Happen?

Some of the answers as to the reasons, or hints thereof, are in the descriptions just given. One important clue is the emphasis on women's purported wish for sons rather than children, which shows societal rather than biological motivation for motherhood. The social and physical situation indeed dictated proliferation of birth if social survival as a whole was to be achieved on any scale. Life expectancy for males and especially for females was extremely low: the personal price for females was the greater burden, not to mention newborn and young children's mortality. The need for birth propaganda is understandable. However, it should not blind us to the fact that women suffered bodily because of it, that their sexuality was controlled much more than men's because of this societal need. There is an existential tension here, a truly fatal one, between society's continuation as a whole and women's relative longevity and well being. And it should be admitted that any attempt to haze knowledge of birth control/pregnancy termination, especially women's knowledge in this regard, is not moral or religious or ideological in origin but socioeconomic. So in the Hebrew Bible, at any rate (see Guillaume 2015).

It should be emphasized that there is no lack of knowledge about birth control, proactive and reactive, in other cultures of the southern Levant before our era and beyond. This is borne out by written texts of varying provenance from ancient Egypt, Mesopotamia, Greece, and Rome. The medical preparations prescribed are mostly of plant origin; they appear in medical literature or literature about medicine. Their knowledge is once again attributed to male practitioners (see Brenner 1997: 52–89).

Further Discussion

Centuries of Bible exegesis and interpretation have complied with biblical propaganda by idealizing the figure of the Mother. Many a Bible feminist critic has collaborated generously with and even appropriated this idealized picture of biblical desire for motherhood as their own: after all, the ability to conceive and give birth is uniquely female/feminine. I have no quarrel with this tendency: motherhood is great, but perhaps not equally for all and at all times and circumstances. And I do want to point out the facts, easily obscured by pro-motherhood propaganda, that so-called "pro-life" policies might have meant early death for its ancient female adherents; and that female birth control, although almost completely eradicated [by males?] from the Hebrew Bible, must have been practiced in ancient Israel—as in several other ancient cultures of the southern Levant. It appears impossible that whereas contraception and other antifertility measures were known and practiced all around ancient Israel and in early Judaism, and in earlier as well as later times, they were totally unknown in "ancient Israel" itself. The knowledge, part of which was certainly women's knowledge, was available but never explicitly disclosed in biblical literature.

An accidental omission of such data from the Bible is possible but not plausible, in the light of biblical procreation ideologies. The existence of Jewish sources, scanty as they are, is another pointer in this direction: even there, contraception and antifertility are generally not discussed for their own sake but as incidental to other superordinate concerns. Finally, the association of antifertility as well as fertility-advancing knowledge with women might have contributed to its neglect (at best) or suppression (at worst). Female oral traditions, transmitted from mother to daughter in guild fashion, are known from other fields of women's knowledge, such as composing and performing lament (Jer 9:16–20, Lamentations). No reason to deny it in this connection too, within the framework of female experience and self-help.

It could have been expected that, if biblical writers/compilers—especially of the law codes—knew about [female] contraception but objected to it in principle, they would have prohibited it explicitly by formulating laws against it. In other words, are we here faced with author ignorance, disinterest, indifference, or suppression? Ignorance can be ruled out, I think. So can disinterest and indifference, as evidenced by procreation ideologies. It is perhaps relevant to re-remember at this point that most of the biblical materials were authored, compiled, preserved, transmitted, and later studied by males and for males, the true members of the community construct. "F" (female/feminine) voices were largely edited out or muted out of it. If birth control was felt as also in other cultures in general, including later Judaic sources, to fall primarily within the province of women's interest and praxis, then the silence about it fits in with other silences on women's lives. At any rate, as in the case of other F voices in biblical literature, only traces of birth control practices can be found. It remained for postbiblical Judaic sources, as we have seen, to acknowledge female (and male) contraceptive measures incidentally to other concerns.

And yet, the tracing of contraception information in "biblical Israel" might prove helpful not only for the reconstruction of a segment of ancient realia. It might also and simultaneously contribute to the interpretation of some biblical texts. Therefore, by way of attempting to expand our understanding, I would like to mention two texts on female involvement in some kind of performing magic.

Exodus 22:17 (Eng. 18): A Strange Collection

Magicians and sorcerers of both genders are acknowledged in the Hebrew Bible, and their practices forbidden (if at times taken over by the Priests). However, females are singled out in Exod 22:17 [Eng. 18]:

מכשפה לא תחיה

"You shall not tolerate a sorceress," *JPS 1985*;

"You shall not permit a female sorcerer to live," *NRSV*.

This verse certainly appears in an immediate textual context of forbidden sexual behavior: it is inserted in between a prescription for forced marriage between a male seducer and a seduced virgin, or payment to the father (vv. 15–16); and death punishment for having sex with an animal (the next verse). Here is the text of vv. 15–18 (16–19):

> 15 (16) When a man seduces a virgin who is not engaged to be married, and lies with her, he shall give the bride-price for her and make her his wife. But if her father refuses to give her to him, he shall pay an amount equal to the bride-price for virgins.
> 17 (18) You shall not permit a female sorcerer to live.
> 18 (19) Whoever lies[5] with an animal shall be put to death.

So, if we ask ourselves, what does the female sorcerer do here, what is her transgression out of all the available practices? We usually assume, in such cases of apparent loose connection, that some principle of association was brought to bear on the arrangement of individual "laws" one after the other. The association between the virgin seduction and bestiality is clear enough: illicit sex; but this association seems to jump a verse. The association between the recommended fate of the female sorcerer and the

---

5. The translation obliterates the grammatical form of the Hebrew: the verb translated "lies" (Heb. שכב) is grammatically a singular masculine participle, hence the proper translation here would be: "He who lies"... when both genders are prohibited from practicing sex with animals (properly speaking domestic animals, בהמה), this is stated by including both males and females—as in Lev 18:23 and 20:15–20. In the latter text, as in Exod 22, the punishment is death for both human and animal.

animal-lover is clear too: the death sentence. But what is the association between the male seducer and the female sorcerer that seems to disturb the flow to the last verse?

It seems to me that we are directed by the word context to assume two things: one, that the female sorcerer exercises power in the sex[6] realm; and two, that it is forbidden power. Like many views of magic in the Hebrew Bible, it is officially condemned because it is in competition with Yhwh's power. Remember? It is Yhwh who opens and shuts wombs. And this leads us to the next passage.

Ezekiel 13:17–21

... set your face against the daughters of your people, who prophesy out of their own imagination; prophesy against them, and say, Thus says the Lord God: *Woe to the women who sew bands on all wrists, and make veils for the heads of persons of every height, in the hunt for human lives!* Will you hunt down lives among my people, and maintain your own lives? You have profaned me among my people for handfuls of barley and for pieces of bread, *putting to death persons who should not die and keeping alive persons who should not live,* by your lies to my people, who listen to lies. Therefore thus says the Lord God: I am against your bands with which you hunt lives; I will tear them from your arms, and let the lives go free, the lives that you hunt down like birds. I will tear off your veils, and save my people from your hands; they shall no longer be prey in your hands; and you shall know that I am the Lord (*NRSV*, italics mine).

This passage is against females "prophesying," but it is very different from the previous verses against males "prophesying" (1–16). The males are accused of unauthorized prophecies, including political prophecies and lies. Those men talk and try to influence their audience.

However, the accusations against the women are different from those against their male counterparts, although the title given to their action is similar. They seem to be using magical aids of sorts. What sorts, and for what purposes? Most commentators (see recently Bowen 2010 and Joyce 2007 in their commentaries on the passage) agree that matters of life and death (נפשות) are involved. Once again: from the textual speaker's viewpoint, an irrelevant competition with Yhwh. But how?

Let us advance the notion that these female practitioners indeed deal with life and death matters—not by way of foretelling or influencing such matters for adults, but for preborn. They determine fates. Let us also remember that, if the same author is responsible for both chapters 13 and 16 in the book named Ezekiel, he (for so he introduces

---

6. I would assume here that both the seduction of a virgin and bestiality were considered abhorrent for reasons of theoretically producing mongrel offspring, not necessarily for moral reasons. Such a mongrel offspring will not be a proper *imago dei*!

himself) knows a great deal on birth and after-birth care. So, he will know what women do about birth-and birth control.

What if we read the passage differently, as describing such women's *actions* rather than talk? They are paid (unlike their male counterparts), which means that they are doing a job. They're dealing with life and death—of fetuses and newborn, and being paid for that? What if the "bands on the wrists" are the bands or thread placed on new-born arms for identification, a practice that continues today and is certainly present in biblical literature (a crimson band or thread placed by the midwife on Zerah's arm at birth, Gen 38:27–30)? What if the "veils" mentioned are simply swashes of material to cover the cleaned-up baby, a practice the author of ch. 16 is familiar with, a blanket to warm the newborn—or a piece of cloth to hide an aborted fetus?

Perhaps. To the best of my knowledge, no satisfactory explanation has been of-fered so far to "Ezekiel's" rage in this passage, or to the identity or functionality of the accused women's tools of trade as magical tools. The advantage of the present interpre-tation might be the restoration of the other side of midwifery—birth control by abor-tion—to the same female practitioners who assist life into the world, thus also adding to our knowledge of the scanty catalogue of female professions traditionally allowed in biblical times. And, of course, this is another interpretation for a difficult text that cer-tainly requires more research. And reading ch. 16 again in this light: isn't the metaphor-ical, abandoned female infant rescued by Ezekiel's god and taken care of in precisely the manner those condemned "prophesying" women should have done, properly cleaned and wrapped up, a fitting counterpoint to their attempt to assume divine responsibility? A pity, though, that Yhwh is disappointed in the orphan he rescues later on.

This is perhaps a good time to return to the *sôṭâh* ritual (Num 5). As it seems, in the biblical text a woman guilty of fornication will be pregnant; the concoction the priest makes her drink will cause termination of pregnancy, if she is guilty. Clearly, the contents of the "cursed water" includes no natural abortifacient; the location, and the holy earth, will do the job. This will be a case of Yhwh intervening—by priestly proxy—directly in the guilty woman's womb: he interferes with women's wombs regu-larly, for better or for worse. His proxy has no medical knowledge in this case and no power, just a mission of faith. Hence he, the male priest, is allowed to perform a non-medical abortion, or cause a miscarriage if you wish. The "prophesying" women, also cultic personnel, whose methods are different, are denied legitimate basis for their acts and knowledge by the claim that they do not serve Yhwh's mission or purpose. One thing, however, is not denied, and is perhaps the reason for Ezekiel's angry rant: they seem to be successful in their profession.

By Way of Summary

In contemporaneous Western cultures the objection to female self-regulated reproduc-tion, in whatever form, proactive or reactive, is claimed to be religiously and divinely ordained: certainly so in orthodox Judaism and in orthodox Christianity. Furthermore, prioritizing the life of a fetus over its mother is certainly an innovation, compared to the ancient sources. Men tend to deny women the right to regulate their productivity, anchoring that denial in the Sacred. The women who suffer most are the devout, and the poor; they are firmly placed in an inferior, even deadly, personal place.

By way of detour let me say that in Islam, although contraception and abortion are not encouraged, they are not forbidden in the Qur'an explicitly, and not totally forbidden beyond it. Even Shi'a Islam is, ironically, perhaps more lenient here that present-day American Evangelicals: in 2004 Iran accepted as law that abortion in case of maternal risk is allowed up to 120 days of pregnancy. But I digress here.

It is therefore worth noting, once again. The Hebrew Bible does not contain explicit prohibitions against either female or male birth control. It does, nevertheless, obliterate details of current practices, and their being largely a matter of female traditions. Only traces remain.

My wish, in writing this piece, is to illustrate that women always have known how to cope medically with their situation as vessels for societal survival, more or less successfully; that pious claims for divine ordinance did hang on contemporaneous patriarchal needs and the social needs of a bygone age, but are not to be found explicitly in the Hebrew Bible. Furthermore, such claims are irrelevant to a world where population explosion threatens to deplete global resources, not to buttress them; and that society should applaud contraception and the right to abortion, when justified and wished for by women, rather than find excuses for making them unattainable. Finally, and foremost from my viewpoint: it seems that women of the biblical worlds, like other women of antiquity, did understand the need for regulating their own reproduction, and were prepared and able to step out of the "Be Fruitful and Multiply" command that could cost them their lives. And this, as well as the glory of parenthood, should be remembered.

Let us state the obvious, once more. Medical research and knowledge are gendered, and have always been so, from three viewpoints: that of the researchers, that of the practitioners, and that of the ones helped or left by the wayside. Knowledge is power; the withholding of knowledge, as well as the withholding of available practice, is a matter of social dominance or the strife for it. It is not by chance that birth control is medically available for women, but then socially denied to them because of religious claims; it is not by chance that birth control for males lags behind. This is a social, not a divine or medical, matter.

And finally. Savina Teubal published three books, two of which are *Sarah the Priestess* (1984) and *Hagar the Egyptian* (1990). Teubal discusses the possibility that Sarah, at least, regulated her own fertility and delayed having children (until nearly too late) because of her function as a priestess—as did, probably, other ancient Near Eastern priestesses, allowed to marry but not to have children while on the job. This implies, once more, professional female knowledge about contraception and birth and abortion. Surely, if correct or even just viable, this could be a "pro-choice" model from the Hebrew Bible, rather than using the good book as a "pro-life" manifesto.

A Personal Note to Norma

Dear Norma,

In 2015 you and Jennie Ebeling gave me a lovely tour of the Jezreel dig you co-directed, generously spending time and effort. It was lovely to see the dig, to realize how well it was organized, to see female power at work. As we all know, a dig run by woman scholars is a rare find. It was especially meaningful to me since, as you know, I was a member of Kibbutz Jezreel a long time ago and seldom go back there. This is where I came fresh out of high school, learned that birth control was unofficially available, got married, and then left for other things. So I thought of writing for you about this topic. And not only because of that, but mainly because you are a real warrior for ethical causes, for women and beyond. So here's to you, to your scholarship and humanity, and—not least—your wonderful sense of personal style. A small tribute from the heart.

References

Bowen, Nancy R. 2010. *Ezekiel*. Abingdon Old Testament Commentaries. Nashville: Abingdon.
Brenner, Athalya. 1983. "Aromatics and Perfumes in the Song of Songs." *JSOT* 25:75–81.
———. 1997. *The Intercourse of Knowledge: On Gendering Desire and 'Sexuality' in the Hebrew Bible*. Leiden: Brill.
Cassuto, Umberto. 1967. *A Commentary on the Book of Exodus*. Translated by I. Abrahams. Jerusalem: Magness (originally in Hebrew, 1951).
Childs, Brevard. S. 1974. *The Book of Exodus: A Critical, Theological Commentary*. Philadelphia: Westminster.
Guillaume, Philippe. 2015. "פְּרוּ וּרְבוּ and the Seventh Year: Complementary Strategies for the Economic Recovery of Depopulated Yehud." Pages 123–50 in *The Economy of Ancient Judah in Its Historical Context*. Edited by Maxwell L. Miller, Ehud Ben Zvi, and Gary N. Knoppers. Winona Lake, IN: Eisenbrauns.
Joyce, Paul M. 2007. *Ezekiel: A Commentary*. London: T&T Clark.
Rosen Zvi, Y. 2012. *The Mishnaic Sotah Ritual: Temple, Gender and Midrash*. Leiden: Brill.
Teubal, Savina J. 1984. *Sarah the Priestess: The First Matriarch of Genesis*. Athens, OH: Swallow.
———. 1990. *Hagar the Egyptian: The Lost Tradition of the Matriarchs*. San Francisco: HarperSanFrancisco.

Qumran in the Iron Age, with Cross-Temporal Reflections on the Hasmonean and Early Roman Periods

Joan E. Taylor and Shimon Gibson

Abstract: While the site of Qumran has been of great interest in connection with the period relating to the depositing of the Dead Sea Scrolls in nearby caves, with the later periods of occupation at the site heavily prioritized, the earlier Iron Age II period of occupation (seventh–sixth centuries BCE) has been relatively neglected. In this paper, the existing evidence for the Iron Age II settlement of Qumran is dealt with thoroughly. The authors propose that in this period Qumran consisted of a rectangular enclosed settlement with a central courtyard, a separate domestic unit, a round cistern and water system, and an industrial area with two pottery kilns. It was clearly not an insignificant cluster of huts, as has recently been suggested. It is demonstrated that it belonged to a string of settlements along the western coast of the Dead Sea. Understanding the structural layout of the Iron Age site is vital because the template of the site was largely maintained in the subsequent Hasmonean resettlement.

Keywords: Qumran, Roland de Vaux, Buqeiʻa plateau, ʻEin Feshkha, Iron Age Judah

From 2005 onward, the present authors have been engaged in understanding Qumran within its wider landscape, particularly in regard to the paths connecting Qumran to other localities around the Dead Sea and inland to the Buqeiʻa, the Judaean wilderness that stretches from the top of the Qumran pass to Hyrcania and beyond.[1]

The conclusions we have reached in this study are important for Qumran, in that we were able to determine that the pathway systems around the site were fundamentally Iron Age in terms of their basic template and character.[2] These paths—including

1. This article is dedicated with affection to Dr. Norma Franklin, an indefatigable and perceptive researcher of the Iron Age in the southern Levant, and a good friend of one of the authors of this paper (Gibson). Norma joined us, together with Louise Hitchcock, for an unforgettable visit with a picnic in January 2009 to view the Iron Age sites investigated by the late Professor Lawrence E. Stager in the Buqeiʻa plateau above Qumran to the west.
2. Taylor and Gibson 2008, 2011. To further the research for this article, the authors made a number of visits to Qumran and environs in April and August 2004, February 2005, November 2010, May 2011, June 2012, and August 2014, to clarify various architectural and stratigraphical details, and

Figure 1. A map of the northern end of the Dead Sea showing sites mentioned in the text. Map prepared by
J. E. Taylor.

the pathways of the pass—were more or less maintained for local traffic in later periods,
but there was never any significant further development, meaning that the old paths

to visit ongoing excavations. We are grateful to the Palestine Exploration Fund for financial support,
also to the late Yuval Peleg for showing us the results of his excavations at the site with Yitzhak Magen,
and to Randall Price and Oren Gutfield for showing us their digging operations in the area of the
southern esplanade. A draft of this paper was delivered to the International SBL conference in London
in 2011, and we are also grateful to the audience at this event for comments received, especially to
Stephen J. Pfann, Jodi Magness, and Dennis Mizzi.

sufficed for the limited use made of them during the ages that followed. In research-ing the "road system" around Qumran, our work was continually pulled away from the well-known settlement of Qumran in the time of the Dead Sea Scrolls, to another time hundreds of years earlier (the Iron Age II) when this region, including the hinterland of the Judaean wilderness, was seemingly much more developed.

After exploring the Iron Age II at Qumran with a view to understanding the road system more holistically, our study has led us to understand Qumran itself as lying at a crossroads in the Iron Age, situated on the main route along the Dead Sea coast, where settlements were dotted between Jericho and 'Ein Gedi, and located at the junction that led to the pass and the Judaean wilderness settlements (fig. 1). Researchers who have seen Qumran as being on this important crossroads in the Herodian and Early Roman periods have made a fundamental error of dating. The connectivity of Qumran was far more apparent in the Iron Age than at any other time, just as these settlements were more numerous and significant in the Iron Age: in the Hasmonean and Herodian periods, none of the settlements of the Buqei'a Plateau existed.

Here we will not focus on the material objects discovered from the Iron Age[3] but rather consider the architecture of the site on the basis of the remnants of walls and reports of excavations. It will be argued that the extent of the Iron Age at Qumran has been considerably underestimated by previous scholars, and that some features previ-ously attributed to the late Hellenistic/Hasmonean period, particularly from Period Ia, are more likely to be of Iron Age origin.

The Iron Age II at Qumran has been attributed to the late eighth century to the early sixth century BCE based on pottery finds—a period of about one hundred years or so—and so it is likely that this period might itself be divided into different architec-tural phases.[4] At present, however, we will focus on the main delineations of walls and other features, and consider their significance.

---

3. We are very grateful to Mariusz Burdajewicz and Jean-Baptiste Humbert who kindly permitted us to read the report on the Iron Age pottery intended for the final Qumran publication. Burdajewicz notes that there are 350 diagnostic pieces from the period that he dates from the late eighth to the early part of the sixth century BCE from both the site of Qumran and the caves. The pottery comprises basic common ware well known at Judahite sites from the Iron Age IIC: jars, jugs, cooking pots, large bowls/ kraters, smaller bowls, plates, and lamps, but the assemblage did not include any interregional imported wares or luxury vessels. See now the suggested second half of the seventh century to early sixth century BCE date for the Iron Age assemblage at Qumran, and its Judahite "uniformity," in Yezerski 2018. Yezerski illustrates seventy-seven items in her publication, but it is unclear what percentage this is of the overall Iron Age assemblage that was examined from the site. Vessel types are the same as those studied by Burdajewicz, except for a few basins, a stand, a lid, a tripod-bowl, and flasks. Yezerski also notes the particular importance in terms of quantity of the different kinds of bowls evident in the Iron Age Qumran assemblage.

4. This last phase of the Iron Age from the seventh and sixth centuries BCE is generally referred to in publications as the Iron Age IIC and now more frequently as the Iron Age III. See Gitin 2015.

The History of Qumran Excavations and the Iron Age

When Qumran excavations in the 1950s were jointly undertaken by the Palestine Archaeological Museum, the Department of Antiquities of Jordan, and the École Biblique et Archéologique Française de Jérusalem, headed by Fr. Roland de Vaux of the École Biblique[5] (figs. 2–4), it was determined that the first constructions at the site were from Iron Age II (referred to as "israélite" in de Vaux 1956: 535–37; 1973: 1–3). A significant amount of fragmentary Iron Age pottery was discovered dated to the eighth (at the earliest) to early sixth centuries BCE (see above, n. 3). In his synthesis of results, presented as the Schweich Lectures and published in 1973, de Vaux concluded that a rectangular building with a large open courtyard and residential quarters existed on the eastern side of the site, with a water system on the west (fig. 5).

In his field notes, further details were supplied (Humbert and Chambon 1994). De Vaux noted that some wall foundations dating to the first century BCE appeared to be at a lower level than others. These lower walls originated in the Iron Age since they relate to a layer of ash with ceramic finds dating from that time (de Vaux 1973: 1). This layer was noted at the angle of the southeast corner between L.73 (Humbert and Chambon 1994: 315) and L.80, and extended further south to L.68. It was found also in the area outside the wall of L.6 (and L.40), in a zone later designated L.145 (Humbert and Chambon 1994: 338).

At the south of L.66, de Vaux observed that the later water channel running to cistern L.71 cuts through a large wall 0.90 m wide, probably dating to the Iron Age (Humbert and Chambon 1994: 314, photos 174 and 176). The deep ashy deposit was found north of L.38 and throughout this area, where the layer is associated with earlier walls, against the north wall and under the south wall of L.77, and in the room L.86 –L.87/89 (Humbert and Chambon 1994: 316, 320). Since de Vaux did not explore beneath many of the floor levels of Period I, it is striking that when he did so he invariably recorded Iron II remains, though the picture is patchy. The Iron Age was clearly not his interest: in L.125 de Vaux indicated some disappointment when after opening a small trench, it yielded nothing except Iron Age sherds (Humbert and Chambon 1994: 332).

The foundations of the wall running north–south along the east of cistern L.117 were identified as belonging to the Iron Age along with other walls associated with L.106, L.109, L.113, L.114, L.119b, and L.108, with an opening to the north between L.114 and L.119, through which surface rainwater from the surrounding area was drained into a large round cistern L.110 (de Vaux 1973: 2).

---

5. Preliminary reports: de Vaux 1949, 1953, 1954, 1956, 1959, 1961, 1973. See also Laperrousaz 1966, 1976, 1980. We express reservations regarding some of his interpretations. The first final report of de Vaux's excavations, including significant reinterpretations, has now appeared in Humbert, Chambon, and Mlynarczyk 2016. For the purposes of this paper we will continue using de Vaux's locus numbers.

Figure 2. Father de Vaux at Qumran in 1966.
Photograph courtesy of Gibson Picture Archive.

Figure 3. General view of Qumran in the 1950s to the northeast. Note the tents of de Vaux's expedition next to the site. Photograph courtesy of Gibson Picture Archive.

In addition, de Vaux identified the long wall running south along the southern es-planade as Iron Age, suggesting that it served to demarcate this region. It is of the same orientation as the eastern side of the Iron Age enclosure, and the type of construction is

Figure 4. Qumran at the time of de Vaux's excavations in 1953, from L.49/L.50 to the west. Photograph courtesy of Gibson Picture Archive.

similar to the northern wall of this enclosure. The pottery identified by de Vaux did not seem to predate the seventh century BCE. He noted, however, that in L.68 there was a jar handle with a stamped seal impression in Palaeo-Hebrew characters, "to the king" (*lmlk*), of apparent late eighth century BCE date, a point we will return to presently (de Vaux 1973: 3, 59–60).

De Vaux suggested that the Iron Age settlement was eventually destroyed and burnt in the sixth century BCE; the layer of ash was noted as having associated sherds from that time. De Vaux's view was that this settlement was devastated during the Baby-lonian invasion of Judaea and the sacking of Jerusalem in 587/586 BCE (de Vaux 1973: 91–93), but it might have occurred slightly later in 582 BCE at the time of Nebuchad-nezzar's campaign to Ammon and Moab in Transjordan (Herr 1999).

De Vaux's plan of the Iron Age remains at Qumran, published as plate III in his Schweich Lectures volume, is quite instructive concerning the locations at the site where he thought Iron Age walls must have existed. In graphic terms, the published version of de Vaux's plan is not very clear, and so we have added key locus numbers, and the heavy hatching of the reconstructed lines of walls has been eliminated (fig. 5). It should be compared with our new plan of Iron Age Qumran (fig. 7),[6] and this shows

---

6. Our plan is an accurate reconstruction of the layout of Iron Age Qumran, showing the position of the architectural remains, based on the wall remnants as reported by the excavators and on early wall foundations seen by different observers (including ourselves) below later Period Ib architecture, and with the addition of the findspots where Iron Age fills, floors, and artifacts were found. But we

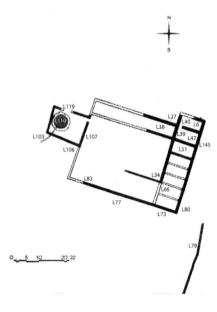

Figure 5. Plan of Qumran in the Iron Age as published by de Vaux, with the addition of locus numbers and the clarification of the appearance of the reconstructed walls. Plan adapted with modifications from de Vaux 1973: pl. III.

in red the architectural features we think existed in the Iron Age and in yellow stratigraphic locations where Iron Age levels were encountered. While these attributions cannot be absolutely certain, these will be explained during the course of this discussion.

Clearly, de Vaux's plan does not represent the exact position of the Iron Age wall fragments as he found them; instead it shows the general alignment of walls based on his field observations (shown in fig. 5 in black), and hypothetical reconstructed lines of walls (shown in white with broken lines). What emerges is that de Vaux was absolutely certain of the Iron Age date for the entire outer perimeter wall of the compound seen on the east (from L.6 and L.145 to L.80) and south (L.73 to L.83), or at least for their lower foundations (now largely buried). Based on the shape of the three rooms he identified at the northeast corner of the compound (L.40 and L.6; L.39 and L.47; L.51), de Vaux thought there may have been five additional rooms of similar size extending to the south along the interior eastern perimeter wall.

In addition to what was previously published of de Vaux's excavations, there has now been a substantial reinterpretation undertaken by Jean-Baptiste Humbert, along with detailed plans, drawings and photographs from the archives of the de Vaux excavations (Humbert, Chambon, and Mlynarczyk 2016). This allows for some further testing of some of de Vaux's conclusions, and clarifications of his field notes. Along with this, archival photographs of de Vaux's excavations, taken by John Allegro in 1954, have enabled us to further understand the site, as have our own observations.[7]

---

must emphasize that it is still not an excavation plan and therefore it incorporates a certain amount of reasoned and well-considered conjecture. Thus it should be taken only as a useful working guide to the original appearance of Iron Age Qumran.

7. The photographs come from the Manchester Museum Allegro Collection, and have been digitized as part of the Dispersed Qumran Caves Artefacts and Archival Sources (DQCAAS) project, funded by the Leverhulme Trust. They are reproduced here with the permission of the copyright holder Judith Brown (© Allegro Estate), Allegro's daughter.

Figure 6. A sounding made in the 1950s revealing the Iron Age ashy layer beneath the floor at the western end of L.77. Photograph by John Allegro, © Allegro Estate, courtesy of Manchester Museum/Judith Brown.

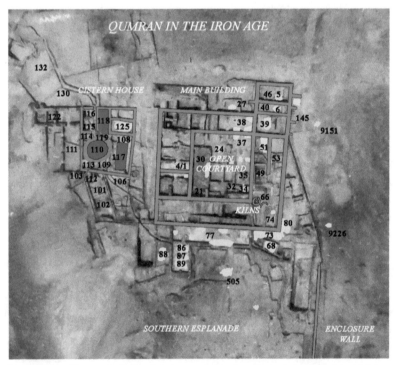

Figure 7. Plan of Qumran in the Iron Age, as suggested by the authors, on the basis of an aerial photograph published in de Vaux 1973: pl. II. Map prepared by S. Gibson.

For example, on the basis of his field notes, it appears that de Vaux's working hypothesis was that the large south wall of L.66 was from Period I and the principal channel from Period II; but, at the time of his synthesis, he changed the latter period to Period Ib and the former to the Iron Age, continuing into Period Ia. This conclusion is preferable, because the wall met the eastern wall of the Iron Age enclosure at the southeast corner of L.74, where, as we have seen, de Vaux mentioned there was evidence of ash and sherds dating to the Iron Age. In his field notes he mentions this ash in relation to L.73, commenting that this lay against cistern L.68 very deeply, being around 0.50 m thick there, while it was less thick in other places. This ash contained many (150) sherds from Iron Age II, though without complete forms. The ashy layer passes under the exterior drain of the bath of L.68. An ostracon with two lines of Palaeo-Hebrew was discovered at this point in L.68 (KhQ 1236).[8] In Humbert's reexamination, de Vaux's helpful stratigraphical drawing of a cut through L.68 to L.72 is reproduced, along with photographs illustrating the ashy layer.[9] Humbert suggests that the ash, which lies thicker toward L.72–73, is the result of the cleaning out of the kilns into what is designated as L.178 (lower L.66; see below and Humbert, Chambon, and Mlynarczyk 2016: 243). Humbert notes that this Iron Age deposit of ash appears to lie against the bath of L.68 and is also found in the older basin in L.72, thus the bath of L.68 was dug into this ashy layer and the ash was flung into the former basin of L.72 (Humbert, Chambon, and Mlynarczyk 2016: 243).

In regard to the Iron Age ashy layer of L.77, a photograph by John Allegro from 1954 illustrates the sounding de Vaux made was on the west side of L.77 against wall 850. De Vaux noted in his diary that the sounding, in the vicinity of the stone circle, showed that there was under the plaster (of the upper floor) a deeper place, then some ashes and finally the virgin earth. He observed that they collected Iron II sherds in the ash layer, and that it extended under the south wall of L.77[10] (fig. 6). Humbert has understood this layer to be part of the spread of ash from the kiln installation,[11] and

---

8. This was analyzed by André Lemaire and published in the second volume of the Qumran excavations, with a reading indicating the letters: ויין (line 1) and רשים (line 2), the first line reading "and wines" and the second we suggest may be "poor" (plural): Lemaire 2003: 353, and see PAM 42–683. The second line is read differently by Lemaire, as רשים[פ], "two horse-riders."

9. See Humbert, Chambon and Mlynarczyk 2016: fig. 92c, 92d, 94d and see the drawing on p. 249. Humbert notes (p. 243) that more accurately it is not so much directly about L.68 and L.73 but the junction of L.72 and L.73. It is not a cut across L.68 and L.73, but exterior to the former and cutting through the latter.

10. De Vaux wrote on 23 March 1954: "Un sondage autour du cercle de pierres montre qu'il y a sous le plâtre [du sol] enduit plus profond, puis des cendres et enfin la terre vierge. Dans les cendres, on ne recueille que quelques tessons du Fer II. La couche de cendres passe sous le mur sud de 77" (Humbert and Chambon 1994: 316).

11. Humbert, Chambon, and Mlynarczyk 2016: 321, though he also observes the ashy layer continued into L.86 (329, 342).

suggested that the cut was in the middle of L.77, due south of the kiln, but Allegro's photograph now shows it was beside the western wall (850).

In his field notes for L.5 de Vaux recorded the appearance of a wide wall running east–west over L.5 and L.46 with not only potsherds but also the rim of an Iron Age II hole-mouth jar (Humbert and Chambon 1994: 233), found by the southern part of the wall (Humbert and Chambon 1994: 27, photo 25). This probably indicates that the thick wall (272) is the northern edge of the Iron Age enclosure. A photograph by John Allegro from 1954 from L.19 looking east appears to show an earlier foundation wall below the Period Ib wall (274) on the west side of room L.46. (fig. 9) In addition, beyond this area to the east, in what is now identified as L.145, there were at least three small walls jutting eastwards at right angles from the main wall beyond L.6 and L.47, but these were not shown on de Vaux's plan, and, in the publication of the field notes and photographs by Humbert and Chambon, these walls appear only in the plan of Period Ib (plates IV and VIII). They do now appear also in Humbert's new analysis, labeled walls 396, 397 and 398 (Humbert, Chambon, and Mlynarczyk 2016: pl. I). These may perhaps be identified as small lean-to outbuildings adjacent to the northern room in L.5 and L.46, and further south, dating to the Iron Age.

Humbert notes regarding L.145 that the presence of Iron Age sherds witnesses to a level from this time (Humbert, Chambon, and Mlynarczyk 2016: 229–30). He notes also that de Vaux tended to refer to excavations in this area as "east of 44" or "exterior to 44" (even "east of 45" or "84") without specificity, but de Vaux's archives have shown that he cut a trench exterior to wall 900 (running north–south) beyond L.84 in 1953 and continued this work in 1954. In this trench de Vaux observed an earthquake fissure running north–south, and also the lower ashy level associated with the end of the Iron Age site lying on virgin soil (feature 145.4). The ashy level sinks down into the fissure, but continues eastward to the edge of the trench.

Publication of the drawings of these zones enables the relevant walls to be determined more precisely. The plans drawn by Chambon in the latest Qumran volume are very helpful in determining Iron Age wall remains attested by de Vaux. Evidence of the thick north–south perimeter wall (272, 284, 285) and other associated walls of this period are sometimes shown as looking stony (not colored in black), where they differ from later walls. As mentioned in his synthesis, further west in L.38, at its southeast angle, de Vaux uncovered part of a north–south wall (267) and an east–west wall (262) with associated ash and potsherds from the Iron Age (Humbert and Chambon 1994: 305, photo 41). In the excavation notes de Vaux wrote that the wall between L.35 and 49 (292), like that between 35 and 34 (306), descends deeper than the excavated floor, and that these walls were perhaps "Israelite," but the material was missing to date them.[12] De Vaux's comments here do not always relate clearly to published photo-

---

12. Humbert and Chambon 1994: 304. "le mur entre les loci 35 et 49, comme celui entre 35 et 34,

Figure 8. The wall of the esplanade near L.78 towards the west. Photograph from the 1960s, courtesy of Gibson Picture Archive.

Figure 9. View from L.14 toward L.27 in a photograph from the 1950s. Note the Iron Age stone foundation at the base of the wall. Photograph by John Allegro, © Allegro Estate, courtesy of Manchester Museum/ Judith Brown.

Figure 10. The kiln at L.66. Photograph de Vaux 1973: pl. Vb.

graphs, but his observations in L.38 and L.34–L.35 formed the basis for his reconstruction of an inner Iron Age wall running parallel to the outer perimeter wall.

De Vaux also noted traces of an east–west Iron Age wall running to the southwest
corner of L.34, between L.32 and L.36, continuing the southern wall of L.36 (295)
(Humbert and Chambon 1994: 304). A lower foundation, which is probably a western
continuation of this wall, is evident at L.21 at the southern end of L.30 (240).

The evidence of de Vaux's surviving exposed walls suggests that the eastern perimeter wall ran from the northeast corner of L.6 to the southeast corner of L.74, a distance
of 37 m. The question of the north, south, and west walls of the Iron Age enclosure
are, however, not clarified by de Vaux's notes, or by the reexaminations by Humbert.
This is because the lowest level of the site was not substantially explored. In general, de
Vaux did not dismantle walls from Period I in order to define the extent of the Iron Age
settlement beneath it, preferring instead to focus on the periods related to the Dead Sea
Scrolls. He made only occasional soundings, but these are quite instructive (as we shall
see below).

Regarding the Iron Age date for the potters' kilns, close to the inner wall of the
Iron Age enclosure de Vaux identified two kilns (L.66), one quite destroyed but the

descend plus bas que le sol dégagé. Murs peut-être israélites mais le matériel manque pour le dater."
The intersection of these two walls may be shown in photos 76 and 77, but this is unclear.

other in a relatively good state (fig. 10). These had been covered over by a stone pavement following changes in the ground level owing to the creation of the later cistern
L.48–49 (Humbert and Chambon 1994: 314). De Vaux wondered in his field notes
whether these may be dated to Iron II, but by the time of his synthetic publication
(De Vaux 1973) he had changed his mind, and assigned these instead to Period Ia.
During this period, which de Vaux dated to Qumran's resettlement in the late second
century BCE, a similar enclosure to the one from the Iron Age was identified, but with
certain additional features. Despite the destruction of the Iron Age settlement, de Vaux
concluded that "what remained of the Israelite buildings served as a point of departure
for the constructions of the new occupants" (de Vaux 1973: 4).

In L.66 de Vaux indicated that the two kilns, built side by side, were obliterated
during the development of the site in the next period (Ib), when a large cistern was
built to the north (L.48–49, de Vaux 1973: 16–17). He stated simply that "there is
nothing to indicate that these kilns were already in service during the Israelite [=Iron
Age] period" (de Vaux 1973: 4). This is curious as we have seen that he identified the
inner wall very near the kilns at the southeast corner of L.34 as Iron Age, meaning that
their alignment and positioning fits well with these. De Vaux did not record that there
was any layer of Iron II ash and sherds there. Instead, he associated pottery from Period
Ib from the southern area of the main building with these kilns. The levels he refers to
are unclear. The absence of a record of Iron II pottery fragments does not in fact mean
there were none, since de Vaux did not undertake pottery seriation during his sort-
ing procedures, and many of the supposedly nondiagnostic body sherds he may have
thrown away. In general, one must be wary of some of the stratigraphical associations
provided by de Vaux, owing to the sparse details provided in his field notes.

Jodi Magness has pointed out, on the basis of the evidence de Vaux provided for
Period Ia as a whole, that "de Vaux found no coins associated with Period Ia, and there
were only a few potsherds which he could not distinguish in type from those of Period Ib" (Magness 2002: 64). This has led her to assign most of the supposed Period
Ia developments to Period Ib, beginning in the first quarter of the first century BCE.[13]
However, importantly, Magness noted that the kilns in L.66 are more appropriately
seen as Iron Age, since they "represent a kind of circular kiln with a central pillar that
is attested in Palestine from the Bronze Age on" (Magness 2002: 64). This seems the
most plausible solution, and one also now adopted by Humbert (see above), and we
therefore assign the kilns to Iron Age II, allowing us to view the southern corner of the
main Iron Age enclosure as a pottery workshop.

As noted, it was south of L.66, near L.73, that the jar handle with the *lmlk* ("for the
king") stamped seal impression was found (KhQ1235).[14] Another of these was found
in the excavations of Magen and Peleg in their L.3000 next to the enclosure wall in

---

13. For a good summary of Period Ia, see Mizzi 2015.
14. Humbert and Chambon 1994: 314; Lemaire 2003: 353; see PAM 42-683. De Vaux 1973: 2

the southern esplanade (see below). It has formerly been accepted that the particular type of stamp in KhQ1235 should be dated to 705–701 BCE, to the time of the revolt of King Hezekiah against the Assyrian king Sennacherib (Ussishkin 1977). However, Oded Lipschits has proposed a new chronological scheme, based on a typology set out by André Lemaire (1981). This type of jar handle is classified by Lemaire as type XII, with a two-winged sun and the inscription *lmlk* appearing above the upper part of the solar disk, with nothing written in the lower part (Lemaire 2003: 353). This is one of the jar handle types that Lipschits has noted appear only in hill-country sites that were not destroyed in 701 BCE, or in strata of the seventh century BCE, one of the "late types" (Lipschits, Sergi, and Koch 2010: 11, 13–17; Lipschits 2012: 1, 8). This would provide evidence consistent with the view that the settlement survived through to the Babylonian invasion of 587/586 or 582 BCE.

We concur with de Vaux in considering that the end of the Iron Age II occupation of Qumran is represented by a destruction layer of ash. Where ash appears at the site, therefore, it is important to review whether it might belong to this level.[15] For example, following the removal of the floor in L.30 de Vaux encountered an oven, which he attributed to Period Ia. At a lower level was a layer of ash that appeared to extend beneath the eastern wall, but he does not indicate the date of the pottery from within this layer. Is this also to be dated to the Iron Age? Along the western wall of L.132 it is clear that in Period Ib a wall that begins in L.142 has been destroyed, leaving no remains (Humbert and Chambon 1994: Period Ib, pl. IV). Water erosion led to the destruction of the western wall of L.132. The preserved wall built in Period II and buttressing on the northwestern corner of the western building was a rebuild from the ground up, with buttressing on the southwest of L.130 that went down to a thin layer of ash (Humbert and Chambon 1994: 333). De Vaux thought that this might be from a fire sometime at or after the end of Period Ib, but is it possible that this is the Iron Age destruction level ash which appears in a confused picture at the corner of this building as a result of the flooding and rebuild, resulting in a partially reversed stratigraphy?

To seek further answers concerning the stratigraphy of Qumran, renewed excavations at the site of Qumran took place between 1994 and 2004, undertaken by Yitzhak Magen and Yuval Peleg.[16] The excavations focused on four "refuse" dumps, to the north, south, and east of the main building, and, in addition, a large paved area immediately

---

cites it as L.68, but de Vaux must have been confusing it with the other Iron Age sherd with Hebrew letters (KhQ 1236).

15. For a discussion of the question of the ash and carbonized materials at the site, see Humbert, Chambon, and Mlynarczyk 2016: 47–55. Humbert links Iron Age II ash in the south with the kilns (p. 50), but it seems too substantial and spread out over the site to be the result of dispersed ash from one locality (L.66 area).

16. Yitzhak and Peleg 2006, 2007, 2018. The authors are grateful to the late Yuval Peleg for showing us around the site in 2004, pointing out to us the exact places where they had uncovered Iron Age II remains, and discussing with us their possible relevance.

to the south of L.77 was exposed. Test squares were also made inside the buildings, all of which revealed the same deep layer of ash and small sherds previously noted by de Vaux (Magen and Peleg 2018: 101–4; 2007: 27). An area on the southern plateau was also excavated (Magen and Peleg 2007: 4, fig. 4).

The southern refuse dump of the later settlement was excavated, located south of pool L.71 and extending west to the paved area south of L.77, and Iron Age pottery was found mixed with Period Ib pottery (L.401 Magen and Peleg 2018: 59). In the paved area south of L.77 Iron Age pottery was found as residuals beneath the pavement (e.g., L.505: Magen and Peleg 2018: fig. 51). In addition, Iron Age II pottery was found in the northern refuse dump, some 25 m north of the site at the edge of the plateau (L.2028), and in an area immediately east of the main building (L.9151, 9226).[17] In the northern part of this area, an intact Iron Age juglet was found (Magen and Peleg 2018: 68–69; 2007: 28; 2006: 76).

During their work inside the main building, Magen and Peleg were able to identify a number of locations with Iron Age remains and pottery.[18] A hint as to the extent of the Iron Age on the west side of the main building was obtained as a result of a sounding Magen and Peleg excavated beneath the eastern side of the floor of room L.4, revealing the top of an Iron Age wall.[19] This wall runs from west to east, where it evidently bonded with another wall with a north to south axis, probably running beneath wall W519, and therefore delimiting the western side of the courtyard. Yet, another early wall which may also be from this period was visible on the interior side of wall W529 at the southern end of room L.30 (Magen and Peleg 2018: cross-section 1-1 in fig. 25). This wall may very well be the western extension of an Iron Age wall running to the west from the direction of L.32 and L.34 (see above). Magen and Peleg assume that the original shape of the central courtyard was determined no earlier than Period Ib, but this flies in the face of the evidence of their own soundings made in 1998 (L.3038, 3045, 3046, 3062, and 3063) which revealed much Iron Age pottery in this area. More-

---

17. Magen and Peleg 2018: 59–60 (eastern refuse dump), 68–69 (northern refuse dump); 2007: 6–10; 2006: 59–64.

18. The exact stratigraphical association between the pottery published by Yezerski and the Iron Age walls, floors and fills at the site is unclear. The locus list in the final report is not particularly helpful in that regard and does not include chronological data or pottery readings, which of course reduces its usefulness: Magen and Peleg 2018: 141–69. The following might be helpful to future researchers: Yezerski published seventy-seven items, out of which eleven came from the main building (L.3038, 3045, 3046, 3062, 3063), three from the western wing of the main building (L9148, 9154, 9164), one from the southeast angle of the main building (L.9160), six from the eastern refuse dump (L.9151, 9226), three from the south side of the building in L.77 (L.9521), three from the paved square (L.505, 3006, 3022), thirty-nine from the southeast side of the site (L.507, 1001, 1002, 1003, 3000), two from the southern esplanade (L.353, 401), seven from the northern refuse dump (L.508, 510, 522, 801, 2023, 2028), and four from unclear locations (L.421, 603, 1101).

19. Magen and Peleg 2018: 23: L.4/1, figs. 22–24, 27. The pottery found in the fill adjacent to this wall was not included in the final report.

over, these soundings confirmed that the walls at the northeast angle of the courtyard at
L.37 had to be from the Iron Age (Magen and Peleg 2018: 48). New work took place on
the southeast side of the building, unearthing the same Iron Age layer previously seen
by de Vaux in L.73, L.80, and under Pool L68. As noted above, this is where de Vaux
found a *lmlk* stamped jar handle. The new excavations revealed Iron Age sherds and
stone weights (L.3033, 9106, 9148; Magen and Peleg 2018: 103).

In room L.6 within the northeast angle of the main building, the removal of a floor
revealed a wall with a west to east axis (W575) and an ashy layer; Magen and Peleg suggested dating it to the Iron Age (Magen and Peleg 2018: figs. 31–32; 103). On the other
side of the east wall of the building, in the area of L.145, Magen and Peleg recorded
three or four "poorly built" walls dating from the Iron Age (Magen and Peleg 2018:
59). In the eastern wing, in the area de Vaux previously designated as L.51, Magen and
Peleg found the foundation of a wall (W600) with a north–south axis, which they attributed to the Iron Age (L.9148, 9154, 9164; Magen and Peleg 2018: 103, figs. 41,
43). A southern extension of this same wall was traced in L.53 and was seen running
beneath W589, which is the eastern wall of the stepped installation L.48/L.49. At least
three underground stone-lined pits identified as silos (L.341/1–3) were found in the
southern esplanade (L.353), but their Iron Age date is not absolutely certain.[20] Seg-
ments of walls made of fieldstones were unearthed, jutting out from the eastern boundary wall of the esplanade (W576); the associated layer was described by the excavators
as "close to and under the eastern outer wall" (L.1005, 3000, 3004). Beneath this ashy
layer was an earthen and cobbled living surface with a number of hearths (Magen and
Peleg 2018: 103). The Iron Age layer of ash and sherds appeared to lie beneath the long
esplanade wall (as de Vaux found under the southern wall of L.77), and here, abutting
the wall on the southeastern side, another *lmlk* seal impression on a jar handle was
found (L.3000; Magen and Peleg 2018: 104; 2007: 27, figs. 29–31; 2006: fig. 3:24).

Further excavations by Randall Price and Oren Gutfield in the area of the southern esplanade uncovered Iron Age pottery, but this has not yet been published.[21] At
any rate, this area to the south of the settlement would undoubtedly have been in use
during the Iron Age. The esplanade is flat and elongated, with a length of approximately
160 m from north to south, and a breadth of 60 m, narrowing considerably to 12 m in
the south. It may have been bounded by a wall on the eastern side. The history of the
construction of this eastern esplanade boundary wall is still not fully understood. It
would appear to have served as an architectural terrace supporting and retaining the

---

20. Magen and Peleg 2018: 69 mentioning four pits, figs. 79–81, and p. 102 mentioning three pits,
with the authors adding: "based on the sherds found between the wall's stones, they date to the Iron
Age"; 2007: 32, fig. 32; 2006: 36, 38: fig. 3.25, We note that these silos have the same appearance as the
circular pits containing Early Roman pottery which have been excavated elsewhere on the southern
esplanade.

21. We are grateful to the excavators Randall Price and Oren Gutfield for graciously showing us
the results of their work in the southern esplanade on a number of occasions between 2004 and 2012.

Figure 11. The esplanade wall to the west, with the late Yuval Peleg on the right in 2004. Photograph by S. Gibson.

Figure 12. The esplanade wall running to the south, as it appeared in 2004. Photograph by S. Gibson.

ground surface to its west; clearly it was rebuilt on a number of occasions[22] (fig. 11). A recent examination suggests that it had to be contemporary with the earliest Iron Age use of the esplanade; otherwise the ground surface within this area would have eroded away (fig. 12). The layer of ash and Iron Age sherds noted by Magen and Peleg probably extends within a breach in a destroyed or collapsed segment of the original wall, which was subsequently rebuilt in the Hasmonean period. The narrow walls jutting out from this esplanade wall may represent an earlier phase of construction within the Iron Age, or perhaps a "casemate" arrangement of rooms or magazines connected to the esplanade wall (as at sites in the Buqeiʿa and at nearby Khirbet Irneh, see below).[23] The fact that this terrace wall was in use during the entire existence of the Qumran settlement down to the first century CE is not at all surprising for architectural terracing, reflecting a continuous use over a long period.[24]

Excavations within the main building uncovered another north–south wall inside L.51 and L.53, continuing east of pool L.48 and pool L.50. This seems to continue the line of a later dividing wall between L.39 and L.47 (fig. 13), which would indicate that later constructions were indeed founded on Iron Age foundations. However, Magen and Peleg conclude from their investigations of the eastern wall, attributed by de Vaux to the Iron Age, that "the said foundations are an integral part of the Hasmonean structure." Nevertheless, in L.6 today it seems that the outer eastern wall is built over the ruins of the Iron Age outer wall, which is used as a foundation (fig. 14). Magen and Peleg, however, assume that it is only the small walls jutting out at right angles from the line of the eastern boundary, and under the long wall of the southern esplanade, that represent the true Iron Age structures, so that the settlement from that period "was composed of clay huts and wooden sheds that rested, in part, on fieldstone building foundations" (Magen and Peleg 2018: 11, 104; 2007: 28). This is curious given the very large amount of Iron Age sherds and ash found throughout the site, and a small settlement of simple huts does not account for the thick wall of L.51, though here they suggest that "life in the settlement possibly revolved around a public structure or stone tower" (Magen and Peleg 2018: 104; 2007: 28). Moreover, a collection of small huts is not a form paralleled in other Iron Age II settlements in the region (Faust 2003, 2018).

Further to the south inside the main building a stone weight calibrated with lead was found; this appears to have been discovered in some proximity to the kilns of L.66 (Magen and Peleg 2006: fig. 3:26). A large amount of ash and sherds of Iron Age II date was found under the Period I floor at the west end of L.77 on top of a lower plaster floor

---

22. Humbert has suggested the extension of the wall south to ʿEin Feshkha as an *eruv*, but this relates to the Hasmonean period; Humbert, Chambon, and Mlynarczyk 2016: 35–45.

23. Our use of the term "casemate" refers to a series of very small rooms running along one side of a long wall, and it does not imply they had any defensive function; Lapp 1976.

24. Indeed, the longevity of this wall as a functioning terrace is quite remarkable and in 1856 it was the most prominent visible feature at the site when visited by one of the early explorers; Isaacs 1857: 66 engraving opposite.

Figure 13. The architectural features at L.51, toward the west. Photograph by S. Gibson.

Figure 14. The east wall of the building complex, just south of L.145, viewed toward the west. Photograph by J. E. Taylor.

(L.9520, 9522 and 9525; Magen and Peleg 2018: 45–46; 2007: 27). This is interesting given de Vaux's observation of this layer under the southern wall (Magen and Peleg's W613), suggesting that there was another southern wall of this Iron Age structure to the south of L.77 (i.e., under the "paved square") that has yet to be found. This may have been an extension of an initial enclosure, since the basic template of an Iron Age site like that of Qumran was generally rectangular, as we see at such nearby single-era sites as Hurvat Shilhah (Kh. Shilheh; Mazar, Amit, and Ilan 1995). This site offers a good comparable structure to the form of Iron Age Qumran.

On the western side of the site, de Vaux's round pool L.110 (fig. 15) was clearly shown not to stand alone. Magen and Peleg were able to determine that the original height of the round pool L.110 was about 1 m below its later form, and it had a close relationship with L.117 and L.118 from the beginning, suggesting to them that both these pools were used for gathering clay in their sediment (fig. 16; Magen and Peleg 2018: 50–57, figs. 57–58; 2007: 13).

Magen and Peleg are doubtful that the round cistern could be Iron Age, believing that the hydraulic plaster is typical of the Hellenistic and Hasmonean periods.[25] Nevertheless, as Yizhar Hirschfeld suggested, the Iron Age cistern might simply have been replastered in order to make it waterproof and useful in later times (Hirschfeld 2004: 57). Indeed, its extended height over which the coating of plaster was attached clearly indicates that some of the plaster dates to the time of this later modification.[26] Magen and Peleg note that they did not find Iron II remains on the western side of the site, and thus they assumed this area was used for collecting rainwater solely in the Hasmonean period (Magen and Peleg 2018: 103–4; 2007: 27). But this very observation seems to suggest that (a) a cistern complex was indeed required in association with any rainwater collection, which would have been necessary also in the case of the Iron Age, and (b) that rainwater collection, involving occasional flooding, could have washed away considerable primary evidence from this lower level. In actual fact, de Vaux did uncover Iron Age remains in L.125, which lies within the cistern complex, immediately to the northeast. It remains to be seen whether further soundings will uncover Iron Age remains there.

In Magen and Peleg's view, the cisterns cannot be Iron Age because, as they state:

> It defies belief that the Iron Age inhabitants of Qumran, who themselves lived in huts, were capable of digging such a huge pool … the powerful character of Pool L-110 is inconsistent with that of the site's Iron Age structures. It is very likely that the Iron Age pools were quite small, and probably dried up before the end of summer. In fact, Iron Age Qumran was quite small, and may well have been inhabited only in winter and spring. (Magen and Peleg 2007: 28)

25. Unfortunately, we still lack good comparative material on plaster types. Impressive first steps have been made by Yosef (Sefi) Porath and Aryeh Shimron in their research, but a greater database of plaster types is essential to make this a viable dating method. In our opinion, the earliest plaster coating near the base of L.110 could very well be Iron Age.

26. This is further complicated by the fact that modern restoration appears to have been made to the plaster coating the interior of this installation, at least in its upper parts.

Figure 15. The round cistern L.110 as seen in 2010. Photograph by S. Gibson.

Figure 16. The cistern house toward the west, with the round cistern L.110 center left, and the stepped installation L.117 on the left, in a photograph taken in 1977. Photograph courtesy of Gibson Picture Archive.

This observation seems to fly in the face of their own excavations that brought to light a large amount of Iron Age artifacts, especially potsherds. The suggestion that the long wall bounding the southern esplanade was not constructed in the Iron Age but in a later period, over the conflagration layer and Iron Age walls, seems unlikely owing to its terrace-like function in supporting the ground surface within the esplanade. This does not, however, negate the possibility of "casemate" rooms built into or adjoining the long wall. Moreover the template for Iron Age (and Persian) settlements usually involved rectangular enclosure structures, with "casemate" rooms or magazines along the perimeter and with an open central area, though there could be outlying buildings at times and animal pens surrounded by stone fences (Faust 2003, 2018). At Qumran, it is possible there were structures abutting the main enclosure, and also various buildings in the southern esplanade.

The evidence of thick Iron Age walls uncovered by de Vaux and forming the basis for a main rectangular Iron Age enclosure still seems clear from his field notes, plan, and photographs. Magen and Peleg's new thick wall of L.51 also fits into this template, as does their evidence of a plastered floor lying underneath L.77, indicating a continuation of the Iron Age presence to the south.

Rather than an area of small huts, we suggest an activity zone with a rectangular compound with a central courtyard, with a possible domestic structure at the northeast angle, and fenced-off areas of Iron Age II date, with possible building extensions to the east and south. Magen and Peleg argue that since Pool L.110 had to have been built at the same time as Cistern L.117 and L.118, which they dated to no earlier than the Hasmonean period, this meant that an Iron Age date for Pool L.110 was untenable. In addition to this they claimed that the Iron Age inhabitants at the site would in any case have been incapable of constructing a large pool with thick hydraulic plaster (Magen and Peleg 2007: 28). In our opinion, the exact opposite can be argued, and both circular reservoirs and stepped cisterns of Iron Age date are paralleled in other sites.[27] The round cistern with the adjoining stepped cisterns L.117 and L.118 and its surrounding walls, would then be lying on the west side of this enclosure, but not necessarily an integral part of the main building, as de Vaux had suggested. In addition, given a possible minimum of seventy years of occupation in the Iron Age II, there need not have been one single timespan of construction after which the site was left exactly in the same state. Indeed, it is more likely that there were successive developments within this time frame, with at least a couple of phases of building construction.

In regard to the notion that the Iron Age settlers could not build a sophisticated water system, it is apparent throughout the Kingdom of Judah in urban and industrial contexts, and in the neighboring region of the Buqei'a where the art of water harvesting in fields was extremely developed. We contend that an advanced water system would

---

27. Tsuk 2001–2002; Miller 1980. On the Iron Age water system at Suba with a stepped cistern, see Gibson 2009.

have been imperative for the pottery works at the site in the Iron Age. Apart from kilns, a pottery workshop would have required storage and stacking surfaces, clay prepara- tion installations, and of course an ample source of water. Hence, the Qumran system must have included the round pool (L.110) for the collection of water and the stepped cisterns (L.117 and L.118) for the preparation of the clay, and all this would be appro- priate given the presence of the Iron Age pottery kilns within the main building (L.66). [28] If the clay preparation area was on the west where there was access to water, with the kilns inside the building to the east, then the drying floors, where vessels were stacked until leather-hard and ready to be fired, might have been in the intervening courtyard, or alternatively toward the southern esplanade (perhaps the plastered floor under L.77 was one such working surface).

In his synthesis of the chronology of the site, de Vaux concluded that in Period Ia new occupants expanded the water collection and storage system in the western area around the old round cistern. A channel was built to supply water more effectively to the round cistern and two other rectangular cisterns built close by, L.117 and L.118, with a decantation or silting basin (L.119) serving all three cisterns. It is now possible to determine, on the basis of Magen and Peleg's excavations, that this in fact describes the form of the original construction of the cistern complex. In addition, de Vaux (1973: 3–4) noted that a small channel was seen running underneath an Iron Age wall, in or- der to collect rain water from the south, and a covered building was constructed in the south (L.101–102), with other rooms added to the north (L.115–116 and 125–127).

From his field notes it seems that an early wall lay along the north of L.106 and L.101 (L.112) and was cut into by the main water channel developed in Period Ib (Humbert and Chambon 1994: 329). Another lower and narrow water channel was first encountered in L.103, to the west, running from L.112. In L.122 de Vaux dug to de- termine the continuation of this but found it disappeared in L.112. But it seemed pos- sibly linked with another channel, on virgin soil, running from L.111, which he found turning to L.113. On lifting a wall between L.109 and L.113, he found the first lower floor, coated with plaster, which communicated by a narrow opening with the supply channel to L.110. In L.109 on lifting the lower threshold between L.109 and L.101, an- other lower floor was encountered anterior to the principal channel and without doubt contemporary with the first circular cistern (Humbert and Chambon 1994: 326). In L.119 de Vaux was clearly fascinated in tracing the progress of the lower channel sys- tems, and in his field notes he concluded that water was drained from a roof above L.101 and L.106, and that therefore the three cisterns L.110, L.117 and L.118 "sont contemporaines" (Humbert and Chambon 1994: 329). Strangely, he decided against his own field observations in his later synthesis. However, Magen and Peleg's new exca- vations now affirm the integral connections between all three installations, as de Vaux

---

28. For the various installations associated with a clay-production plant from the Iron Age, see Gibson 2009.

himself had observed, and they have also uncovered the earlier system of channels, with an entrance channel in the north wall of L.116, running beneath the floor of L.116 and L.115, ultimately ending up in the silting basin L.119 (Magen and Peleg 2006: 66).

To sum up, we suggest the original layout of the rectangular building complex surrounding Pool L.110 and Cisterns L.117 and L.118, is from the Iron Age and it should not be attributed to the elusive (and now apparently nonexistent) Period Ia, as de Vaux assumed. Rainwater was channeled into the installations from the surroundings, as well as collected from the roofs of the rooms round about. This covered cistern-house system may conceivably be similar to the *beth ha-bor* mentioned in Jeremiah (37:15–16, 38:6). A complex water system would not be surprising for this period and numerous water-collection and storage installations, many exhibiting a high degree of technological and engineering skills, have hitherto been investigated at both urban, village, and countryside locations, as for example at Beersheba, the Amman Citadel, Beth Shemesh, Suba, and elsewhere (Faust 2008c; Haiman 2002).

This sophisticated water installation fell into disuse at the time of the destruction of the settlement in the sixth century BCE. It was subsequently restored and put back into use when the site was redeveloped at the beginning of Period I, ca. 100 BCE. When the aqueduct was built, new covered water channels were made and large pools of this era were also constructed, and the old installations were put back into use. The major overhaul and restoration of this installation complex in Period Ib, has ultimately confused the overall stratigraphic picture of the western side of the Iron Age settlement, despite the fact that the architectural evidence clearly indicates the cisterns must predate the Hasmonean development of the site.

We therefore offer a new plan of Qumran in the Iron Age. De Vaux's suggestion that there may have been five additional rooms of similar size extending to the south along the interior eastern perimeter wall is unlikely owing to the discovery by Magen and Peleg of a wall with a north to south axis, running at the center of de Vaux's room L.51, and also because we suggest assigning the kilns in L.66 to the Iron Age (see below), which makes the existence of de Vaux's two southern rooms unlikely. Our reconstruction of the walls at the northeast corner of the compound differs from that of de Vaux, and it is based on the alignment and visual appearance of the underlying walls in this area. Moreover, the wall stubs at L.145, and possibly also at L.27, suggest an additional northern room must have existed at the northeast angle enclosing L.5 and L.46. What emerges is that the compound had a separate and integrated building at the northeast angle with at least two distinct rooms; it is likely to have been used for dwelling purposes and perhaps even for basic defensive purposes as well. Long corridors ran along the interior of the northern (L.38), eastern (L.55 to L.66), western (L.4/1), and southern (L.74 to L.83) perimeter walls; some of these may have been subdivided into rooms for storage. These corridors surrounded an open rectangular courtyard at the center of the compound (extending from L.37 on the north, to L.34 at the inner southeast angle, and to L.30 on the west).

De Vaux also attributed the earliest use of the cistern house (L.110), on the western side of the compound, to the Iron Age, and indicated that it was surrounded by four walls (L.106, L.107), with a possible doorway at L.119 (shown reconstructed on his plan), and a water channel entering the cistern from L.103. Our plan of the cistern house includes the installations L.117 and L.118, and additional rooms to the north. De Vaux identified the retaining wall on the eastern side of the southern esplanade as Iron Age and traced it as far north as L.78 (fig. 8), but he was uncertain as to its northern continuation and where it connected with the earlier compound.

The Identification of Iron Age Qumran

Iron Age Qumran has featured very little in the comprehensive discussions dealing with the archaeology of the site, but it has been of interest to scholars of the Hebrew Bible, especially in regard to discussions on the identification of the toponyms mentioned in Josh 15. Even prior to the discovery of the Scrolls, there was some speculation that the ruins of Qumran might represent the remains of a biblical site. F. M. Abel (1938: 386) identified Qumran with Middin. Martin Noth (1938: 72; also Cross 1956: 12–17) identified the site as Ir ha-Melah, the "City of Salt," mentioned in Josh 15:61–62: "In the wilderness: Beth-Araba, Middin and Secacah and Nibshan and the City of Salt and Engedi; six cities with their villages."

De Vaux followed Martin Noth's identification, including the suggestion that the other Judaean settlements of the Judaean monarchy were sequentially indicated in this passage.[29] Pessah Bar Adon likewise identified Ain el-Ghuweir as the City of Salt and Qumran with biblical Secacah (Josh 15:61; Bar Adon 1977). This suggestion is followed also by Jodi Magness (2002: 24–25). Hanan Eshel (2009: 8) has also agreed that the site was Secacah (or Sokokah in the LXX), stating its name is "likely from the root s-k-k ('to cover'), referring to the date-palm leaves used to cover the roofs of the houses." John H. Allegro (1959–1960: 64) suggested a relationship between Qumran and the name of the Kippah torrent mentioned in the Copper Scroll, near which there is a place called Sekaka (3Q15 IV, 13; V, 2, 5, 13).

However, while the general town list of Josh 15, does approximate the geographical scope of the small kingdom of Josiah (639–609 BCE), one must be cautious (Ahituv 1993). The identification of the Iron Age sites of the Judaean wilderness, which include 'Ein Gedi, would need to be on the basis of substantial "cities" that could have smaller "villages" in their environments. Since there are many more Iron Age sites known now than those indicated by the named localities in Josh 15:61–62, we would need first to determine where the larger "cities" might have been, apart from Jericho and 'Ein Gedi.

---

29. See de Vaux 1973: 91–92; Cross and Milik 1956. The LXX deviates from the Masoretic Text here, and not only in the forms of the names, but there is no reference to "in the wilderness." Most likely, these names indicate other actual sites known at the time of the composition of the LXX, at which time there were no settlements in the wilderness.

The area of the wilderness would need to encompass the region of the higher hinterland (the Buqei'a) and also the coastal region of the Dead Sea. Altogether this is a wide
area, and unknown sites may yet come to light.

Iron Age Context: Eastern Judah in the Eighth–Sixth Centuries BCE

De Vaux pointed out that in 2 Chr 26:10, King Uzziah (781–740 BCE) is described
as having large herds and loving the soil, that he "built towers" (*migdalim*) in the wilderness and hewed out many cisterns. Prior to this, Jehoshaphat (870–848 BCE) was
said to have built in Judah fortresses and store cities, but there are no archaeological
indications of building efforts in the wilderness (2 Chr 17:12; de Vaux 1956). One
could argue therefore that the earliest structures in the wilderness should be Uzziah's
"towers" constructed in the eighth century BCE. However, the archaeological picture
we encounter is entirely different: apart from large settlements such as Jericho (Tell
es-Sultan), with settlement remains extending from as early as the ninth and eighth
centuries BCE, the landscape on the eastern edge of Judah consists of a plethora of
small sites, all thriving during the seventh century BCE, but only a fraction of them
have pottery finds extending back to the late eighth century BCE.

As Magen and Peleg note (2007: 25, fig. 28; 2006: 73–79, fig. 3.22), the establishment of the settlement of Qumran in the Iron Age was part of a great wave of settlement in this area in the late eighth and early seventh centuries. Their map indicates the
variety of known categories of Iron Age sites in the wider region, with solitary towers,
cave-dwellings, fortified enclosures, industrial locations, and town sites. They suggest
that settlement of this region was not a result of a specific state strategy relating to the
initiatives of individual Judahite kings, but was the direct result of the settlement of
refugees following the fall of Samaria in 720 BCE; these refugees are mentioned in Jer
41:5 and 1 Chr 30:10–11; 34:9. Avraham Faust, however, has argued that Judah was at
its settlement peak in the seventh century BCE, especially in what he calls the "fringe
areas" of the Judaean Desert and the Negev, despite the catastrophe of Sennacherib's
invasion of 701 BCE. During the seventh century BCE this region "suddenly witnessed
an unparalleled wave of settlement activity" (Faust 2008b: 170; Stern 1994: 406–7).

In terms of the main Iron Age sites in the region which were contemporary to the
settlement of Qumran, there is of course the city of Jericho (Tell es-Sultan), which was
in continuous occupation from the eighth through sixth centuries BCE, though it had
an earlier occupation in the Iron Age as well.[30] Further south is Kh. el-Uja (Bar Adon
1977: 109, no. 26), Ard al-Mafjar (Bar Adon 1977: 113–14 site no. 59), and Tell es-
Samarat (Bar Adon 1977: 114, site no. 61). Following this, there is Vered Yericho, and

---

30. On Kathleen Kenyon's work on the Iron Age II at Jericho (Tell es-Sultan), see Kenyon and
Holland 1982. For recent work on the third phase of the Iron Age II stratum at Jericho ("Sultan VIc,"
dated 732–535 BCE), see Nigro 2014. For a survey of this area see Bar Adon 1972.

another Iron Age site without a name, 3 km south of Tell es-Sultan, followed by a large site of 30 dunams 3 km north of Vered Jericho and in Wadi Qelt (Eitan 1983; Horowitz, Tchernov, and Lernau 2018). Further south is Kh. Muhalhil (Bar Adon 1977: 114, 117–33). To the east, on the northern side of the Dead Sea, Rujm el-Bahr is a small stony island which served as an artificial anchorage (Bar Adon 1989; Hirschfeld 2006: 221–22). Various Iron Age II sherds were found by Bar Adon at the site but recent researchers believe these to be intrusive, i.e., they were brought to the site as residuals during later construction activities.[31] At Wadi Mukallik (Nahal Og) south of Kibbutz Almog, there is a cluster of three Iron Age II sites, and finally we reach Qumran.

At the top of the rocky pass to the west of Qumran is the Buqei'a plateau and on it are several Iron Age II sites, with the main ones situated at Kh. el-Maqari, Kh. es-Samrah, Kh. Karm Abu Tabaq, Kh. Abu Tabaqi, as well as two further unnamed sites; all of these were explored by Frank Cross and Józef Milik in the 1950s, and later by Lawrence E. Stager in the 1970s (fig. 17; Stager 1975, 1976; Cross and Milik 1956: 7; Cross 1993; Master 2009; Ilan 1973: 186–94). These Iron Age sites had sophisticated water harnessing systems, particular in the case of Kh. Abu Tabaq, Kh. es-Samrah, and Kh. al-Maqari, which also had large open reservoirs.[32] The landscapes immediately surrounding these sites were divided up into fenced plots of land with well-defined irrigation systems, dams, and retaining walls, now also partly destroyed. The appearance of these sites and the pottery found there suggested to Cross and Milik that the agricultural farming at these Buqei'a sites was a centrally organized activity conducted by the ruling authorities at the time of the reigns of Hezekiah or Josiah. What was grown in the fields on the plateau is unknown,[33] but we suggest they were sown primarily to provide green pasturage and irrigated using flood-farming techniques. Grazing would have been in the late winter and spring, with herds relying on stored fodder, dry stubble and natural shrubs for the rest of the year, with some transhumance occurring as well toward higher rainfall areas in the summer months. We suggest therefore that the settlements on the plateau were used as protected havens for semi-sedentary specialized pastoralists, with corrals for livestock, storage facilities, and access to water, probably used on a seasonal basis, during the seventh–sixth centuries BCE. While there are evident ecological constraints in the Buqei'a, with limited and unpredictable water sources and a lack of arable soil and other resources, aspects typical of a marginal environment, the archaeological evidence actually suggests otherwise and the region clearly thrived in the Iron Age II.[34]

---

31. On the new work at Rujm el–Bahr see Oren et al. 2015.

32. The Iron Age sites on the Buqei'a plateau were examined by the authors in October 2007, together with Rafael Y. Lewis and Mareike Grosser, as part of our roads investigation funded by the PEF. Another visit was made in January 2009 by Gibson, together with Norma Franklin and Louise Hitchcock.

33. Stager 1976: 146 suggested the cultivation of cereals and legumes.

34. On other marginal environments that were not so marginal, see Berger and Juengst 2017; Legge 2004.

Figure 17. An aerial view of the Buqei'a plateau toward the north. Photograph by S. Gibson.

Just south of Qumran, less than 1 km away, is an area with a few scattered ruins, which appears on Jack Ziegler's map under the name "Airneh" (fig. 18). It is here that de Vaux identified and partly excavated an Iron Age II structure, with a set of "casemate" rooms at the southwest corner of a large square enclosure (60 × 64 m) with two square "towers" at the southeast and northeast corners respectively (Humbert and Chambon 1994: 367, pl. XLVIII). It was never fully published, and it is now in a very bad state of preservation, with the modern road going through the eastern part of the structure. We reexamined the site, remeasuring the structural remains, and tentatively naming it Khirbet Irneh[35] (fig. 19). Our reexamination revealed the entire western boundary wall (1 m thick) belonging to the structure (62 m in length), with two separate ranges of "casemate" rooms along the inner side, at the southwest angle (23 × 3.50 m) and at the northwest angle (16.5 × 3.50 m). A gap (4 m wide) in the wall may have been the entrance into the compound (No. 5). The southwest range of rooms (Nos. 1–4) was excavated by de Vaux, consisting of four narrow and small rooms (4.80 × 1.50 m; 2.50 × 2.00 m; 4.70 × 2.00 m; 2.00 × 1.50 m), one which had a stone-cobbled floor (No. 1). We traced the northwest range of rooms (No. 6), not seen by de Vaux, and one can

---

35. The site was visited by the authors in October 2007 and November 2010, and measurements were taken with the assistance of Rafael Y. Lewis and Mareike Grosser.

detect the outlines of at least two small rooms (No. 7–8), but they remain unexcavated. The northern boundary wall (0.50 m thick) was traced for 19 m, and the southern wall for 28 m. It had pottery that was dated by de Vaux to the eighth century, suggesting it was superseded by the building on the plateau.[36] The surface Iron Age pottery we examined, however, was not particularly diagnostic, and it could very well be from the seventh century BCE.[37] The overall size of the enclosed compound (0.37 ha) suggests it was used primarily as a corral to contain livestock.[38]

Nearby, to the east, was another isolated Iron Age structure (12 × 12 m) which was linked to a zig-zagging Iron Age stone wall, running close to the dried-up spring of 'Ein Ghazal, which was also explored by de Vaux[39] (fig. 20). This wall and small building appear to have been destroyed in modern agricultural clearance work, and our repeated attempts to locate the original position of these remains have been unsuccessful.

The lower wall associated with the Israelite fortress extending toward 'Ein Feshkha was most likely built to delineate the plantation region irrigated by small springs. It resembled the construction method of the southern esplanade wall at Qumran, even though the latter was a terrace not a stone fence. In addition, there were various walls and small stone structures between Irneh and 'Ein Feshkha.[40] At 'Ein Feshkha, Yizhar Hirschfeld (2004: 171, 184) excavated an Iron Age structure on the hill to the west of the present road.

A late Iron Age fortified settlement existed at Kh. Mazin (Qasr el-Yahoud), south of 'Ein Feshkha,[41] but recent work shows the anchorage there is of later date because sea levels in the Iron Age were quite low (ca. 405 to 408 mbsl; Oren et al. 2015: 90). At 'Ein el-Ghuweir a structure was excavated dated to the eighth century BCE (Bar Adon 1989), and south of the site there is a long wall with rooms and houses, with structures running to 'Ein et-Turaba (Ofer 1998: 20, 29). 'Ein el-Ghuweir was established in the

---

36. De Vaux 1973: 58–59, and No. 35 on the general map in de Vaux 1956: pl. XL. Patrich 1994: 74, n. 4: structure No. 35 refers to this same Iron Age structure.

37. A later cemetery with at least six tombs made of piled stones with a north–south axis, was noticed within the courtyard of the Iron Age structure (No. 11). We examined this cemetery further to the south and it appears to be quite extensive. Most of the tombs were built of small heaped stones, but there are occasionally larger more prominent tombs as well, marked with rows of stones around their edges. Most of the tombs have a north–south axis, but there are a few with an east–west axis. Scattered sherds of nineteenth–early twentieth-century jars and water jugs (including those of the "Black Gaza Ware" variety) were visible on the surface.

38. By comparison the Khirbet es-Samrah compound in the Buqei'a has an area of 0.26 ha.

39. De Vaux 1973: 58–60; 1953: 540–61. This wall was so impressive that it figured prominently on a map of the region made in 1850/51: de Saulcy 1853: second map labeled "Itinéraire du pourtour de la mer morte."

40. De Vaux 1973: 59. A similar wall was found also running 600 m between 'Ein el-Ghuweir and 'Ein et-Turaba; see Blake 1966: 595; Bar Adon 1970: 399.

41. Bar Adon 1989, possibly related to a nearby village and caves; Bar Adon 1977: 126; Ofer 1998.

Figure 18. The northern angle of the Iron Age building at Khirbet Irneh toward the south. Photograph by S. Gibson.

late Iron Age, reestablished in the Hasmonean period, and continued to be used in Early Roman times. At 'Ein et-Turaba the same chronological parameters appear at a similar altitude (Ofer 1998: 41–49). 'Ein et-Turaba was a large well built structure with a courtyard in front, possibly dating to the eighth century BCE. At Rujm esh-Shajra, there was a late Iron Age fortified settlement near the coast (Bar Adon 1989: 86).

'Ein Gedi (Tel Goren) was undoubtedly a very important town along the western shore of the Dead Sea, thriving particularly in the seventh century BCE (Period V), with a perfume industry at the oasis.[42]

In addition to these sites with remains of built structures, Iron Age II material, dated to the eighth to early sixth century BCE, has been found in caves in the vicinity of Qumran (Burdajewicz 2016). The 1952 survey of caves close to Qumran uncovered such material in GQ6, 13, 27, 39, "Cave A" and "Cave B" (de Vaux 1962). A small fragment from the side of a bowl was found in Cave 9Q, one of the marl caves below the end of the esplanade (de Vaux 1961: 31). In 11Q jar fragments, a rounded juglet and two Iron Age II lamps were found (de Vaux 1956: 574; 1973: 51; Humbert and Chambon 1994: 265–66 and 344). Józef Milik (Milik 1959: 151; see Taylor 2016) excavated a cave with a protruding terrace above 'Ein Feshkha, (wrongly) identified as GQ37 in

---

42. Mazar, Dothan, and Dunayevsky 1966; Stern 2007: 23–27. At the top of the 'Ein Gedi ascent leading from Tel Goren westwards toward Tekoa is an Iron Age II fortress; Meshel and Ofer 2008; Porat and Davidovitch 2008: 73 map of road fig. 1.

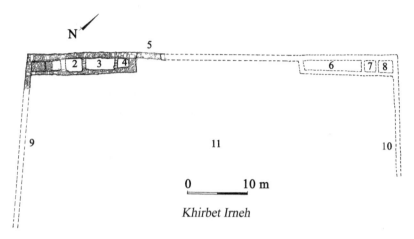

Figure 19. A plan of the range of 'casemate' rooms along the northwestern edge of the site at Khirbet Irneh, adapted from a drawing published by Humbert and Chambon (1994, pl. XLVIII), but with corrections and additions based on new measurements made by the authors in Nov 2010. Plan by S. Gibson.

Ziegler's map, with a stratum of Iron Age II sherds. Joseph Patrich's excavations of Cave 13 (probably cave GQ 2 in the 1952 survey)[43] also revealed Iron Age II pottery as well as a mud and palm-frond floor.[44] Patrich found the true GQ37, further north than on Ziegler's plan, also with a terrace and a mud and palm-frond floor, and containing a great deal of Iron Age II material, including two burials, one a child. There were also Iron Age II wooden beams, possibly from a ploughshare, and a juglet.[45] The University of California Long Beach found Iron Age II pottery in their survey at a site they designated as Cave 11, near the Kidron (Eisenman 2000: 126). The Operation Scroll Survey, which ranged over a large zone northwest of the Dead Sea, found 16 caves with Iron Age remains, nine of which are in the wider area around Qumran (Burdajewicz 2016: 248).

Further south, in caves 1, 2, and 3 in Wadi Murabba'at (Nahal Darga), there was pottery and other items from Iron Age II, including a letter dated to the eighth century BCE (Mur 17; Harding 1952; Benoit, Milik, and de Vaux 1961). Pessah Bar Adon identified Iron Age II sherds in caves west of Ain et-Turaba and Ain el-Ghuweir (Bar

---

43. Burdajewicz 2016: 247 wonders if Cave 13 was GQ37 as described in DJD 3, but actually this was another cave.

44. Patrich and Arubas 1989; see also Patrich 1994: 92 on the problem of dating this and other floors in caves.

45. Eisenman 2000: 123; Patrich 1989: 34. A decorated arrow shaft was originally thought to be Iron Age but it is now understood to be Roman, thanks to the reclassification by Guy Stiebel, see Taylor 2016: 20.

Adon 1989: 41–49). In the caves of Nahal Hever and Nahal David, close to 'Ein Gedi, several contain Iron Age II pottery (Amit and Eshel 1998), notably the Cave of the Pool (Avigad 1961).

Mariusz Burdajewicz has suggested from the pottery that most of these caves is from the eighth to sixth centuries and in some of the caves this can be narrowed to late seventh to early sixth centuries. He suggests most caves would have served as temporary shelters, for seasonal occupation, or as hideaways (Burdajewicz 2016: 253). One may note though that there is a burial in GQ37. There is some question about the marl caves at the end of the Qumran esplanade, overlooking the wadi. In an interview with Hershel Shanks, Frank Moore Cross suggested that the marl caves (4Qa, 4Qb, 5Q, 7Q–9Q) might be former Iron Age tombs.[46] Cross's suggestion may be supported somewhat by the fact that at Megiddo and Tell es-Saideyeh there are tombs cut into the edge of the Iron Age tells themselves, close to the settlements, and other hewn cave tombs of the Iron Age occur on the edge of wadis (Bloch-Smith 1992: 20, 39, figs. 17 and 18, cf. 256–57). Elizabeth Bloch-Smith notes that cave tombs are found in the "soft chalk and limestone outcrops of the foothills and highlands east and west of the Jordan River" and that such tombs were "initiated during the tenth through the sixth century BCE at the eastern Cisjordanian foothill and highland sites of Khirbet Beit Lei, Bethlehem, Lachish, Tell Judeidah, Ras-et-Tawil, Khirbet Rapud and Ez Zahariyah, and at Amman and Mt Nebo in Transjordan" (Bloch-Smith 1992: 39). Such tombs "cluster on the slopes below or outside a settlement, in rock cliffs facing a settlement" (Bloch-Smith 2013: 254).

Alternatively, as Burdajewicz suggests, it is possible that the marl caves do date from the Iron Age, but they were used for habitation. Burdajewicz (2016: 254) notes importantly that the majority of caves used in Iron Age II lie close to Qumran: "It is a marked cluster of caves in close proximity to the settlement on the plateau" (and see his fig. 17.1), and thus they deserve to be called "Qumran caves."

Cross-Temporal Study: Qumran in the Iron Age and in the Hasmonean Era

Having reviewed the evidence for Qumran in the Iron Age II, and considering also the contemporaneous environment, it appears that the settlement at the site was much more extensive than has previously been supposed, even by de Vaux's estimation, which is perhaps the reason why he decided not to define the cultural material from this time frame as an independent "period" in his overall chronological scheme of the site. Indeed it is surprising, but scholars continue to ignore or minimize the existence

---

46. This identification is not widely known, and we are grateful to Sidnie White Crawford for pointing this out to one of the authors (Taylor); Shanks 1994: 114. Alternatively, Magen and Peleg (2018: 100) surmise that the cemetery of trench-dug graves on the east side of Qumran had its beginnings in the Iron Age but they offer no evidence to support this idea.

BÂTIMENT ISOLÉ

Figure 20. A plan of the Iron Age "bâtiment isolé." Adapted from Humbert and Chambon 1994, pl. XLVIII.

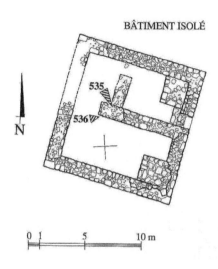

535

536

N

0 1 5 10 m

of this significant pre-Hasmonean stratum at the site, especially given that it has largely not been excavated down to this level.[47] What has been probed suggests a substantial settlement. This oversight is largely due to the great interest in periods that relate to the Dead Sea Scrolls, rather than in earlier centuries. This is unfortunate because, as we shall see, the overall architectural layout of the Iron Age settlement had a significant impact on the eventual appearance of the early phase of the Period Ib Late Hellenistic/ Hasmonean building complex at the site (fig. 7).

Analysis of the architectural remains dating from the Iron Age suggests an overall rectangular building complex (33 × 36 m), roughly resembling in character known building plans of that period elsewhere,[48] with stone-built foundations and a superstructure built of mud bricks (fig. 21). It comprised a tower-like domestic area protruding at the northeast angle of the compound (10 × 10 m), an industrial area in a corridor (10 m wide) within the southeast angle, probably open to the sky, another two corridors (10 m wide) to the south and west (L.4/1), which may have been subdivided originally into rooms, a very narrow corridor (L.38) on the north (6 m wide), and a large open square courtyard at the center of the complex (16 × 16 m), with open-air

---

47. Magen and Peleg 2018: 101–4 perpetuate this by not including a chapter on the stratigraphy of the Iron Age remains at Qumran in their final excavation report, except for a summary of the period in a chapter on the history of the site. Magen and Peleg 2018: 11, 103 sum up the Iron Age remains at Qumran as reflecting a temporary civilian and/or seminomadic settlement used on a seasonal basis in the winter months, with flimsy structures and tents.

48. For example, the Iron Age IIC site of Khirbet Abu et-Twein: Mazar 1982: 174. It had a rectangular plan with rooms surrounding a courtyard, and some of the surrounding long rooms were partitioned with rows of stone pillars. This might suggest that we should identify the north–south partition wall in L.51 at Qumran not as a full constructional wall but as the stone foundation for a row of monolithic stone pillars, such as can be seen at many Iron Age II sites in Judah.

working surfaces situated further to the south (e.g., the plastered floor beneath L.77). In addition , there was a smaller self-contained building on the west (19 × 15 m) which had a round cistern, conduits, and adjacent installations. The western building was sep- arated from the main building by an alley in L.107 (8 m wide). Various add-on build- ings probably existed as well, to the east and south, and a long wall ran along the eastern edge of the southern esplanade. Altogether, the built-up area covered an area of only 1.5 dunam, or 0.15 ha. The domestic area was limited, and most of the space was given over to water-harvesting, industrial activities, and storage. It is difficult to suggest a figure for the number of inhabitants living at the site in the Iron Age II because some of them may have been living in tents on the esplanade to the south,[49] but it is reasonable to assume that it was no more than two to three extended families.

The main dating evidence for the Iron Age occupation at the site is based on the pottery derived from de Vaux's excavations, which remains unpublished, but the overall assemblage of common wares is attributable to the seventh–sixth centuries BCE.[50]

While the Period I building complex at Qumran was evidently constructed some- time in the Late Hellenistic/Hasmonean era, various opinions have been given in re- gard to the date of its initial phase (Period Ia), with a starting date ranging between 150 and 100 BCE.[51] Our impression of the few intact artifacts that might be attributed to Period Ia, notably an intact cooking pot from under an oven in L.30, and a few bowls, is that they belong to ceramic types generally attributable to the last third of the second century BCE, but equally they could date from the very end of this time range as well, that is, to ca. 100 BCE, and thus to the very beginning of Period Ib as defined by de Vaux. This is also true of the late Hellenistic range of lamps from the site (Types 031, 032–035, 041–044), which conceivably might be of late second-century BCE date but are more likely to be from ca. 100 BCE at the earliest (Mlynarczyk 2013). Importantly, the Period Ib pottery at Qumran is identical to Hasmonean pottery from Jericho, which is attributed to no earlier than 90 BCE (Bar-Nathan 2006). One should also mention the evidence of Hellenistic coinage (Ptolemaic and Seleucid) indicating a general date in the last quarter of the second century BCE, which might be significant, but one has to take into account the possibility that some of these coins, especially the silver ones, remained in circulation until very late in that century and beyond. [52] The foundation

49. On the evidence for the use of tents at Qumran, albeit in later periods, see Homan 2002: 54–55.

50. One cannot deny that the settlement at Qumran might have been established already in the late eighth century BCE, but we think this unlikely. In the conclusion to Yezerski's study of the Iron Age pottery from the Magen/Peleg excavations, she suggests a mid-seventh century to early sixth century BCE date for the assemblage, though how this fits with the evidence of the two *lmlk* stamped handles from the site is left unresolved; Yezerski 2018: 347.

51. Davies 1982: 54; Cargill 2011. For a summary of the various views see Mizzi 2015.

52. De Vaux 1973: 18–19; and for the coins from L.120: Humbert and Chambon 1994: 329–30. A tetradrachm of Demetrius II from 129 BCE has recently come to light in the southern esplanade: Farhi

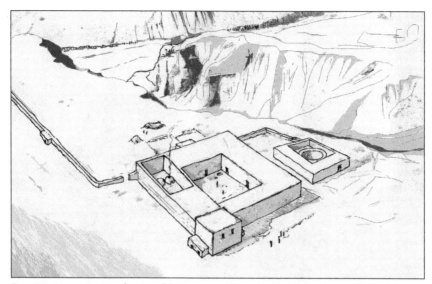

Figure 21. A reconstruction drawing of the Iron Age settlement toward the southwest with Wadi Qumran behind. Drawing by S. Gibson.

Figure 22. Leveled areas immediately to the north of Qumran which were probably adapted in antiquity for green pasturage. Note the remnants of a terrace wall in the foreground. Photograph by S. Gibson.

Figure 23. The authors, Taylor and Gibson, in Pool L.49, deliberating the architectural and stratigraphic phasing of the site at Qumran. Photograph by D. Gibson.

date in ca. 100 BCE places the Hasmonean settlement of Qumran in the reign of Alexander Jannaeus (103–76 BCE).[53]

This suggests that de Vaux's subsequent Period Ia in the second century BCE did not in fact exist, as originally suggested by Magness (2002: 64–68; Mizzi and Magness 2016: 301–2). It consists of fills with an amalgamation of mixed cultural materials derived from two strata: residual items from the earlier Iron Age level, on the one hand, and intrusive items from the very first phase of the Late Hellenistic/Hasmonean era (Period Ib, i.e., from no earlier than ca. 100 BCE), on the other. As we have seen, quite a few Iron Age stratigraphical features were incorporated erroneously by de Vaux into his Period Ia. Added to this, we have the new Iron Age material uncovered by Magen and Peleg that confirms the importance of the Iron Age stratum at Qumran, despite their own interpretations. There is now a growing understanding that the chronological scheme of periods employed by de Vaux at Qumran no longer works, and that his Period Ia is actually a conflation of a number of different phases of construction (Mizzi 2015; Mizzi and Magness 2016).

While the first cohesive Hasmonean settlement at Qumran appears to have been established no earlier than the very beginning of the first century BCE, with the Period Ia phase of the late second century BCE now quite dubious, it is clear that there was an initial building phase in which there was a Hasmonean square enclosure, but floors have not survived in situ (except for traces of an oven in L.30). A few residual Late Hellenistic pottery types are in mixed contexts from Period Ib. If we retain de Vaux's terminology, for the purpose of the present paper, we need at least to see Period Ib as a phase that had two stages of development: (1) an initial Hasmonean square enclosure and (2) an expanded form with complex water systems and industrial units.[54] For the overall layout of the Hasmonean phase of Qumran, we follow what has been presented previously in the work of Humbert.[55]

But how does our reconstruction of the layout of the Iron Age settlement compare with the layout of the subsequent Hasmonean (Period I) settlement and its Roman successor?

Without going into any minor issues, the overall points of similarity are:

1. *A need for a viable and sophisticated water collection system.* In the Iron Age, the harsh environment made water harvesting an imperative at Qumran. The "cistern

---

and Price 2010. See now seven additional Ptolemaic and Seleucid coins from excavations at Qumran in Ariel 2018.

53. For further on the historical background and dating of what should just be called Period I, see Taylor 2012: 225, 227, 251–52.

54. The form of this initial Hasmonean construction has been explored most extensively in Humbert and Chambon 1994: 419–44, 467–82.

55. We are grateful to Jean-Baptiste Humbert for sending us a forthcoming paper that summarizes his arguments to be published in the next Qumran volume, and focuses on comparanda of other square structures.

house," on the west side of the settlement, functioned sufficiently well for it to be ser-
viced by two direct access stepped reservoirs. The pottery-making procedures would
have required a variety of features and water was of course essential for other purposes
as well. During the Hasmonean era this water-collection system was expanded, but initially, during the early phase of Period I, the original Iron Age water system was simply
cleaned, repaired and put back into use. The continuity in the use of water installations
spanning different periods is a well known phenomenon at Iron Age to Roman sites in
the southern Levant.

2. *Pottery-making.* Pottery making is a feature of both the Iron Age and the Hasmonean-Roman periods (Periods I–II). There appears to have been two kilns functioning
simultaneously in the Iron Age, accessed from different directions. Petrographic studies
should now be made on the Iron Age pottery from Qumran to see if it is possible to
ascertain which of the pottery vessels were made locally and which types were brought
in from elsewhere.[56] In the Hasmonean-Roman era there were also two kilns, one kiln
in L.64 for making larger ceramic vessels and one for smaller vessels, also accessed from
different directions just as they were in the Iron Age. Pottery-making was undoubtedly a key activity in Iron Age Qumran, but not necessarily the only one. Our lack of
information concerning the nonceramic finds from the Iron Age levels at the site (e.g.,
animal bones, carbonized seeds, fibres, etc.), does not mean we should just assume
the settlement at that time was only a pottery-making facility. Other multiresourcing
activities may have included: the gathering of salt and bitumen from the Dead Sea for
trade, weaving and rug-making, the up-keep of areas for green pasturage to the north
and south of the settlement on leveled and terracing land,[57] and the herding of livestock
(sheep/goats) and exploitation of their secondary products (milk, wool, and hair; fig.
22).

---

56. Yezerski 2018: 339, but she does not dwell much on fabrics. The vessels were moderately
well-fired, with slips, some of the red variety, and many ring burnished. The ware contained varying
quantities of large and small white limestone grits. The percentages of nonslipped vessels and
burnished vessels were not calculated. Yezerski does, however, indicate that similarities of material
in terms of techniques of production and surface treatment imply that some vessels were made in a
"shared workshop" (p. 340). In his petrographic study of the Iron Age II pottery assemblage from the
Buqei'a sites on the plateau west of Qumran, Master 2009: 308 notes that "a surprising amount of the
domestic pottery was made locally."

57. Clearly, straightforward agricultural pursuits would not have been possible in the immediate
Qumran environment during the Iron Age, owing to the constraints of a harsh arid climate and a
lack of water, notwithstanding the fact that the climate at that time was a little better than it is today
(see below, n. 62). Later, during Hasmonean/Roman times, the growing of date trees was a major
commercial venture practiced in the region, and these plantations required high maintenance. We
believe a few date trees were probably grown on the southern esplanade of Qumran, and the press
unearthed at L.75 was probably used for making date wine (contra Magen and Peleg 2018: 90 and fig.
108, who argue that it was used for water sedimentation). In addition, a date palm grove must have
existed at 'Ein Feshka; Broshi 2006.

3. *Orientation.* The orientation of the Iron Age structures is replicated in the later
Hasmonean-Roman constructions. As was common, a ruin provided readily available
building materials and a template for the layout of later buildings. Fallen walls were
raised and new walls were built on old foundations. This resulted in the "disappearance"
of Iron Age walls beneath the lower parts of Hasmonean walls. Additional Iron Age
walls were likely to have been quarried for building stones, during the sinking of foundations in later periods, which further resulted in the diminishing of the preservation
of the earliest remains at the site. It is not surprising therefore that the oldest remains
are also the worst preserved.

4. *Burning.* Given the extent of the ubiquitous ashy layer, it is likely that the Iron
Age settlement was destroyed by a devastating fire caused by an invading army in
587/586 or 582 BCE. Another fire from the invading army of the Romans devastated
the site in 68 CE. In between, there may have been occasional localized fires (see Wagemakers and Taylor 2011).

Differences

1. *Size.* Overall, it seems the size of the occupied space of the main enclosure in the two
periods is not considerably different. However, as Period Ib developed, the western sector of the site was expanded and divided up into much smaller interior spaces, and the
overall layout became more complex, with the addition of a very large defensive tower
on the north. The water systems were much expanded and developed with many more
pools. The need for expanded water systems, given the relatively small size of the site, is
striking, but it does not seem to be a direct result of the clay-preparation procedures as
Magen and Peleg have suggested. The extension of the water system might indicate an
increasing need for water in the Hasmonean-Roman periods for the special activities
of the site, with a greater reliance on capturing the flood waters from the wadi to the
west, with water carried down by aqueduct.[58] By comparison the Iron Age water system

---

58. Ilan and Amit 2002. The original date of the aqueduct is uncertain, but it was undoubtedly in
use during Period II; de Vaux 1973: 8 attributed it to Period Ib, but Humbert in Humbert, Chambon,
and Mlynarczyk 2016: 425–32 now suggests it was established after ca. 31 BCE. In November 2009
a trip was organized by one of the authors of this paper (Gibson) to examine the outlet at the eastern
end of the aqueduct, with the participation of the late David Amit, Stephen Pfann, the late David
Stacey, and the late Yuval Peleg. We examined the following locations: (1) the base of the "waterfall";
(2) the supposed barrage/dam and its axis, and the area behind where water might have been
intentionally "ponded"; (3) the rock-cut aqueduct; (4) the tunnel and its relationship to a segment of
looped aqueduct; and (5) the possible rock-cut spillways to the south. Peleg was of the opinion that
the barrage/dam never existed, and that the aqueduct only collected water from the gullies leading
from the southern side of the wadi, that the "loop" was a first and unsuccessful attempt to create the
aqueduct, and that it was eventually superseded by the tunnel. He also thought the spillways (one or
all three of them) are natural. Peleg indicated that he had prepared a new map of the aqueduct, which
he planned to update as a result of our November field trip. David Amit disagreed with Peleg in regard

seems quite small, and was entirely dependent on rainwater and surface flooding from the immediate area round about.

2. *Complexity.* Along with the size of the settlement, the later settlement has a much more complex layout, indicating it had numerous new functions, though this assessment must take into account that much of the Iron Age architectural remains are either unexcavated or in a bad state of preservation. This becomes increasingly apparent as the site develops through the first century BCE and first century CE, with a nonsymmetrical pattern which deviates from the symmetry of both the Iron Age and initial Hasmonean phase building complexes. The nonsymmetrical and expansive developments include a meandering water system, the industrial complex on the west, and the extensive use of marl and limestone caves in the vicinity of the site (Broshi and Eshel 2004).

3. *Continuity.* While the Iron Age site did not recover after its destruction in the sixth century BCE, the site of Qumran in Period II did not suffer the same devastation that made reuse of it impossible, and it continued to be occupied in Period III, at least until the 90s of the first century CE and finally in the Bar Kokhba period (Taylor 2006; 2012: 261–65).

4. *Relationship.* While in the Iron Age it is easy to see the close relationship Qumran had with its many surrounding settlements, to which it was connected via a network of roads and paths, the relationship between Qumran in the Hasmonean–Roman period and other settlements is less than clear. In other words, Qumran of the Hasmonean–Roman period was apparently much more isolated in its regional setting than in the

---

to the looping aqueduct being an abandoned attempt at creating an aqueduct, and pointed out that plaster was visible adhering to the side wall of this aqueduct, at the point where it linked up to the tunnel, and therefore the plaster must indicate that it had functioned at some point. Amit also believed that at least one of the spillways to the south was artificially cut, notably the one leading from the wadi to the southeast, which he said was much better preserved in tunnel form and with tooling seen on its sides when he first investigated it more than 20 years earlier (this feature is No. 5 on his published map), extending to a deep cut in the rock scarp which is clearly an outlet for surplus water dropping down to the wadi below. The existence of a barrage/dam does fit the topography and would have been a logical feature, so as to collect the maximum of water especially at times when the flow of water was at a minimum. Hence, water ponding behind the barrage wall would have reached a height of at least 2 m. Nothing is now visible of any construction or wall, but this is probably because it was washed away by flash floods which in the winter descend in this area with a ferocious energy. The spillway channel (No. 5) would have taken surplus waters away to the southeast from behind the dam when flooding occurred. Moreover, on the opposite side, there is a level area which may represent the remnants of a channel linking the area behind the barrage to the v-junction to the east of the aqueduct and its southern loop. All the participants agreed that the construction of this aqueduct would have required substantial engineering expertise and financial investment. Compare these comments to those in Stacey and Doudna 2013. Magness 2014 disagrees with Stacey's date for the original construction of the aqueduct in Period II, and follows de Vaux's dating for it in the Hasmonean Period Ib. The Hasmonean date is also maintained by Magen and Peleg 2018: 75–80, figs. 86–88 who compare it to the Hasmonean aqueduct known from nearby Jericho and thus date it accordingly.

previous Iron Age.[59] The nearby site of 'Ein Feshkha was developed in the Hasmonean period, as were other Iron Age settlements to the south (Kh. Mazin, 'Ein el-Ghuweir) and to the north (Rujm el-Bahr), but these by comparison are smaller and much further apart in distance than the corresponding Iron Age settlements (e.g., the short distance between Qumran and Kh. Irneh). There are no settlements in the Buqei'a until later in the Roman period, perhaps corresponding to Period III in Qumran. Qumran therefore appears much more isolated in these later periods (fig. 23). Pastoralist groups in this region may have been impoverished, or intentionally excluded from the region owing to the development of date plantations and with the build-up along the coast of sea-faring activities for the gathering of bitumen, sulphur, and salt.

Conclusions

The Iron Age building complex at Qumran fits very well the picture of expanding and burgeoning settlements along the eastern border of the Kingdom of Judah in the seventh century BCE.[60] It is during this century that the central state authority was actively strengthening its eastern defences against possible pillaging and encroachment of military incursions from Transjordan (Ammonites and/or Moabites), by building very small fortified outposts, by developing networks of roads/paths, by encouraging economic advantages, such as the extraction of salt and bitumen from the Dead Sea, by providing safe passage for caravans of traders crossing through this area, by instigating industrial and agricultural activities, and by supporting the needs of local nomadic and semipastoralist groups in order to gain their loyalty (Stern 1994).

Hence, we argue against the notion that the catalyst for the flourishing of settlements along the eastern border of Judah was the direct result of an influx of refugees into the Kingdom of Judah from the north, following Sennacherib's successful invasion of Samaria in 720 BCE, who were forced by circumstances to adopt a seminomadic existence (Magen and Peleg 2018: 101–4; 2006: 73–79), on the grounds that at times of major stress and hardship refugees from towns/cities head toward urban centers and not into marginal environments, such as the Judaean Desert, which had limited water sources. The oasis of Jericho would be a good destination, but not the Buqei'a plateau. In general terms, the settlement process in this region was most likely the result of a state initiative concerned with protecting the eastern border of Judah against military incursions from the east. This was not done by erecting large numbers of forts, but by "filling the vacuum" by establishing a plethora of very small enclosed *ḥṣr* (חצר) settlements with different functions,[61] and by securing the allegiance of nomadic, semisedentary and pastoralist groups in the area.

---

59. For an alternative approach, see Zangenberg 2004.

60. On the economic prosperity of the southern Levant in the seventh century BCE under Assyrian control, see Faust and Weiss 2005.

61. The *ḥṣr* (חצר) could equally refer to a small enclosed agricultural farmstead in highland

Technological know-how might also have been provided by the Judahite state in facilitating the establishment of water collection and harvesting systems at sites, as can be seen at Qumran and perhaps also in the Buqeiʻa, which would have encouraged people to settle in such marginal arid environments.[62] In addition, there can be no doubt that the road and path systems of the region were substantially improved and developed at this time, and this was unprecedented, as we were previously able to show through our work in the region of Qumran (Taylor and Gibson 2011). The opening up of these roads and paths to human traffic, clearing them of stones and maintaining them from winter flooding, was not done on an ad hoc basis; protecting them was imperative for the safety and economy of the Kingdom of Judah in the seventh century BCE and it provided considerable political and financial advantage.

The Hasmonean settlement at Qumran (beginning ca. 100 BCE) was far more isolated than its Iron Age predecessor, and it was connected to only a few local sites along the Dead Sea. The Hasmonean complex had a defensive tower, but was otherwise built very much on the same template as the preceding Iron Age structure, adopting the same kind of symmetrical plan and utilizing surviving walls, to such an extent that it is sometimes impossible to separate out the Iron Age and Hasmonean phasing in individual walls. In addition to this problem, the Period I settlement at Qumran undoubtedly had at least two construction stages during the course of the first half of the first century BCE, and distinguishing between the architectural features of the two is complicated. The basic plan of the initial Hasmonean-period resettlement, which may be closely associated with the early building works at Rujm el-Bahr and Khirbet Mazin/Qasr el-Yahoud, was eventually replaced with a far more-developed water system, an industrial center, cave use, and a complex of buildings that deviates from the original symmetrical plan. While these new developments may be the direct result of the economic advantages of maintaining large date plantations in the area, they also indicate that the site of Qumran, in terms of its layout and functions, had now become

---

environments (e.g., in the region of Jerusalem), or to an enclosed small settlement used by semi-sedentary pastoralists (e.g., in the Judaean Desert), as one of the present authors already pointed out long ago, based on archaeological surveys of Iron Age sites around Jerusalem: Edelstein, Gat, and Gibson 1983 (Hebrew). See now a comprehensive discussion on the terms בית החצרים and חצר in Faust 2008a: 109. On settlements in the Iron Age II with clearly defined boundary walls or fences, see Faust 2017.

62. Notwithstanding the current low rainfall in the Dead Sea region, it would appear the climate of the southern Levant was wetter in the Iron Age. However, this does not mean that the Qumran environment in the Iron Age was markedly different from today's. One must take into consideration the variable climatic fluctuations that existed at that time, and the impact these might have had on human populations at the micro level, especially to those vulnerable to drought, which can occur even in regions with temperate climates. Indeed, very small shifts in climate in an arid zone can be disastrous for the survival of pastoralist groups and their flocks. On the evidence for the climate in the Iron Age, see Neumann et al. 2010: 760–62; and the summary in Langgut et al. 2015: 230.

fundamentally distinct from the much older Iron Age and earlier Hasmonean building complexes that preceded it.

References

Abel, F.-M. 1938. *Géographie de la Palestine*, vol. 2. Paris: Gabalda.

Ahituv, Shmuel. 1993. "The Missing District: A Study in the List of the Cities and Districts of Judah in Joshua 15:21–62." *Eretz-Israel* 24:7–11 (Hebrew).

Allegro, John. 1959–1960. *The Copper Scroll from Qumran*. Glasgow: Glasgow University Oriental Society.

Amit, David, and Hanan Eshel. 1998. "The Bar Kokhba Period Finds from the Tetradrachm Cave." Pages 189–204 in *Refuge Caves of the Bar Kokhba Revolt*. Edited by Hanan Eshel and David Amit. Tel Aviv: Israel Exploration Society (Hebrew).

Ariel, Donald T. 2018. "Coins from the Renewed Excavations at Qumran." Pages 403–30 in *Back to Qumran: Final Report (1993–2004)*. Edited by Yitzhak Magen and Yuval Peleg. Jerusalem: Israel Antiquities Authority.

Avigad, Nahman. 1961. "Expedition A – Nahal David." *IEJ* 12:169–83.

Bar Adon, Pessah. 1970. "Rivage de la Mer Morte: Un établissement essénien." *RevB* 77:398–400.

———. 1972. "The Judean Desert and Plain of Jericho." Pages 92–152 in *Judaea, Samaria and the Golan: Archaeological Survey 1967–1968*. Publications of the Archaeological Survey of Israel 1. Edited by Moshe Kochavi. Jerusalem: Carta (Hebrew).

———. 1977. "Another Settlement of the Judean Desert Sect." *BASOR* 227:22–23.

———. 1989. "Excavations in the Judaean Desert." *'Atiqot* 9:3–14 (Hebrew).

Bar-Nathan, Rahel. 2006. "Qumran and the Hasmonean and Herodian Winter Palaces of Jericho: The Implication of the Pottery Finds on the Interpretation of the Settlement at Qumran." Pages 263–77 in *Qumran, the Site of the Dead Sea Scrolls: Archaeological Interpretations and Debates; Proceedings of a Conference Held at Brown University, November 17–19, 2002*. Edited by Katharina Galor, Jean-Baptiste Humbert, and Jürgen Zangenberg. Studies on the Texts of the Desert of Judah 57. Leiden: Brill.

Benoit, P., Józef T. Milik, and Roland de Vaux, eds. 1961. *Les grottes de Murabba'ât*. DJD 2. Oxford: Clarendon.

Berger, Elizabeth, and Sara L. Juengst. 2017. "Humans in Marginal Environments: Adaptation Among Living and Ancient Peoples." *American Journal of Human Biology* 29:e23022. https://doi.org/10.1002/ajhb.23022.

Blake, Ian. 1966. "Chronique archéologique." *RevB* 73:595.

Bloch-Smith, Elizabeth. 1992. *Bronze and Iron Age Burials and Funerary Customs in the Southern Levant*. Sheffield: JSOT Press.

———. 2013. "Death and Burial: Bronze and Iron Age." Pages 254–62 in *The Oxford Encyclopedia of the Bible and Archaeology*. Edited by Daniel Master. Oxford: Oxford University Press.

Broshi, Magen. 2006. "Was There Agriculture at Qumran?." Pages 249–52 in *Qumran, the Site of the Dead Sea Scrolls: Archaeological Interpretations and Debates. Proceedings of a Conference held at Brown University, November 17–19, 2002*. Edited by Katharina Galor, Jean-Baptiste Humbert, and Jürgen Zangenberg. Studies on the Texts of the Desert of Judah 57. Leiden: Brill.

Broshi, Magen, and Hanan Eshel. 2004. "Three Seasons of Excavations at Qumran." *JRA* 17:321–32.

Burdajewicz, Mariusz. 2016. "History of the 'Qumran Caves' in the Iron Age in the Light of the

Pottery Evidence." Pages 247–60 in *The Caves of Qumran: Proceedings of the International Conference, Lugano 2014*. Edited by Marcello Fidanzio. Studies on the Texts of the Desert of Judah 118. Leiden: Brill.

Cargill, Robert R. 2011. "The State of the Archaeological Debate at Qumran." *CBR* 10:101–18.

Cross, Frank M. 1956. "A Footnote to Biblical History." *BA* 19:5–17.

———. 1993. "El-Buqei'a." *NEAEHL* 1:267–69.

Cross, Frank M., and Józef T. Milik. 1956. "Explorations in the Judaean Buqe'ah." *BASOR* 142:5–17.

Davies, Philip R. 1982. *Qumran*. Grand Rapids: Eerdmans.

Edelstein, Gershon, Yosef Gat, and Shimon Gibson. 1983. "Food Production and Water Storage in the Jerusalem Area." *Qadmoniot* 16:16–23 (Hebrew).

Eisenman, Robert. 2000. "The 1988–1992 California State University Dead Sea Walking Cave Survey and Radar Groundscan of the Qumran Cliffs." *Qumran Chronicle* 9: 123–30.

Eitan, A. 1983. "Vered Jericho." Pages 106–7 in *Excavations and Surveys in Israel* 2. Jerusalem: Israel Antiquities Authority.

Eshel, Hanan. 2009. *Qumran: Scrolls, Caves, History*. Jerusalem: Carta.

Farhi, Yoav, and Randall Price. 2010. "The Numismatic Finds from the Qumran Plateau Excavations 2004–2006, and 2008 Seasons." *DSD* 17:210–25.

Faust, Avraham. 2003. "The Farmstead in the Highlands of Iron II Israel." Pages 91–104 in *The Rural Landscape of Ancient Israel*. Edited by Shimon Dar, Aren M. Maeir, and Zeev Safrai. Oxford: Archaeopress.

———. 2008a. "Cities, Villages, and Farmsteads: The Landscape of Leviticus 25:29–31." Pages 103–12 in *Exploring the Longue Durée: Essays in Honor of Lawrence E. Stager*. Edited by J. David Schloen. Winona Lake: IN: Eisenbrauns.

———. 2008b. "Settlement and Demography in Seventh-Century Judah and the Extent and Intensity of Sennacherib's Campaign." *PEQ* 140:168–94.

———. 2008c. "Water Systems in Bronze and Iron Age Israel." Pages 2234–35 in *Encyclopaedia of the History of Science, Technology and Medicine in Non-Western Cultures*. Edited by Helaine Selin. Dordrecht: Kluwer.

———. 2017. "The Bounded Landscape: Archaeology, Language, Texts, and the Israelite Perception of Space." *JMA* 30:3–32.

———. 2018. "Forts or Agricultural Estates? Persian Period Settlement in the Territories of the Former Kingdom of Judah." *PEQ* 150:34–59.

Faust, Avraham, and Ehud Weiss. 2005. "Judah, Philistia, and the Mediterranean World: Reconstructing the Economic System of the Seventh Century B.C.E." *BASOR* 338:71–92.

Gibson, Shimon. 2009. "The Suba Water System as a Clay-Production Plant in the Iron Age II." *Eretz-Israel* 29:45*–56*.

Gitin, Seymour. 2015. "Chapter 3.3: Iron Age IIC: Judah." Pages 345–64 in *The Ancient Pottery of Israel and Its Neighbors from the Iron Age Through the Hellenistic Period*, vol. 1. Edited by Seymour Gitin. Jerusalem: Israel Exploration Society.

Haiman, Mordechai. 2002. "Water Sources and the Iron Age II Settlement Pattern in the Negev Desert." Pages 23–31 in *Cura Aquarum in Israel Proceedings of the 11th International Conference on the History of Water Management and Hydraulic Engineering in the Mediterranean Region, Israel, 7–12 May, 2001*. Edited by C. Ohlig, Yuval Peleg ,and Tsvika Tsuk. Siegburg: Deutsche Wasserhistorischen Gesellschaft.

Harding, Gerald L. 1952. "Khirbet Qumran and Wadi Muraba'at: Fresh Light on the Dead Sea Scrolls and the New Manuscript Discoveries in Jordan." *PEQ* 84:104–9.

Herr, Larry G. 1999. "The Ammonites in the Late Iron Age and Persian Period." Pages 219–37 in *Ancient Ammon*. Edited by B. MacDonald and R. W. Younker. Leiden: Brill.

Hirschfeld, Yizhar. 2004. *Qumran in Context: Reassessing the Archaeological Evidence.* Peabody, MA: Hendersen.

———. 2006. "The Archaeology of the Dead Sea Valley in the Late Hellenistic and Roman Periods." Pages 215–29 in *New Frontiers in Dead Sea Paleoenvironmental Research.* Edited by Yehouda Enzel, Amotz Agnon, and Mordechai Stein. Geological Society of America Special Paper 401. DOI: https://doi.org/10.1130/SPE401.

Homan, Michael M. 2002. *To Your Tents, O Israel! The Terminology, Function, Form, and Symbolism of Tents in the Hebrew Bible and the Ancient Near East.* CHANE 12. Leiden: Brill.

Horowitz, Liora Kolska, Eitan Tchernov, and Omri Lernau. 2018. "The Archaeozoology of Vered Yericho, an Iron Age II Fortified Structure in the Kingdom of Judah." Pages 966–1007 in *Studies in the History and Archaeology of Israel: Essays in Honor of Aren M. Maier on the Occasion of His Sixtieth Birthday.* Edited by Itzhaq Shai, Jeffrey R. Chadwick, Louise Hitchcock, Amit Dagan, Chris McKinny and Joe Uziel. Münster: Zaphon.

Humbert, Jean-Baptiste, and Alain Chambon. 1994. *Fouilles de Khirbet Qumrân et de Ain Feshkha I: Album de photographies. Répertoire du fonds photographique. Synthèse des notes de chantier du Père Roland de Vaux.* Novum Testamentum et Orbis Antiquus, Series Archæologica 1. Fribourg: Editions universitaires; Göttingen: Vandenhoeck & Ruprecht.

Humbert, Jean-Baptiste, Alain Chambon, and Jolanta Mlynarczyk. 2016. *Khirbet Qumrân et Aïn Feshkha, Fouilles du P. Roland de Vaux,* vol. IIIa, *L'archéologie de Qumrân, Reconsidération de l'interprétation; Corpus of the Lamps.* Novum Testamentum et Orbis Antiquus, Series Archæologica 1B. Göttingen: Vandenhoeck & Ruprecht.

Ilan, Zvi, ed. 1973. *The Judaean Desert and the Dead Sea.* Tel Aviv: Society for the Protection of Nature in Israel (Hebrew).

Ilan, Zvi, and David Amit. 2002. "The Aqueduct of Qumran." Pages 380–86 in *The Aqueducts of Israel.* Edited by David Amit, Joseph Patrich, and Yizhar Hirschfeld. Portsmouth, RI: Society for the Promotion of Roman Studies.

Isaacs, Albert Augustus. 1857. *The Dead Sea: Notes and Journeys Made during a Journey to Palestine in 1856–7.* London: Hatchard & Son.

Kenyon, Kathleen M., and Thomas A. Holland. 1982. *Excavations at Jericho,* vol. 3. London: British School of Archaeology in Jerusalem.

Langgut, Dafna, Israel Finkelstein, Thomas Litt, Frank Harald Neumann, and Mordechai Stein. 2015. "Vegetation and Climate Changes during the Bronze and Iron Ages (~3600–600 BCE) in the Southern Levant Based on Palynological Records." *Radiocarbon* 57.2: 217–35.

Laperrousaz, E. M. 1966. "Brèves remarques archéologiques concernant la chronologie des occupations esséniennes de Qoumran." *RevQ* 12:199–212.

———. 1976. *Qoumran, l'établissement essénien des bords de la Mer Morte, histoire et archéologie du site.* Paris: Picard.

———. 1980. "Problèmes d'histoire et d'archéologie qoumrâniennes: à propos d'un souhait de précisions." *RevQ* 10:269–91.

Lapp, Nancy L. 1976. "Casemate Walls in Palestine and the Late Iron II Casemate at Tell el-Ful (Gibeah)." *BASOR* 223:25–42.

Legge, Anthony J. 2004. "Margins and Marginality." Pages 118–20 in *Colonisation, Migration, and Marginal Areas.* Edited by Marina Mondini, Sebastián Munoz, and Stephen Wickler. Oxford: Oxbow.

Lemaire, André 1981. "Classification des estampilles royales judéennes." *Eretz Israel* 15:54*–60*

———. 2003. "Inscriptions du khirbeh, des grottes et de 'Ain Feshkha." Pages 341–88 in *Khirbet Qumran and 'Ain Feshkha II: Études d'anthropologie, de physique et de chimie.* Edited by Jean-Baptiste Humbert and Jan Gunneweg. Novum Testamentum et Orbis Antiquus,

Series Archæologica 3. Fribourg: Editions universitaires; Göttingen: Vandenhoeck & Ruprecht.

Lipschits, Oded. 2012. "Archaeological Facts, Historical Speculations and the Date of the *lmlk* Storage Jars: A Rejoinder to David Ussishkin." *JHebS* 12.4:1–14, DOI:10.5508/jhs.2012.v12.a4.

Lipschits, Oded, O. Sergi, and I. Koch. 2010. "Royal Judahite Jar Handles: Reconsidering the Chronology of *lmlk* Stamp Impressions." *TA* 37:3–32.

Magen, Yitzhak, and Yuval Peleg. 2006. "Back to Qumran: Ten Years of Excavation and Research, 1993–2004." Pages 55–113 in *Qumran, the Site of the Dead Sea Scrolls: Archaeological Interpretations and Debates; Proceedings of a Conference Held at Brown University, November 17–19, 2002*. Edited by Katharina Galor, Jean-Baptiste Humbert, and Jürgen Zangenberg. Studies on the Texts of the Desert of Judah 57. Leiden: Brill.

———. 2007. *The Qumran Excavations 1993–2004: Preliminary Report*. Jerusalem: Israel Antiquities Authority.

———. 2018. *Back to Qumran: Final Report (1993–2004)*. Jerusalem: Israel Antiquities Authority.

Magness, Jodi. 2002. *The Archaeology of Qumran and the Dead Sea Scrolls*. Grand Rapids: Eerdmans.

———. 2014. "Review of Stacey and Doudna." *RevQ* 26:638–46.

Master, Daniel. 2009. "From the Buqê'ah to Ashkelon." Pages 305–17 in *Exploring the Longue Durée: Essays in Honor of Lawrence E. Stager*. Edited by J. David Schloen. Winona Lake, IN: Eisenbrauns.

Mazar, Benjamin, Trude Dothan, and Immanuel Dunayevsky. 1966. *En Gedi: The First and Second Seasons of Excavations 1961–1962*. Jerusalem: Israel Exploration Society.

Mazar, Amihai. 1982. "Three Israelite Sites in the Hills of Judah and Ephraim." *BA* 45.3:167–78.

Mazar, Amihai, David Amit, and Zvi Ilan. 1995. "Hurvat Shilhah: An Iron Age Site in the Judean Desert." Pages 193–211 in *Retrieving the Past: Research and Methodology in Honour of Gus Van Beek*. Edited by Joe Seger. Starkville, MS: Cobb Institute of Archaeology.

Meshel, Zeev, and Avraham Ofer. 2008. "A Judahite Fortress and a First-Century Building Near the Top of the 'En-Gedi Ascent." *IEJ* 58:51–72.

Milik, Józef T. 1959. *Ten Years of Discovery in the Wilderness of Judaea*. London: SCM.

Miller, Robert. 1980. "Water Use in Syria and Palestine from the Neolithic to the Bronze Age." *World Archaeology* 11:331–41.

Mizzi, Dennis. 2015. "Qumran Period I Reconsidered: An Evaluation of Several Competing Theories." *DSD* 22:1–42.

Mizzi, Dennis, and Jodi Magness. 2016. "Was Qumran Abandoned at the End of the First Century BCE?." *JBL* 135:301–20.

Mlynarczyk, Jolanta. 2013. "Terracotta Oil Lamps from Qumran: The Typology." *RevB* 120:99–133.

Neumann, Frank Harald, E. J. Kagan, S. A. G. Leroy, and Uri Baruch. 2010. "Vegetation History and Climate Fluctuations on a Transect along the Dead Sea West Shore and their Impact on Past Societies over the Last 3500 Years." *Journal of Arid Environments* 74:756–64.

Nigro, Lorenzo. 2014. "Aside the Spring: Tell es-Sultan/Ancient Jericho: The Tale of an Early City and Water Control in Ancient Palestine." Pages 25–51 in *A History of Water*. Vol. 1: *Water and Urbanization*. Edited by Terje Tvedt and Terje Oestigaard. London: Tauris.

Noth, Martin. 1938. *Das Buch Joshua*. Tubingen: Mohr.

Ofer, Avraham. 1998. "The Desert Towns of Judah." *Cathedra* 90:7–32 (Hebrew).

Oren, Asaf, Ehud Galili, Gideon Hadas, and Mich Klein. 2015. "Two Artificial Anchorages off the Northern Shore of the Dead Sea: A Specific Feature of an Ancient Maritime Cultural Landscape." *International Journal of Nautical Archaeology* 44:81–94.

Patrich, Joseph. 1989. "Hideouts in the Judean Wilderness: Jewish Revolutionaries and Christian Ascetics Sought Shelter and Protection in Cliffside Caves." *BAR* 15.5:32–42.

———. 1994. "Khirbet Qumran in Light of New Archaeological Explorations in the Qumran Caves." Pages 73–95 in *Methods of Investigation of the Dead Sea Scrolls and the Khirbet Qumran Site*. Edited by Michael O. Wise et al. New York: New York Academy of Sciences.

Patrich, Joseph, and Benny Arubas. 1989. "A Juglet Containing Balsam Oil (?) from a Cave near Qumran." *IEJ* 39:43–59.

Porat, Roi, and Uri Davidovitch. 2008. "A Newly Discovered Cistern Near the 'First-Century Building' near the Top of the En-Gedi Ascent." *IEJ* 58:73–78.

Saulcy, Louis Félicien de. 1853. *Voyage autour de la Mer Morte et dans les terres bibliques*. Paris: Gide et J. Baudry.

Shanks, Hershel. 1994. *Frank Moore Cross: Conversations with a Bible Scholar*. Washington, D.C.: Biblical Archaeology Society.

Stacey, David, and Gregory Doudna. 2013. *Qumran Revisited: A Reassessement of the Archaeology of the Site and Its Texts*. Oxford: Archaeopress.

Stager, Lawrence. 1975. "Ancient Agriculture in the Judean Desert: A Case Study." PhD Diss. Harvard University.

———. 1976. "Farming in the Judean Desert during the Iron Age." *BASOR* 221:145–58

Stern, Ephraim. 1994. "The Eastern Border of the Kingdom of Judah in its Last Days." Pages 399–409 in *Scripture and Other Artifacts. Essays on the Bible and Archaeology in Honor of Philip J. King*. Edited by Michael D. Coogan, J. Cheryl Exum, and Lawrence E. Stager. Louisville, KY: Westminster John Knox.

———, ed. 2007. *En Gedi Excavations. Final Report (1961–1965)*. Jerusalem: Israel Exploration Society.

Taylor, Joan E. 2006. " Kh. Qumran in Period III." Pages 133–46 in *Qumran, the Site of the Dead Sea Scrolls: Archaeological Interpretations and Debates*. Edited by Katharina Galor, Jean-Baptiste Humbert and Jürgen Zangenberg. Studies on the Texts of the Desert of Judah 57. Leiden: Brill.

———. 2012. *The Essenes, the Scrolls and the Dead Sea*. Oxford: Oxford University.

———. 2016. "The Qumran Caves in their Regional Context: A Chronological Review with a Focus on Bar Kokhba Assemblages." Pages 7–33 in *The Caves of Qumran: Proceedings of the International Conference, Lugano 2014*. Edited by Marcello Fidanzio. Studies on the Texts of the Desert of Judah 118. Leiden: Brill.

Taylor, Joan E., and Shimon Gibson. 2008. "Roads and Passes Round Qumran." *PEQ* 140:225–27.

———. 2011. "Qumran Connected: The Paths and Passes of the North-Western Dead Sea." Pages 1–51 in *Qumran und Archäologie: Wechselseitige Perspektiven*. Edited by Jörg Frey and Carsten Claussen. Tübingen: Mohr Siebeck.

Tsuk, Tsvika. 2001–2002. "Urban Water Reservoirs in the Land of the Bible during the Bronze and Iron Ages (3000 BC–586 BC)." *ARAM* 13–14:377–401.

Ussishkin, David. 1977. "The Destruction of Lachish by Sennacherib and the Dating of Royal Judean Storage Jars." *TA* 4:28–60.

Vaux, Roland de. 1949a. "Post-Scriptum. La cachette des manuscrits hébreux." *RevB* 56:234–37.

———. 1949b. "La grotte des manuscrits hébreux." *RevB* 56:586–60.

———. 1953a. "Fouille au Khirbet Qumrân." *RevB* 60:83–106.

———. 1953b. "Exploration de la région de Qumrân." *RevB* 60:540–61.

———. 1954. "Fouilles au Khirbet Qumrân: rapport préliminaire sur la deuxième campagne." *RevB* 61:206–36.

————. 1956. "Fouilles de Khirbet Qumrân: rapport préliminaire sur les 3e, 4e et 5e campagnes." *RevB* 63:533–77.

————. 1959. "Fouilles de Feshkha: rapport préliminaire." *RevB* 66:225–55.

————. 1961. *L'archéologie et les manuscrits de la Mer Morte.* Oxford: Oxford University Press.

————. 1962. "Archéologie." Pages 3–36 in *Les 'petites grottes' de Qumrân: Explorations de la falaise; Les grottes 2Q, 3Q, 5Q, 6Q, 7Q à 10Q; Le rouleau de cuivre.* Edited by M. Baillet, Jósef T. Milik, and Roland de Vaux. DJD 3. Oxford: Clarendon.

————. 1973. *Archaeology and the Dead Sea Scrolls.* Oxford: Oxford University Press.

Wagemakers, Bart, and Joan E. Taylor. 2011. "New Photographs of the Qumran Excavations from 1954 and Interpretations of L.77 and L.86." *PEQ* 143:134–56.

Yezerski, Irit. 2018. "Iron Age III Pottery Vessels from the Renewed Excavations in Qumran." Pages 179–338 in *Back to Qumran: Final Report (1993–2004).* Edited by Yitzhak Magen and Yuval Peleg. Jerusalem: Israel Antiquities Authority.

Zangenberg, Jürgen. 2004. "Opening up Our View: Khirbet Qumran in a Regional Perspective." Pages 170–87 in *Religion and Society in Roman Palestine: Old Questions, New Approaches.* Edited by D. R. Edwards. New York: Routledge.

FROM MAKER'S MARK TO MASON'S MARK: CYPRIOT MASON'S MARKS IN THEIR AEGEAN AND LEVANTINE CONTEXTS

LOUISE HITCHCOCK

Abstract: *Engraved signs begin to appear in the Aegean as early as the Middle Bronze Age (ca. 1900–1700 BCE) on Crete. They proliferate in the Late Bronze Age on Crete, in the Aegean islands and Mycenaean mainland. In Israel, Yigal Shiloh documented their appearance in palatial architecture at Megiddo and Samaria. In addition, one appears on a block from the great horned altar in Beersheba. Although they have been conventionally termed "mason's marks," they did not function as such in the accepted sense as aids in the positioning of blocks in the construction of a building. The marks from Israel received detailed attention from Norma Franklin, who associated them with guilds of Carian builders, an association that has not been irrefutably confirmed or disputed. This article considers twenty-five such marks from Cyprus and concludes that meanings assigned to them may vary and need not be mutually exclusive.*

Keywords: Crete, Cyprus, mason's marks, Caria, Samaria, Megiddo

It is with the greatest pleasure that I dedicate this paper to my friend and colleague Norma Franklin.[1] I met Norma on my first visit to Israel, and we became colleagues over our love of and curiosity about ancient architecture and its foreign connections in

1. I am grateful to Sinclair Hood for sharing his unpublished typology of mason's marks with me as an eager student many years ago. This typology will be superseded by Hood's (2020) long awaited publication of the 1,600 mason's marks from Knossos, which was not available to consult by the time this paper went to press. The following excavation directors gave me permission to study the Cypriot marks: Paul Åström, Gerald Cadogan, Sophocles Hadjisavvas, Vassos Karageorghis, Franz Maier, and Alison South. Madaline Harris-Schober and Brian O'Neill gave me assistance in preparing my drawings and tracings for publication. This study was funded by the Fulbright Commission in Cyprus to undertake research at the Cypriot American Archaeological Research Institute and by a USAID Fellowship to undertake research at the Albright Institute in Jerusalem. I am grateful to the staff of both institutes. It was at the Albright that I met Norma Franklin, learned about her work, and formed a lasting friendship. Any mistakes are mine.

the east Mediterranean, particularly "mason's marks." We became friends over a shared love of adventure, good food, and all things British.

Engraved signs begin to appear in the Aegean, mostly on worked stone blocks, as early as the Middle Bronze Age (ca. 1900–1700 BCE) on Crete. Their numbers proliferate on Crete in the Late Bronze Age (ca. 1700–1470/50 BCE), and they appear, in fewer numbers, in the Aegean islands at Akrotiri in Thera where there are about sixty[2] (Palyvou 1990), with one in Aegina, and a handful on the Mycenaean mainland. Although they have been conventionally termed mason's marks in the literature, they did not function as such in the accepted sense as aids in the positioning of blocks in the construction of a building.

Mason's marks appear in the Aegean in differing contexts, multiple designs, varying occurrence from site-to-site, and diverse visibility within a building, resulting in divergent interpretations as to their symbolic, religious, and regional significance, or their link to the social and/or ethnic identities as well as the skill level of the masons. By the thirteenth century BCE, mason's marks appear, primarily in token numbers, in monumental administrative centers and cult sites in Cyprus. In Israel, Shiloh (1979) first systematically documented their appearance in palatial architecture at Megiddo and Samaria. In addition, a notable one depicting a snake appears on a block from the great horned altar in Beersheba.[3] The marks from Israel received detailed attention from Norma Franklin (2001), who associated them with guilds of Carian builders, an association that has not been irrefutably confirmed or disputed. This paper considers mason's marks anew based on their appearance in Cyprus, where the author has documented sixteen of twenty-five known marks in widely varying architectural contexts.[4]

The Cypriot marks I published in Hitchcock (2003) and those published by others (see Hitchcock 2003, 2009, 2008) will be mentioned briefly, with the remaining nine marks presented here for the first time. The marks were cataloged using a format developed for cataloging architectural fragments, traced 1:1 using mylar-film and waterproof ink, photographed, and with the blocks drawn on a scale of 1:10. I will begin with a brief overview of previous and ongoing studies of mason's marks, summarize the views cited in the most recent work on them in the Aegean, and then focus on the types of marks in Cyprus that are also found in Israel. My examination concludes that several meanings can be ascribed to the marks and that the various meanings need not be mutually exclusive.

---

2. It is possible that some of those from Akrotiri were pry holes as discussed below for the entry under Koulia-*Palaepaphos*.

3. A handful of other marks have been noted for other sites in Israel (Franklin 2001: 107 n. 2). On horned altars, see Hitchcock (2002).

4. Begg 2004a, 2004b; Devolder 2018 noted the presence of mason's marks in Israel and Cyprus, but I have not looked at them in detail.

Bronze and Early Iron Age Mason's Marks in the Mediterranean:
A Summary of Meanings and Methods of Interpretation

The term "mason's mark" is conventionally applied to incised or engraved symbols typically found on the top, base, or face of an ashlar block, and most famously associated with Minoan "palatial" architecture on Crete (ca. 1900–1450 BCE), with more thickly engraved marks interpreted as chronologically earlier.[5] The Minoan marks did not function as mason's marks in the utilitarian and conventional sense ascribed to them in classical architecture where they served to determine the positioning of other blocks (see Shaw 1971: 109). The different functions they have been attributed with are either of a symbolic and/or religious character or as the distinguishing mark of guilds or groups of skilled masons. Although he was not the first to notice them (Begg 2004b: 8–9), Evans (1921: 134) first referred to them as craftsmen's signs, an observation that seems to have been missed in later studies. Graham (1987) famously promoted Evans' other interpretation: as having a religious function, noting that twenty-nine were engraved on eight blocks of the two pillars in the so-called "pillar" crypts at Knossos.[6]

A number of scholars have argued against the religious-symbolic function as well as against a decorative function for the marks, observing that those that were plastered over or engraved on the top or base of blocks would not be seen. Müller-Celka et al. (2003) have pointed out that one was engraved on a block found in a quarry that probably served the palatial center at Malia and another was found in a quarry at the town site of Palaikastro (Driessen 1984: 143–49, fig. 9, pl. 13f). Fotou (1993: 43) has shown that they were engraved on mud bricks at Gournia. As mud bricks do not survive well in the Aegean, Fotou's observation may indicate that they were more prevalent than assumed, or even that apprentices may have been imitating the practices of more experienced builders.[7] Devolder (2018: 361–62; also Begg 2004a: 222; 2004b; Sakellarakis 1967) has gone so far as to say that if a mark did have a clearly symbolic context such as the two marks placed on an altar at Malia, then they could not also have functioned as mason's marks.

Mason's marks are rare in Greece outside of Crete (Hood 1984) and Thera. One mark was found on a block beneath the palace at Pylos, tantalizingly suggesting builders trained in Minoan building techniques were working there, while two marks (a double axe and a branch) found on the Mycenaean tholos tomb at Peristeria are interpreted

---

5. There are a few examples of multiple mason's marks carved on different surfaces of a block on Crete (Hood 1987; Devolder 2018), and one example in Israel (Franklin 2001: 107).

6. Pillar crypts are small dark rooms interpreted as architectural representations of sacred caves attested in at least thirteen different structures, see Hitchcock 2007.

7. The term master builder is attested later in Linear B or Mycenaean Greek as a *pan-tēkton* (Palaima 2008: 385–86).

as a Minoan inscription.[8] Another mark is known from the remains of a structure on the island of Aegina near Athens (Niemeier 1995). Despite the numerous palatial features known from the buildings at the site of Akrotiri on Thera, the closest of the Cyclades to the island of Crete, only a loose block with a trident, simple crosses, and engraved lines ranging from one to three in number are known, though these number over eighty (Palyvou 2005: 120–21, 180; Hitchcock 2003: 261).[9] The lack of visible marks at Akrotiri may be a result of preservation of the buildings to the second and third story. Minoan marks of a particular type often tend to be concentrated in certain areas of the "palaces" (Hood 1987: 209). Other incised marks that take the form of an elaborate graffiti (Phaistos monumental stairway 67; also in Kition Cyprus, Temple 1, probably an inscription, see Hitchcock 2003) are not treated here or elsewhere as being part of the same class.

Objections that mason's marks did not have religious or symbolic value can easily be dispatched based on more recent approaches to the agency of objects and the increased interest by Aegean scholars in foundation deposits. Herva (2005; also Hunt 2006: 190–97; Maeir et al. 2015) argues that the deposition of objects beneath buildings as foundation or repair deposits was the beginning of a new phase in an object's biography, rather than the end of its life. In this new phase, the buried, no-longer-visible object might serve to maintain positive relations with ancestral and/or other spirits that resided in the site, or create a positive relationship between the building and its inhabitants, or again, maintain continuity with the past. I would like to propose that, just as foundation deposits did not need to be visible to have powerful symbolic meanings through communication with a divine realm, neither did mason's marks.

General Characteristics of Cypriot Mason's Marks

Like many Minoan mason's marks, which were not always engraved on visible surfaces of the block, Cypriot marks seem to have been generally (but not always) placed in areas not intended to be seen. The only clear exceptions are three examples from Hala Sultan Tekke, two of which are finely incised. Such incised or engraved marks only account for four out of approximately twenty-five marks documented for Cyprus.[10] The placement of Cypriot marks on the tops of blocks suggests that more marks may exist than it is possible to document. Given their scarcity, however, it is unlikely their num-

---

8. Conventional scholarly practice regards two or more signs as an inscription (Godart and Olivier 1976: xi).

9. The possibility should be considered that the thickly engraved, oblique parallel lines were not mason's marks, but functioned as pry or wedge holes, used to help manoeuvre a higher block into place (Oleson 2010: 123). Graham (1987: 154) suggests that small round holes found on the sides of Minoan blocks functioned as lifting holes.

10. The number is approximate as it was not possible to see all of the marks, and it is argued below that perhaps some of the marks were cuttings of another type and not symbols.

ber would reach a level comparable to the Cretan marks. Like Aegean marks, there is no indication that Cypriot marks (with two exceptions) served any kind of practical use. With the exception of Hala Sultan Tekke, sites with several marks tend to depict the same symbol. This is especially true at Kition where the same sign is repeated six times. Here it is tempting to relate the sign to the identity or purpose of the site, although the identity of the guild of masons working there remains another possibility. Finally, most of the marks tend to be consistent with signs found in the Cypro-Minoan script while others find a parallel in Minoan mason's marks. Marks such as the cross or the vertical stroke are regarded here as generic enough to suggest their occurrence is based on coincidence rather than an intentional act of borrowing.[11] In contrast, the so-called "*bras-levés*" that is part of the ligature from Hala Sultan Tekke is unusual enough to suggest foreign influence. It should be noted that the most well-known Minoan marks, the double axe and trident, are not present as mason's marks in Cyprus.

Any conclusions that might be drawn from these observations are necessarily hypothetical and represent an attempt to explain the evidence. These explanations should not be regarded or clung to as evidence in their own right. At the same time, to just mindlessly document the marks and not attempt to assign some meaning to them ignores their potential significance. It is hoped that the explanations put forward here will generate more useful explanations in an ongoing dialectic of interpretation. While the Cypriot marks and their context may largely be distinct from Aegean marking conventions, the practice of marking architectural elements may have been inspired by an emulation of building customs from abroad. This clearly seems to be a case of expressing a foreign usage in a local way.

Adopting the practice of marking or engraving blocks may be linked to masons emulating the exclusivity of writing and an attempt to link marking to the exclusivity of the masonry craft, hence communicating status, perhaps even secrecy in the transmission of skills. Neither possibility is mutually exclusive. Although it is not necessarily an appropriate analogy, it is interesting to remember that guilds of medieval masons shrouded their techniques in mystery, later giving rise to Freemasonry (Wright 1992: 368). Other Bronze Age technologies such as writing (Hood 1987: 210) and metallurgy (e.g., Knapp 1986) were similarly shrouded in mystery as a means of maintaining exclusivity in the profession.

---

11. Shaw and Costaki (2006: 89, no. 19; 90) regard the cross as the most popular of Minoan mason's marks, with the closest parallel to the one from Building T at Kommos to be found at Archanes.

Figure 2. Alassa-*Palaiotaverna*, ashlar building, cross incised on ashlar block, LC IIC thirteenth century BCE, drawing of block with mark.

Figure 1. Alassa-*Palaiotaverna*, ashlar building, cross incised on ashlar block, LC IIC thirteenth century BCE, photo of block. All photos and drawings by Louise A. Hitchcock with preparation assistance from Madaline Harris-Schober and Brian O'Neill.

Figure 3. Alassa-*Palaiotaverna*, ashlar building, cross incised on ashlar block, LC IIC thirteenth century BCE, tracing of mark.

List of Cypriot Mason's Marks and Description of Previously Unpublished Ones

*1. Alassa-*Palaiotaverna *(Hadjisavvas 1986, 1994): one cross (figs. 1–3)*

The block at Alassa-*Palaiotaverna* was discovered by looking at the top and exposed face of every block in the building. Given the state of preservation of the pithos hall, it is possible that more mason's marks are yet to be discovered. Ashlar foundation block; in situ; fair to poor condition with a longitudinal crack extending east–west near the north edge of the block with four additional cracks extending out from it; lichen in the crack will likely cause further degradation; brownish-gray sandstone; shape: trapezoidal; section: likely trapezoidal; L 53.4 × W 40.2 (max) × H (exposed) 5.5 (max) cm. Top is roughly chiseled (sample of marks: 3.2 × 1.1; 4.0 × 0.7; 3.0 × 0.7 cm) to create a flat surface. Mason's mark: cross; faintly incised on east half of block; north stroke: L 3.8 × W 0.5 cm; south stroke: L 3.8 × W 0.4 cm; the north and south strokes of cross are not aligned indicating that they were chiseled separately, and there is a small gouge at the east end of the stroke extending east–west. The block itself is set into the soil, located in the second room to the south of the room containing the drain emptying into the street in the west wing (room 27); the block is the fourth block to the east in the inner north wall; the joins to adjacent blocks are close-fitting at the front, tapering back, as is typical for this type of building technique. The room is square, likely a storage area.

2. Enkomi: one arrow or half star?

It was not possible to undertake research at Enkomi, however Webb (1999: 254 n. 16) notes that two anchors, one bearing unidentified Cypro-Minoan signs, were found in rooms 42 and 39B in the Sanctuary of the Horned God. Based on the presence of half-stars or arrows on all other anchors, it is likely that it was also an arrow.

3.–12. Hala Sultan Tekke: nine signs (2 parallel lines [pry hole?], 1 arrowhead on paver, 1 cross on drain, 2 blocks with parallel lines or scratches, 1 ligature composed of two signs on a weight, 2 arrows on anchors from the lake)

Hala Sultan Tekke in southern Cyprus, just west of Larnaca has the greatest number and widest variety of mason's marks, totaling in all nine signs in six different designs. They are now found in the Larnaca Museum, in situ, or in publications.

    3. *Worked block with two parallel lines* (figs. 4–5). Inventory No. N1039, Larnaca District Museum No. 1972/42a. Area 8, House A, worked block from wall F 1023, north wall of Room 1; broken, about half preserved; white medium hard limestone; L 32 (max) × W 25 (base), 26 (top) × H 13 cm; depth of trough: 4 cm (depth); rim thickness 3–4 cm. This is also known as the "Hollowed Block with Carved Sign" and a description was published by Hult (1977: 77, 85, fig. 80, 90, fig.111, 91, fig. 114). Hult notes that it was found reused as a building stone in wall F 1023, the north wall of the "basin" room (Hitchcock 2009). The mark on the flat side consists of two parallel engraved lines with V-shaped cross sections. Hult also notes that the opposite side was hollowed leaving rough chisel marks and that the edges were left smooth. In one corner, approximately one-quarter of the block has broken off. The block has the appearance of an *auge*, a stone with a one-two small trough-like depression in it that was frequently found in east Cretan Minoan architecture, probably used as a pot stand, and frequently repurposed as a building stone (see Hitchcock 2000: 112–14, with further references). It is possible that the marks were added later as pry holes used to maneuver another block into position (see below for Kouklia).

    4. *Arrowhead on the top of a pavement stone from Hala Sultan Tekke.* Inventory No. N 1172A, Larnaca District Museum No. 1979/30. This is probably Late Cypriote IIIA 1 or possibly IIIA 2, published in Hitchcock (2003: 262, pls. 54a–b).

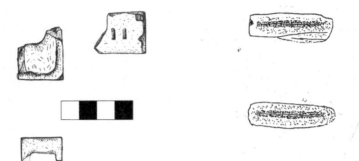

Figure 4. Hala Sultan Tekke, Inventory No. N1039, Larnaca District Museum No. 1972/42a. Area 8, House A, worked block from wall F 1023, auge fragment with pry holes, LC IIIA?, drawing of block.

Figure 5. Hala Sultan Tekke, Inventory No. N1039, Larnaca Dustrict Museum No. 1972/42a. Area 8, House A, worked block from wall F 1023, auge fragment with pry holes, , LC IIIA?, tracing of pry holes.

Figure 6. Hala Sultan Tekke, Inventory No. N 1572, Larnaca District Museum No. 1983/15; found in Area 8, Room 36, cross incised on stone drain segment, LC IIIA?, photo of drain.

5. *Cross finely incised on stone drain segment* (figs. 6–8). Inventory No. N 1572, Larnaca District Museum No.1983/15; found in Area 8, Room 36, Layer 3, a layer that contained debris from fallen walls and possibly later intrusions; L (preserved) 112 × H 10 × W 23–24.5 cm; lip is 3–3.5 cm wide; good condition, but restored from ten fragments of hard white limestone; an 8 × 20.5 cm triangular fragment is missing from

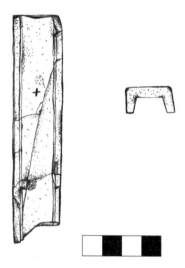

Figure 8. Hala Sultan Tekke, Inventory No. N 1572, Larnaca District Museum No.1983/15; found in Area 8, Room 36, cross incised on stone drain segment, LC IIIA?, tracing of mark.

Figure 7. Hala Sultan Tekke, Inventory No. N 1572, Larnaca District Museum No.1983/15; found in Area 8, Room 36, cross incised on stone drain segment, LC IIIA?, drawing of drain.

Figure 10. Hala Sultan Tekke, Worked ashlar block with two lines angling inward to form a V that doesn't join at base, or likely a half star with the third line broken away; the block is located in room 22, LC IIIA?, tracing of mark.

Figure 9. Hala Sultan Tekke, Worked ashlar block with two lines angling inward to form a V that doesn't join at base, or likely a half star with the third line broken away; the block is located in room 22, LC IIIA?, drawing of block.

the bottom end; a 3 × 5–10 cm fragment is missing from the top end; shape is rectangular; section is a flat U-shape; there are 2 × 3–4 cm broad chisel marks;[12] and short sharp 2.5 × 0.2 cm chisel marks where the side of drain meets the base; there is some thickening of the drain toward the center; there is some damage around the cross, likely from the process of chiseling; date is Late Cypriote IIIA1 or later; the cross is noted in

---

12. On the broad chisel in Cyprus, Philistia, and the Aegean, see Hitchcock 2012; Blackwell 2011: 40, 118, 146–49, 152–68.

Daniel (1941) Class I, no. 16. At least twelve mason's marks, including three crosses, are reported from the drainage system at Knossos (MacDonald and Driessen 1988: 238–46, pls. 37–39), although these are on slabs and blocks rather than a flat U-shaped channel section.

6. *Scratches or parallel lines, F1636, Room 26, middle of north wall, south row of stones.* It is not clear as to whether or not this is a mark of intentionally incised lines or scratches. It was not studied further.

7. *In the area of Feature 1357; No Inv. No.* Roughly rectangular stone with four vertical accidental slashes, natural fissures or signs (a long, a short, a long and a short one) on one of its sides. L 37 × W 30.5 × Th15 cm. This is an excavated area comprising 5 × 4 m in a surface layer (layer 2) in FGf-k 501–504 (Åström 1989: fig. 3, "Pithos room"). It was not found in a dateable layer. Theoretically it could be anything from the Late Bronze Age to Hellenistic times and was not studied further.

8. *Worked ashlar block with two lines.* The lines angle inward to form a V that does not join at base, or likely a half star with the third line broken away (figs. 9, 10); the block is located in room 22, at the top of the west end of the north doorway. In situ; fair condition, some lichen on top with a little along the edge of face; hard grayish sandstone; L 67 × W 25 × H 37 cm; there is a 6 × 15.5 cm oblong chip on the top edge of the stone; the north face has a half ovoid 11 × 3.5 cm chip; a 4 Th × 10 W × 29 L cm section of the face of the block has exfoliated; two chisel marks are evident in each line of the V mark; Shape: Trapezoidal with rectangular face; Section: Trapezoidal/rectangular; Top is roughly dressed, with a few 1 × 3–4 cm chisel marks visible; face of block has a smooth finish with a few 0.7 × 2.5–5 cm chisel marks visible; the adjacent block appears to be a reused threshold block with pivot hole. Date is assumed to be LC IIIA or twelfth century BCE, based on dating of the settlement, see Åström (1986a, 1986b).

9–10. *Ligature.* Inventory No. N 1046, was published by Hult (1978: 2, 6,10, fig. 12; 14, fig. 30; 15, fig. 38) who describes it as a "stone with large carved sign" found in layer 3 immediately north of and outside of the north wall of room 8 associated with feature F 1040. The stone is described (Hult 1978: 6) as dark green dacite and has a flattened rounded front, rounded corners, a flat uneven back, a convex top, and a slightly convex base. Connected funnel-shaped cavities drilled through the base and the back evidently served to fasten it to something. At L 40 × W 27 × Th 10 cm, it is the size of a small building block, although the unusual color of the stone seems to militate against this. The surface and the sign or mark appear extremely worn, suggesting reuse.

According to Hood's (1987: 207) typology of mason's marks it appears to be a composite of two Minoan signs known as the six-pointed star and "hockey sticks," both signs are primarily attested at Knossos. Hult (1978: 6) notes that the sign has no exact parallel, but also notes that similar signs without the cross bar appear in Linear A and B, and in Daniel's (1941: 263, fig. 9) "Class II" of signs not found in the Cypro-Minoan script. The sign without the cross bar is identical to Hood's (above) "hockey sticks" mason's mark and corresponds specifically to Daniel's (1941) sign of Class II: 20. In-

Figure 11. Kalavasos-*Ayios Dhimitrios*, Building X, the ashlar building, pithos hall, cross is thickly engraved on maneuvering boss of rusticated central panel of a plinth, LC IIC, photo of boss with cross.

Figure 12. Kalavasos-*Ayios Dhimitrios*, Building X, the ashlar building, pithos hall, cross is thickly engraved on maneuvering boss of rusticated central panel of a plinth, LC IIC, tracing of boss with cross.

terestingly, Daniel (1941: 264–65) regards this particular sign as being one of several of Minoan origin that comes into Cyprus on Mycenaean pottery. A new tracing of the block is published in Hitchcock (2008: 21, fig. 3) and its symbolic significance in relationship to the basin building is discussed in Hitchcock (2009).

11–12. *Two Signs.* Four stone anchors were reported from the border of the Salt Lake, which Karageorghis (1968: 10) believes were within the harbor of the ancient site. Two of these have the same Cypro-Minoan sign of half-stars engraved on them: 11. 1968/V-18/1 (Karageorghis 1968: pl. 2.1) and 12. 1967/VIII-9/1 (Karageorghis 1968: pl. 2.2). On the symbolic deposition of anchors, see Boucher (2014).

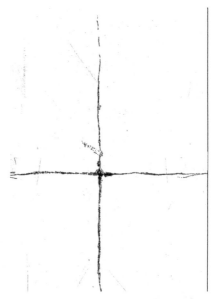

Figure 13. Kalavasos-*Ayios Dhimitrios*, Building X, the ashlar building, courtyard, cross is thinly engraved on pillar base, LC IIC, drawing of boss with cross.

Figure 14. Kalavasos-*Ayios Dhimitrios*, Building X, the ashlar building, courtyard, cross is thinly engraved on pillar base, LC IIC, tracing of boss with cross.

*13.–14. Kalavasos-*Ayios Dhimitrios: *two crosses*

13. *Cross.* The cross is thickly engraved on maneuvering boss of rusticated central panel of a plinth block in the inner west wall of the west wing, the second block from the south end (figs. 11, 12), the pithos hall, of Building X, the Ashlar Building; in situ; a drawing of the entire block can be found in Hitchcock (2008: 21, fig. 4); dark, calcareous "Tochni" sandstone; good condition; L 177 × W 54 × H (exposed) 25.5 cm; it extended at least 4–8 cm beneath the ground level; shape was trapezoidal; section was rectangular; the top of the block and the drafted margin were very finely worked; the cross mason's mark begins near the top of the maneuvering boss; it has a depth of 0.8 cm; the north–south part of the cross is distinguished by a second chisel mark below the first; there is a pry hole (discussed for Kouklia below) on top of the block, near the north end; L 8 × W 2.4 × D ca. 3.5 cm; the north part of the cross was originally L 5 cm but was lengthened to 8 cm at some point; dated by ceramics to LC IIC (thirteenth century BCE).

14. *Pillar base with finely incised cross.* At the northeast end of courtyard of Building X, the Ashlar Building, space A.157 (figs. 13, 14) the pillar base on the northwest end of the courtyard was robbed out leaving a pit of ca. 26–30 cm around the edge and as deep as 60–70 cm in the center allowing us to estimate a similar thickness for the in situ base under discussion here; the base block was irregularly shaped, with a

raised rectangular area in the center suggesting the irregular part was buried beneath the pebble pavement of the courtyard, leaving the raised rectangular area to carry the pillar; South (1983: 96) provides measurements of 1.73 × 1.26 m and at least 0.20 m thick; for the raised area bearing the mark, she gives measurements of 1.20 × 0.80 m; the mark is a thinly incised cross that trails off at its ends, measuring 29.5 north–south and 32 east–west cm. South believes that the incised cross was used as a mark to position a now missing pillar support or that it was used for the purpose of cutting the block down, positions taken for Cretan marks by Begg (2004a, 2004b) and Devolder (2018). I agree with South's conclusion that this was a true mason's mark, used for the practical purpose of positioning a pillar. Its unusually large size and fine engraving render it distinct from other marks known from the Aegean and the Levant. On the Aegean connections to Building X, see Hitchcock (1999). It is likely that the missing pillar was carved from a monolithic block of Tochni sandstone as Cypriot builders seemed to have a preference for more expensive monolithic pillars[13] as seen in the west wing of Building X as well as at the Temple at Kouklia-*Palaepaphos*. It is likely that the two bases would have supported a small portico at the north end of the courtyard.

15–22. Kition: eight marks: five half stars or arrows, one three-sign graffiti

Blocks at Kition frequently employed drafted margins on three sides, with some blocks over 3 m in length and close-fitted joints (Sandars 1986). This is particularly the case in Temple 1. The corpus of mason's marks from Kition consists of six blocks with the same engraved Cypro-Minoan sign on them, which correspond to Hood's (1987: 207, fig. 5; also Evans 1921: 135, fig. 99, 33b) arrow or a half-star. In addition, there is ship graffiti published in the report (Basch and Artzy: 1985) and discussed at great length along with all of the temples by Webb (1999: 37–44; 64–83) and a three-sign graffiti or inscription published in the report.

15. *Temple 4.* Bench, sign engraved on external face of bench (Karageorghis and Demas 1985: pl. 105.1)

16. *Temple 4.* Bench, sign engraved on external face of bench (Karageorghis and Demas 1985: pl. 105.2)

17. *Temple 5.* Altar, Floor 3, Ashlar Block with "Cypro-Minoan" sign (Karageorghis and Demas 1985: pls. 92.6, 105.3). Regrettably this sign is no longer visible on site.

18. *Temenos B.* East facade wall of entrance (Karageorghis and Demas 1985: pl. 105.4, also Plans: pl. 40.1, elevation 19)

19. *Anchor stone.* A thickly incised arrow or half star in situ in Temple 2 (figs. 15–18), in the northwest corner of the west wall of Room 24B, a vestibule or "adyton,"

---

13. Monolithic pillars would have been more expensive as a mistake would result in having to start over. In contrast, the Minoans primarily made segmented pillars with blocks stacked one atop the other, so that if one was damaged, it would be less laborious to replace.

Figure 15. Kition, Temple 2, Anchor stone with thickly incised arrow or half star in the northwest corner of the west wall of Room 24B, vestibule or "adyton," LC IIC–LC IIIA, photo of anchor.

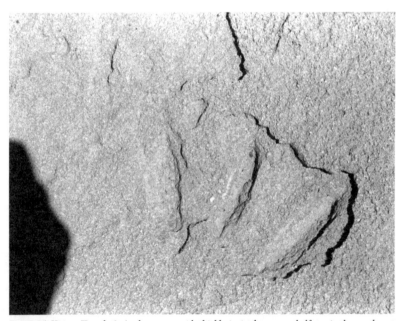

Figure 16. Kition, Temple 2, Anchor stone with thickly incised arrow or half star in the northwest corner of the west wall of Room 24B, vestibule or "adyton," LC IIC–LC IIIA, photo of mark.

Figure 17. Kition, Temple 2, Anchor stone with thickly incised arrow or half star in the northwest corner of the west wall of Room 24B, vestibule or "adyton," LC IIC–LC IIIA, drawing of anchor.

(Webb 1999: 43–44; 65–71);[14] in situ medium brown soft sandstone; fair condition; L 78 × W 60 × Th 17.5 cm; two layers of ca. 0.6 cm each around the mason's mark have exfoliated away and are shown in the tracing with dashed lines, indicating that the mark was originally deeper; the stone is anchor shaped with a small, round top; wide flat base; and flat sides that angle out at the bottom; it is rectangular in section; there is a larger round hole (diameter 19.5 narrowing to 12 cm in the center) with visible chisel marks located 19.5 cm from the small end taking a rope and two smaller holes (diameter ca. 5 cm) placed 15–16 cm from the wider bottom end to take sharpened sticks to catch in place; however, Webb (1999: 184–87) has shown that the anchors built into the Kition temples lack use wear, indicating that they were deliberately intended to be used symbolically as building stones, they are assigned to LC IIC or IIIA.

20–22. Orthostat. Three-sign inscription or graffiti on an orthostat block with drafted margins, east wall of Temple 1. The inscription published by E. Masson (1985: 280–84) was retraced with greater accuracy in Hitchcock 2003.

23. Maroni-Vournes

One box or square on an ashlar block, published in Hitchcock 2003: 261–62; pl. 52a–c; one end was worn away leaving open the possibility that there was a short "tail" extending from it.

24.–25. Kouklia-Palaepaphos Two V-with tail; two parallel lines (pry holes)

24. Sanctuary of Aphrodite. Mason's mark on possibly reused block in Roman pavement (figs. 19–21). A small paved area composed of four limestone blocks is adjacent to the north end of the shallow basin within the Late Bronze Age temenos. One of these

---

14. Webb (1999: 254, n. 16) notes that two anchors, one bearing unidentified Cypro-Minoan signs, was found in rooms 42 and 39B of the Sanctuary of the Horned God at Enkomi. Based on the other anchors from Kition, it is possible that it was also an arrow.

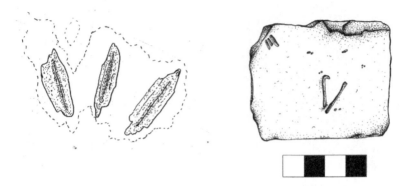

Figure 18. Kition, Temple 2, Anchor stone with thickly incised arrow or half star in the northwest corner of the west wall of Room 24B, vestibule or "adyton," LC IIC–LC IIIA, tracing of mark.

Figure 20. Kouklia-*Palaepaphos*, Sanctuary of Aphrodite, mason's mark of V with tail, on possibly reused block in Roman pavement, date uncertain, drawing of block with V.

Figure 19. Kouklia-*Palaepaphos*, Sanctuary of Aphrodite, mason's mark of V with tail, on possibly reused block in Roman pavement, date uncertain, photo of pavement.

blocks carries a mason's mark, which Maier (1977: 137) regards as similar to those at Kition. The Kouklia mark, however, is somewhat different in that it forms a V with a hook at one end whereas the Kition marks all take the form of a Cypro-Minoan sign forming a three-stroke arrow. Maier (pers. comm. Sept. 11, 2000) believes that it is a reused Bronze Age block, however it cannot be dated with confidence.

25. *Sanctuary of Aphrodite.* Ashlar plinth block with drafted margins and pry holes previously identified as a mason's mark (figs. 22–24) in situ as the fourth block of south wall of sanctuary I/north wall of temenos; L 79 × W 45–52 × H (exposed) 16 cm; as the exposed height of other blocks is different, it is likely that this was a levelling course; material is hard, sandy limestone; trapezoidal in shape and rectangular in section; the pry holes con-

Figure 21. Kouklia-Palaepaphos, Sanctuary of Aphrodite, mason's mark of V with tail, on possibly reused block in Roman pavement, date uncertain, tracing of V.

sist of two ovoid gouges on top near the west end of the block; measuring L 11 × W 5 × D 1.25 cm and L 9 × W 5 × D 1.25 cm; the top is finely chiseled and the front has a finely finished border around a rusticated central panel; Hult (1983: 17, 79, 111, fig. 10) reports what may be mortises or mason's marks visible on the top two courses. Hult (1983: 79) believes that they are mason's marks rather than mortises because of their "shallowness." Upon investigating this feature, I believe it is more likely that they are pry holes, as such features are common on the tops of blocks in Building X at

Figure 22. Kouklia-*Palaepaphos*, Sanctuary of Aphrodite, pry holes on plinth block, the fourth block of south wall of sanctuary I/north wall of temenos, LC IIC or IIIA, photo of block.

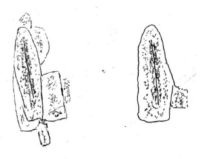

Figure 23. Kouklia-*Palaepaphos*, Sanctuary of Aphrodite, pry holes on plinth block, the fourth block of
south wall of sanctuary I/north wall of temenos, LC
IIC or IIIA, drawing of block.

Figure 24. Kouklia-*Palaepaphos*, Sanctuary of Aphrodite, pry holes on plinth block, the fourth block
of south wall of sanctuary I/north wall of temenos,
LC IIC or IIIA, tracing of pry holes.

Kalavasos-*Ayios Dhimitrios* and now at Tell eṣ-Ṣafi/Gath (Hitchcock et al. 2019). They
occur always in roughly the same position. As pry holes, they may have been used to
leverage an upper course of blocks into position. Such features have typically been associated with classical architecture where they are a well-known feature. Initially dated to
the twelfth century BCE. However, given the later discovery of monumental thirteenth
century ashlar buildings at Maroni, Kalavasos, and Alassa, and the shallowness of the
deposits at Kouklia, an LC IIC date can be suggested as a possibility.

Cypriot Marks: Their Levantine and Aegean Connections

The marks found in Cyprus that are also attested in the Levant date largely to the thirteenth century BCE and include the following:

- Crosses, four: occurring once at Hala Sultan Tekke, twice at Kalavasos-*Ayios Dhimitrios* Building X, and once at Alassa-*Palaiotaverna*.
- Stars and half stars, occurring frequently at Kition, in numerous, well-published
  contexts.
- Box, occurring in one instance at Maroni-*Vournes* (see Hitchcock 2003).
- V- a variation on the V, at Kouklia-*Palaepaphos*, which was originally regarded as
  a sort of altar base for a stepped block or possibly a "horns of consecration" (cf.
  Maier 1977: 137), it has since been dated stratigraphically as Roman (Webb 1977:
  128; Maier pers. comm. Sept. 11, 2000). One block of this pavement displays a
  mason's mark, compared by Maier (1977: 137) to those at Kition, though the
  hook on it distinguishes it from Kition. Nevertheless, the block may have been
  reused.
- Vertical lines, which have been primarily reinterpreted here as pry holes, based on
  their depth and placement on the tops of plinth blocks.

Given the generic nature of the cross and vertical line or pry hole marks, the most convincing Cypriot *comparanda* that have commonalities with both the Aegean and Levant are the box (with or without tail), the V with tail which could be a variation of the Y with tail found in the Levant.

The most frequently attested mark, the half-star or arrow, and arrow with shaft are only attested in the Levant as full-stars; but are well-known in the Aegean along with the bras-levés. These types are based on Sinclair Hood's unpublished typology as well as Hood (1987). The cross, box or box with tail, and arrow or half-star are also well known in the Cypro-Minoan script, while one of the signs in the Kition Temple 1 inscription is Cypro-Minoan sign 91; only the cross is found in Linear A and Linear B, while the V with tail is found in Linear B, and the arrow or half-star is found in Cretan hieroglyphic; this is based on Davis (2010, 2011).

Vertical lines are found in all *corpora* considered. It can be provisionally suggested that Cypriot mason's marks enjoy their closest parallels with Aegean mason's marks, the Cypro-Minoan script, and the very early Cretan hieroglyphic script. Similarities to the Levantine mason's marks are not convincing. However, given the small size of the Cypriot corpus, not too much should be read into this observation, although the lack of parallels with Linear A and Linear B are startling.

Conclusions

The chronological distinction between finely and thickly engraved marks known from Crete, does not seem to be operative in Cyprus, where the marks appear within a very limited time frame, from the thirteenth century and perhaps as late as the eleventh century BCE. Wright (2000: 399; also Hitchcock 2005, 2008) assigned regional distinctions in Cypriot masonry in part to varied foreign connections, although a specific Cypriot masonry technique developed independently. This is shown in the common use of drafted margins with maneuvering bosses as a technique of forming close joins. This was a common technique in Cypriot architecture, but rare on Crete, with just three early and isolated examples documented by Hood (1980) at Ayia Triada, Phaistos, and Malia. The trapezoidal shape giving the blocks six surfaces where the back of the block receives a chinking of mud brick and smaller stones is also a typical Minoan building characteristic (see Begg 2004b).

I agree with Shaw who has remarked (comments section in Hägg and Marinatos 1987: 211) that it may be an oversimplification to assume that the marks had one function. Although Devolder (2018) makes the most reasonable argument that the Minoan marks might be associated with quarry persons, based on their context, clustering (also Graham 1987: 155; Begg 2004b: 3–4; Palyvou 1990), and analogies to Egyptian work gangs, it can be proposed that all of the marks also had a symbolic function. That certain symbols were preferred to the exclusion of others indicates that choice and agency were involved in the selection of which symbols were used as marks. A corresponding symbolic function can be assigned based on analogies with the functions of writing and foundation deposits, which does not detract from their practical meaning as markers of identity. Shanks and Tilley (1987; also Leone 1984: 32–33) have demonstrated that distinctions between the functional and symbolic are arbitrary, linked to modern industrial and postindustrial concepts of time, whereby time becomes segmented and commodified as something to be saved, spent, or otherwise measured.

Only two Cypriot marks seem unlikely to be associated with any symbolic function or function linked to the identity of quarry persons, and that is the cross on the pillar base from Kalavasos-*Ayios Dhimitrios* Building X, which seems to have been placed for the purpose of positioning a pillar or column support. Its finely incised form and enormous size is out of character in comparison with all other Cypriot marks, and the idea that it was meant to promote maneuvering of a support into place seems more plausible. In addition, the two parallel lines from Kouklia-*Palaepaphos* and tentatively interpreted by Hult (1983: 79) as a mason's mark, were more likely a set of pry holes.

The ligature of "star" and "hockey sticks" found on a weight in Building A at Hala Sultan Tekke shows a particular affinity with Crete given the combination of signs (star and hockey sticks) common to Minoan mason's marks. Marks combined to form ligatures are also known from Minoan architecture, with specific examples of varying types coming from Knossos (Evans 1921: 135, fig. 99. 3–6, 14; Hood 1987: 208, fig. 9) and Malia (Pelon et al. 1980: 183, fig. 3). Ligatures were also used in the Minoan writing system, Linear A (Hood 1987: 210). The presence of a ligature in Cyprus with signs exhibiting links to Crete is not surprising given the context of the basin room and cattle skull found in the same building (Hitchcock 2009). In terms of transference of the symbols given the temporal gap between the Minoan civilization and the construction of monumental buildings with marks found in Cyprus, multiple explanations are possible and plausible. First of all, the undeciphered Cypro-Minoan script, as its name implies, derives from the Minoan Linear A script, suggesting that connections with Crete have a long history.[15] In addition, despite their destruction, the remains of the Minoan palaces and villas not only remained visible well into the Iron Age, they became sites of "ruin cult" that were periodically visited and venerated (Prent 2003, 2004).[16]

In terms of the foreign connections of the Cypriot marks, the crosses and the single strokes or pry holes must be eliminated, as they are too generic to be regarded as culturally meaningful, although both types are found in the Aegean and in the Levant. This leaves just six types of signs to be considered in relation to Minoan and Levantine architecture: the half star or arrow, the arrowhead, the ligature (star and "hockey sticks"), the V-with hook, and the box. In terms of numbers, there are far fewer marks in Cyprus than on Crete where the major palatial sites have hundreds of marks (Hood

---

15. For an overview of Cypro-Minoan, see Davis 2010, 2011.

16. As the term implies, newly emerging elites engaged in ritual activities among the ruins of the "palaces" and "villas," where mason's marks were presumably visible.

1987; Devolder 2018). However, there seem to be more marks in Cyprus than are known from the Greek Mainland.[17]

The only evidence for clustering comes from Kition, where six of the same mark (arrows or half stars) are found, and the only deviation from this pattern takes the form of the ship graffiti (already mentioned, and beyond the scope of this paper) and the three-sign inscription.[18] In addition, this symbol also occurs on several anchors. It is worth investigating further whether this symbol has any connections to maritime cult and seafaring.

The box at Maroni, which is damaged, is paralleled by the Israelite marks corresponding to Carian marks 27 (square or box) and 28 (box with tail), and attested at Samaria (Franklin 2001). The mark is also attested on Crete as Hood (n.d.; 1987: 207, fig. 5) Type 17.i square or 17.iii square with tail.

A cross with hook is identified at Malia (Devolder 2018: 352, table 1), while a Y with hooked tail from Megiddo and Samaria (Carian sign 19; Franklin 2001), form a close but imprecise and speculative parallel to the V with hooked end from Kouklia-Palaepaphos. A V, labeled as a gamma is Hood's (n.d.) 20.iii on Crete. A V with hook is also found in Linear B as mentioned above. The hockey sticks in the ligature from Hala Sultan Tekke is known from Crete, where it is Hood's (n.d.) mark type 2.

The arrow on the paving stone at Hala Sultan Tekke differs from the Minoan one in having a long shaft, extending beyond the flights, which are narrower (but see Evans 1921: 135, fig. 99, 33a).

In terms of comparison, if we eliminate the generic marks such as the vertical stroke(s) and the cross (Hood 1987: 207, fig. 5; Franklin 2001: 111, fig. 1), Cyprus shares an affinity with Crete and/or the Levant in terms of the marks discussed below, however, the closest affinity is with Crete. Given that Linear A is the parent script of Cypro-Minoan this is not surprising. Although the similarities are relevant, I find it is possible to accept Franklin's argument regardless. This assessment is based on limited evidence Franklin presents such as the terms Kar-ki-sa (Carian in Hittite), the island of the Weshesh, and biblical references to Cherethites, that link Luwian-speaking Carian builders to the Sea People and the Aegean. It can now be bolstered by further evidence from Anatolia including the Luwian title Tarwanis ("*seren*") for war lord (Davis et al. 2016), the Lydian names Alyattes and Wlattes attested at Gath (Maeir et al. 2008), and the geographical location of Caria. Caria encompassed Miletus or ancient Millawanda,

---

17. It was not possible to examine the sites of Myrtou-*Pighades* or Enkomi in northern Cyprus when this study was undertaken, however it is not unreasonable to suspect that marks are not present there. I discovered the cross mark at Alassa-*Palaiotaverna* by dint of will, inspecting the top of every exposed block on the site.

18. The only other possible evidence for clustering on Cyprus is at Kalavasos-*Ayios Dhimitrios* where there are two crosses, though of very different character as discussed in the text. If an inscription is to be defined as two or more signs (Davis 2011: 46, n. 5), they are also known in the Aegean at Peristeria and at Knossos (Hood 1987: 209, figs. 14–15).

which had a long Aegean history, first as a Minoan colony,[19] that was taken over by the Mycenaeans who continuously skirmished with the Hittites. In addition, Caria was just to the north of Lycia, associated with the Lukka, a name adopted by one tribe of Sea Peoples, and to the south of Lydia where a linguistic connection was noted above. The site of Bademgedği Tepe, where Mycenaean IIIC krater sherds depicting the scene of a ship with rowers below deck and armed warriors wearing spiked helmets on the top deck (Mountjoy 2011: 485), is also located in the region of Lydia. All of these things contribute to a picture of maritime piracy and banditry with an Aegean component (Hitchcock and Maeir 2018) in this region that bolsters Franklin's conclusions.

References

Åström, Paul. 1986a. "Hala Sultan Tekke. An International Harbour Town of the Late Cypriot Bronze Age." *Opuscula Atheniensia* 16:7–17.

———. 1986b. "Hala Sultan Tekke and Its Foreign Relations." Pages 63–68 in *Acts of the International Archaeological Symposium "Cyprus Between the Orient and Occident."* Nicosia 8th–14th September 1985. Edited by V. Karageorghis. Nicosia: The Department of Antiquities, Cyprus.

———. 1989. *Trenches 1972–1987: with an Index for volumes 1–9; Hala Sultan Tekke 9.* Göteborg: Åströms.

Basch, Lucien, and Michal Artzy. 1985. "Ship Graffiti at Kition. Appendix II." Pages 322–36 in *Excavations at Kition V: The Pre-Phoenician Levels. Areas I and II, Part I.* Edited by V. Karageorghis. Nicosia: The Department of Antiquities, Cyprus.

Begg, D. J. Ian. 2004a. "An Interpretation of Mason's Marks at Knossos." Pages 219–23 in *Knossos: Palace, City, State.* Edited by Gerald Cadogan, Eleni Hatzaki, and Antonis Vasilakis. London: British School at Athens.

———. 2004b. "An Archaeology of Palatial Mason's Marks on Crete." Pages 1–26 in *Charis: Essays in Honor of Sara A. Immerwahr.* Edited by Anne P. Chapin. Athens: American School of Classical Studies.

Blackwell, Nicholas G. 2011. "Middle and Late Bronze Age Metal Tools from the Aegean, Eastern Mediterranean, and Anatolia: Implications for Cultural/Regional Interaction and Craftsmanship." PhD diss., Bryn Mawr College.

Boucher, Amanda. 2014. "Interpreting the Wine-Dark Sea: East Mediterranean Marine Symbolism." PhD diss., University of Melbourne.

Daniel, John F. 1941. *Prolegomena to the Cypro-Minoan Script.* Philadelphia: University of Pennsylvania.

Davis, Brent E. 2010. "Introduction to the Aegean Pre-Alphabetic Scripts." *KUBABA* 1:38–61.

———. 2011. "Cypro-Minoan in Philistia?" *KUBABA* 2:40–74.

Davis, Brent E., Aren M. Maeir, and Louise A. Hitchcock 2016. "Philistine Names and Terms Once Again: A Recent Perspective." *Journal of Eastern Mediterranean Archaeology and Heritage Studies* 4.4:321–40.

Devolder, Maud. 2018. "The Functions of Masons' Marks in the Bronze Age Palace at Malia (Crete)." *AJA* 122:343–65.

---

19. Miletus contained the full Minoan cultural package including frescoes, loom weights, Linear A writing, and locally made Minoan pottery (see Niemeier and Niemeier 2002).

Driessen, Jan. 1984. "II. Notes on Building Materials and Quarries: Minoan Building Materials at Roussolakkos." *Annual of the British School at Athens* 79:143–49.

Evans, Arthur J. 1921. *The Palace of Minos at Knossos*, vol. 1. London: Macmillan & Co.

Fotou, Vasso. 1993. "New Light on Gournia: Unknown Documents of the Excavation at Gournia and Other Sites on the Isthmus of Ierapetra by Harriet Boyd." Liège: University of Liège.

Franklin, Norma. 2001. "Masons' Marks from the 9th Century BCE Northern Kingdom of Israel: Evidence of the Nascent Carian Alphabet." *Kadmos* 40:107–16.

Godart, Louis, and Jean-Pierre Olivier. 1976. *Recueil des inscriptions en Linéaire A: 1. Tablettes éditées avant 1970*, Paris: Geuthner.

Graham, J. Walter. 1987. *The Palaces of Crete*. Princeton: Princeton University Press. Repr. of 1962 edition.

Hadjisavvas, Sophoklis. 1986. "Alassa. A New Late Cypriote Site." *RDAC* 1986:62–67.

———. 1994. "Alassa Archaeological Project 1991–1993." *RDAC* 1994:107–14.

Hägg, Robin, and Nanno Marinatos, eds. 1987. *The Function of the Minoan Palaces*. Stockholm: Svenska Institutet i Athen.

Herva, Vesa-Pekka. 2005. "The Life of Buildings: Minoan Building Deposits in an Ecological Perspective." *OJA* 24:215–27.

Hitchcock, Louise. A. 1999. "Cult(ural) Continuity and Regional Diversity: The Encoding of Aegean Form and Function in Late Bronze Age Cypriote Architecture." *JPR* 13:11–21.

———. 2000. *Minoan Architecture: A Contextual Analysis. Studies in Mediterranean Archaeology Pocket Book* 155. Jonsered: Åströms.

———. "Levantine Horned Altars: An Aegean Perspective on the Transformation of Socio-Religious Reproduction." Pages 223–39 in *"Imagining" Biblical Worlds: Spatial, Social, and Historical Constructs; Essays in Honor of James W. Flanagan*. Edited by P. M. McNutt and D. M. Gunn. JSOTSup 359 Sheffield: Sheffield Academic.

———. 2003. "'And above Were Costly Stones, Hewn according to Measurement…': Documentation of Pre-classical Ashlar Masonry in the East Mediterranean." Pages 257–67 in *METRON: Measuring the Aegean Bronze Age, the 9th International Aegean Conference, Yale University, New Haven, Connecticut, April 18–21, 2002*. Edited by Karen P. Foster and Robert Laffineur. Leuven: Peeters.

———. 2007. "Naturalizing the Cultural: Architectonicized Landscape as Ideology in Minoan Crete." Pages 91–97 in *Building Communities: House, Settlement and Society in the Aegean and Beyond, Cardiff University, April 17–21, 2001*. Edited by Ruth Westgate, N. R. E. Fisher, and James Whitley. London: British School at Athens.

———. 2008. "'Do You See a Man Skillful in His Work? He Will Stand before Kings': Interpreting Architectural Influences in the Bronze Age Mediterranean." *Ancient West and East* 7:17–49.

———. 2012. "Dressed to Impress: Architectural Adornment as an Exotic Marker of Elite Identity in the Eastern Mediterranean." Pages 663–71 in *KOSMOS: Jewelry, Adornment and Textiles in the Aegean Bronze Age, Proceedings of the 13th International Aegean Conference, Copenhagen, 19–22 April 2010*. Edited by Marie Louise Nosch and Robert Laffineur. Leuven: Peeters.

———. 2009. "Building Identities: Fluid Borders and an 'International Style' of Monumental Architecture in the Bronze Age." Pages 165–71 in *Crossing Cultures: Conflict, Migration and Convergence, Proceedings of the 32nd International Conference of Art History (CIHA), University of Melbourne, 13–18 January 2008*. Edited by J. Anderson. Melbourne: Miegunyah.

———. 2018. "Fifteen Men on a Dead Seren's Chest: Yo Ho Ho and a Krater of Wine." Pages 147–59 in *Context and Connection: Essays on the Archaeology of the Ancient Near East in Honour of Antonio Sagona*. Edited by Atilla Batmaz, Giorgi Bedianashvili, Aleksandra Michalewicz, and Abby Robinson. Leuven: Peeters.

Hitchcock, Louise A., Shirah Gur-Arieh, Madaline Harris-Schober, Pietro Militello, Aren M. Maeir, and Laura Pisanu. 2019. "All in All It's Just Another Stone in the Wall: From Safi to Sicily, 12th Century Monumental Architecture in the Mediterranean." Paper presented at the American Schools of Oriental Research Annual Meeting, San Diego, 20–23 November 2019.

Hood, Sinclair. 1984. "A Minoan Empire in the Aegean in the 16th and 15th Centuries B.C.?" Pages 33–37 in *The Minoan Thalassocracy: Myth and Reality*. Edited by R. Hägg and N. Marinatos. Stockholm: Åströms.

Hood, M. S. F. 1980 "Masonry with Drafted Margins in Bronze Age Crete." *Eirene* 36: 20–26.

———. 1987. "Mason's Marks in the Palaces." Pages 205–12 in *The Function of the Minoan Palaces*. Edited by R. Hägg and N. Marinatos. Stockholm: Svenska Institutet i Athen.

———. 2020. *The Masons' Marks of Minoan Knossos*. L. Bendall BSA Supplementary Volume 49. London: British School of Archaeology at Athens.

———. No date. "Corpus of Minoan Mason's Marks in the Knossos Area" (Typewritten/ Hand Drawn manuscript).

Hult, Gunnel. 1977. "Architecture." Pages 73–91 in *Hala Sultan Tekke 3*. Edited by P. Åström, G. Hult, and M. Strandberg Oloffsson. Studies in Mediterranean Archaeology 45.3. Göteborg: Åströms.

———. 1978. *Hala Sultan Tekke 4*. Studies in Mediterranean Archaeology 45.4. Göteborg: Åström.

———. 1983. *Bronze Age Ashlar Masonry in the Eastern Mediterranean*. Studies in Mediterranean Archaeology 66. Göteborg: Åström.

Hunt, Gloria R. 2006. "Foundation Rituals and the Culture of Building in Ancient Greece." PhD diss., University of North Carolina at Chapel Hill.

Karageorghis, Vassos. 1968. "Notes on a Late Cypriote Settlement and Necropolis Site Near the Larnaca Salt Lake." *Report of the Department of Antiquities Cyprus*, 1–11.

Karageorghis, Vassos, and Martha Demas 1985. *Excavations at Kition V: The Pre-Phoenician Levels; Areas I and II, Part I*. Nicosia: Department of Antiquities, Cyprus.

Knapp, A. Bernard. 1986. *Copper Production and Divine Protection: Archaeology, Ideology, and Social Complexity on Bronze Age Cyprus*. Göteborg: Åströms.

Leone, M. P. 1984. "The William Paca Garden in Annapolis Maryland." Pages 25–35 in *Ideology, Power, and Prehistory*. Edited by D. Miller and C. Tilley. Cambridge: Cambridge University Press.

MacDonald, C. F., J. M. and Driessen. 1988. "The Drainage System of the Domestic Quarter in the Palace at Knossos." *Annual of the British School at Athens* 83:235–58.

Maeir, Aren M., Brent E. Davis, Liora K. Horwitz, Yotam Asscher, and Louise A. Hitchcock. 2015. "An Ivory Bowl from Early Iron Age Tell es-Safi/Gath (Israel): Manufacture, Meaning and Memory." *World Archaeology* 47:413–38, https://doi.org/10.1080/0043 8243.2015.1009154.

Maeir, Aren M., Stefan J. Wimmer, Alexander Zukerman, and Aaron Demsky 2008. "A Late Iron Age I/Early Iron Age II Old Canaanite Inscription from Tell eṣ-Ṣâfî/Gath, Israel: Palaeography, Dating, and Historical-Cultural Significance." *BASOR* 351:39–71.

Maier, Franz-Georg. 1977. "Excavations at Kouklia (Palaeopaphos) Ninth Preliminary Report: Season 1976." *RDAC* 1977:133–40.

Masson, Emilia. 1985. "Inscriptions et marques chypro-minoennes à Kition." Pages 280–84 in *Excavations at Kition V: The Pre-Phoenician Levels; Areas I and II, Part I*. Edited by Vassos Karageorghis and M. Demas. Nicosia: Department of Antiquities, Cyprus.

Mountjoy, Penelope. 2011. "A Bronze Age Ship from Ashkelon with Particular Reference to the Bronze Age Ship from Bademgediği Tepe." *AJA* 115:483–88.

Müller-Celka, Sylvie, Robert Laffineur, and Jean N. Anslign 2003. "Prospection archéologique de la plaine de Malia." *BCH* 127:456–69.

Niemeier, Wolf-Dietrich. 1995. "Aegina: First Aegean 'State' Outside of Crete?" Pages 73–80 in *Politeia: Society and State in the Aegean Bronze Age; Proceedings of the 5th International Aegean Conference. V. 1.* Edited by Robert Laffineur and Wolf-Dietrich Niemeier. Leuven: Peeters.

Niemeier, Wolf-Dietrich, and Barbara Niemeier. 2002. "The Frescoes in the Middle Bronze Age Palace." Pages 254–85, 288–98 in *Tel Kabri: The 1986–1993 Excavation Seasons.* Edited by N. Scheftelowitz and R. Oren. Tel Aviv: Emery and Claire Yass Publications in Archaeology.

Oleson, John P. 2010. *The Oxford Handbook of Engineering Technology in the Classical World.* Oxford: Oxford University Press.

Palaima, Thomas G. 2008. "The Significance of Mycenaean Words Relating to Meals, Meal Rituals, and Food." Pages 383–89 in *DAIS: The Aegean Feast; Proceedings of the 12th International Aegean Conference University of Melbourne, Cemtre for Classics and Archaeology, 25–29 March 2008.* Edited by Louise A. Hitchcock, Robert Laffineur, and Janice L. Crowley. Leuven: Peeters.

Palyvou, Clairy. 1988. "Akrotiri, Thera: Building Techniques and Morphology in Late Cycladic Architecture." PhD diss., Athens Polytechnic Institute (Greek) .

———. 1990. "Architectural Design in Late Cycladic Akrotiri." Pages 44–56 in *Thera and the Aegean World III.* Edited by D. A. Hardy, C. G. Doumas, J. A. Sakellarakis, and P. M. Warren. London: Thera Foundation.

———. 2005. *Akrotiri, Thera: An Architecture of Affluence 3500 Years Old.* Philadelphia: INSTAP.

Pelon, Olivier, Elga Andersen, and Jean-Pierre Olivier. 1980. *Études crétoises.* Paris: Geuthner.

Prent, Mieke. 2003. "Glories of the Past in the Past: Ritual Activities at Palatial Ruins in Early Iron Age Crete." Pages 81–103 in *Archaeologies of Memory.* Edited by Ruth M. van Dyke and Susan E. Alcock. Malden, MA: Blackwell.

———. 2004. "Cult Activities at the Palace of Knossos from the End of the Bronze Age: Continuity and Change." Pages 411–19 in *Knossos: Palace, City, State.* Edited by Gerald Cadogan, Eleni Hatzaki, and Antonis Vasilakis. London: British School at Athens.

Sakellarakis, Yannis. 1967. "Mason's Marks from Archanes." Pages 277–88 in *Europa: Festschrift für Ernst Grumach.* Edited by William C. Brice. Berlin: de Gruyter.

Sandars, N. K. 1986. "Some Early Uses of Drafted Masonry around the East Mediterranean." Pages 67–73 in *Philia Epi: Festschrift for George Mylonas,* vol. 1. Athens: Athens Archaeological Society.

Shanks, Michael, and Christopher Tilley. 1987. "Abstract and Substantial Time." *Archaeological Review from Cambridge* 6:32–41.

Shaw, Joseph W. 1971. *Minoan Architecture: Materials and Techniques.* Padova: Bottega d'Erasmo.

Shaw, Joseph W., and Leda Costaki. 2006. "Architectural Blocks, Mason's Marks, and Column Bases from the Southern Area." Pages 86–91 in *Kommos V. The Monumental Minoan Buildings at Kommos.* Edited by Joseph W. Shaw and Maria C. Shaw. Princeton: Princeton University Press.

Shiloh, Yigal. 1979. *The Proto-Aeolic Capital and Israelite Ashlar Masonry.* Jerusalem: Hebrew University Press.

South, Alison K. 1983. "Kalavassos—Ayios Dhimitrios 1982." *RDAC* 1983:92–105.

Webb, Jennifer M. 1999. *Ritual Architecture, Iconography and Practice in the Late Cypriot Bronze Age.* Jonsered: Åströms.

Wright, G. R. H. 1992. *Ancient Building in Cyprus*. HdO 7. Leiden: Brill.

————. 2000. "Schools of Masonry in Bronze Age Cyprus." Pages 399–422 in *Proceedings of the Third Cypriological Congress, Nicosia, 16–20 April 1996*. Nicosia: Leventis Foundation.

A Fourth-Century BCE Chian Stamped Amphora Toe from Tel Akko, Israel

Ann E. Killebrew, Gerald Finkielsztejn, Yiftah Shalev, Jane C. Skinner, and Vassiliki E. Stefanaki

Abstract: A Chian Straight-Neck amphora with an unusual stamped toe, dating to the third quarter of the fourth century BCE, was excavated at Tel Akko, Israel, in 2015. The stamp impression depicts the profile of a sitting sphinx facing left, with an amphora positioned in front of it. What makes this impression unique is its location on the toe of the vessel rather than the usual placement on the rim, neck, or shoulders of the amphora. Very similar seated sphinxes facing amphoras appear on fourth-century BCE silver Chian coins. We suggest the contemporaneity of this motif on both Chian amphora stamps and coins indicates a centralized administrative control of measures within a common political-economic context.

Keywords: Tel Akko, Chian Straight-Neck amphora, stamped amphora toe, Chian coins, Chian tetradrachm, sphinx

During the Tel Akko 2015 excavation season, a unique Chian amphora toe stamped with the image of a sphinx facing an amphora was recovered from Area A in L. 3123, a pit stratigraphically assigned to the mid- to late fourth century BCE. The mound, situated to the east of the modern Mediterranean coastal city of Akko and its old town, the UNESCO World Heritage site of Acre, served as a major Canaanite and Phoenician maritime commercial and industrial center for over three millennia. Two series of excavations at Tel Akko, directed by Moshe Dothan (1973–1989) and co-directed by Ann E. Killebrew and Michal Artzy (2010–present), have revealed impressive architectural remains and industrial activities from the Middle Bronze, Late Bronze, Iron, Persian, and Hellenistic periods, spanning the early second millennium through late second century BCE (Dothan 1976, 1993; Artzy and Beeri 2010; Killebrew and Olson 2014; Killebrew and Quartermaine 2016). Located in Area A, the northernmost region of the tell, a massive iron-smithing industrial-scale workshop was uncovered, which was in operation during the Persian period (ca. sixth–mid-fourth centuries BCE; fig. 1). Pit 3123 was dug into this smithy following the cessation of iron forging in Area A, most likely sometime during the mid-fourth century BCE. In this article, dedicated to our friend and colleague Norma Franklin in recognition of her important contribu-

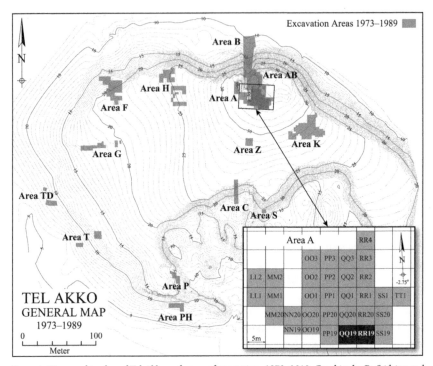

Figure 1. Topographic plan of Tel Akko and areas of excavation: 1973–2018. Graphics by R. Stidsing and J. C. Skinner; © Tel Akko Total Archaeology Project.

tions to the archaeology of the Levant, we present the archaeological context and typology of this Chian amphora and unusual stamped toe. This is followed by a stylistic and comparative analysis of the impression and a discussion of the significance of the Tel Akko Chian stamped amphora toe.

Archaeological Context and Vessel Typology

The Tel Akko Chian stamped amphora toe (Reg. No. 23131/6) was recovered from the fill inside Pit 3123, an ovoid pit straddling the southeastern quadrant of Square QQ19 and continuing into the southwestern quadrant of Square RR19 (fig. 2). At its maximum, Pit 3123 measures 3.6 m in width with a depth of 0.6 m. It is one of several disturbances, along with Pit 2665 and a robber's trench, P2850, that cut into the floors (FL2766), surface build-ups (SB2664, SB2716, and SB2782.2), and floor make-up (FM2821 and FM2778) of the Stratum A4 Persian-period (sixth–mid-fourth centuries BCE) iron-smithing industrial area (figs. 3 and 4). All these disturbances occurred prior to the construction of early Hellenistic architectural features assigned to Stratum A3, patches of which were found on top of Pit 3123 (Debris 2633 and Floor 2603) and Robber's Trench 2850 (Floors 2612, 2603 and Floor Make-up 2731). Thus, strati-

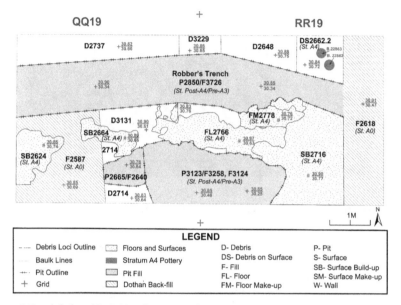

Figure 2. Detailed plan of Pit 3123 and its stratigraphic context in squares QQ19 and RR19. Graphics by J. C. Skinner; © Tel Akko Total Archaeology Project.

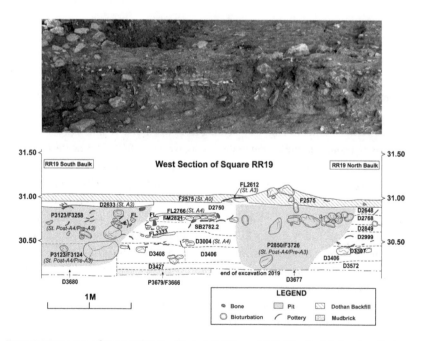

Figure 3. West section of square RR19. Graphics by J. C. Skinner; © Tel Akko Total Archaeology Project.

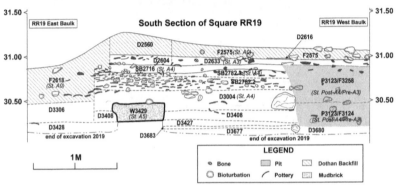

Figure 4. South section of square RR19. Graphics by J. C. Skinner; © Tel Akko Total Archaeology Project.

graphically Pit 3123 and the other disturbances can be assigned to post-Stratum A4/ pre-Stratum A3, dated to the mid- to late fourth century BCE.

The stamp impression appears on a massive, long, and narrow cone-shaped toe of an Aegean amphora identified as originating from the island of Chios (fig. 5). Chian amphoras first appear in the Levant in the late sixth century BCE. During the following century, they become one of the most common imported amphora types. Fifth-century BCE Chian amphoras are easily recognized by their bulging necks. They appear at almost all coastal sites in the eastern Mediterranean basin, being the second most common amphora type after the southeast Aegean types from Samos and Miletus. During the last quarter of the fifth century BCE, the Chian amphora shape evolves into what is commonly referred to as the Chian Straight-Neck (Shalev 2014: 370–72).

From the late fifth through the second century BCE, Chian Straight-Neck amphoras are characterized by cone-shape toes dubbed as either the "cuff toe" (Lawall 1995: 104, n. 67) or "dunce capped toe" (Monakhov and Rogov 1990: 129; Demesticha 2011: 41). The Tel Akko amphora toe discussed here belongs to this shape (fig. 6). Although relatively larger than most parallels, its specific shape—wide and long with a deep hollow in its lower part, measuring ca. 10 cm in height and 8 cm wide—is quite

distinctive and can be dated to the second half of
the fourth century BCE (Lawall 1995: 104 n. 67;
2005: 43–45; Monakhov 2003: 21–22, 242, pls.
11:6, 12:1 Type V-B).

Initially, Chian Straight-Neck amphoras were
quite common in the eastern Mediterranean. However, their distribution seems to decrease during
the course of the fourth century BCE. Although
a large assemblage of Chian amphoras contemporary with the Tel Akko example discussed here was
found on the Mazotos Shipwreck on the southern
coast of Cyprus near modern Larnaca (Demesticha 2011), they appear less frequently at sites along
the Levantine coast than the earlier Chian types
(Shalev 2014: 373–74). Documented fourth-century BCE examples include one from Tell er-Ras
(Rochman-Halperin 1999: 94, fig. 10:18), one
from the Atlit harbor, and one found at the sea off
the coast of Ashkelon (Zemer 1977: 37, pl. 10:30).
The Tel Akko Chian amphora is an important addition to this assemblage.[1]

What were the contents of the Tel Akko Chian
Straight-Neck amphora? Since Chian wine was
highly praised by several ancient writers (for example, Strabo, *Geog.* 14.1.35; Pliny, *HN*14.16.97),
Chian amphoras are usually interpreted as contain-

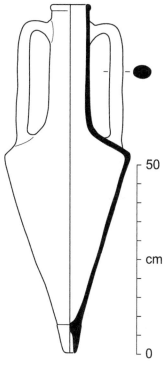

Figure 5. Chian Straight-Neck amphora, Monakhov Type V-B. Graphics by
R. Stidsing; © Tel Akko Total Archaeology Project).

ers for the wine trade. However, residue and DNA analyses conducted on several such
vessels clearly indicate that these were also used for other commodities, such as olive
oil (Foley et al. 2009: 294; Foley et al. 2012). Additionally, according to the third-cen-
tury BCE Zenon Papyri, which list amphora origins and their contents, Chian amphoras could also contain honey, hazelnuts, and olives (Lawall 2011: 43; listed in Panagou
2016: 326, with n. 35).

The Stamp Impression and its Iconography

The design on the Tel Akko stamp impression depicts the profile of a sitting sphinx facing left, with an amphora standing in front of it (see fig. 6). The impression is circular

---

1. Recently, several fourth-century BCE Chian amphora toes have also been recovered from salvage excavations directed by Amani Abu Hamid to the north of Tel Akko at the railway station (Gerald
Finkielsztejn, pers. comm.).

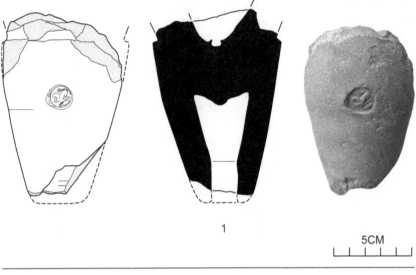

1

5CM

Legend

= Fresh break
= Uncertain and reconstructed

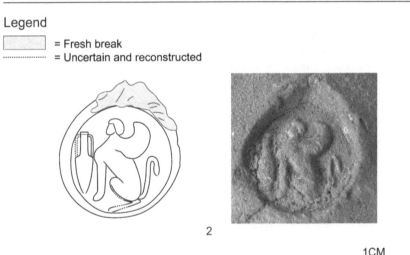

2

1CM

Figure 6. Photos and drawings of Chian amphora toe and stamped amphora impression. Graphics and photographs by R. Stidsing; © Tel Akko Total Archaeology Project.

in shape, with a diameter of 1.25 cm. The die had been pressed into the unfired clay of the amphora. The sphinx is shown somewhat schematically. The visible folded back leg of the sphinx displays a strong thigh, but its left side was not clearly impressed and the leg itself not at all. The front leg is a mere straight upward cylinder, prolonged by a poorly designed paw. The head bears no features of the face and has a compact hairdo. The wing is thick and prolongs the shoulder. The tail is sharply impressed, but it is not visible where it is attached to the lower back of the sphinx. It raises from the bottom and then folds down, the tip located at the mid-level of the raised part.

The amphora is standing parallel to the front leg. Its neck is elongated with a slight (however exaggerated) thickening at the rim. The body appears as an asymmetrical elongated oval—almost flat to the right, as if hidden by the leg of the sphinx—with a discreet shoulder. The body seems prolonged by a high cylindrical base or toe. Only the right handle is visible, represented by a very thin vertical line running between the shoulder and the rim, and a perpendicular short line that seems to reach the rim. This unusual representation is due to flaws in the clay and maybe in the engraving of the die. It is corrected on the drawn illustration of the stamp in figure 6. The closest parallel to the depicted vessel is Monakhov's Chian amphora Type V-B, corresponding with the fourth century BCE date of the Tel Akko amphora toe.

Similar impressions depicting a sphinx with an amphora are relatively common at the end of the fifth century (ca. 430–425 BCE), coinciding with the period Chian amphoras were evolving from the bulging-neck to the Straight-Neck amphora type. However, on these earlier examples the impressions generally appear on the rim, neck, or shoulders.[2] A stamp on an amphora from the Athenian Agora is located at the base of one handle. In the case of another example from Panticapaeum the impression was stamped on the rim of a Straight-Neck amphora (Šelov 1957: 203, 215, pl. III, fig. 6). It depicts a Straight-Neck amphora with a seated sphinx facing right. In difference to our stamp, it is completely imprinted, but the design is more schematic, in flat relief, and occupies the whole field of the die. However, the features of the face are visible, as well as the feathers of the wing and two claws of the paw. The body of the amphora is wider than the one depicted on the Tel Akko impression, and the neck appears shorter. The handles are set on the shoulder and apparently just below the rim. In shape and proportion, this representation of a rather squat amphora resembles Monakhov's Type V-A, dated to the end of the fifth century BCE.[3]

All the above-mentioned examples were stamped on either the base of one handle or on the rim. Therefore, the Tel Akko stamp adds to the corpus (1) another, and un-

---

2. Lawall 1995: 103–4, 108; Monakhov 2003: 20–21, pls. 8–10, Types IV–V-A. See also Grace 1979: Comment on illustrations 44, 45, 48, and 49 (no page numbers). For the Athenian Agora, see catalog in Lawall 2000: 28–29, no. 12, 30–31, no. 17 (both stamped with same die at base of the handle), no. 18 (stamped at top of neck), all dated 430–425 BCE. This could be interpreted as signaling that the new Straight-Neck form's capacity was the same as that of the former bulging-neck one (Stefanaki and Seroglou 2019: 11, with n. 81; 12, with n. 90).

3. Monakhov 2003: 24, 240, pl. 10, 1. See the numismatic analysis of the depiction of the stamp, below. Contrary to the description of the latter by the authors, it does not seem that a grape cluster is set above the amphora, as is the case with the coin. A grape cluster does not appear on any of the amphora stamps; perhaps it was not needed because it was understood that Chian amphoras usually contained wine. The coins of Chios, due to the value of the wine grown on this island, however, were deemed to be suitable advertising vehicles. Similar imagery is known on coins from Samos that depict a local amphora with an olive branch next to it (Mattingly 1981: pl. I, h).

usual, stamping practice, and (2) another, late, chronological point for the stamping of Chian amphoras with the sphinx and amphora, the *parasemon* of the island. The Tel Akko Chian stamped amphora toe appears to be unique, at least in that it is larger than other toes of this shape and carries a stamp impression previously documented only on amphora necks or handles. This new location of the stamp bears on the interpretation of the stamping of amphoras. The toe discussed here was stamped at the production center on Chios while the amphora was drying, turned upside down, before firing. Therefore, after the amphora was unloaded from the ship and stored in the emporion of destination, the stamp was not visible to the buyer or the local comptroller. On the other hand, some sort of production control on the island of Chios itself can be inferred.[4]

The iconography that most closely compares to the Tel Akko amphora stamp stems from Chian coins. As has been noted by Stefanaki and Seroglou (2019), in several Greek cities during the fifth–fourth centuries BCE, such as Mende, Chios, Kos, Rhodes, and Samos, amphora stamps "faithfully" mirror depictions on coins. The stylistic and metrological development of Chian amphoras from the Late Archaic to the Roman period can be traced in their depictions on Chian coin series. Representations of Chian amphoras, which appear on the obverse of Chian silver coins from the late 490s, are probably contemporary with the amphoras they appear to have copied. During the early fifth century, an amphora and a bunch of grapes were added as "secondary" symbols in front of the sphinx, which became a permanent feature of the Chian coin type (Hardwick 1993: 211–22). However, the amphora depicted as "secondary" symbol on Classical Chian coins minted until the third quarter of the fourth century BCE, is small in size in comparison with those that appear as the sole reverse type on later Hellenistic silver and bronze issues (Lagos 1999: 77–100). Thus, in certain cases, the depiction's attribution to a specific amphora type is rendered difficult due to its small size. Nevertheless, it is clear that the bulging-necked amphora is depicted on Chian silver coins issued from the late 490s to ca. 425 BCE. This corresponds with the production of the bulging-neck amphoras that date from the end of the sixth century until ca. 425 BCE, when this type was completely superseded by the Straight-Necked style. These Chian Straight-Neck amphoras are depicted on Chian coins (ca. late fifth–mid-fourth century BCE) minted on a reduced Chian or "Chian-Rhodian" weight standard of 15.30 g. and on later issues dating to the third quarter of the fourth century BCE minted on a debased local standard of 13.70 g (fig. 7).[5] Some amphoras of this type, including the one from Tel Akko, carry circular stamps that "faithfully" reproduced the

---

4. For thoughts on the purpose(s) of amphora stamps, see Finkielsztejn 2006 and 2012 passim.

5. On the chronology and the weight standard of Chian silver coins of the Classical period, see Hardwick 1993 and 2010. See also Meadows 2002: 105 and Hardwick 2002: 212–16. On the Chian, "Chian-Rhodian," and Rhodian weight standards, see also Stefanaki 2012: 65–66, with the bibliographical references.

Figure 7. Photo of Chian tetradrachm (13.39 g), 350–325 BCE from the collections of the Museum of Fine Arts, Boston (accession no.: 04.1047; https://collections.mfa. org/objects/1725/tetradrachm-of-chios-with-sphinx-struck-under-kephisokritos [public domain]; Brett 1974: no. 1949).

image on the contemporary coin types, apart from the bunch of grapes above the amphora that does not appear.[6]

The Chian amphora stamped toe from Tel Akko supports the suggestion of a parallel development and the contemporaneity of amphora stamps and coin types that corresponds to administrative control of measures within a common political-economic context (Stefanaki and Seroglou 2019). Indeed, since the amphora toe in question dates to the third quarter of the fourth century BCE, the Straight-Neck amphora that figures on its stamp dates probably to the first to third quarters of the fourth century BCE. The closest type of amphora depicted on Chian coins is depicted on examples dated to this period (see Hardwick 1993: pl. XIII, nos. 13, 18, and 20). Therefore, by "faithfully" imitating coin depictions, the amphora stamps of Chios create a mental

---

6. The sphinx with amphora, the parasemon of Chios, appeared on other official *instrumenta* and items: scale weights (Tekin 2016: 202–3, pls. 28–29, figs. 216–221), also with amphora only and the name of the city (Tekin 2016: 202–3, pls. 28–29, figs. 222–224), scale weight with amphora and countermark depicting the parasemon (Zacharou-Loutrari 1998: 67–71, fig. 40), and water pipes (Zacharou-Loutrari 1998: figs. 43–44).

connection between local coinage and the actual vessels, resulting in the association of one "emblem of the city" and probably "standard of the city" (the *nomisma*) with another, the amphora (see Stefanaki and Seroglou 2019: 48–49).

References

Artzy, Michal, and Ron Beeri. 2010. "Tel Akko." Pages 15*–23* in *One Thousand Nights and Days: Akko through the Ages*. Edited by Ann E. Killebrew and Vered Raz-Romeo. Haifa: Hecht Museum.

Brett, Agnes B. 1974. *Catalogue of Greek Coins, Museum of Fine Arts, Boston*. New York: Attic Books.

Demesticha, Stella. 2011. "The 4th-Century-BC Mazotos Shipwreck, Cyprus: A Preliminary Report." *The International Journal of Nautical Archaeology* 40:39–59.

Dothan, Moshe. 1976. "Akko: Interim Excavation Report First Season, 1973/4." *BASOR* 224:1–48.

———. 1993. "Tel Akko." *NEAEHL* 1:17–23.

Finkielsztejn, Gerald. 2006. "Production et commerce des amphores hellénistiques: Récipients, timbrage et métrologie." Pages 17–34 in *Approches de l'économie hellénistique*. Edited by R. Descat. Saint-Bertrand-de-Comminges: Musée archéologique départemental.

———. 2012. "Réflexions additionnelles sur le marquage des instruments et récipients à l'époque hellénistique." Pages 77–84 in *Stèphanephoros: De l'économie antique à l'Asie Mineure; hommages à Raymond Descat*. Edited by K. Konuk. Bordeaux: Ausonius.

Foley, Brendan P., Katerina Dellaporta, Dimitris Sakellariou, Brian S. Bingham, Richard Camilli, Ryan M. Eustice, Dionysis Evagelistis, Vicki Lynn Ferrini, Kostas Katsaros, Dimitris Kourkoumelis, Aggelos Mallios, Paraskevi Micha, David A. Mindell, Christopher Roman, Hanumant Singh, David S. Switzer, and Theotokis Theodoulou. 2009. "The 2005 Chios Ancient Shipwreck Survey: New Methods for Underwater Archaeology." *Hesperia* 78:269–305.

Foley, Brendan P., Maria C. Hansson, Dimitris P. Kourkoumelis, and Theotokis A. Theodoulou. 2012. "Aspects of Ancient Greek Trade Re-evaluated with Amphora DNA Evidence." *Journal of Archaeological Science* 39:89–98.

Grace, Virgina R. 1979. *Amphoras and the Ancient Wine Trade*. Princeton, NJ: American School of Classical Studies at Athens.

Hardwick, Nicholas. 1993. "The Coinage of Chios from the VIth to the IVth c. B.C." Pages 211–22 in *Proceedings of the XIth International Numismatic Congress, Brussels, September 8th–13th 1991*. Edited by T. Hackens and G. Moucharte. Louvain-la-Neuve: Association Professeur Marcel Hoc.

———. 2002. "Chios." Pages 212–16 in *Coin Hoards* 9. London: Spink & Son.

———. 2010. "The Coinage of Chios 600–300 BC: New Research Developments 1991–2008." Pages 217–45 in *Coins in the Aegean Islands: Proceedings of the Fifth Scientific Meeting, Mytilene, 16–19 September 2006*. Vol. 1. Edited by P. Tselekas. Athens: Friends of the Numismatic Museum.

Killebrew, Ann E., and Brandon R. Olson. 2014. "The Tel Akko Total Archaeology Project: New Frontiers in the Excavation and 3D Documentation of the Past." Pages 559–74 in *Proceedings of the 8th International Congress on the Archaeology of the Ancient Near East, 30 April–4 May 2012, University of Warsaw*. Vol. 2: *Excavation and Progress Reports—Posters*. Edited by P. Bieliński, M. Gawlikowski, R. Koliński, D. Ławecka, A. Sołtysiak, and Z. Wygnańska. Wiesbaden: Harrassowitz.

Killebrew, Ann E., and Jamie Quartermaine. 2016. "Total Archaeology@Tel Akko (the 2013 and 2014 Seasons): Excavation, Survey, Community Outreach and New Approaches to Landscape Archaeology in 3D." Pages 491–502 in *Proceedings of the 9th International Congress on the Archaeology of the Ancient Near East, 9–13 June 2014, Basel.* Vol. 3. Edited by O. Kaelin and H.-P. Mathys. Wiesbaden: Harrassowitz.

Lagos, Constantinos. 1999. "Chian Coins and Amphoras during the Hellenistic and Roman Periods." *Nomismatika Chronika* 18:77–100.

Lawall, Mark L. 1995. "Transport Amphoras and Trademarks: Imports to Athens and Economic Diversity in the Fifth Century B.C." PhD diss., University of Michigan.

———. 2000. "Graffiti, Wine Selling, and the Reuse of Amphoras in the Athenian Agora, ca. 430 to 400 B.C." *Hesperia* 69:3–90.

———. 2005. "Negotiating Chronologies: Aegean Amphora Research, Thasian Chronology, and Pnyx III." Pages 31–67 in *Chronologies of the Black Sea Area in the Period c. 400–100 BC.* Edited by V. Stolba and L. Hannestad. Black Sea Studies 3. Aarhus: Aarhus University Press.

———. 2011. "Greek Amphorae in the Archaeological Record." Pages 37–50 in *Pottery in the Archaeological Record: Greece and Beyond.* Edited by Mark L. Lawall and John Lund. Gösta Enbom Monographs 1. Aarhus: Aarhus University Press.

Mattingly, Harold B. 1981. "Coins and Amphoras: Chios, Samos and Thasos in the Fifth Century B.C." *JHS* 101:78–86.

Meadows , Andrew. 2002. "Chios." Pages 95–158 in *Coin Hoards 9.* London: Spink & Son.

Monakhov, S. I. 2003. *Grecheskie amfory v Prichernomor'e. tipologiia amfor vedushchikh tsentrov-éksporterov tovarov v keramicheskoĭ tare (Greek Amphoras in the Northern Black Sea: Amphora Typology of Leading Commercial Export Centers in Ceramic Containers).* Moscow (Russian).

Monakhov, S. I., and E. I. Rogov. 1990. "Amfory nekropolia Panskoe I (Amphoras of the Panskoe I Necropolis)." *Antichnye Mir i Arkheologiia* 7:128–53 (Russian; English translation available at http://projects.chass.utoronto.ca/amphoras/trans/sym-pans.htm).

Panagou, Tania. 2016. "Transport Amphoras and Their Contents." Pages 312–34 in Ἡχάδιν:Τιμητικός τόμος για τη Στέλλα Δρούγου (Caress: Volume in Honor of Stella Drougou). Edited by M. Giannopoulou and C. Kallini. Part 2. Athens: ΕΚΔΟΣΗ ΤΟΥ ΤΑΜΕΙΟΥ ΑΡΧΑΙΟΛΟΓΙΚΩΝ ΠΟΡΩΝ ΚΑΙ ΑΠΑΛΛΟΤΡΙΩΣΕΩΝ.

Rochman-Halperin, Arieh. 1999. "Excavations at Giv'at Yasaf (Tell er-Ras)—1984–1985." 'Atiqot 37:83–123 (Hebrew; English summary Pages 172*–73*).

Šelov, D. B. 1957. "Stamps on Amphoras and Tiles Found in the Excavations of Panticapaeum in 1945–1949." *Materiali i issledovaniya po arkheologii* 56:202–26 (Russian).

Shalev, Yiftah. 2014. "The Mighty Grain-Lands: Demographic and Economic Aspects of 'Southern Phoenicia' under the Achaemenid Regime." PhD diss., University of Haifa (Hebrew with English abstract).

Stefanaki, Vassiliki E. 2012. Νομίσματα-Νομισματική Αιγαίου. Κως I (*Coins-Coinage of the Aegean. Kos I*). Athens: Αρχαιολογικό Ινστιτούτο Αιγιακών σπουδών (Greek with summary in French: 411– 36).

Stefanaki, Vassiliki E., and Fani K. Seroglou. 2019. "Coin Types on Amphora Stamps of the Classical and Early Hellenistic Periods." Pages 45–58 in *Analyse et exploitation des timbres amphoriques grecs: actes du colloque organisé par l'École française d'Athènes et l'université de Rennes 2 Haute Bretagne sous le haut patronage de l'Académie des inscriptions et belles-Lettres (Athènes, 3–5 février 2010).* Edited by N. Badoud and A. Marangou. Rennes: Université de Bretagne.

Tekin, Oğuz. 2016. *Balance Weights in the Aegean World: Classical and Hellenistic Periods.* Istanbul: Turkish Institute of Archaeology.

Zacharou-Loutrari, Athina K. 1998. *Χιακή Σφίγγα. Η διαχρονική πορεία ενός τοπικού συμβόλου* (*The Chian Sphinx: The Diacronic Evolution of a Local Symbol*). Chios: Ομήρειο Πνευματικό Κέντρο Δήμου Χίου.

Zemer, Avshalom. 1977. *Storage Jars in Ancient Sea Trade.* Haifa: National Maritime Museum Foundation.

OF SHEKELS AND SHACKLES:
A WADI SOREK ROMANCE (JUDGES 16)

JACK M. SASSON

Abstract: This essay focuses on Samson in Delilah's chamber (Judges 16). It explores the use of love charms in antiquity to clarify the bonds between the two major characters. It also offers an alternative understanding for why Samson gave in to Delilah's serial insistence that he reveals the secret of his strength.

Keywords: Samson, Delilah, Judges 13–16

> *Amare et sapere vix deo conceditur*
> (Publilius Syrus, first century BCE)

To Norma Franklin, a good friend for a generation and a respected colleague for twice as long, I offer frothy thoughts about Samson's final moments as a free human being. A first-rate archaeologist with scrupulous attachment to historical facts and realities, Norma is also a lover of good stories. On this occasion, therefore, I avoid commenting on the origin(s), date(s), and permutations of traditions on which hard-core scholarship grooves.[1] Rather, I will trust the Hebrew editor to have redacted a version that, however episodic, has proven its power to please through countless reformulations, in poetry, art, musical settings, and films.

No one, Norma least of all, needs reminding of the essentials of the Samson stories that unfold from Judges 13 through 16. Having given up on raising a family, a childless couple from the tribe of Dan receives divine news that they are to have a son. Repeated threefold in the span of chapter 13 (at 3–5, 7, and 13–14), extraordinary instruction consistently assigns the wife (conspicuously unnamed) the burden of consecrating her body, perhaps for the duration of her pregnancy. She is to abstain from intoxicants and unclean food. The child is to be a Nazir, his hair remaining unshorn throughout his life, for "he will begin to rescue Israel from Philistine control" (13:5).

---

1. I explore these issues (and more) in my forthcoming *Judges 13–21* (Anchor Yale Bible). Most any decent Judges commentary will review issues on these matters.

So much for how Samson's story begins. The scene that will interest at chapter 16 features Samson, Delilah, the Philistines, and God. Here is a thumbnail review of their attributes.

The Protagonists

Samson

When we first meet Samson, he is of uncertain age, but old enough to wish for marriage. He has a taste for forbidden fruit, intending to marry from among his people's oppressors. From his rejection of parental advice, we surmise also that he is headstrong. From that incident, too, we learn that he is an instrument in games God periodically plays against his people's adversaries as well as against their gods (14:1–5). When suffused with divine power, Samson can kill a (young) lion barehanded (14:5–7), savage a bunch of Philistines (14:17–19), and batter hundreds of their armed men (15:14–17). Even when left to his own mettle, he can unleash scarcely believable prowess to leave a fortified city defenseless (16:1–3). Samson can be devious in seeking to best his adversaries (14:12–18), righteous in seeking revenge (15:1–3), and inventive when doing so (15:4–8). Yet, he could be protective of his kin (15:9–15) and cognizant of the source of his strength (15:18–19). When we are about to feature him in a drama set in a bedroom, Samson had already displayed a carnal appetite by visiting a whore in Gaza (16:1–3).

Delilah

Delilah is unheralded when she comes on stage and, if we ignore the postbiblical enhancements of her single appearance, she will fade into the twilight when she leaves it.[2] She is, however, the unique woman in the Samson tales to have a name, albeit scarcely transparent in meaning.[3] She lives in Wadi Sorek (*naḥal śōrēq*), named for its vineyards, a porous demarcation between Hebrew and Philistine lands, so likely inhabited by

---

2. Delightful tidbits about Delilah's portraits in literature and art are in Gunn 2005: 211–20. In the movies and elsewhere, she perishes with Samson's destruction of the Gaza temple. More inventive is the late haggadic lore by the fabulist Eldad ha-Dani (ninth–tenth century). There, Samson and Delilah had children and lived in the land of Havilah ("Where the gold is," Gen 2:11); see Neubauer 1889: 105; and note 4 below. Scholars needlessly attach her to the mother of Micah of chapter 17.

3. The name's construction (*qātīl*, denoting a condition, with a feminine ending), certainly looks Semitic if not Hebraic. Several Hebraic words build on the root **dll*, having to do with "poverty," "scarcity," but also with dangling (a baby?) hair. Akkadian offers several constructions based on *dalālum*, "to praise," among them the name Dalal-Ishtar, a devotee of a (love) deity. The rabbis, however, gave us all a chance to derive moral lessons: "Rabbi says: 'Even if her name had not been Delilah, she deserved to be called by such a name: She enfeebled (*dīldělâ*) his strength, she enfeebled his actions, she enfeebled his determination'" (m. Num. Rab. 9:24).

elements from both communities. Consequently, there is debate about her ethnicity. She is widely presumed to be Philistine because the adult Samson seems drawn to its women, for marriage or dalliance. She might be a Hebrew, but given her trade and her fondness for its income, her ethnicity may be irrelevant. Strikingly, Delilah is linked to no parents, husband, or sons, so is independent of male protection, a much more prevalent status for women than is realized in scholarly literature. In Rabbinic literature, however, she is Samson's wife (m. Naz. 2), presumably to sharpen her betrayal as well as to warn of alliances with foreign women.[4]

In the Hebrew account, Delilah does not earn the label *zônâ* as did the whore of Gaza or, earlier in Judges, Jephthah's mother (11:1). Nonetheless, Delilah is often cited as a prostitute, in ancient literature a label (Greek: πόρνη) attached to women who ply their trade in brothels, streets, or open space, as did Enkidu's guide to civilization (Gilgamesh Epic) or the pseudo-prostitute Tamar (Gen 38). However, Delilah connects with rulers and commands tons of cash. Her home is large enough to hide ambushers and to accommodate admirers for longer stretches than might the hovel of a hustling prostitute. Therefore, I rather consider her a courtesan (Greek: ἑταίρα). Greek culture teems with such personalities as Aspasia, Rhodopis, and Thais; but for me Delilah conjures up the unforgettable Tabubu of Demotic tales regarding Prince Setne Khamwas, son of Ramses II.[5] Setne falls in violent lust for Tabubu ("The moment Setne saw her, he did not know where on earth he was ..."). Daughter of the prophet of Bastet though she may have been, the woman was actually for hire, but at the highest price and at her own staging. Tabubu ("She of Splendor") does not easily surrender to Setne; but at successive inflammations of his desire, she cajoles from him his fortune, his property, and his own children's death. Unlike in the romances and the movies, however, professionals like Tabubu hardly return a customer's love, a point we might keep in mind when we get back to our story.

The Philistines

Aside from (incongruent) mention in Genesis (21 and 26) where, grudgingly or otherwise, they assist the patriarchs, the Philistines are not yet the formidable military force that thwarted Israel's incipient monarchy. Earlier in Judges (3:31, 10:6–7), the Philistines are a menace to Israel and an instrument for God's punishment of a stiff-necked people. In the Samson story, they are settled folks who tend vineyards, olive groves, and wheat fields. Their citizens dress fashionably enough to embolden bandits into raiding them. Sophisticated and urbane, they do not shun intercourse with Hebrews and do not object to their daughters marrying one of their (barbarically) circumcised male

---

4. Cited from Danby 1933: 281. The same for Pseudo-Philo (LAB 44.1, where she is Dedila; cited from Harrington 1985) and Milton (*Samson Agonistes*).

5. Translation in Lichtheim 1980: 127–51. Citations are from pages 133 and 134. A fine study that brings out the humor of the tale is Jasnow 2001; see especially 73–81.

neighbors. In all, hardly the material for an uncouth "philistine" as enshrined in our dictionaries.[6] Still, the image we have of them in our pages reminds most of the Roman legions in the Gaul of Asterix and Obelix, the famous French-language cartoon characters. Domineering and ferocious though they were, the Philistine fighters would receive repeated drubbings from Samson, who bludgeons them with delight and abandon.

God

In this scene, the Hebrew God is not a conspicuous character until its final moments, when he begins to take charge of the ensuing staging. Until then, God had dominated Judges, from its opening giving it pulse and trajectory. As the Hebrew historiographers have it, God was testing how best to transit a people from slavery to dominance over nations not willing to be dispossessed. He would remain their God and King, sole proprietor of the conquered land he wishes to distribute among Hebrew tribes.[7] Subsequently, he would rely on an unpredictable series of selected leaders (*šōfēṭ*, traditionally "judge"), from diverse tribes (mostly northern), from both sexes, and different in character or temper. Each would rescue penitent Israel from its harassers, giving it stability and dominance that was expected to endure when the judge leaves the stage a generation or so later. The plan hardly worked effectively, such that at one point (10:16), and totally exasperated by Israel's cyclical failures, God withdraws from the rescue business, leaving it for manipulators like Jephthah to fill the vacuum. There will be more judges, of course, among them Ibzan, Elon, Abdon; but with Samson and soon also Eli and Samuel, their titles will hardly match God's original notion of their function.[8] God could not remain in sole control of kingship for much longer. As Mesopotamians recognized generations earlier (The Sumerian King List, among others), it will need to come down to earth for humans to govern themselves adequately.

Love

In the Hebrew Bible, love sings in poetry (Song of Songs), preaches in prose (Proverbs), and expounds on divine ardor in a variety of prophetic modes. Tales abound about human affection, constancy, but also lust and revulsion. To express love, there are metaphors construing *nefeš* ("soul") with *dāvaq* and *ḥāšaq bĕ-* or *lĕ-* ("attaching" or "joining" to something or someone). Several derivatives of the verb **ydd* share an asso-

---

6. A slew of excavation reports supports this vision of them, perhaps marred only by their apparent consumption of dogs; see Killebrew and Lehmann 2013; Maier and Hitchcock 2017; and Maier 2018. For dog consumption, see Lev-Tov, et al. 2018.

7. Judges 10:16b, *vattiqṣar nafšô baʿāmal yiśrāʾel*, hardly "he could not bear the miseries of Israel" (TNT) as it is commonly translated, but "he lost patience with Israel's behavior."

8. I have deployed reasons and arguments for these positions in many pages of Sasson 2014, especially at 412–16. A succinct picture is in Sasson 2013.

ciation with "love, lovemaking, loving." None of these terms in their amatory sense occurs in Judges, a book given over to wars and power plays; ʾāhēv, however, does. Except for one pietistic expression (at 5:31), its few attestations there are all from the Samson tales. In one striking moment, frustrated for denying her an answer to a riddle, Samson's Timnah bride-to-be accuses him of hating rather than loving her (14:16). Who knows whether she was delusional or merely crafty in her expectations? |

In Delilah's case, however, the narrator reveals that Samson is in love (16:4)—not unusual when a young man experiences a practiced lover. Yet, this striking detail invites us to consider the emotional state in which Samson might wish to prompt an equivalent response in a partner. Unlike the one-night stand he had with the Gaza whore, when we meet God's chosen judge in Delilah's chamber he had already confessed his love (16:15). We have no idea how long he nurtured his crush before doing so; but it must have been lengthy enough for the Philistines to learn his whereabouts, caucus on a strategy to capture him, and travel to meet with Delilah. Using the same language as when haranguing the Timnah bride, the leaders want Delilah to "deceive him" (pattî ʾôtô), this time wisely using carrots (mindboggling stacks of shekels; 16:5) rather than sticks ("... lest we set you and your family on fire; 14:15) to persuade her. They wish her to find out "what makes his strength so great and what would give us control of him so as to bind him for degradation" (bammeh kôḥô gādôl ʾûvammeh nûkal lô va ʾăsarĕnûhû lĕʿannōtô). Delilah may (or may not) have needed the Philistines to explain what they hoped to achieve once in possession of Samson's secret; but they make it clear that having this knowledge would permit them to neutralize its effect.[9] With it, they will no longer fear a repeat of what had happened earlier: Samson breaking his chains and massacring hundreds of them (15:14–16). Little did the Philistines know that his strength came from an infusion of divine power rather than any secrets Samson could reveal. They were now in the realm of fantasy, if not also magic, which is where our story will take us next.

The Staging

I now offer just a smidgen of excerpts from ancient instructions on how to improve a love life:

> You weave together into a single strand the tendons of a gazelle, [hemp,] and red wool; you tie it into fourteen knots. Each time you tie a knot, you recite the incantation. The woman places this cord around her waist, and she will be loved.[10]

---

9. They say that they wish to bind him. As we recall from execration texts excavated in the ancient world, binding is itself a magical prelude to overpowering an enemy. On the execration texts, see conveniently Seidlmayer 2001: 487–89.

10. Reiner (1966: 93, cited in English from Faraone 1999: 101–2). This advice is for a Mesopotamian

To make a woman "talk," you wrap in goat hair: *mēsu*-wood, boxwood, ...-stone, cress, and the tongue of a partridge(?). You place it at the head of your bed. Then that woman will "talk" to you, wherever you meet her; she will not be able to help it. You can make love to her.[11]

You take a harp string (and) tie three knots in it; you recite the incantation seven times, you tie it around his right and left hands and then he will recover potency.[12]

She hangs these (i.e., the clothes or hair of the man) from a peg and heats them up with burning sulfur, sprinkling salt over the fire, and says in addition the names of both people, his and yours...[13]

For quieting the anger of a man: take a six-ply thread and double it/ twice and tie it into seven knots. You should say on each and every knot/ (...) that you may quiet the anger of such-and-such and he should revert from his anger and he will do the words of his lovers and friends who are such-and-such (adapted from Saar 2017: 53 n. 66).

With these useful amatory lessons in mind, let us go back to our drama.

We do not know how soon after her commission Delilah puts her plan to action; but the narrator moves into it promptly. Amit (1999: 286; 2014: 531) points out that the construction relies on a pattern already observed in Jotham's fable (Judg 9:8–15): three failed attempts, capped by a successful fourth. As she seeks to ferret out Samson's secret, Delilah will harass him with four reiterations of the Philistine rulers' own directives (at vss 6, 10, 13, 15). Yet, at each rehearsal, she either trims the formula or accents a segment of it. For example, in her first address to Samson, Delilah simply rephrases the original directive. For obvious reasons, she drops the middle phrase, "... what would give us control of him?" She also avoids revealing who might be doing

---

woman with an angry husband. Incantations for the lovelorn (addressing Ištar) commonly repeat seven times, either before or after the act itself. Geller (2002) notes similarity between Mesopotamian love-magic and other lore from antiquity. This type of magic is widely practiced across time and space. Faraone's chapter (1999: 119–30) "Narcotics and Knotted Cords: The Subversive Cast of Philia Magic" is delightful. Ogden (2002) collects much lore on erotic magic as practiced in antiquity; see in particular chapter 11. Rabbinic Judaism struggled (to little avail) against such magical practices, ranging them among "Amorite practices"; see Bloom 2007: 133, 168 and elsewhere.

11. Cited after Biggs 1967: 71 (KAR 61). *šudbubum* literally is to "make someone talk"; in this context it connotes compliant sexually; see Geller 2002. The text gives other instructions for a successful seduction of a woman.

12. See Biggs 1967: 35–36 (#15). The incantation reads, "Let the wind blow! Let the grove quake! Let the clouds gather! Let the moisture fall! Let my potency be flowing river water! Let my penis be a (taut) harp string so that it will not slip out of her!"

13. Faraone 1999: 150–51, citing Lucian (*Dialogues of the Courtesans* 4.1) who reports on a Syrian sorceress's formula for retrieving a lover.

OF SHEKELS AND SHACKLES

Table 1. Queries and Answers in Judg 16

16:5 Rulers to Delilah	16:6–7 Delilah to Samson I	16:10–11 Delilah to Samson II	16:13 Delilah to Samson III	16:15, 17 Delilah to Samson IV
Beguile him and find out	Do tell me	You deceived me just now, speaking lies to me!	Even now you are deceiving me, speaking lies to me!	How could you say, I love you, when your heart is not with me,
what makes his strength so great	what makes your strength so great			not revealing to me what makes your strength so great?
and what would give us control of him. We will bind so as to humiliate him.	and how might you be bound so as to humiliate you?	Now, you must reveal to me how you might be bound?	You must reveal to me how you might be bound?	
	If I were bound with seven fresh sinews that have yet to dry up … I would then weaken and become as any other man.	If I were firmly bound by ropes that are new and that were never used on any job, I would weaken and become as any other man.	If you would weave the seven braids on my head into the fabric on a loom…	… If my hair is cut, my strength would desert me. I would weaken then and become as any other man.

the binding by relying on the passive conjugation of the relevant verb (*tēʾāsēr*, "you might be bound"). Not as obvious is why she would retain *lěʿannôtekā*, "for degradation," unless the form also conveys the promise of esoteric sensuality. Table 1 might help shape an overview for pair of query-answer.

Sinews and Ropes

It is difficult to gauge over how many séances Delilah deployed her wiles. Aristotelian poetics would favor a threefold unity, of which we have undoubtedly two: of action and of space. The third, of time, is harder to sustain due to the diverse appeals to Philistine leaders/ambushers and the reference to occasional naps Samson takes. Nonetheless, the narrator intimates such a triune temporal concord in covering the fourfold requests and responses. The pattern is repetitious: Delilah poses her question; Samson gives her an answer. She follows his instruction, then tests each trial by sounding the same alarm ("Philistines upon you, Samson!").

Samson manages to fool her three times; so much so, that he hardly bothers to search for ambushers. The fourth one, as we all know, proves the charm (for her).[14] While I leave it to my Commentary to discuss the particulars in each of the tests, I would note that the first two aim to immobilize Samson by using implements of diverse properties as well as by multiplying their numbers—seven being a particular favorite for its presumed effectiveness. In the first case, seven *yětārîm*, "tendons, sinew" (elsewhere used to string bows, as in Ps 11:2), still fresh (*laḥîm*, elsewhere said of grapes or rods) and beyond withering (*lōʾ ḥōrāvû*).[15] In the second, she is to truss him with "ropes" (or "garlands," as in Ps 118:27) that are brand new (*ʿăvōtîm ḥădāšîm*) and "never put to use." Once again, we are in the realm of sympathetic magic, in which fate is subject to human manipulation of symbolic objects.

Fabric, Peg, and Loom

On the third attempt to discover Samson's secret, Delilah repeats her jeremiad, but displays her impatience by substituting *ʿad-hennâ*, "even now," for the previous *hinnê*, "just now." Samson's latest instruction to her completely skips over the usual detailing of the consequences, leaving it to Delilah (and to us) to surmise the outcome. The clause is brief; yet two of its nouns occur nowhere else in Scripture, so deciphering its meaning is circumstantial albeit fairly certain. One is *maḥlěfôt* (plural of *maḥlāfâ*): There are

---

14. We do notice, however, that the Philistines (or the narrator) tire from the exercise, as they stay in ambush just on the first two installments.

15. Not fully appreciating the magical allusion, some translations (among them JPS's) give "rope" or the like. The Greek versions similarly alludes to sinew (νευρά, Latin nervis). Josephus gives "fresh vine-shoots." On discussing two divergent notions for *yětārîm*, Marcos (2011: 96*) hints, "both materials… may be connected with magical practices."

seven of them; Delilah cuts them (16:19); but when at 16:22 they are cited as head-hair (śēʿar-rōʾš), they sprout once again. The other *hapax* in this passage is *masseket*. Debated is whether to derive it from the root *skk, (from which *sukkâ*, "tent" likely derives) or, as plausible, from *nsk (as in *massekâ*, "a molten object," as in idols). This *masseket*, however, will shortly prove to be a woven fabric, perhaps as in the *massēkâ* of Isa 25:7 and 28:20. The key to our phrase, however, is Samson's counsel ʾim-taʾargî ("if you would weave …") for elsewhere the verb ʾārag clearly has to do with weaving. How to tie all three elements—the locks, the fabric, and the weaving—is a challenge. In the literature, there are many philological contortions about it (including mine), much of it relying on expansive Greek versions to surmount the terse obscurity of the Hebrew.[16] As observed above (at 16:6–7), weaving and tying knots are essential components of love charms and there is reason to suppose that infatuated Samson is concocting yet another magical path by which to inflame Delilah's sexual desire.[17] It is essential to real-ize, therefore, that we are not dealing with a dimwit who repeatedly cannot decipher Delilah's unsubtly couched objectives; rather, we are observing a besotted swain who, having thrown caution to the wind, would use magic to ensnare a beloved. What is deli-cious in the scene as plotted is how clashing motivations run contrapuntally: Samson obstinately plays for love; Delilah only has shekels in mind.

Final Attempt

Of greater import to our saga is Delilah's fourth try, this time seemingly crowned with success. Citing the reference to hair in the previous account, some commentators sug-gest that Delilah had already breached his resolve. Still, she had to vex him much be-fore he blurted out what seemed to her a completely truthful answer. Samson's strategy here is camouflaged by the narrator's notice that he "poured his heart out" to Delilah (*vayyagged-lāh ʾet-kol-libbô*), thus deceptively suggesting that the true source of Sam-son's power is now hers to know. In fact, Samson was trying a new way to sharpen her desire, as this was the primary goal of invoking magical practices. We need to keep in mind that in the Timnah episode, when his panicking companion coaxed from him a solution to the riddle he had posed to her compatriots, Samson revealed only its partial solution.[18] The Philistines echoed the deficient solution he had fed his potential bride,

---

16. Josephus (*Ant.* V, 311), simply summarizes "… he told her the third time that his hair should be woven into a web."

17. Niditch (2008a: 169) is not alone to suspect "subversive play in an erotic context"; but the insight is hardly sustained and Niditch does not develop thematic implications from it. Joshua Berman (Bar-Ilan) kindly referred me to Isaac Abravanel's comments on 16:10–13c in his Former Prophet commentary, where he highlights the erotic potential of the scene.

18. I explore the details fully in my forthcoming Commentary and succinctly in an upcoming study (Sasson forthcoming) dedicated to a colleague. The riddle had two phrases of three words each, both of which share the same verb, and each contains more or less contrastive elements. The first, "from the eater out came the eaten" might apply to many carnivores. The second, "from the powerful out

allowing Samson to recognize the true source of their response, thus justifying the successive havoc he wrecked on them.

This strategy may obtain here as well. I will not dwell now on how she soothed him to sleep, how his hair got cut, and how the Philistines seized and blinded him, each a topic with its own *megillah*; see for now Sasson 2008. Yet it is important to stress the narrator's comment (at 16:20), "... for [Samson] did not realize that the LORD was fully deserting him." That highly intrusive assertion proves to be clue to the architecture of the Samson's stories, for it invites us to link what might be a motif in Samson's fall with a theme that runs through the entire series of his tales.

Headhair of a Nazir

I've never really understood Samson's hair:
Its immense secrecy, its Nazirite mystery,
The prohibition (perfectly understandable) against talking about it,
The constant fear of loss of locks, the endless dread
Of Delilah's light caress... (Natan Zach, "Samson's Hair")[19]

How to groom headhair is the subject of many monographs. It was manipulated to characterize status, accent gender distinction, symbolize transitions in and out of sacrality, assert personal choices, as well as impose humiliation. A fine one relating to our topic is Niditch (2008b), subtitled "Hair and Identity in Ancient Israel." It reviews major biblical episodes in which hair has a role to play.[20] Naturally, Niditch writes about

---

came the sweet," is more slippery as the words suggest multiple applications. Nonetheless, with their solution, "What is sweeter than honey and what is stronger than a lion?" the Philistines successfully resolved only *the contrasts* among the pairings. They connected "sweet" with "honey" and "powerful" with "lion." Understandably, however, they remained clueless about the *linkage* between the two phrases, namely, how honey can come out from a lion. To explain this association, they had to be there ... but they were not. Samson could have declared victory; but he did not!

19. Natan Zach (1930–), "*Samson's Hair ('et se'aro shel Shimshon)*" cited from Bargad and Chyet 1986: 132–33. He goes on to versify on Absalom's hair.

20. As a vehicle for contrast (Jacob versus hairy Esau, Gen 27), as an agent of death (Absalom, 2 Sam 18), as an instrument of humiliation (David's envoys, 2 Sam 10), as a channel for holiness (Nazir, Num 6), as a medium for transformation (captive bride, Deut 2:10–14), and as a catalyst in ordeals (Sotah, Num 5). Whether to keep the hair free-flowing, shaping it into bun(s), braiding into ropes, or twisting it into locks (as did Samson), was apparently a personal decision. From the literature about hair-growth I learned that when left unshorn the head-hair of men goes through an anagen stage, increasing by half an inch a month, so about six inches (fifteen cms) a year. It will continue to grow decreasingly for a handful of years, virtually stopping by the fifth year. When it falls out naturally during that period, it replaces itself. Only occasionally does it reach beyond thirty inches (75 cm). Sikh men, who do not cut their hair (anywhere) during their lifetime, roll their head-hair under a headgear, most often a turban. In Israel, men trimmed their long head-hair to avoid becoming hirsute (2 Sam 14:26), keeping it just below the nape, perhaps on visiting barbers (*gallāvîm*, Ezek 5:1). Ideally, they might oil their locks shiny (*qĕvuṣṣôt*) and shape them curled (*taltallîm*), perhaps in imitation of Mesopotamia grooming where elite wore theirs either bobbed or curled at the base of the nape. Comments on hair

Samson's, but (in my opinion) she muddies the issues when coupling Samson's singular tenure as a Nazir with elements of the practice presented in legal formulation (Num 6). In fact, they are barely harmonizable, as are most biblical examples that straddle genres.

Hair as a motif in narratives is common to many literatures. From Enkidu's luxuriant growth and Medusa's venomous curls, to Rapunzel's endless tresses, lore linking the corporeal and the magical inherent to headhair is driven by human physiognomy and therefore is not likely unique to any culture. While cutting a protagonist's hair can be an element for plots (Haase 2007: 435–36), surprisingly, the lore linking hair and strength is not plentiful. D1831 in Stith Thompson's remarkable compendium of motifs cites a few (among them Samson's) with such a conjunction, although restoration to happiness is also a feature.[21] A Greek myth tells of Scylla (not of Charybdis fame), daughter of a king (Nisos) who was unconquerable as long as he sported a bright lock of hair. Besotted with Minos, an enemy of her father, Scylla drugs Nisos before snipping the magical lock. Her betrayal results in her father's death, her lover's rejection, and her own dismal end (Graves 1955: 308–11 §91). Actually, Delilah pays the ultimate price only in the Byzantine *Palaea Historica* (136) and in Cecil B. DeMille's immortal *Samson and Delilah*.[22]

The Plot

Hair Again

Still, a number of questions about the famous scene come to mind. To begin with, there is absolutely no suggestion anywhere in Scripture that a Nazir morphed into Hercules just by avoiding cutting his hair. There is no hint of such an eventuality, neither when the angel spoke to Samson's mother nor when Samson stumbles into Dagon's temple. It might therefore be unreasonable to conjecture that only in this scriptural context (at 16:19, 22) does the link between uncut hair and human strength occur. Samson himself had a cavalier attitude toward his own hair, displaying no apprehension about its manipulation into a loom. Too, given that Delilah had always followed his instruction on defusing his power, Samson could expect her to shear him no matter what her motivation. Delilah certainly wished to betray Samson for wealth; but neither she nor the Philistines learned (until too late) that cutting his hair was hardly the path to neutralize him.

---

and grooming in Israel and neighboring lands (with bibliography) are in Wilson and Rodriguez in the *DDL* 2:381–94. In the Lachish reliefs from Sennacherib's palace (late eighth century BCE), Judeans sport shortish hairdos, somewhat curly. The scholarly convention is that Assyrian artists strove for accuracy. I have my doubts.

21. Thompson, 1956: 338. Accessible online at https://archive.org/details/B-001-002-579/page/n341. Notice an addition from Chios to the collection is in Argenti and Rose 1949: 531–32.

22. Less prudent modern scholars have proposed (after rabbinic lore) that she survived to mother Micah of Ephraim, a character in a later chapter of Judges.

All these observations suggest to me that far from revealing the true source of his extraordinary power (divine infusion), Samson was proposing yet another method by which to coax Delilah's ardor. A confirmation is that on awakening—and despite the likelihood of spotting tons of hair about him—Samson never doubted his capacity to muscle his way back into normalcy. Once again, he felt ready to hammer any attacking Philistines: "I will breakout as time after time, and will shake free" (16:20). The formulaic language applies to the previous trials but it is hardly relevant here. An even stronger corroboration for Samson's deceitful strategy is the narrator's insertion (also at 16:20) that credits God—not the shorn hair—for weakening his chosen judge.[23] We also note that by waxing autobiographical on the fourth go-round with Delilah— a strategy he had already employed in a Timnah bedchamber (14:16)—Samson was once again conveying partial truth, this time implying a connection between hair and power, just as earlier in their involvement he had made similarly false conjunctions. Finally, as we turn to the concluding scene, we hear nothing more about hair. Never once does the blinded Samson display trust in its magical powers by checking on its growth. Neither did the Philistines, for that matter.

The Fallout

Over the centuries, the narrator's notice about Samson's hair sprouting even as it was cut (16:22) has misdirected many commentators into pursuing an equation between hair shorn and power lost. In fact, the observation does serve as a clue; but it is that as far as God was concerned Samson breached his Nazir status, but it can be restored; for legal formulations did indeed provide for both its interruption and resumption.[24] Unfolding from this juncture, however, is the gathering of intriguing threads deployed earlier in the Samson narratives. An explanation shapes the concluding paragraph, with supporting evidence reserved for my Commentary; see for now Sasson 2019.

Countless reports from Mesopotamia to Rome inform us on the fate of an especially hated yet worthy antagonist. The captured nemesis is often maimed but kept alive to be paraded in chains. At a festive moment, in public and normally within sight of the gods, the victim is led out for execution. Gideon executed in this manner the Midianite chieftains Zebah and Zalmunna (Judg 8:18–21). The same fate likely pursued

---

23. Amit (2009: 305) makes the same observation but draws from it a different conclusion. Others offer a similar opinion, for example, Guillaume (2004: 189) "There is no magical power in Samson's hair, his comes from YHWH and he is like any other man as soon as YHWH turns away from him (v. 20)." Less felicitous is his equation of Delilah's deed with Shamhat's taming of Enkidu in the Gilgamesh Epic.

24. As far as the ritual status of a Nazir, even those who are contaminated could restore it by shaving their heads and resume their practice of unshorn hair after the proper sacrifices; see Num 6:9–13. Amusing is the take in the *Palaea Historica* (Adler 2013: 655), where a servant (obviously not a Philistine) helps Samson (and God) by pouring water on Samson's head to speed hair sprout.

Adoni-bezeq by Jerusalem, after his captors severed his thumbs and toes (Judg 1:6-7). Therefore, as Samson entered the temple and heard the bellows of a thousand throats, he knew that the jig was up: he would not be returning to his cell. Only in an extended sense, therefore, might we apply the term suicide (as is frequently done) to how he ended his own life.

Once Samson sets himself between the central pillars of a Gaza temple, the entire series of his tales refocuses on the narrator's famously obtrusive insertion early in the Samson saga, when Samson expressed a desire for forbidden flesh. We learned then (at 14:4) that his parents did not know "that this was from the Lord, for he was prodding a reaction from the Philistines." In this phrase, the antecedent "he" is indefinite: while it certainly refers to God, it might also have Samson in mind. This ambiguity therefore alerts us to the unfolding of two parallel programs, neither one of which excludes the other.

With his final words, Samson shows no remorse; rather, he solicits one more proof of God's favor by which to turn the Philistines' celebration into monumental grieving. In effect, Samson is now completing the final act in a *picaresque* tale, wherein he would be the one "prodding a reaction from the Philistines." Yet, Samson may also have sensed that he had become a human instrument in an embryonic *theomachy*, a battle among the gods. For this take, I am reminded of the second version of a Hittite tale in which the Storm god Tarḫunz uses a mortal to confound his enemy, the dragon Iluyankas (Hoffner 1998: 13). Noteworthy is that this young man, like Samson, was also destined to die for his role in the divine confrontation. Applied to our case, then, God would now be the subject of the phrase, "he was prodding a reaction from the Philistines." This particular manifestation of the heavenly contest would pit the God of Israel against the Philistine god Dagon. It was to be just one volley in a longer match between them. I need not spoil it for Norma by divulging who will emerge triumphant in this (lopsided) battle.

References

Amit, Yairah. 1999. *The Book of Judges: The Art of Editing*. Translated by J. Chipman. Leiden: Brill [Hebrew version, 1992]).

———. 2009: "The Book of Judges: Dating and Meaning." Pages 297–322 in *Homeland and Exile: Biblical and Ancient Near Eastern Studies in Honour of Bustenay Oded*. Edited by Gershon Galil, Mark Geller, and Alan Millard. VTSup 130. Leiden: Brill.

———. 2014. "Judges." Pages 495–543 in *The Jewish Study Bible*. 2nd edition. Edited by Adele Berlin and Marc Z. Brettler. New York: Oxford University Press.

Argenti, Philip Pandely, and Herbert Jennings Rose. 1949. *The Folk-Lore of Chios*. 2 vols. Cambridge: Cambridge University Press.

Bargad, Warren, and Stanley F. Chyet. 1986. *Israeli Poetry: A Contemporary Anthology*. Bloomington: Indiana University Press.

Biggs, Robert D. 1967. *Šà.zi.ga, Ancient Mesopotamian Potency Incantations*. TCS 2. Locust Valley, NY: Augustin.

Danby, Herbert. 1933. *The Mishnah: Translated from the Hebrew with Introduction and Brief Explanatory Notes*. Oxford: Clarendon.

Faraone, Christopher A. 1999. *Ancient Greek Love Magic*. Cambridge: Harvard University Press.

Geller, Markham J. 2002. "Mesopotamian Love Magic: Discourse or Intercourse?" Pages 129–39 in *Sex and Gender in the Ancient Near East: Proceedings of the 47th Rencontre Assyriologique Internationale, Helsinki, July 2–6, 2001*. Edited by Simo Parpola and Robert M. Whiting. Helsinki: Neo-Assyrian Text Corpus Project.

Graves, Robert. 1955. *The Greek Myths*, vol. 1. Baltimore: Penguin.

Guillaume, Philippe. 2004. *Waiting for Josiah: The Judges*. London: T&T Clark International.

Gunn, David M. 2005. *Judges*. Blackwell Bible Commentaries. Malden, MA: Blackwell.

Haase, Donald. 2007. *The Greenwood Encyclopedia of Folktales and Fairy Tales*. 3 vols. Westport, CT: Greenwood.

Harrington, Daniel J. 1985. "Pseudo-Philo (First Century A.D.)." Pages 297–377 in *The Old Testament Pseudepigrapha*. Vol. 2: *Expansions of the "Old Testament" and Legends, Wisdom and Philosophical Literature, Prayers, Psalms, and Odes, Fragments of Lost Judeo-Hellenistic Works*. Edited by James Charlesworth. New York: Doubleday.

Hoffner, Harry A., Jr. 1998. *Hittite Myths*. 2nd ed. WAW 2. Atlanta: Scholars Press.

Jasnow, Richard. 2001. "'And Pharaoh laughed …': Reflections on Humor in Setne 1 and Late Period Egyptian Literature." *Enchoria* 27:62–81.

Killebrew, Ann E., and Gunnar Lehmann. 2013. *The Philistines and Other "Sea Peoples" in Text and Archaeology*. ABS 16. Atlanta, GA: Society of Biblical Literature.

Lev-Tov, Justin, Ann E. Killebrew, Haskel J. Greenfield, and Annie Brown. 2018. "Puppy Sacrifice and Cynophagy from Early Philistine Tel Miqne-Ekron Contextualized." *Journal of Eastern Mediterranean Archaeology & Heritage Studies* 6:1–30.

Lichtheim, Miriam. 1980. *Ancient Egyptian Literature*. Vol. 3: *The Late Period*. Berkeley: University of California Press.

Maier, Aren M. 2018. "'The Philistines Be upon Thee, Samson' (Jud. 16:20): Reassessing the Martial Nature of the Philistines; Archaeological Evidence vs. Ideological Image?" Pages 158–68 in *Change, Continuity and Connectivity: North-Eastern Mediterranean at the Turn of the Bronze Age and in the Early Iron Age*. Edited by Łukasz Niesiołowski-Spanò and Marek Węcowski. Philippika 118. Wiesbaden: Harrassowitz.

Maier, Aren M., and Louise A. Hitchcock. 2017. "The Appearance, Formation and Transformation of Philistine Culture: New Perspectives and New Finds." Pages 149–62 in *The Sea Peoples Up-To-Date: New Research on the Migration of Peoples in the 12th Century BCE*. Edited by Peter M. Fischer. Contributions to the Chronology of the Eastern Mediterranean 35. Vienna: Austrian Academy of Sciences.

Marcos, Natalio Fernández. 2011. שפטים *Judges*. Biblia Hebraica Quinta 7. Stuttgart: Deutsche Bibelgesellschaft.

Neubauer, Adolf. 1889. "Where Are the Ten Tribes? II. Eldad the Danite." *JQR* 1:95–114.

Niditch, Susan. 2008a. *Judges, a Commentary*. The Old Testament Library. Louisville: Westminster John Knox.

———. 2008b. *"My Brother Esau Is a Hairy Man": Hair and Identity in Ancient Israel*. New York: Oxford University Press.

Ogden, Daniel. 2002. *Magic, Witchcraft, and Ghosts in the Greek and Roman worlds: a Sourcebook*. New York. Oxford University Press.

Reiner, Erica. 1966. "La magie babylonienne." Pages 69–98 in *Le monde du sorcier: Égypte Babylone-Hittites-Israël-Islam-AsieCentrale-Inde-Népal-Cambodge-Viet Nam-Japon*. Paris: Seuil.

Saar, Ortal-Paz. 2017. *Jewish Love Magic: From Late Antiquity to the Middle Ages*. Leiden: Brill.

Sasson, Jack M. 1988. "Who Cut Samson's Hair? (and Other Trifling Issues Raised by Judges 16)." *Prooftexts* 8:333–46.

———. 2013. "Jephthah: Chutzpah and Overreach in the Portrayal of a Hebrew Judge." Pages

405–19 in *Literature as Politics, Politics as Literature: Essays on the Ancient Near East in Honor of Peter Machinist*. Edited by David S. Vanderhooft and Avraham Winitzer. Winona Lake, IN: Eisenbrauns.

———. 2014. *Judges 1–12. A New Translation, with Introduction and Commentary*. The Anchor Yale Bible. New Haven: Yale University.

———. 2019. "A Gate in Gaza: An Essay on the Reception of Tall Tales." Pages 178–91 in *Biblical Narratives, Archaeology and Historicity: Essays in Honour of Thomas L. Thompson*. Edited by Emanuel Pfoh and Łukasz Niesiolowski-Spanò. London: T&T Clark.

———. Forthcoming. "Samson as Riddle." In *Essays in Biblical and Ancient Near Eastern Studies*. Edited by Peter Machinist.

Seidlmayer, Stephan J. 2001. "Art. Execration Texts." *OEAE* 1:487–89.

Thompson, Stith. 1956. *Motif-Index of Folk Literature*. Vol. 2. Bloomington: Indiana University Press.

THE CASE OF THE ENIGMATIC
"CYPRO-PHOENICIAN" JUGLETS IN MOAB

MARGREET L. STEINER

Abstract: In several Iron Age tombs in ancient Moab in Transjordan, large quantities of small painted juglets have been found. In excavation reports these juglets are commonly called "Cypro-Phoenician" and are seen as products of the interregional trade over the King's Highway and as direct proof of contacts with Phoenicia. However, the Jordanian juglets differ significantly from those found in either Cyprus or Phoenicia. This analysis of a number of the juglets from Mudayna, Sahab, and Dhiban show that these luxury items were most likely locally made. In the emerging state of Moab they may have been used as markers of status and identity by the elites buried in the tombs.

Keywords: Moab, Cypro-Phoenician juglets, Iron II, tombs, Mt. Nebo, Dhiban, Khirbet al-Mudayna

Iron Age Moab has been a focus of archaeological debate since the nineties of the last century, when several modern excavations in the region started. When Bruce Routledge published his book on Moab in the Iron Age in 2004, interest deepened. It seems that currently every aspect of this ancient region has been thoroughly discussed, from tribes to towns, from state formation processes to trade routes, and from agricultural towers to kingly things, not to mention new interpretations and translations of the Mesha Stele (overview and literature in Steiner 2014).

However, the pottery of Iron Age Moab is still little known, several published surveys and excavations notwithstanding. I am in the lucky position of studying the pottery of three Iron Age sites in northern Moab for publication: Khirbet al-Mudayna in the Wadi Thamad, a fortified Iron II town (Steiner 2006, 2009); Site WT-13, an Iron II open-air sanctuary with and earlier Iron I occupation layer (Steiner 2017); and Khirbet Lehun, a fortified Iron I village with a later fort, possibly from Iron II (Steiner 2013; Steiner and Jacobs 2008).

When comparing this pottery corpus with other Iron I and II assemblages from Jordan, I stumbled upon several rock-cut tombs full of pottery, which have not received the attention they certainly deserve. In the current discussion these tombs play no role at all and are seldom mentioned. In Routledge's book the word "tomb" does not even make it into the index. And yet, these tombs may enlighten us as to several aspects of the culture of the ancient Moabites.

I want to focus here on the small painted juglets of which several hundred specimens have been found. They are commonly called "Cypro-Phoenician" juglets, a name that suggests a relationship with Cyprus and Phoenicia and also suggests that these juglets were imported into Transjordan and were part of the long-distance trade along the King's Highway.

It can be questioned whether these juglets originated in Cyprus or Phoenicia. But even if they were not imported, they differ remarkably from the other local juglets and do betray a foreign origin. So what do these juglets represent? Were they locally made or imported? And why are they found mainly in funerary contexts?

Most of the juglets found in Jordan are described by their excavators as small two-handled painted juglets. All have a high, ridged neck, and handles that go from ridge to shoulder. Their bodies are bag-shaped, and the rim is everted. The painted motifs generally consist of horizontal bands or lines on the neck and the body, while a few have concentric circles on two sides of the body. The lines are mostly colored black, sometimes red and black, and, more rarely, white.

The ware of most juglets is described as a fine buff or light cream ware, with a red or orange slip, or a light cream slip, and the juglets are generally burnished. Others are made of a fine, hard, polished red ware. Most juglets have two handles, some have one handle or, more rarely, no handles at all. The two-handled specimens consistently have a small disc base, while the one-handled juglets have a round base. As far as I know no study has yet been made of either the technology or the ware of these juglets.

Juglets Found in Moab

In Moab such juglets have been found in great quantities in several tombs, roughly dated to Iron IIB, the ninth and eighth centuries BCE. I have been able to view and photograph a number of these juglets.

Father Saller published his finds from two tombs excavated at Mt. Nebo. In Tomb 20 he counted 36 complete or almost complete Cypro-Phoenician juglets, as well as more than 500 fragments, of which 131 were bases. The majority had two handles and a small disc base; only some had one handle or were without handles. In the second tomb (Tomb 84) about 50 Cypro-Phoenician juglets were found, and the majority had two handles. The decoration is described as "horizontal bands or lines on the neck and on the body, a few have concentric circles on two sides of the body. The color is exclusively black or both black and red. The lines are executed in such a neat fashion that they make a very good impression." (Saller 1966) All in all at least 200 juglets were counted in these two tombs (fig. 1).

During the excavations of Dhiban, the capital of ancient Moab, several Iron Age tombs were excavated, three of which (Tombs J5, J6, and J7) were full of pottery

Figure 1. Juglets from Mt. Nebo. Photographs by M. Steiner.

Figure 2. Juglets from Dhiban. Photographs by M. Steiner.

(Tushingham 1972). Together with other specimens of pottery, these tombs contained more than fifty Cypro-Phoenician juglets. Tushingham describes the juglets as cream or buff wares, some with slip, mostly burnished. Most juglets have a black decoration, but some show thick lines in white and red paint (fig. 2).

Recently, four complete Cypro-Phoenician juglets as well as several sherds have been excavated in a disturbed tomb (Tomb WT-200) near Mudayna Thamad (Chadwick 2017).

From most of the excavated Moabite settlement sites, such as Madaba, Ataruz, and Hesban, no Cypro-Phoenician juglets have (yet) been reported.

At the tell of Khirbet al-Mudayna in the Wadi ath-Thamad, however, several dozen fragments of such juglets were found, among which thirteen were bases, making it possible to study these more thoroughly (fig. 3).

The color of their wares differs from cream to greyish to reddish. Some are slipped, some are not, and all but one are burnished from the handles down and over the base. Most have a decoration of three dark lines on the shoulder, rather more brown to brownish-red than black, 0.1–0.2 cm thick, sometimes very poorly executed with the paint dripping. In some cases the paint has faded away almost completely. Two juglets have additional spirals painted on the neck. Most necks are either too blackened by soot (from the destruction of the site) or too eroded for the decora-

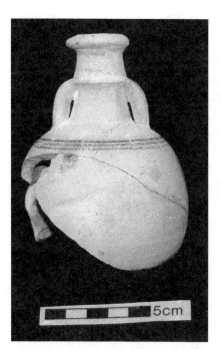

Figure 3. Juglets from Mudayna Thamad. Photographs by M. Steiner.

tions to be seen. Most bodies below the handles are undecorated, and one juglet has lines and circles on the body.

Juglets in Ammon

Cypro-Phoenician juglets have not been found only in Moab. Several tomb complexes in ancient Ammon yielded many juglets as well, although some are slightly different in shape and decoration. I have not handled these juglets myself.

From a tomb (Tomb B) at Sahab, a site located east of Amman, Harding (1948) illustrated six Cypro-Phoenician juglets, but counted many more. He writes that there are many of fine hard-polished red ware with black lines, but some are of a much thicker ware and covered with a cream slip on which bands of broad and very fine black lines are painted. All are two-handled except one (fig. 4).

Figure 4. Juglets from Sahab. From Harding 1948: pl. XXXV.

In a tomb found at Jebel al-Joffeh, south of the Amman citadel (Tomb E), Dajani (1966) found many Cypro-Phoenician juglets. The juglets are described as "fine hand-polished red ware with black lines, some covered with a creamy slip." According to Dajani these juglets are similar to the ones found in Sahab Tomb B.

Dornemann (1983) dates these two tombs in his so-called "middle range," that is Iron IIB. Just a few Cypro-Phoenician juglets were found in earlier tombs (Iron IIA) such as Amman Tomb C (Hardin 1951) and Madaba Tomb B (Piccirillo 1975). In later tombs, for instance in the Adoni Nur tombs and the graves at Tell Mazar, no such juglets have been found.

More than Three Hundred Cypro-Phoenician Juglets Excavated in Jordan

So all in all at least three hundred painted juglets have been recorded from the four tomb complexes in Ammon and Moab containing seven tombs still full of pottery and other finds. Smaller numbers were found in several other tombs in Moab and Ammon, and a sizeable number was excavated at the tell of Mudayna Thamad (fig. 5).

Context	Number of Cypro-Phoenician juglets
Mt. Nebo Tombs 20 and 84	Ca. 200
Dhiban Tombs J5, J6 and J7	57
Sahab Tomb B	Many
Amman Tomb E	Many
Total number of Cypro-Phoenician juglets found in these seven tombs	At least 300
Other tombs	At least 10
Khirbet Mudayna	At least 20

A characteristic of these juglets is that they are mostly two-handled and have a bag-shaped body and a disk base. From the description several kinds of juglets can be inferred. The first one is made of "fine hard-polished red ware" while the other type is thicker and cream-colored. It is not yet clear if all of these juglets were slipped. Some are decorated with small lines; others have concentric circles as well. The color of the decoration is mostly black or blackish lines; in other cases the lines are black and red, while red and occasionally white paint is used to make wider stripes. Some juglets have a longer neck, decorated with painted lines.

In general the Moabite tombs at Mt. Nebo and Dhiban only contained the thicker, cream-colored juglets. This is in accordance with the general trend for the rest of the pottery found in these tombs, which is mostly unslipped and unburnished. In the Ammonite tombs of Amman and Sahab, on the other hand, there were more reddish juglets and juglets with a longer neck. The pottery in Ammon is famous for its red-slipped and burnished wares.

Comparative Material

It is easy to see that these juglets are very dissimilar to the unpainted locally made juglets of the region, which are neither burnished nor painted, made of a course buff ware and mostly do not have a ridged neck. And, notwithstanding their name, the "Cypro-Phoenician" juglets from Transjordan are also quite dissimilar to the black-on-red Phoenician and Cypriot juglets.

These black-on-red juglets are made of reddish-brown or dark-brown clay, with a red or reddish-brown slip, and are often burnished. Generally they have a spherical body, one handle and a flat base. The Jordanian juglets, on the other hand, are mostly made of cream or buff wares with an orange, light-red, or cream slip. They have a bag-shaped body, two handles and a disc base (fig. 6). In the Ammonite tombs at Sahab and Amman "fine hard-polished red wares" are reported, but generally this also refers to bag-shaped juglets with two handles.

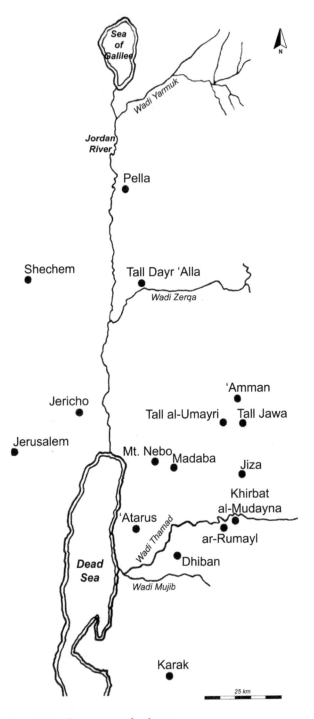

Figure 5. Map of sites mentioned in the text.

Figure 6. Black-on-red juglet with two handles. Photograph Metropolitan Museum of Art, CC0.

The Jordanian Cypro-Phoenician juglets thus differ from the real black-on-red juglets in their wares, shapes, and overall impression and cannot count as Cypriot black-on-red juglets, as described by Schreiber (2003).

Most Jordanian juglets were found in graves. Large quantities were deposited in tombs found at Mt. Nebo, Dhiban, Amman, and Sahab. The quantities presented here are remarkable. Although not every excavator has counted the juglets, it seems that over 300 specimens were found in only seven tombs. The site of Mudayna Thamad and Tomb WT-200 in Moab yielded another 25 juglets at least. This contrasts sharply with the quantity of real black-on-red juglets found in the Levant. From the immense area of the Levantine mainland, including Israel, Palestine, Jordan, Syria, Lebanon, Egypt, and parts of Turkey, Schreiber counted only 364 black-on-red juglets, mostly from tombs— just slightly more than the 7 that the Jordanian tombs yielded. Schreiber dated these juglets to the Iron IIB period, the late ninth and eighth centuries BCE. The Jordanian juglets seem to occupy the same time span, although Jordanian pottery has not been well-dated up until now.

This is not to say that no real black-on-red juglets were ever found in Jordan. A possible imported black-on-red juglet was recorded from site WT13 in ancient Moab (Daviau 2017: 26, fig. 3.5:13). Some sherds of small, well-levigated and finely painted juglets were also recorded from Mudayna Thamad. However, the large number of juglets found in the Iron II B tombs and in Mudayna Thamad are certainly of a different origin. I am quite confident that these juglets were locally made in Transjordan, although no ware analysis has so far been carried out to my knowledge. They were a local imitation of the real black-on-red juglets, which (almost) never reached Transjordan. The question is then: why, and why there and then? As these juglets were found in great numbers in tombs and only occasionally in settlements, it is reasonable to assume that they played a role in funerary rituals. Schreiber's assertion that the real black-on-red juglets were filled with scented oil or perfume seems reasonable; note, however, that earlier Phoenician bichrome juglets have now been established to contain cinnamon and nutmeg, two spices that had to be imported from southeast Asia (Gilboa and Namdar 2015).

Conclusions

The majority of the so-called Cypro-Phoenician juglets found in Transjordan (> 300) comes from tombs in a very restricted area: from Amman and Sahab in the north to Dhiban in the south, and they seemingly played a role in rituals surrounding the deposition of the dead. In most settlements only a few juglets have been found. This may be due to the very restricted areas excavated at Ammonite and Moabite sites or to a general absence of these juglets in residential areas. However, at Mudayna Thamad some twenty Cypro-Phoenician juglets as well as many more sherds have been recorded so far. It is not clear if they were made at or in the vicinity of the site, or were imported at the site for specific functions.

These decorated juglets did not originate in Cyprus or Phoenicia nor were they part of the long-distance trade in incense. They are most likely locally made as containers for scented oil. Note that several subtypes can be distinguished, pointing to a variety of production centers for these juglets.

Chronologically they seem to be restricted to the Iron IIB, the late ninth and the eighth centuries BCE, although they could have extended into Iron IIC. The original black-on-red juglets have the same time frame, and we may safely assume that the Jordanian Cypro-Phoenician juglets are a local imitation of the original Cypriot juglets, which were exported to the Levantine mainland in small quantities only.

What did Amman, Sahab, Mt. Nebo, Dhiban, and Mudayna Thamad have in common during the ninth and eighth centuries BCE? Why then, why only there? We know that in this period the emerging kingdoms of Moab and Ammon had their centers at Amman and Dhiban, while Sahab, Mt. Nebo (Khirbet al-Mukkhayat) and Mudayna Thamad may have been important settlements.

The tombs belonged to the elite of the emerging kingdoms of Ammon and Moab. Routledge (2004) has coined the phrase "kingly things," which refers to the things the elites surrounded themselves with. These include palaces, inscriptions, sculpture, and luxury objects, and the consumption of wine and scented oil.

In the ninth century BCE, an elite emerged in Moab and Ammon that wished to distinguish itself from the common people by conspicuous consumption and the ostentatious display of wealth, as clearly observed in the contents of these tombs: luxury objects such as jewelry, censers, decorated kraters and bowls, and fine painted juglets containing expensive scented oils. These juglets are a clear imitation of the more exotic but very rare Cypriot black-on-red juglets. Such was the demand for these perfume juglets that local production centers developed in the region.

A large-scale research project for the study of these Jordanian juglets, their wares, production processes, decoration techniques, and typology seems in order. A new name would need to be given to these juglets too, as they are certainly not of Cypro-Phoenician origin.

Acknowledgements

I thank Michèle Daviau for the opportunity given to me to study the juglets from Mudayna Thamad. The late Father Piccirillo kindly allowed me to see and photograph the material from the Mt. Nebo tombs, now in Jerusalem. The Royal Ontario Museum in Toronto houses the material from the Dhiban tombs and kindly let me study and photograph the juglets.

References

Chadwick, Robert. 2017. "A Newly Discovered Iron Age II Cave Tomb near Khirbat Al-Mudayna on the Wadi ath-Thamad." Pages 25–38 in *Walking through Jordan: Essays in Honor of Burton MacDonald*. Edited by M. Neeley, G. Clark, and P. M. M. Daviau. Sheffield: Equinox.

Dajani, R. W. 1966. "An Iron Age Tomb from Amman." *ADAJ* 11:41–47.

Daviau, P. M. Michèle. 2017. *A Wayside Shrine in Northern Moab: Excavations in Wadi ath-Thamad*. Oxford: Oxbow.

Dornemann, Rudolph. H. 1983. *The Archaeology of the Transjordan in the Bronze and Iron Ages*. Milwaukee, WI: Public Museum.

Gilboa, Ayelet, and Dvory Namdar. 2015. "On the Beginnings of South Asian Spice Trade with the Mediterranean Region: A Review." *Radiocarbon* 57:265–83.

Harding, G. L. 1948. "An Iron Age Tomb at Sahab." *QDAP* 13:92–102.

———. 1951. "Two Iron-Age Tombs in Amman." *ADAJ* 1:37–40.

Piccirillo, Michele. 1975. "Una Tomba del ferro I a Madaba (Madaba B, Moab)." *Liber Annus* 25:199–224.

Routledge, Bruce. 2004. *Moab in the Iron Age: Hegemony, Polity, Archaeology*. Philadelphia: University of Pennsylvania Press.

Saller, S. 1966. "Iron Age Tombs at Nebo, Jordan." *Liber Annuus* 16:165–298.

Schreiber, Nicola. 2003. *The Cypro-Phoenician Pottery of the Iron Age*. Leiden: Brill.

Steiner, Margreet L. 2006. "The Pottery of Khirbet al-Mudayna and Site WT-13 in Jordan." *Leiden Journal of Pottery Studies* 22:101–11.

———. 2009. "Khirbet al-Mudayna and Moabite Pottery Production." Pages 145–64 in *Studies on Iron Age Moab and Neighbouring Areas in Honour of Michèle Daviau*. Edited by P. Bienkowski. Leuven: Peeters.

———. 2013. "The Iron I Pottery of Khirbat al-Lehun." *ADAJ* 57:519–33.

———. 2014. "Moab during the Iron Age II Period." Pages 770–81 in *The Oxford Handbook of the Archaeology of the Levant (c. 8000–332 BCE)*. Edited by Margreet L. Steiner and Ann E. Killebrew. Oxford: Oxford University Press.

———. 2017. "WT-13 Pottery and the Central Jordan Tradition." Pages 171–78 in *A Wayside*

Shrine in Northern Moab: Excavations in Wadi ath-Thamad. Edited by P. M. Michèle Daviau.. Oxford: Oxbow.

Steiner, Margreet L., and L. Jacobs. 2008. "The Iron Age Pottery of al-Lehun, Jordan: Fabrics and
Technology." *Leiden Journal of Pottery Studies* 24:133–41.

Tushingham, A. D. 1972. *The Excavations at Dibon (Dhiban) in Moab: The Third Campaign 1952–
53.* AASOR 40. Cambridge, MA: American Schools of Oriental Research.

FAME AND FORTUNE: IRON AGE II ARABIAN TRADE IN SCHOLARLY IMAGE AND IN REALITY

YIFAT THAREANI

Abstract: Frequent references to Arabs, camels, and exotic goods making their way to the Iron Age II imperial and royal courts have led many scholars to assume that the Assyrian expansion and conquests stimulated the growth of the long-distance trade route across the Arabian desert. The growing corpus of archaeological data attests to extensive Arabian trade ever since the late second–early first millennia BCE. Assyrian conquests in the region led to limited and indirect imperial involvement in the conduct of trade. Management and maintenance of the trade system were carried out by local authorities.

Keywords: Arabia, trade, Assyria, tribe, imperial control, Negev, Edom

> *"... because vast wealth from Rome and Parthia accu-*
> *mulates in their [Arab] hands, as they sell the produce*
> *they obtain from the sea or their forests and buy nothing*
> *in return."*
>
> (Pliny, *HN* 6.162)

Camel caravans crossing the desert, bearing frankincense and myrrh to markets along the Fertile Crescent—such images have sparked the imagination of archaeologists and historians ever since the inception of the study of the ancient Near East. Illustrious figures such as St. John Philby (Monroe 1973), Sir Richard Burton (Burton 1879), Lawrence of Arabia (Tabachnick 1997; Anderson 2013), and Nelson Glueck (Brown and Kutler 2006) were among the first to explore the unknown territories of the desert in both Arabia and the Levant, and to lay the foundations for the current vibrant research of these regions.

Inspired by the frequent appearance of Arabs in Assyrian inscriptions and reliefs and in the biblical account, as well as an ever-growing assemblage of archaeological finds attesting to far-reaching cultural contacts between Iron Age II empires and local Mesopotamian and Syro-Levantine kingdoms with remote desert societies, scholars of the past century have developed numerous theories concerning the nature of Assyria's imperial involvement in Arabian trade and the role that the latter played in the economic arena of ancient Near Eastern societies.

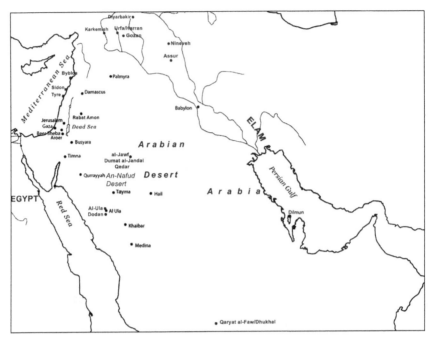

Figure 1. Map of the main sites of the ancient Near East during the Iron Age. Drawing by Noga Zeevi.

In the common view, Arabian trade is depicted as a network of major land and sea routes linking ancient Near Eastern polities with sources of incense, spices, and other luxury goods (Van Beek 1960; Elat 1977, 1978; Edens and Bawden 1989). Commodities originating in Arabia and northeastern Africa found their way to the Assyrian imperial core as well as to local Syro-Levantine kingdoms via several major trade routes (fig. 1): one road connected Arabia with the Persian Gulf by crossing the desert; the King's Highway linked Arabia and the south with the important commercial centers of Damascus and Tyre by traversing the Transjordanian Plateau; and another route connected Arabia with the Mediterranean ports and the international highway via the southern Levantine Negev Desert and Coastal Plain.

Intensive archaeological surveys and excavations conducted along these three geographic axes have uncovered a large quantity of objects and sites associated with the trade (Finkelstein 1992; Liverani 1992; Singer-Avitz 1999; Magee 2004; Jasmin 2006; Thareani 2007; Potts 2010; Knauf et al. 2010; Hausleiter 2011). When combined with the frequent mentions of Arabs, camels and exotic goods in Assyrian administrative records and reliefs (Eph'al 1984; Reade 1998) and in historiographic sources such as the Bible (e.g., 1 Kgs 10; Song 1:5), the result is a patchwork image of Arabian trade inspired by a mixture of bias and facts, impressions and wishful thinking.

The aim of this paper is to assess how modern views of the Assyrian Empire have influenced and fueled perceptions of Arabian trade. This scholarly trend shall be examined against Assyrian sources, other historical records, and archaeological remains. The tension between the scholarly image of the trade and its reality will be addressed in light of the archaeological evidence, increasing our scientific awareness and resulting in a more balanced view of this ancient phenomenon.

Enemies, a Love Story: Assyrian View of Arabs and Trade in the Early First Millennium BCE

While throughout most of the Bronze Age there was little apparent contact between Arabs and Assyrians, the transition to the Iron Age in the first half of the first millennium BCE witnessed a sharp change. During this period contacts between Assyria and the Arabs became notably more visible, evolving into fully developed commercial and political interactions.

This uptake should not be surprising. After all, it was during the Iron Age II that Assyria became the greatest power the ancient world had known. Highly motivated by clear economic interests and armed with a strong ideological message, the Assyrians were convinced that the Mediterranean (the "Upper Sea") and the Persian Gulf (the "Lower Sea") represented the two extremities of the entire world and therefore should be unified under the hegemony of a single Mesopotamian ruler (K. Yamada 2005: 31).

It was this hegemonic outlook that undergirded the Assyrian expansion and conquests westward in the eighth–seventh centuries BCE. Cities and kingdoms situated between the Assyrian heartland and the Mediterranean Sea became targets of repeated Assyrian invasions. By the zenith of the empire's territorial expansion in the seventh century BCE, Assyria controlled the entire eastern Mediterranean basin (Parpola 2003).

Assyria's conquests created a new sociopolitical reality, in the framework of which imperial officials and soldiers encountered "the Other." Interaction with new cultures and distant communities opened up an array of novel experiences and necessitated the creation of a constant dialogue between the empire and its new subjects—violent at times, peaceful at others (Parker 2003; Thareani 2016).

Of all "strange others" that the Assyrians met in their western ventures, desert dwellers were very likely the most outlandish of all. As was the case with other "others" (see the case of the Aramaeans: Sader 2010), the name "Arabs" first appeared in the Kurkh Monolith inscription of Shalmaneser III, dated to 853 BCE. There it appeared as a generic name given by the empire to all seminomadic populations that resided in the desert frontiers and deserts of Sinai, Arabia, and Syria (S. Yamada 2000: 159, 162). Characterized by raising camels and sheep, living in tents and unfortified camps, moving from place to place with their flocks, sporadically raiding the permanent settlements in nearby regions (Eph'al 1984: 5–6), in Assyrian eyes these seminomadic groups were all the same: Arabs.

An attestation to this sense of "ignorance" that accompanied the Assyrian approach toward the Arabs (Byrne 2003: 12–13) may be also found in the Khorsabad annals, where Sargon II records his deportation of Arab groups to recently conquered Samaria (721 BCE): "far away, living in the desert, with whom no overseer or governor was familiar, [people who] had never before brought a king their tribute" (Fuchs 1994: 110).

Ideologically, the Assyrians saw the desert frontier as a boundary between the civilized world and its chaotic periphery. This dichotomy marked the opposition between the known and the unknown, between the reassuring and the hostile. Esarhaddon's succession treaty graphically illustrates this disposition (Parpola and Watanabe 1988: 45):

> May Sîn, the brightness of heaven and earth, clothe you with leprosy and forbid your entering into the presence of the gods or the king. Roam the desert like the wild ass and the gazelle.

Other than ideological formulas, the Assyrian royal inscriptions and imperial administrative records constitute almost the only references to the Arabs of the Iron Age II.

At some point in the mid-eighth century BCE, just before Tiglath-pileser III completed the empire's final outline and consolidated the frontiers, his eponymous annals describe the capture of a large caravan coming from Sheba via Tayma by the king of Suhhu in the Middle Euphrates (Cavigneaux and Ismail 1990: 346–47, iv 26b–38a, 351):

> People from Teima' and Sheba, whose abode is far away, whose messenger did not come to my presence, and who did not advance up to my presence: a caravan of theirs approached to the Martu-well and the Halatum-well, and went (even) beyond, and entered the city of Hindanu. I got the news at noon in Kar-apladad. I harnessed my yoke, in the night I crossed over the river, and on the next day before noon I reached Azlanu. Three days I remained in Azlanu and on the third day they arrived. 100 of them I took alive, and 200 of their dromedaries with their loads: purple-wool ... wool, iron and alabaster, all of their consignments I took away. A great booty I plundered, and I took it inside Suhhu.

Two hundred dromedaries bearing purple-dyed textiles, iron and alabaster were brought by the rich Arabian caravan. The justification for it being attacked was that this caravan had avoided paying the usual tolls and tariffs required in the region, as well as the province's right to be the first to choose its goods (Na'aman 2007: 111).

In a period of increasing contacts with the outside world and growing demand for luxury commodities, the ascension of Tiglath-pileser III to the Assyrian throne in 745 BCE brought about frequent encounters with Arab tribes. In his annals from 733–732 BCE, the Assyrian king reported an incursion into the territory of Sheba, Maas'aa, and Tayma during his first western campaign (Tadmor and Yamada 2011: 42 27'b–33').

> 10,000 soldiers ... The people of the cities Mas'a (and) Tema, the tribe Saba, the people of the cities [Hayappa, Badanu], (and) Hatte, (and) the (tribes) Idiba'ilu [...], who are on the border of the western lands, [whom none (of

my predecessors) had known about, and whose country is remo]te, [heard about] the fame of my majesty (and) [my heroic deeds, and (thus) they beseeched] my lordship. As one, [they brought before me] gold, silver, [camels, she camels (and) all types of aromatics] as their payment [and they kissed] my feet.

Zabibe, a queen of Mat-Aribi (the west land or land of the Arabs) is reported to have paid Tiglath-pileser III tribute, a synonym for exchanging goods (Tadmor and Yamada 2011: 15 2; 27 6; 32 8; 35 iii 19). By contrast, another Arabian queen experienced a different fate: the notorious Assyrian wrath (42 19′–24′).

> As for Samsi, queen of the Arabs, at Mt. Saqurri [I] de[feated 9,400 (of her people)]. I took away (from her) 1000 people, 30,000 camels, 20,000 oxen [...] ..., 5,000 (pouches) of all types of aromatics, ..., thrones of her gods, [the military equipment (and) staffs of her goddess(es)], (and) her property.
>   Moreover, she, in order to save her life, [... (and) set out] like a female onager [to the de]sert, (a place where one is always) thirsty. [I set the rest of her possessions] (and) her [ten]ts , her people's safeguard within her camp, [on fire].

Samsi, who was accused of violating the oath sworn by Shamash, followed the lead of Rezin, king of Damascus, in forsaking her allegiance to Assyria, probably in order to protect the economic interests of her people. She was defeated by Tiglath-pileser near Mount Saquri. Many of her people were killed, a great deal of booty was taken including captives, camels, sheep, and many spices, and she fled for her life—"like a wild she-ass"—into the desert. Nevertheless, Samsi was never imprisoned and continued to rule her people, albeit with an Assyrian qēpu now inspecting her commercial activities (Frahm 2017: 301).

Later on, Sargon II boasted of exacting exotic tribute, ivory and aromatics, both from Samsi and from It'amar the Sabaean (Hausleiter 2012). Furthermore, in the Nimrud Prism the Assyrian monarch explicitly stated (Tadmor 1958: 34):

> I opened the sealed-off harbour [kāru] of Egypt, mingled Assyrians and Egyptians together and made them trade with each other.

Sennacherib, his successor, reported that the gift of Karibilu, king of Sheba, was placed in the foundations of the Bit-Akitu temple (Potts 2003). From another building project were preserved the words (E. Bennett 2015: 26) "[que]en of the Arabs, together with...pappardilû-stones ...-stones, ... spices of all kinds." During this time one of Nineveh's gates was somewhat unusually called "The Desert Gate through which the Gifts of the People of Te-e-me and Su-mu-' Enter." (Eph'al 1984: 124–25).

In order to return the divine images that were taken from the Arabs by his father Sennacherib, Esarhaddon demanded from Hazael the Qedarite an extra tribute in addition to that which had been levied by his father, namely, sixty-five camels (Eph'al 1984: 124).

Finally, Ashurbanipal's attempts in the mid-seventh century BCE to encourage direct trade between Assyrians and Arabs are recorded in his treaty with Hazael's son Yauta', also king of the Qedarites, who later revolted only to be defeated once more. So much booty was taken that the price of camels and slaves in the Assyrian markets dropped drastically (Eph'al 1984: 149; Gerardi 1992).

It thus seems that in Assyrian royal inscriptions the term "Arabs" is applied specifically to the Qedarites, people of Sumu'ilu and the Idiba'ilu, Thamud, Ibadidi, Marsimani and 'Ephah. Yet, the term likewise fits other groups associated with desert regions and with the characteristic lifeways of nomads. It should be noted that not one of the thousands of inscriptions found in southern Arabia and produced by the kingdoms that existed in the region from the beginning of the first millennium BCE (among them Sheba, Qataban, Ma'in, Hadhramaut, and Himyar) contains the slightest hint of a connection between these kingdoms and the term "Arabs," indicating that it was not the designation that the nomads applied to themselves (Eph'al 1984: 7–8).

The use of a general label along with a slanted representation of Arabs in the imperial records derived mainly from the Assyrian strong sense of identity and can be seen as both a cause and an outcome of their view of the "Other" (Parpola 2004). These peoples residing on the empire's remote frontier were looked upon as static, timeless, and threatening outsiders who lacked the qualities of "civilized" life (Bahrani 2006: 51).

With such a prejudiced view of desert dwellers being deeply rooted within that ancient imperial ideology, have some of these ideas found their way into current scholarly thinking?

Modern Scholarship through Ancient Eyes

References to the pre-Islamic cultures of Arabia were recorded by early Greek, Ptolemaic, and Roman historians and geographers in connection with the ancient Arabian spice trade (Miller 1969; Groom 1981; Young 2001; Hoyland 2002: 103–12). The appealing references to flourishing nomadic kingdoms with lavish tastes and elaborate economic systems were bound to kindle the curiosity of scholars (Talhami 1982: 283) and bolster their fantasies of remote exotic destinations (Philby 1981).

Foundations for the modern exploration of both Arabia and the desert were laid in the first half of the nineteenth century CE. Of special value are the works of Burckhardt (1829) and Musil, the latter of whom traversed the deserts from the Negev and northern Arabia through Wadi Sirḥān and the Syrian Desert to the Euphrates in the years 1896–1902 and 1908–1915 (Musil 1907, 1930).

The first visits and journeys of European travelers in the Arabian Peninsula portrayed the tribes simply as nomads who provided camel caravans for trade (Musil 1928; Köhler-Rollefson 1993) as they did until the building of the Hijaz railway in the

1920s. For the European travelers this "nomadic spirit" embodied the wish to depart upon that distant journey into unknown lands where "man feels once more happy," as Sir Richard Burton put it (Burton 1879).

Early investigations of the Negev Desert went through similar processes, only here the Western quest for the east was deeply influenced and accompanied by the mighty authority of the Bible (Robinson and Smith 1867: 205; Albright 1956: 14). And like Tiglath-pileser III and Esarhaddon in ancient times, Nelson Glueck described the Amalekites and "other Bedouin groups ... that for centuries had roamed about the Negev like untamed beasts of the field ..." (Glueck 1959: 169).

Thus in these early days of systematic research, the dominating paradigm of archaeology in the Near East was culture-historical in nature. The main concern of this prevalent model was to isolate and characterize the specifics of each culture in order to explain chronology, geographical developments, and cultural influences created by movements of peoples, objects, and ideas through space and time (Bunimovitz 2001; Matthews 2003: 20–22).[1] Hence, most of the historical and archaeological studies dealing with Arabian trade that were written in the mid-nineteenth and early twentieth centuries may be seen as following this culture-historical perspective.

In these early days of research, the dominating perception of local Arabian and southern Levantine society heavily relied on the common concept of a "struggle between the desert and the sown" (Reifenberg 1955; Shaw 1982–1983). According to this view, nomads and seminomads live in arid zones not suitable for agriculture, and thus their livelihoods are characterized mainly by raising livestock. The natural environment determines the seasonal movements of these nomads, who live in autonomous groups, maintain autarchic households that rely on livestock products, and have little contact with sedentary societies. These people are hostile to central authority and wait for windows of opportunity in which to take advantage of sedentary populations' weaknesses. In this view, nomadic life patterns remain static, and nomads do not become sedentary (Patai 1971: 42; Musil 1928; Barth 1961: 111).

The second half of the twentieth century saw the systemization of archaeological excavations and surveys in both Arabia and the Levant, and the development of a new anthropological paradigm for nomadic societies in the Near East. While the previous scholarly treatment of Arabian and Levantine cultures emphasized hostile relations, difficulties in coexistence and social integration of seminomadic societies with their sedentary counterparts, studies published since the 1960s have demonstrated that this approach was misleading and suffered from bias and stereotypes.

Anthropological and ethnographic works conducted among traditional seminomadic communities showed that relations between sedentary groups and nomads are symbiotic (Barth 1961: 93–100; Marx 1977, 1992: 256–58; Khazanov 1994: 202–12).

---

1. For a critical overview of the culture-historical paradigm, see Lyman, O'Brien, and Dunnell 1997.

At about the same time, the decipherment and publication of the Assyrian kings' inscriptions and imperial economic and administrative records brought the ancient Arabs into center-stage and called for a comprehensive historical reconstruction of the long-distance Arabian trade system. A direct consequence of this trend was that scholars such as Eph'al (1984), Cavigneaux and Ismail (1990), and Liverani (1992) chose to locate Arabian trade within the framework of an imperial context, focusing on the Near Eastern demand for exotic commodities originating from Arabia and on the Assyrian economic revenue from the trade. These sorts of explanations relied mostly on historical considerations, while archaeology was marginal and included merely as supporting evidence.

The ancient Assyrian line of thinking thus survived in the common Western perception of the ancient Arabs and trade,[2] a view that was itself an outcome of a contemporary colonial and imperial historical reality.[3] While the Assyrian occupation of Syria and the Levant was perceived as the prime mover behind the development and intensification of local settlement systems, the ancient Arabs were simply seen as "nomads" representing stagnation and backwardness. Arabian trade was understood as a unidirectional movement of commodities from the uncivilized periphery to the well-organized imperial center, intermediated by nomads and client kingdoms with an emphasis on the trade's contribution to the imperial economy. These rather simplistic theories disregarded the benefits and the social responses of the indigenous societies to this kind of globalization—a denial that once again turned the Arabs into the passive object of their history.

Now, it seems that we have finally reached the point where we can no longer discuss the scientific treatment of Arabian trade without recalling the words of Edward Said (1978: 11): "All academic knowledge about the cultures of the Orient is somehow tinged and impressed with, or violated by, the gross political fact—the reality of imperialism and colonialism."

In broad terms, the history of Arabian trade was written in modern times and in Western thought much as it was transmitted by the Assyrian kings and scribes to their audience. Needless to say, being propagandist in nature, the Neo-Assyrian kings' inscriptions and reliefs are compositions that follow particular iconographic traditions as well as aiming toward an ideological glorification of king and empire. As part of Assyria's global perception, the Assyrio-centric view of the Arabs had sealed the fate of Iron Age II desert societies, which were to remain just as marginal in modern scholarly consciousness as they were in antiquity.

---

2. For a similar influence of the Hellenistic-Roman empires on the way classical Arabia was perceived by Western scholars, see Otaibi 2006.

3. For a discussion on the orientalist trend in Near Eastern archaeology, see Larsen 2005.

Reality behind Arab-Assyrian Relations Revealed

In order to unveil the reality behind Arabian trade, the economic networks involved, the ways in which the trade was conducted and the sociopolitical agents who took part in this commercial activity, it is of the utmost importance to differentiate between Assyria's rigid propaganda and *de facto* imperial policy.

While ideologically the Assyrians saw the desert as a concrete expression of the chaotic periphery (see references above), various lines of archaeological and historical evidence illustrate that Assyrian imperial policy toward desert regions and their communities was far more moderate and flexible than the ideological formulae followed by royal inscriptions and other imperial texts.[4]

Much archaeological work conducted at sites along the three main land routes connecting Arabia with the Assyrian empire to its northeast and other ancient Near Eastern kingdoms (fig. 1) has yielded rich material-culture assemblages of the Iron Age IIb that provide a detailed portrait of the trade.

One major route connected Arabia with the Mediterranean ports and the international highway (the *via maris*) that crossed the southern Levantine Coastal Plain.[5]

Another important road was the King's Highway that linked Arabia and the south with the principal entrepôt of Damascus and Tyre by crossing the Transjordanian Plateau (for archaeological results see, e.g., Busairah [Bienkowski 2002]; Tawilan; Um al-Biarah [C. M. Bennett 1978; Bienkowski 2000]; Tall Jawa [Daviau 2001]).

Finally, a third road—its major importance having been revealed only recently—connected Arabia with the Persian Gulf, via the Arabian Desert. Recent archaeological work at various sites located along the three main north Arabian oases of Duma, Dedan, and Tema and an array of epigraphic sources attest to this route's significance and close contacts between the region and Mesopotamia during the Iron Age (for archaeological results see, e.g., Macdonald 1997; Magee 2004; Abu al-Hassan 2010; al-Said 2010; Hausleiter 2012).

Assyria's efforts to gain control over the border with Egypt and the vibrant trade with Arabia were motivated by imperial desire for access to raw materials and luxury items, as well as the various economic revenues and tolls to be gleaned from the trade, and by the well-established Assyrian appetite for political supremacy over competing or independent-minded entities. Under imperial patronage and with an ever-increasing demand for luxury items originating in Arabia, the Levantine and Arabian Desert regions experienced settlement growth and economic prosperity.

---

4. For an anthropological-archaeological discussion of diverse imperial control strategies practiced by the Assyrians in frontier regions, see Parker 2001, 2003.

5. Archaeological results: Tel Jemmeh (Ben Shlomo and Van Beek 2014); Tel Beersheba (Singer-Avitz 1999); Tel Malhata (Beit Arieh and Freud 2015); Tel 'Aroer (Thareani 2011).

Elsewhere I have discussed the imperial control strategies by which Assyria exerted its power over remote desert regions, mainly the Negev and its wild population (Thareani 2017). I shall briefly describe those points that are germane to the current discussion.

At the basis of Assyrian imperial rule lay the perception that the desert frontier differed significantly from the imperial core regions in its cultural, social, and political essence. The Assyrians themselves boasted of their ability to control and pacify Arabian Desert societies (see detailed discussion and references above). Indeed, given the conditions on the eve of the Assyrian conquest—the unique ecological and cultural settings of desert communities—it is clear that the empire practiced a creative combination of control strategies in these regions.

Imperial authorities unceasingly encouraged local tribal elites to take advantage of their traditional position of power by offering social advancement through the likes of luxury items and land, in exchange for loyalty. By these means, ancient empires created a new social status for seminomads, who were converted into land and property owners (Mattingly 1995: 144–53; Grahame 1998: 97–100). With this transition, contacts with governmental representatives and sedentary populations were facilitated, as well as the ability for tribal leaders to significantly influence local affairs.

The imperial treatment of tribal elites as landowners and high-ranking nobles generated the creation of a new social class—a strategy that ensured tribal leaders' support and led to peace and internal stability on the empire's frontiers. This phenomenon is well documented in a *longue durée* historical view, for instance the nomads of southern Iran (Barth 1961: 96–97); of Jordan (Bienkowski and Van der Steen 2001) and of the Negev (Thareani 2017). At the same time, other, more direct Assyrian imperial strategies were at play.

Administrative buildings were constructed and imperial personnel were stationed in client kingdoms that were never annexed but were considered desirable by Assyria. Instead, imperial agents were attached to local courts in such client states, and local craftsmen were employed directly by the imperial public administration (Postgate 1979: 210–12; 1992: 256–57).

This is evinced by the presence of Assyrian architecture and construction methods on both sides of Wadi Arabah: to the east, at Busayra in the heart of the Edomite tribal kingdom (C. M. Bennett 1978; Bienkowski 2000, 2002), where Assyria's administrative affairs were handled and contacts were maintained with the local population; and to the west, in the Philistine southern Coastal Plain (Kogan Zehavi 2006), the northwestern Negev (Ben Shlomo and Van Beek 2014) and in the Judean Arad-Beersheba Valley (Thareani 2007, 2017).

Though limited in their presence, the watchful eyes of imperial representatives in local centers situated at key locations safeguarded imperial assets in desert areas, in exchange for certain material benefits—a policy from which both sides benefitted.

Conclusions

Contrary to the common view, according to which Arabian trade is depicted as a unidirectional movement of commodities from a static passive periphery to an active imperial core, the anthropological, archaeological, and historical evidence support a set of reciprocal relations that existed between seminomadic groups residing in the desert areas of Arabia and the Levant and an imperial power that managed to decipher the sociopolitical codes typical of these regions, and to reach out to local seminomadic elites who would function as intermediaries in exchange for material incentives.

Similarly to its successor empires, Assyria adapted ecologically to these remote arid zones and managed to calibrate a unique control strategy that best suited such regions. Nevertheless, while the diachronic chain of events in terms of relations between the Assyrians and the Arabs is relatively clear, it was the imperial ideology that generated the image of the desert and desert-dwellers in the Assyrian elite psyche.

A survey of prominent studies treating Arabian trade suggests that current scholarly perspectives have been influenced—and to a large extent are still dominated—by the Neo-Assyrian power of imperialism. The ancient reality, however, as revealed by archaeological investigation of these desert regions has been shown to be far more multifaceted than the image portrayed by written evidence.

No doubt the Assyrians' desire to extend the empire's economic activities and sources of revenue beyond the borders of Assyria proper and to gain control over exotic commodities was the driving force behind increasing contacts between Assyrians and Arabs during the *pax Assyriaca* and throughout the Iron Age. But while imperial ideology aimed at inferiorizing the Arabs, the *de facto* Neo-Assyrian policy was flexible and appeasing. The very same Tiglath-pileser III who conquered, destroyed and dismantled Aram-Damascus and Israel did not displace Samsi—the rebellious queen—but accepted her repeated surrenders and merely appointed a supervisor to watch over her. Moreover, both Tiglath-pileser III and Sargon II boasted of settling Arab leaders in urban environments and entrusting them as proxies of imperial interests on the southwestern frontier. This strategy stemmed from the Assyrian desire to avoid disturbing the governmental framework and social organization in the frontier regions of their realm. Inhabitants of those zones were a vital mediating link in international trade, and the orderly conductors of activity that was essential to the imperial economy. The tribes were rewarded for their loyalty, probably by an increase in their imperial social status and by all kinds of gifts and material benefits—a policy not without parallels in later imperial comparanda.

Thus, the Neo-Assyrian control strategy for Arabian trade was mostly restricted to indirect imperial involvement. Management and maintenance of the trade system was conducted by elaborate arrangements largely in the hands of local authorities—settled populations, client kingdoms, and seminomads—all of whom benefited from the trade. The fact of the trade's uninterrupted continuation throughout the late seventh

century BCE and beyond—even after the Assyrian retreat from the region—supports
this view.

References

Abu al-Hassan, H. 2010. "The Kingdom of Lihyan." Pages 270–75 in *Roads of Arabia: Archae-ology and History of the Kingdom of Saudi-Arabia*. Edited by A. al-Ghabban, B. André-Salvini, F. Demange, C. Juvin, and M. Cotty. Paris: Musée du Louvre.
Albright, William F. 1956. "The Biblical Tribe of Massa and Some Congeners." Pages 1–14 in *Studi orientalistici in onore di Giorgio Levi Della Vida* 1. Rome: Istituto per l'Oriente.
Anderson, Scott. 2013. *Lawrence in Arabia: War, Deceit, Imperial Folly and the Making of the Modern Middle East*. New York: Doubleday.
Bahrani, Zainab. 2006. "Race and Ethnicity in Mesopotamian Antiquity." *World Archaeology* 38: 48–59.
Barth, Frederik. 1961. *Nomads of South Persia: The Basseri Tribe of the Kamseh Confederacy*. Oslo: Oslo University Press.
Beit Arieh, Itzhaq, and Liora Freud, eds. 2015. *Tel Malhata: A Central City in the Biblical Negev*. Winona Lake, IN: Eisenbrauns.
Ben Shlomo, D. and Van Beek, G. W., eds. 2014. *The Smithsonian Institution Excavation at Tell Jemmeh, Israel, 1970–1990*. Washington DC: Smithsonian.
Bennett, C. M. 1978. "Some Reflections on Neo-Assyrian Influence in Transjordan." Pages 164–71 in *Archaeology in the Levant: Essays for Kathleen Kenyon*. Edited by P. R. S. Moorey and Peter Parr. Warminster: Aris & Phillips.
Bennett, E. 2015. "Trade or Gender: Which Was More Influential in Relations between the Royalty of Neo-Assyrians and the 'Queens of the Arabs'?" PhD diss., University of Birmingham, https://etheses.bham.ac.uk/id/eprint/6038/1/Bennett15MRes.pdf.
Bienkowski, Piotr. 2000. "Transjordan and Assyria." Pages 44–58 in *The Archaeology of Jordan and Beyond: Essays in Honor of James E. Sauer*. Edited by Lawrence E. Stager, Joseph A. Greene, and Michael D. Coogan. Winona Lake, IN: Eisenbrauns.
———. 2002. *Busayra Excavations by Crystal-M. Bennett 1971–1980*. Oxford: Oxford University Press.
Bienkowski, Piotr, and Eveline Van der Steen. 2001. "Tribes, Trade and Towns: A New Framework for the Late Iron Age in Southern Jordan and the Negev." *BASOR* 323: 21–47.
Brown, Jonathan M., and Laurence Kutler. 2006. *Nelson Glueck: Biblical Archaeologist and President of the Hebrew Union College Jewish Institute of Religion*. Cincinnati: Hebrew Union College Press.
Bunimovitz, Shlomo. 2001. "Cultural Interpretation and the Bible: Biblical Archaeology in the Postmodern Era." *Cathedra* 100: 27–46 (Hebrew).
Burckhardt, J. L. 1829. *Travels in Arabia: An Account of those Territories in Hedjaz which the Mohammedans Regard as Sacred*. London: H. Colburn.
Burton, Richard F. 1879. *The Land of Midian*. London: Kegan Paul.
Byrne, Ryan. 2003. "Early Assyrian Contacts with Arabs and the Impact on Levantine Vassal Tribute." *BASOR* 331:11–25.
Cavigneaux, A., and B. K. Ismail. 1990. "Die Statthalter von Suhu und Mari im 8. Jh. v. Chr. anhand neuer Texte aus den irakischen Grabungen im Staugebiet des Qadissiya-Damms." *BagM* 21:321–456.
Daviau, P. M. Michèle. 2001. "Assyrian Influence and Changing Technologies at Tall Jawa, Jordan." Pages 214–38 in *The Land That I Will Show You: Essays on the History and Archaeol-

ogy of the Ancient Nera East in Honour of J. Maxwell Miller. Edited by John A. Dearman and Matt P. Graham. Sheffield: Sheffield Academic.

Edens, C., and G. Bawden, 1989. "History of Tayma and Hejazi Trade during the First Millennium BC." *JESHO* 32:48–103.

Elat, Moshe. 1977. *Economic Relations in the Lands of the Bible: c. 1000-539 B.C.* Jerusalem: Bialik (Hebrew).

———. 1978. "The Economic Relations of the Neo-Assyrian Empire with Egypt." *JAOS* 98:20–34.

Eph'al, Israel. 1984. *The Ancient Arabs: Nomads on the Borders of the Fertile Crescent 9th–5th Centuries B.C.* Leiden: Brill.

Finkelstein, Israel. 1992. "Horvat Qitmit and the Southern Trade in the Late iron Age II." *ZDPV* 108:156–70.

Frahm, Eckart. 2017. "Assyria and the Far South: The Arabian Peninsula and the Persian Gulf." Pages 299–310 in *A Companion to Assyria.* Edited by Eckart Frahm. New Haven, CT: Yale University Press.

Fuchs, Andreas. 1994. *Die Inschriften Sargons II aus Khorsabad.* Göttingen: Cuvillier.

Gerardi, P. 1992. "The Arab Campaigns of Assurbanipal: Scribal reconstruction of the Past." *SAAB* 6:67–103.

Glueck, Nelson. 1959. *Rivers in the Desert: A History of the Negev.* New York: Farrar, Straus & Cuhady.

Grahame, Mark. 1998. "Rome without Romanization: Cultural Change in the Pre-Desert of Tripolitania (First–Third Centuries AD)." *OJA* 17:98–111.

Groom, Nigel. 1981. *Frankincense and Myrrh: A Study of the Arabian Incense Trade.* New York: Longman.

Hausleiter, Arnulf. 2011. "Ancient Tayma': An Oasis at the Interface between Cultures. New Research at a Key Location on the Caravan Road." Pages 102–20 in *Roads of Arabia: The Archaeological Treasures from Saudi Arabia.* Edited by Ute Franke and Joachim Gierlichs. Tübingen: Wasmuth.

———. 2012. "North Arabian Kingdoms." Pages 816–32 in *Blackwell Companions to the Ancient World: A Companion to the Archaeology of the Ancient Near East.* Edited by D. T. Potts. Malden, MA: Wiley-Blackwell.

Hoyland, Robert G. 2002. *Arabia and the Arabs from the Bronze Age to the Coming of Islam.* London: Taylor & Francis.

Jasmin, Michael. 2006. "The Emergence and First Development of the Arabian Trade across the Wadi Arabah." Pages 143–50 in *Crossing the Rift: Resources, Routes, Settlement Patterns and Interaction in the Wadi Arabah.* Edited by Piotr Bienkowski and Katharina Galor. Oxford: Oxbow.

Khazanov, Anatoly M. 1994. *Nomads and the Outside World.* Madison: University of Wisconsin Press.

Kogan Zehavi, Elena. 2006. "Tel Ashdod." *Hadashot Arkheologiyot* 118, http://www.hadashot-esi.org.il/report_detail_eng.aspx?id=340&mag_id=111.

Knauf, Ernst A., André Lemaire, Edouard Lipinski, Eveline van der Steen, and Yifat Thareani. 2010. "Arabian Trade in the Iron Age." Pages 39–54 in *From Antiquity to the Present: The 2008 European Association of Biblical Studies Lisbon Meeting.* Edited by J. A. Ramos, P. R. Davies, and M. A. Travassos Valdez. Lisbon: Centro de História da Universidade de Lisboa.

Köhler-Rollefson, Ilse. 1993. "Camels and Camel Pastoralism in Arabia." *NEA* 56:180–88.

Larsen, Mogens Trolle. 2005. "Orientalism and Near Eastern Archaeology." Pages 228–38 in

Domination and Resistance. Edited by Daniel Miller, M. J. Rowlands, and Christopher Y. Tilley. One World Archaeology. London: Routledge.

Liverani, Mario. 1992. "Early Caravan Trade between South Arabia and Mesopotamia." *Yemen* 1:111–15.

Lyman, R. L., Michael J. O'Brien, and Robert C. Dunnell. 1997. *The Rise and Fall of Culture History.* New York: Plenum.

MacDonald, M. C. A. 1997. "Trade Routes and Trade Goods at the Northern End of the 'Incense Road' in the First Millennium BC." Pages 333–49 in *Profumi d'Arabia.* Edited by Alessandra Avanzini. Rome: "L'Erma" di Bretschneider.

Magee, Peter. 2004. "The Impact of Southeast Arabian Intraregional Trade on Settlement Location and Organization during the Iron Age II Period." *Arabian Archaeology and Epigraphy* 15:24–42.

Matthews, Roger. 2003. *The Archaeology of Mesopotamia.* London: Routledge.

Mattingly, David J. 1995. *Tripolitania.* London: Batsford.

Marx, Emanuel. 1977. "The Tribe as a Unit of Subsistence: Nomadic Pastoralism in the Middle East." *American Anthropologist* 79:343–63.

———. 1992. "Are There Pastoral Nomads in the Middle East?" Pages 255–60 in *Pastoralism in the Levant: Archaeological Materials in Anthropological Perspectives.* Edited by Ofer Bar-Yosef and Anatoly M. Khazanov. Madison, WI: Prehistory.

Miller, J. Innes. 1969. *The Spice Trade of the Roman Empire: 29 BC to AD 641.* Oxford: Clarendon.

Monroe, Elizabeth. 1973. "Arabia. St. John Philby's Contribution to Pre-Islamic Studies." Pages 29–35 in *Proceedings of the Seminar for Arabian Studies.* Vol. 3: *Proceedings of the Sixth Seminar for Arabian Studies held at the Institute of Archaeology, London 27th and 28th September 1972.* London: Archaeopress.

Musil, Alois. 1907. *Arabia Petraea.* Hildesheim: Olms.

———. 1928. *The Manners and Custom of the Rwala Bedouins.* New York: American Geographical Society.

———. 1930. *In the Arabian Desert.* New York: H. Liveright.

Na'aman, Nadav. 2007. "The Contribution of the Suḫu Inscriptions to the Historical Research of the Kingdoms of Israel and Judah." *JNES* 66:107–22.

al-Otaibi, Fahad M. 2006. "Towards a Contrapuntal Reading of History: Orientalism and the Ancient Near East." *Journal of King Saud University – Arts* 19:55–66.

Parker, Bradley J. 2001. *The Mechanics of Empire: The Northern Frontier of Assyria as a Case Study in Imperial Dynamics.* Helsinki: Neo-Assyrian Text Corpus Project.

———. 2003. "Archaeological Manifestations of Empire: Assyria's Imprint on Southeastern Anatolia." *AJA* 107:525–57.

Parpola, Simo. 2003. "Assyria's Expansion in the Eighth and Seventh Centuries and Its Long-Term Repercussions in the West." Pages 99–112 in *Symbiosis, Symbolism and the Power of the Past.* Edited by William G. Dever and Seymour Gitin. Winona Lake, IN: Eisenbrauns.

———. 2004. "National and Ethnic Identity in the Neo-Assyrian Empire and Assyrian Identity in Post-Empire Times." *Journal of Assyrian Academic Studies* 18:5–22.

Parpola, Simo, and Kazuko Watanabe, eds. 1988. *Neo-Assyrian Treaties and Loyalty Oaths.* Helsinki: Helsinki University.

Patai, Raphael. 1971. *Society, Culture and Change in the Middle East.* Philadelphia: University of Pennsylvania Press.

Philby, H. St. John. 1981. *The Queen of Sheba.* London: Quarter.

Postgate, J. Nicholas. 1979. "The Economic Structure of the Assyrian Empire." Pages 193–221 in *Power and Propaganda: A Symposium on Ancient Empires.* Edited by Mogens T. Larsen. Copenhagen: Akademisk Forlag.

———. 1992. "The Land of Assur and the Yoke of Assur." *World Archaeology* 23: 247–63.

Potts, D. T. 2003. "The *mukarrib* and Hid Beads: Karib'il Watar's Assyrian Diplomacy in the Early 7th Century B.C." *Isimu* 6:197–206.

———. 2010. "Rethinking Some Aspects of Trade in the Arabian Gulf." *World Archaeology* 24:423–40, https://doi.org/10.1080/00438243.1993.9980217

Reade, Julian. 1998. "Assyrian Illustrations of the Arabs." Pages 221–32 in *Arabia and Its Neighbours: Essays on Prehistorical and Historical Developments Presented in Honour of Beatrice de Cardi*. Edited by C. S. Phillips, D. T. Potts, and S. Searight. Turnhout: Brepols.

Reifenberg, Adolf. 1955. *The Struggle between the Desert and the Sown*. Jerusalem: Jewish Agency.

Robinson, Edward, and Eli Smith. 1867. *Biblical Researches in Palestine and the Adjacent Regions*. London: Murray.

Sader, Hélène. 2010. "The Aramaeans of Syria: Some Considerations on Their Origin and Material Culture." Pages 271–300 in *The Book of Kings: Sources, Composition, Historiography and Reception*. VTSup 129. Edited by Baruch Halpern and André Lemaire. Leiden: Brill.

Said, Edward B. 1978. *Orientalism*. London: Penguin.

al-Said, S. F. 2010. "Dedan (al-'Ula)." Pages 262–69 in *Roads of Arabia: Archaeology and History of the Kingdom of Saudi-Arabia*. Edited by A. al-Ghabban, B. André-Salvini, F. Demange, C. Juvin, and M. Cotty. Paris: Musée du Louvre.

Shaw, B. D. 1982–1983. "Eaters of Flesh, Drinkers of Milk: The Ancient Mediterranean Ideology of the Pastoral Nomad." *Ancient Society* 13–14:5–31.

Singer-Avitz, Lily. 1999. "Beersheba–A Gateway Community in Southern Arabian Long-Distance Trade in the Eighth Century B.C.E." *TA* 26:3–74.

Tabachnick, Stephen E. 1997. "Lawrence of Arabia as Archaeologist." *BAR* 23:40–71.

Tadmor, Hayim. 1958. "The Campaigns of Sargon II of Assur: A Chronological-Historical Study." *JCS* 12:22–40, 77–100.

Tadmor, Hayim, and Shigeo Yamada. 2011. *The Royal Inscriptions of Tiglath-Pileser III (744–727 BC) and Shalmaneser V (726–722 BC), Kings of Assyria*. Royal Inscriptions of the Neo-Assyrian Period 1. Winona Lake, IN: Eisenbrauns.

Talhami, G. 1982. Review of *Frankincense and Myrrh: A Study of the Arabian Incense Trade*, Nigel Groom. *Arab Studies Quarterly* 4:283–86.

Thareani, Yifat. 2007. "Ancient Caravanserai: An Archaeological View from 'Aroer." *Levant* 39: 123–41.

———. 2011. *Tel 'Aroer: An Iron Age II Caravan Town and a Hellenistic and Early Roman Settlement in the Negev; Avraham Biran (1975–1982) and Rudolph Cohen (1975–1976) Excavations*. Jerusalem: Hebrew Union College-Jewish Institute of Religion.

———. 2016. "The Empire and the 'Upper Sea': Assyrian Control Strategies along the Southern Levantine Coast." *BASOR* 375:77–102.

———. 2017. "Empires and Allies: A *longue durée* View from the Negev Desert Frontier." Pages 409–28 in *Rethinking Israel: Studies in the History and Archaeology of Ancient Israel in Honor of Israel Finkelstein*. Edited by Oded Lipschits, Y. Gadot, and Matthew J. Adams. Winona Lake: IN: Eisenbrauns.

Van Beek, Gus W. 1960. "Frankincense and Myrrh." *BA* 23:70–95.

Yamada, Keiko. 2005. "From the Upper Sea to the Lower Sea: The Development of the Names of Seas in the Assyrian Royal Inscriptions." *Orient* 40:31–55.

Yamada, Shigeo. 2000. *The Construction of the Assyrian Empire: A Historical Study of the Inscriptions of Shalmaneser III (859–824 BCE) relating to His Campaigns to the West*. CHANE 3. Leiden: Brill.

Young, Gary K. 2001. *Rome's Eastern Trade: International Commerce and Imperial Policy 31 BC–AD 305*. London: Routledge.

CONTRIBUTORS

Deborah Appler is professor of Hebrew Bible at Moravian Theological Seminary in Bethlehem, PA, and an Elder in the Eastern Pennsylvania Conference of the United Methodist Church. Her academic interests and publications center on the intersections of religion, gender, social justice, and sexuality in the Hebrew Bible and how biblical texts and their interpretations impact communities. She has also excavated at many sites in Israel/Palestine including Megiddo and Jezreel. Moravian Theological Seminary was a consortium member of the Jezreel Expedition.

Eran Arie is the curator of the Iron Age and Persian period at The Israel Museum, Jerusalem, and a research associate at the Leon Recanati Institute for Maritime Studies, The University of Haifa. He also teaches in the Martin (Szusz) Department of the Land of Israel Studies and Archaeology at Bar-Ilan University. He specializes in the social and historical value of pottery and small finds from the Iron Age in northern Israel and excavated at Tel Megiddo until 2013.

Julye Bidmead is director of the Center for Undergraduate Excellence and associate professor of Religious Studies and Peace Studies at Chapman University, Orange, CA. Her publications include *The Akitu Festival: Religious Continuity and Royal Legitimation in Mesopotamia* (Gorgias Press, 2004), *Invest Your Humanity* (Pickwick, 2016), and articles on Near Eastern religion, ritual studies, and gender. She has participated in several archaeological digs in Israel including the Jezreel Expedition. Chapman University was a consortium member of the Jezreel Expedition.

Athalya Brenner-Idan is professor emerita of the Hebrew Bible/Old Testament at the Universiteit van Amsterdam and served as professor in the Department of Biblical Studies at Tel Aviv University. She also taught in Hong Kong and at Brite Divinity School in Fort Worth, TX, was "Extraordinary Professor" at Stellenbosch University, South Africa, and is currently a research associate with the Orange Free State University, South Africa. She received an honorary PhD from the University of Bonn in 2002 and was president of the Society of Biblical Literature in 2015. Her publications include *The Israelite Woman: Social Role and Literary Type in Biblical Narrative* (English: Sheffield Academic and Bloomsbury, 1985, 2014; Hebrew: Tel Aviv University Press, 2018), as well as twenty edited volumes in the series *A Feminist Companion to the Bible*, and six edited volumes (with Archie C. C. Lee and Gale Yee) in the Texts@Contexts series. Her latest edited book (with Meira Polliack) is *Jewish Biblical Exegesis from Islamic Lands: The Medieval Period* (SBL Press, 2019).

Tony W. Cartledge is professor of Old Testament at Campbell University Divinity School in Buies Creek, NC. He also writes a weekly Bible study curriculum and serves as contributing editor for *Nurturing Faith Journal and Bible Studies*, now a part of Good Faith media. He and his wife Susan have dug with Yosef Garfinkel at Lachish (2015) and with Franklin and Ebeling at Jezreel (2017–2018). Campbell University was a consortium member of the Jezreel Expedition in 2018.

Ian Cipin is a PhD candidate in the Zinman Institute of Archaeology at the University of Haifa with a background as a senior archaeologist in commercial archaeology in the United Kingdom. His research interests are the later Neolithic to Early Bronze Age in the southern Levant with a focus on daily life practices and social organization from the perspective of the individual and smaller scale dynamics within societies, and his dissertation focuses on food processing technologies in the late Chalcolithic from the perspective of ground stone tools. He has excavated extensively in the United Kingdom, Romania, Turkey, and Israel and is the field director of the Jezreel Expedition.

Eric H. Cline is professor of Classics and Anthropology in, and former chair of, the Department of Classical and Near Eastern Languages and Civilizations at The George Washington University. He is also currently director of the Capitol Archaeological Institute at GWU. His research interests include trade and interconnections during the Bronze Age in the Aegean and eastern Mediterranean and he is the author or editor of twenty books and nearly one hundred articles. He is an active field archaeologist with more than thirty seasons of excavation and survey experience in Israel, Egypt, Jordan, Cyprus, Greece, Crete, and the United States, including ten seasons at Megiddo (1994–2014), where he served as co-director before retiring from the project in 2014, and another ten seasons at Tel Kabri, where he currently serves as co-director.

Karen Covello-Paran is a senior field and research archaeologist for the Israel Antiquities Authority Research Department. She also teaches part-time for the International MA Program in Archaeology and Ancient Near Eastern Cultures at Tel Aviv University. She specializes in the social and economic aspects of the Bronze and Iron Ages and has excavated extensively throughout northern Israel, where she also served as the chief scientific advisor.

Jennie Ebeling is associate professor of Archaeology at the University of Evansville in Indiana and, with Norma Franklin, co-director of the Jezreel Expedition. Her research interests include ancient food and drink technology, women in antiquity, and religion and cult in the Bronze and Iron Age Levant. She has co-edited volumes on household archaeology and ground stone artifacts and is the author of *Women's Lives in Biblical Times* (T&T Clark, 2010).

Gerald Finkielsztejn is a retired senior researcher and archaeologist at the Israel Antiquities Authority. He is currently a staff member of the South Tiberias Harbour Project team, University of Haifa.

Nimrod Getzov is a senior research archaeologist for the Israel Antiquities Authority. He is the author of numerous excavation reports and other publications and has directed or co-directed excavations at Ein Zippori and many other sites.

Shimon Gibson is a professor of practice in the History Department at the University of North Carolina at Charlotte. His principal research interests are landscape archaeology, history of archaeology, history and archaeology of Jerusalem, early Judaism and early Christianity, and the history of photography in the Middle East. He edited (with D. Vieweger) *The Archaeology and History of the Church of the Redeemer and the Muristan in Jerusalem* (Oxford, 2016). His popular book *The Final Days of Jesus: the Archaeological Evidence* (HarperOne, 2009) has been translated into nine languages. During the past thirty years, he has directed numerous archaeological excavation projects in different parts of Israel/Palestine, notably in Jerusalem.

Philippe Guillaume is an adjunct lecturer at the University of Berne, Switzerland. His publications include *A History of Biblical Israel* (Equinox, 2016) with Ernst Axel Knauf and he is currently preparing several volumes on the economy of the ancient Levant and the laws of Deuteronomy with Diana Edelman's research group at the University of Oslo. He is a member of the Jezreel Expedition.

Martha Hellander makes art and writes poetry, fiction, and nonfiction. She won a Minnesota Book Award for *The Wild Gardener: Life and Selected Writings of Eloise Butler* (North Star Press, 1992). With Philippe Guillaume, she published "The House of the Forest of Lebanon: A Temple Silenced" in *Biblische Notizen* (2019). She has excavated at Tel Hazor and is a member of the Jezreel Expedition.

Louise Hitchcock is professor of Aegean Bronze Age archaeology in the Classics and Archaeology Program at the University of Melbourne. Her current research is engaged with Mediterranean island identities, globalization, decolonization, interconnections, and entanglements. She is the author of *Minoan Architecture: A Contextual Analysis* (Åströms), *Theory for Classics* (Routledge) (with Donald Preziosi), and *Aegean Art and Architecture* (Oxford), and a co-editor of *DAIS: The Aegean Feast* (Aegaeum 29) and *Tell It in Gath: Studies in the History and Archaeology of Israel; Essays in Honor of Aren M. Maeir on the Occasion of His Sixtieth Birthday* (Zaphon). She has excavated in California, Syria, Greece, and Israel, most recently at Tell eṣ-Ṣafi/Gath.

Ann E. Killebrew is an associate professor of Classics and ancient Mediterranean studies at the Pennsylvania State University and a research fellow at the Leon Recanati Institute for Maritime Studies, University of Haifa. She is currently the co-director of the Tel Akko Total Archaeology Project.

Marilyn Love is a PhD student in Hebrew Bible at the University of California, Los Angeles. Marilyn specializes in Second Temple literature and its reception history with a primary focus on ritual, gender, and the paradigmatic Other. Her research interests also include the function of writing in apotropaic inscriptions. She has participated in archaeological excavations at Megiddo and Jezreel.

Menachem Rogel holds degrees in archaeology and mathematics and is the web designer of the Jezreel database.

Jack M. Sasson is emeritus Kenan Professor of Religious Studies at University of North Carolina Chapel Hill and emeritus Werthan Professor of Biblical and Judaic Studies at Vanderbilt University. He is past president of the International Association for Assyriology and of the American Oriental Society. He publishes widely on biblical as well as Mesopotamian subjects, most recently two volumes, Judges 1–12 (Anchor Yale Bible, 2014) and *From the Mari Archives* (2nd ed., Eisenbrauns, 2017).

Yiftah Shalev is an archaeologist for the Israeli Antiquities Authority and a Teaching Fellow at the University of Haifa. He is currently the co-director of the excavation at Givati Parking Lot, Jerusalem.

Jane C. Skinner is an affiliated researcher at The Pennsylvania State University. She is currently the assistant director of the Tel Akko Total Archaeology Project.

Anastasia Shapiro is a geologist who is employed as a researcher for the Israel Antiquities Authority. Her researches include petrographic and petrologic studies of pottery from the Pottery Neolithic to the Ottoman period, field mineralogical, geological and geomorphological consultation, archaeological surveys, GIS and mapping, ancient technologies of pottery manufacture, and Ottoman clay tobacco pipes. She is the author or co-author of more than thirty professional papers, including recent articles on Mamluk and Early Ottoman Pottery form Ramla and the petrographic examination of pottery from Safed. Since 1992, she has participated in numerous IAA excavations and surveys and international projects.

Vassiliki E. Stefanaki is an archaeologist-numismatist in the Numismatic Museum, Athens. Between 2002 and 2011, she worked at the Archaeological Institute of Aegean Studies in Rhodes on a project untitled "Coins-Coinage of the Dodecanese."

Margreet L. Steiner is an archaeologist with a special interest in the southern Levant. She wrote her PhD thesis on Kenyon's excavations in Jerusalem and authored several books. She has conducted archaeological research in Israel, Jordan, Syria, and Lebanon.

Matthew Susnow is a postdoctoral researcher at the Institute of Archaeology at the Hebrew University in Jerusalem, Israel. His research focuses on Canaanite religion in the Bronze Age, archaeological approaches to reconstructing past behavioral patterns, and more broadly, the history and textual traditions of the ancient Near East during the Bronze and Iron Ages.

Yifat Thareani is a research archaeologist at the Nelson Glueck School of Biblical Archaeology at the Hebrew Union College in Jerusalem and the academic director of the Caesarea Maritima Project at New York University. Following the completion of the final publication of Tel 'Aroer, she was entrusted with the study and publication of the Iron II findings from more than fifty years of excavation at Tel Dan. Exploration of imperial strategies in frontier zones led her to initiate and execute a new archaeological project Tel Achziv with co-directors Philippe Abrahami of Lyon 2 University and Michael Jasmin. She co-directs the Tel Dan excavations with David Ilan.

Joan Taylor is professor of Christian Origins and Second Temple Judaism at King's College London and has published widely on history, literature, and archaeology. While her work has ranged from the Iron Age to the Byzantine period, she has a particular interest in the material history of both early Christianity and the Dead Sea area, and is the principal investigator for the Leverhulme-funded "Dispersed Qumran Cave Artefacts and Archival Sources" (*DQCAAS*) project. Her first book Christians and the Holy Places (Clarendon Press, 1993) won an Irene Levi-Sala Prize from Ben Gurion University for an archaeological study of Israel.

Yotam Tepper is a researcher and archaeologist with the Israel Antiquities Authority. His research focuses on Byzantine period sites in the Negev, particularly relict field systems and the ancient agricultural installations that dot the hinterland of Byzantine settlements. He has directed numerous excavations and surveys in Israel for the last three decades. His latest project includes survey and excavation in the region of the Roman military camp at Legio (el-Lajjun). As part of this work, he conducted extensive excavation at the Megiddo prison compound where a Christian Prayer Hall from the end of the Roman period was discovered.

Subject Index

ANCIENT SOURCES INDEX

Rabbinic Works

Early Christian Writings

.